Psychoanalysis
and
the Bible

A STUDY IN DEPTH
OF
SEVEN LEADERS

Psychoanalysis and the Bible

A STUDY IN DEPTH
OF
SEVEN LEADERS

Dorothy F. Zeligs, Ed. D.

BLOCH PUBLISHING COMPANY · NEW YORK

*Dedicated to the memory of my
father and mother,* JOSEPH *and*
BETTY MIRKIN ZELIGS, *who imparted
to all their children a sense of
the joy of learning.*

Contents

ACKNOWLEDGMENTS   ix

FOREWORD   xi

INTRODUCTION   xv

1. Abraham, A Study in Fatherhood   1

2. Two Episodes in the Life of Jacob   35

3. The Personality of Joseph   59

4. A Character Study of Samuel   91

5. Saul, the Tragic King   121

6. David, the Charismatic Leader   161

7. Solomon, the Man and the Myth   259

Conclusion: A Psychoanalytic Note on the Function of
    the Bible   311

Some Brief Remarks on Biblical Exegesis   315

References and Notes   323

Glossary of Psychoanalytic Terms   333

Index to Biblical References   339

Index   341

Acknowledgments

These studies represent a continuing interest over a number of years. Along the way on this unchartered journey there were a number of people whose thoughtful criticism of the material and personal encouragement were of great help to me. Among them was Dr. Theodor Reik, one of my former teachers and supervising analysts. Although my approach in these biblical studies is along quite different lines than his own well-known contributions to this field, his lively interest in the work, his critical reading of the manuscript and our discussions regarding it, all contributed to a vital experience for me.

My special thanks go also to Dr. Philip Phenix, Professor of Philosophy and Education, Teachers College, Columbia University. As a teacher and writer in the field of religion, he at first had some doubts about a psychoanalytic approach to the biblical content. But after reading the material his response was warm and accepting because of what he regarded as its creative qualities. When he wanted to know why I had not included Moses, I replied that Freud himself had done a study on that awe-inspiring figure. However, Dr. Phenix encouraged me to go ahead with my own approach. I have been working for some time on a series of studies about that great leader. Several of these have appeared in the journal, *American Imago*.

Among others who read this material, in whole or in part, and gave me the benefit of their thinking were the Reverend Eugene S. Tanner, biblical scholar, formerly Professor of Religion, Wooster College, Ohio, the Reverend John Hall Snow, Professor of Pastoral Theology, Cambridge, Mass., Dr. Joachim Flescher, and Dr. John Herma, psychoanalysts and authors, the latter having been one of my valued former teachers. I am indebted, also, to Dr. Raphael Patai, anthropologist in the fields of the Bible and the Near East, for his constructive interest in this work.

My warm appreciation goes to Rabbi Arthur Lelyveld, who took the time from his busy life to read the manuscript critically and contribute Part One of the *Foreword* to this book. Dr. Joost Meerloo, who wrote Part Two, has been from the inception of my work, an encouraging and helpful influence.

I wish to thank the editors of *American Imago* and *The Psychoanalytic Review* for permission to reprint here some of the material which appeared earlier in their journals.

Permission has also been secured from The Jewish Publication Society of America, Philadelphia, for quotations from *The Holy Scriptures, According to the Masoretic Text,* which was published under their aegis in 1917, and for excerpts from *The Legends of the Jews,* by Louis Ginzberg.

The Index was prepared by Mrs. Helen Margalith.

*Foreword**

PART ONE

By Rabbi Arthur J. Lelyveld

In this book, Dr. Zeligs has given us a new and fascinatingly different kind of approach to the biblical text. She has studied this literature with a care and responsibility that testify to her deep love of the material, and she has interpreted it expertly, using the tools and skills of psychoanalytic psychology.

Dr. Zeligs has given emphasis to the received text in which she finds whole human beings who by their real and coherent personalities enable us to understand the perennial power of the story. Indeed, in her analysis of their personalities, she establishes the authenticity of the biblical characters; she makes them "more believable." Her wonderfully suggestive insights add flesh to

---

* Since this book involves two fields of knowledge, it seems appropriate that a scholar from each of these areas but who is knowledgeable about both, should express his thoughts in this *Foreword*. Rabbi Lelyveld, one of the leaders of American Reform Judaism and a past president of the American Jewish Congress, holds the degrees of Master of Hebrew Literature and an Honorary Doctor of Divinity. Dr. Meerloo, a psychoanalyst, is widely known for his many contributions to this field. I am indeed privileged to have them represented here. D.F.Z.

characters whose role and motivations are laconically presented in Scripture: Uzzah, who pays with his life for having sought to protect the Ark; Abishag, the companion of David's last days, and a host of others in the "supporting cast."

Both those who seek to understand the text and those who expound it will find stimulation and new clarity of understanding in Dr. Zeligs' evocation of the hidden factors which motivate the conduct and responses of her Scriptural heroes. She has already had this effect on my own preaching and teaching, deepening my familiarity with biblical personalities about whom I had mistakenly believed I could learn nothing new. A new and seminal idea —what we call a *chiddush*—is her view of these well-known stories as "a remarkable expression of the development of the superego, outgrowth of the oedipal conflict, portrayed as a group drama . . . leading to new paths in morality and religion." This is an understanding of Scripture that gains persuasive strength as we follow Dorothy Zeligs in her re-creation of these biblical characters, enlivened by insights which stem from the comparatively new field of depth psychology. Thus is re-enforced the truth of the rabbinic interpretation (Avot. IV:I) of the Psalmist's words, *"Mikol m'lam'dai hiskalti*—I have learned from all my teachers."

PART TWO

By Dr. Joost A. M. Meerloo

Dr. Dorothy Zeligs looks at the *Old Testament* heroes from a psychoanalytic viewpoint. In her interpretations she uses the enrichment of basic understanding provided not only by her background in the field of psychoanalysis but also by her considerable knowledge of biblical literature.

Many a critic will ask: "Is this method of biblical interpretation valid? May we look at history and the Bible from such a psychological angle?" Our psychoanalytic answer can be: "This is the very method every exegete unobtrusively uses in reading the old texts."

The only difference in Dr. Zeligs' presentation is that she is more aware of the deeply hidden motivations in man's universal need to explain the world around him and his place in that world. Strictly speaking, the scientific method used here to interpret the biblical story is the search for clarifying analogies. We may call it the empathic descriptive method as opposed to the causal deductive method of the natural sciences.

In her study of biblical personalities, the author uses that special form of empathy and understanding provided by insights flowing from the use of psychoanalytic concepts and techniques. And how lively the old stories become in this light! In following her writings I could feel how the descriptions of the biblical characters gained in dramatic impact. The heroes came nearer to me. Her psychological analysis makes the reader much more a direct part of the biblical family.

The drama of human conflict and development can be found everywhere in the great books of mankind. Dr. Zeligs is a fascinating guide into that universal drama and I hope many a reader will enjoy the enlargement of empathy and understanding we can obtain from this form of applied psychoanalysis.

Introduction

Almost as remarkable as the Bible itself is the story of man's continuous efforts throughout the ages to understand more fully the meanings of this unique heritage. Approaches to the biblical literature have been as varied as the climates of the historical epochs through which it has passed. The mystic, the rationalist, the philosopher, the scientist, all have brought their interests and skills to the task of comprehending more fully the words of this ever-challenging Book of Books. The quality of elusiveness that pervades many of its passages lends an additional aura of mystery to its pages while, at the same time, the simplicity and directness that characterize much of its writing often touch at the very core of human experience.

The biblical literature does indeed have a unique place in our lives. No other book in Western culture has maintained its hold upon the human mind and imagination for so long a time. No other book has brought consolation, guidance, and inspiration to so many people throughout the centuries or, on the other hand, been used to evoke feelings of guilt, terror, and the fear of eternal damnation in so many trembling souls.

These unusual qualities of the biblical narrative present a challenge to psychological inquiry. Is it possible to delineate and define the essence of that which has made it such a potent force in the lives of men?

Paul Ricoeur, the French philosopher, maintains that the psychology of religious belief can be understood only by studying the texts in which man has indirectly expressed and formulated his beliefs in the process of feeling and living them. He points out that Freud used the *direct* approach in his *Moses and Monotheism* when he attempted to apply a general theory concerning the origins and growth of religion to a hypothetical reconstruction of Hebraic biblical history.[1] Freud, however, was basically concerned with the wider aspects of the evolution of monotheistic ideas in the light of his theories and, in spite of certain controversial areas, laid the basis for an understanding of religious roots in the nature of man.[2]

The Talmudists of old and their successors throughout the ages had no problem about the source for an understanding of the origins of Hebraic beliefs and traditions. They not only studied the *Holy Scriptures* but were immersed in them, savoring every word and freely allowing their thoughts and fantasies, through identification and empathy, to search out every possible aspect of meaning. The importance of language as symbol was intuitively understood and appreciated by these scholars so that the choice of the word, its exact form, its place in the sentence, gave rise to much speculation and interpretation.

In a sense, my own approach to this literature continues the traditional method of biblical commentary through its efforts to interpret the text as it stands. Thus it falls into the category described above by Ricoeur. These studies seek to penetrate to the underlying, or latent meanings that accompany the manifest content. The techniques, however, are those of applied psychoanalysis which, in its own ways, also draws upon the intuitive qualities so well utilized by Talmudic scholars. But in harmony with the nature and purpose of this work, it is not bound by defensive needs or predetermined conclusions and can thus strive to maintain the goal of objectivity.

The Bible presents the narrative portions of its content through the dramatic, personal experiences of its individual leaders and heroes. In a basic sense the true hero of the biblical

drama is the group itself, the Children of Israel. Its leaders therefore can be understood only in relation to the roles they play in
the group and the functions they serve in regard to it.

We shall find that in a curious, often mystifying way, the
psychic processes at work in the leaders reflect the same psychological forces dominant in the group at a given period of its
history. Yet to see these personalities as abstractions, symbolic of
the group as a whole, which was the tendency among some
biblical scholars not too long ago, is greatly an oversimplifica-
tion.[3, 4] Their highly individual qualities, the sense of *psychic
reality* they convey as people, make such a conclusion unconvinc-
ing.[5] By exploring these familiar figures from a new viewpoint, it
should be possible to determine in specific ways their psychological structures and the relationship of this factor to the development of the group. For it is, in large part, through the narratives
about its leaders and heroes that the biblical theme is dramatized.
That theme is the growth of human conscience, here manifested
in the psychodynamics of its leading personalities as they seek new
pathways in morality and religion along the lines of ethical
monotheism.

The prevailing approach in biblical exegesis during the past
two hundred years or so, has been that of the school of *Higher
Criticism*. The present study seeks neither to affirm nor deny the
various theories involved in that vast and complex field of modern
biblical interpretation. Their scholars have contributed much to
our understanding of the Bible, especially its developmental and
historical aspects. But rarely does any approach encompass all
that it is possible to know about a given field of knowledge. Thus,
in the past half-century and more, the findings of archaeology and
newer trends in biblical scholarship have broadened the horizons
in this area and made the atmosphere more receptive to new kinds
of exploration. For the benefit of the interested layman, a brief
glimpse into the world of modern biblical exegesis is presented
later in this volume so that he can place the present studies in a
more understandable perspective. To the scholarly reader from

other schools of thought, a temporary suspension of judgment and belief is suggested.

The content under consideration here then, is not the fragmented Bible of *Higher Criticism,* valuable though that may be, but the book that is read and treasured and puzzled over by the people. *For it is this Bible of everyday usage that has exerted so powerful an influence throughout the centuries. It is therefore a legitimate object of interest in and of itself, apart from how it came to be.*

My approach assumes an underlying unity in the biblical theme that goes beyond the diversity of the sources and the composite nature of the text. Without such cohesiveness of purpose and meaning, the Bible could not have played the role it has in the history of Judeo-Christian culture.[6] Thus the material of the Bible is viewed as stemming from the same roots psychologically.[7]

The words *leader* and *hero* are used here synonymously to describe the personalities of this study because their roles related to both aspects. In contrast to the heroes of other ancient mythologies, whose aim usually was the gratification of their instinctual wishes, especially in the act of *overcoming* the father, the heroic deed of the biblical hero was to *identify* with the Father and his commandments. This process involved the constructive conquest of the oedipal dilemma along the lines of renunciation and sublimation.

The biblical leader, consecrated by God as his prophet, acted as the voice of the Deity to the people. Thus he fulfilled the function of a superego. But since he was at the same time a human being, with his own inner growth a continuing process, he can be better understood as an example of the superego in *statu nascendi,* the *state of becoming.* Thus the human weaknesses of the biblical personalities, their occasional falls from grace, were an understandable, even a necessary part of the biblical theme, with its emphasis on guilt and redemption.

In terms of the reality functions pertaining to the leadership of the group, scholars have observed that if this literature had not presented us with such heroes as Abraham and Moses, it would have been necessary to assume their existence in order to explain the tasks accomplished in their names.[8]

This reality aspect does not affect the role such leaders played as mythopoeic figures. The narratives of the Bible can be understood as a *folk literature,* expressive of the people as a whole.[9, 10] They mark a kind of halfway point between history and mythology, the events of history being used as a framework within which the psychological functions similar to those that motivate the mythologies of other peoples are performed.

Advances in psychoanalytic ego psychology have led to increased interest in the interpretation of the myth from the viewpoint of how it deals with instinctual wishes and fears in terms of the adaptive functions of the ego. Myths have been described along these lines as shared fantasies which help the individual in his integration with the group, thus serving as a stabilizing and socializing force in society.[11] Another aspect gives emphasis to the role of the mythopoeic hero as the rebel, the inconoclast, breaking established idols and pushing forward to new horizons.[12]

The biblical hero fulfilled both these functions. He served as a model for his people, an ego ideal which they held in common.[13] At the same time, his role as leader was to move the people forward against their own inner resistances, toward the preconceived historic destiny which they themselves had chosen. The mythopoeic process functioned in terms of selecting and emphasizing those aspects of behavior and personality in these heroic figures that were especially meaningful for the group in terms of its stage of psychosocial development.[14] But in a manner peculiarly its own, the biblical story preserves the individual character of its heroes. Each one is a distinctive personality. He reflects in microcosm the psychic forces potent in the group but does so in his own individual fashion.

The Techniques of Applied Psychoanalysis

There are situations when, in order to find new meanings, one must start with the mind as a *tabula rasa,* a clean slate, as it were. This process involves the temporary abeyance of previous formulations concerning a given problem in order to allow the emergence of new impressions. This mental set, so useful in these studies, is the same attitude in which a psychoanalyst listens to the *free associations* of a patient.

Freud considered the potential values of applied psychoanalysis in many areas of life as even more important than the clinical aspects of his discoveries. He utilized this approach in a number of his own studies, particularly in the fields of religion, literature, and art.[15]

Psychoanalysis as a method of research is different in certain respects from its use as a therapy. In the latter situation the chief goal is therapeutic and the interpretation of observed facts is limited by certain rules of technique in which timing and the nature of the transference are of paramount importance. Also, in therapy, the material dealt with is different, since it constitutes not only the attempted *free associations* of the patient but the totality of his behavior.

When used as an instrument of research, psychoanalysis has a different goal. It can make full use of its psychological observations without regard for therapeutic consequences, but is more limited in the area and scope of the material that is under consideration.

These studies were begun some years ago in a mood of curiosity about Jacob's dream. I wondered if it would respond to psychoanalytic exploration. In order to find the answer it was necessary to study the totality of Jacob's life history and view the dream against this perspective. The degree of psychological validity found in his character and the responsiveness of the text to psychoanalytic methods were unexpected. The subject matter became a continuing interest. Every personality under consideration revealed himself as a wholly believable human being, with his own unique ways of behavior. That the separate stories in the lives of these heroes express and reflect significant aspects of human experience has always been appreciated. The special factor that emerged was the psychological consistency of their character traits throughout all the material dealing with their lives, as revealed in the underlying psychodynamics.

Even more unexpected was the finding that there was a significant causal relationship between the childhood experiences of the individual heroes, as reconstructed from the biblical material, and the later development of the adult.

While expressing themselves in individual ways, these leaders of ancient Israel were true culture heroes, for their strivings were closely associated with those aspects of life with which the group as a whole was involved in basic ways.

For readers not familiar with psychoanalytic techniques, I shall try to describe briefly the methods actually followed in arriving at the interpretations presented in this volume.

First, I familiarized myself with the totality of the biblical life history of the individual involved, also utilizing as a secondary source, but clearly delineated as such, certain post-biblical legendary material.[16] I then reconstructed what I felt his childhood environment would have been like, given his specific familial and cultural background. Such conditions varied widely, not only in terms of the immediate family situation but also in accordance with the social and historical era to which he belonged.

A basic assumption was that the story was being told from the viewpoint of the hero.[17, 18] This orientation proved to have an impressive degree of validity in terms of the resulting psychological coherence. The next step was a consideration of each specific episode in the light of its place in the reconstructed developmental life of the person concerned.[19]

The words of the text became the voice of the personality who was being studied. My task was to explore, not only the surface meaning, but also the underlying stream of unconscious fantasy that had colored and motivated the production of the biblical story. Through the process of *empathy* I tried to understand the relationship between the words of the text and what was going on in the mind and heart of the biblical *analysand*. With the use of psychoanalytic techniques, hidden meanings came to light, symbolic expressions lent themselves to interpretations, causal connections could be established between seemingly separate incidents, and underlying motivations could be disclosed.

As is well-known, the biblical narratives are full of baffling features. They contain passages that do not seem to make sense on a rational basis, sentences that appear to be out of context, words or phrases that are omitted, repetitions of incidents that are often contradictory, and so forth. Many attempts have been made by scholars over the years to unravel these mysteries of the text and many theories propounded concerning them.

It was not the purpose of this study to attempt so ambitious an undertaking as a new approach to the problems of the biblical text. But when confronted with puzzling aspects of the material under scrutiny, and finding no satisfactory answers on the basis of available exegesis, my training impelled me to seek psychological explanations. I approached these hindrances to the meaning of the text in the same way that *resistances* in the flow of *free associations* in a patient are dealt with in the psychoanalytic process. This kind of investigation was frequently successful, bringing that moment of surprise so well described by Theodor Reik when a hidden piece of knowledge suddenly comes to light and the fragments of a puzzle fall into place.[20] I found that these textual enigmas often occurred *at those points where the content involved material of a conflictful or forbidden nature, such as sexuality or aggression in relation to incestuous objects.* When interpreted on this level the ambiguous features of the text often made sense.

When one is in a state of unconscious conflict, troubled by opposing feelings, the resulting tension may reveal itself in small ways of which the person is unaware. In the biblical writings, as in the *free associations* of the analysand, seemingly insignificant details which did not fit into the rest of the material, frequently proved to be an important source of insight. Such small disharmonies could signify an eruption of unconscious content into an otherwise rational presentation. Ambiguity is another way in which the unconscious manages both to reveal and conceal its troubled secrets.

Within the undercurrents of this literature could be discerned the vestiges of certain tabooed aspects of instinctual life that biblical man tried to renounce in his forward movement toward a higher level of religion and morality. This long and difficult journey is marked many times by a *return of the repressed* in disguised or symbolic form.

Nor should we be too surprised by these findings. The Bible is primarily a religious literature. Its basic purpose is to set forth the vicissitudes of a people in relation to its God and his commandments. It thus depicts the struggles associated with the emergence of a *collective superego,* most dramatically expressed in the individual lives of its leaders.

As a product of religious feelings and beliefs, the biblical narratives contain those psychological elements that prompt the formation and development of religion. These forces are largely of an unconscious nature. They stem, in part, from man's unfulfilled childhood longings for an Idealized Father, a longing perpetuated by the adversities of adult life.[21] Together with this desire for a protective and loving Father come the feelings of ambivalence and guilt and the wish for absolution that are characteristic of this relationship in its human form as well. Elements of conflict are therefore intimately involved, both in manifest and hidden ways.

The traditions of Judaism, in certain respects, exemplify the Freudian concept of the origins of religion as these involve the figure of the father and have their roots in family life. Beginning with Abraham, the leaders and heroes were father figures. The oedipus complex, having its source in instinctual feelings, influences man's basic development as a human being. But the *source* does not necessarily set the *limits* to man's powers of sublimation, his capacity for spiritual development.[22]

The biblical heroes reveal some of these greater achievements of the human spirit. While the present study does focus most strongly upon the oedipal aspect, the first layer, as it were, of this kind of exploration, the writer feels that much more remains to be deciphered in the ambiguous and symbolic language of this great body of literature.

Although it has been assumed as obvious, perhaps it should

be stated that these studies are not concerned with the problem of the nature of God in an objective or philosophic fashion. Such an approach lies outside the realm of psychoanalytic exploration, as Freud himself has made clear.[23, 24]

Psychoanalysis
and
the Bible

A STUDY IN DEPTH
OF
SEVEN LEADERS

Abraham,
A Study in Fatherhood

 CHAPTER ONE

OF ALL the great biblical personalities, Abraham represents *the father* to the fullest degree. Not even Moses is given this title but is referred to as *Moshe Rabbenu*, "Moses, our teacher."

Abraham has been viewed by certain scholars as the prototype of the people, Israel.[1] As such, he brings the message of ethical monotheism to the world. This image of him is indeed implicit within the larger framework of the biblical theme but the narrative itself depicts Abraham as the progenitor of a people. His monotheism is taken for granted.

The provocative question arises: What is the connection between Abraham's mission as the first Hebrew, the founder of a people, and the narratives of his highly personal life experiences? It could not be mere chance that associated the figure of this leader with the specific episodes and events that are related concerning him.

A religion where the concept of God as *Father* is a basic one, develops from the human experience of the earthly parent within the family group. It is understandable therefore that the account of Hebrew life should begin with the story of an individual father and his progress through the conflicts and strivings associated with that role.

It is the view of this writer that the motive of the biblical account is to portray Abraham in the *process of becoming,* to show the stages of development he had to go through in order to achieve the emotional and spiritual maturity that were necessary for his task as leader and pathfinder.

Significantly, he appears upon the scene as *Abram,* "father of a people." Only considerably later, after he has gone through many experiences, at the point when he makes a covenant with God, accepts the rite of circumcision, and awaits the birth of his son Isaac, is the enlarged name of *Abraham,* "father of a multitude of peoples," bestowed upon him.

As befits a father figure, the biblical story of his life begins, not with any legends of his birth or heroic tales of his initiation into manhood, as with some other biblical heroes, but at the ripe age of seventy-five.

But every father is first a son, even if that status is not highlighted in his biography. Abraham was the son of Terah. He could not therefore escape the psychological problems of sonhood any more than he could those of fatherhood.

Freud has pointed out that Judaism, as a Father religion, is especially sensitive to feelings of ambivalence (conflicting attitudes of love and hate) between fathers and sons. Such emotions could imply hostility toward the Father-God himself and so could not be tolerated. The motive for repressing these feelings would therefore be particularly strong. Freud believed that out of such inner tensions and the accompanying need for atonement came the stimulus that led to higher ethical standards in the development of Judaism.[2]

God represented the Heavenly Father as the sole parental

image. No mother figure was involved in the Hebraic concept of divinity. Psychologically this situation can be understood as indicating an element of repression in feelings for the woman.

In terms of these Freudian concepts, it cannot be without significance that Abraham had to deal with conflicts in those very areas that were of special importance in the growth of a Father-God religion—ambivalence toward his sons and a certain degree of inhibition in his feelings for Sarah, his wife. We shall see that the stories of his life are indeed involved with these problems and that his ways of solving them find expression in new concepts of religion and morality.

At the same time, the biblical traditions present Abraham's situations of conflict in hidden ways. The tendency was to repress and rationalize his human weaknesses although it is more usual in the Bible to disclose freely the faults of its heroes. But Abraham was the exalted father and, as such, had to serve as a model. God says to him . . . "walk before Me and be thou whole-hearted (17:1)," that is, free from doubt about his faith. Freedom from doubt would imply the absence of ambivalence. The verse is sometimes translated ". . . walk before Me and be thou perfect," that is, perfect in his trust of God. Thus, for Abraham, the striving for perfection meant the overcoming of ambivalence.

Abraham's mission begins with a call from the Deity:

> Now the Lord said unto Abram, "Get thee out of thy country, and from thy kindred, and from thy father's house, unto the land that I will show thee. And I will make of thee a great nation, and I will bless thee, and make thy name great; and be thou a blessing . . . in thee shall all the families of the earth be blessed (12:1–3)."*

Abraham sets out on his journey not knowing where God will lead him. This situation may indicate that he himself is not yet fully aware of what his mission is to be or how it will be accomplished. The first step, however, in developing leadership is to leave one's home and kindred, thus achieving independence

---

* All biblical quotations and references in this chapter, unless otherwise noted, are from Genesis.

from early ties. This, Abraham does. His life's pilgrimage can be understood as the psychobiography of the making of a founding father.

The personality of Abraham, while profoundly human in many respects, has an aura of remoteness that sets the first Patriarch apart from the other subjects of study in this volume. Fewer details of his everyday life and ways of behavior are revealed. Moreover, since his biblical history starts with the period of his adulthood, the influences of his early life do not receive much notice.

While the Bible tells us little about the relationship between Abraham and his father Terah, tradition in the form of extra-biblical legend is more expansive. Terah is cast in the role, not only of an idol-worshipper but of an idol-maker, who tries to get his son to follow in his footsteps. But Abraham rebels against the gods of his father and arrives at a concept of the One God.

The purpose of this tradition is, of course, to emphasize Abraham's new religious orientation and to present him as a man who separated himself from his past and became the leader of a new faith and a new people. But this difference in belief must also be indicative of an important source of conflict between son and father. By denying the gods of his father, Abraham, in a sense, rejects the father too.

Abraham and Terah thus represent opponents in a struggle between the forces of monotheism and polytheism. But Hebrew tradition, not being able to tolerate such a hostile relationship between father and son, displaces this conflict to Abraham and a legendary king, Nimrod, who supposedly ruled Babylonia at this time. There are many legends about the struggles between these two, in which the idol-worshipping king unsuccessfully pits his strength against the power of Abraham's God.[3] In these stories Terah plays a subsidiary role but one which reveals his own ambivalence toward his son and a submissive-rebellious attitude to the king, a father figure for Terah also.

Let us now turn to the biblical narrative itself. What indications are there, if any, regarding Abraham's early life, his relationship to his parents and siblings? Only by pursuing slight clues can we move beneath the need for righteousness in Abraham to the stream of unconscious conflict beneath.

The Bible says Terah *took* Abraham and other members of the family and went forth with them from Ur of the Chaldees. Thus it is clearly Terah who initiates this move and we can assume that the father fulfills his role as head of the household.

Abraham's own later migration from Haran to Canaan involves a curious discrepancy in chronology. *Chapter eleven* of *Genesis* ends with the statement, "And the days of Terah were two hundred and five years; and Terah died in Haran." *Chapter twelve* opens with God's call which prompts Abraham's departure. The impression is therefore given that Abraham waited until his father's death before leaving the paternal household.

Now Abraham was born in Terah's seventieth year (11:26). He received the call when he was seventy-five (12:4). If Terah died at the age of two hundred and five, he would have continued to live for sixty years after Abraham left Haran. And indeed the Samaritan text states that Terah was one hundred and forty-five at the time of his death, which would be chronologically harmonious with Abraham's departure when his father died.[4]

Talmudic sources refer to the mathematical incongruity, intuitively recognizing it as an indication of unconscious conflict within Abraham.[5] If he did indeed leave Terah while the latter was still alive, the sequence of the two statements, Terah's death and Abraham's starting out on his mission, may unconsciously have been intended to protect the latter from the appearance of filial disloyalty at thus forsaking his aged parent. But a sense of guilt, as if impelled to reveal itself, although unobtrusively, may have found expression in the mention of the father's age.

Perhaps Abraham was able to break this ambivalent tie only by projecting upon God, the Father who superseded Terah, the command to leave his home and kindred. This mission, which presaged a future role far greater than that of his father, could also have increased feelings of guilt.

Abraham's relationship to his mother is even more obscure than to his father. She is, in fact, not even mentioned in the

Bible. Although genealogy in this literature is usually reckoned through the father, it seems a somewhat conspicuous omission not to refer to the mother of so important a personage as Abraham. Extra-biblical legendary sources have tried to fill this gap. The Talmud has a number of references to the mother of Abraham. She is even given a name, *Emtelai,* the etymology of which is uncertain, its possible meanings being either *mother* or *servant.*[6]

The use of a legendary name which involves such a close relationship between the two concepts, *mother* and *servant,* must have some meaning. In dreams the mother may be represented as a servant, an unconscious fantasy stemming from the time when the child had a need to denigrate her because she was the sexual partner of the father. For the young rival prefers to think of the mother as being forced into this role rather than acceding to it willingly. Such concepts may remain repressed in the unconscious of adults.

Other legendary material strengthens the idea of Abraham's ambivalent feelings toward the image of a frustrating, preoedipal mother. One story is that at the time of his birth a royal edict was issued to the effect that all male infants were to be destroyed. This measure was taken because of predictions by soothsayers that a boy would be born who would displace the king himself. This common element in the myth of the birth of a hero is significant here in terms of the mother's behavior. When the time for her delivery came, Emtelai left the city in order to escape detection. Wandering in the desert, she finally found refuge in a cave, where the baby was born. However, she soon abandoned him and returned to her home, declaring that since he had to perish, it was better that he do so alone in the cave so she would not behold him dead at her breast. Evoking God's blessing upon him, she departed.

God sends Gabriel down to help the deserted child. The angel causes milk to flow from the little finger of the infant's right hand so he could feed himself.[7] Another legend adds that Abraham could also draw honey from a second finger.[8] Like the Promised Land of his later life, Abraham flows with milk and honey. He thus gives up the frustrating maternal object and identifies with her instead, incorporating her nurturing qualities.

At the time when the story in *Genesis* begins, Abraham presumably had already lost his mother. Otherwise she probably would have been mentioned among those joining the family migration to Haran.

A fuller understanding of Abraham's relationship with the mother is bound up with a view of his feelings toward siblings. Are there any indications about Abraham's attitudes in this respect? These emotions are deeply disguised in the Bible.

We have the factual statement that Terah had three sons, Abram, Nahor, and Haran. Abram is evidently the eldest. We are then informed that Haran died in Ur. It is the latter's son, Lot, who joins in the family migration to Haran, the city by the same name as his father's, and later accompanies Abraham to Canaan.

This material must have some bearing upon the life of Abraham or it would not be recorded. Again, extra-biblical legends come to our assistance. One of these relates that when Abraham was tossed into the fiery furnace by the king as punishment for denouncing idol-worship, he was saved by God. Seeing this miracle, Haran also declared his belief in Abraham's God. But when he too was thrown into the fire, he perished, for his faith had not been sincere. We have here a contrast between the faithful Abraham and his unworthy brother.

According to one commentary, Haran's death was the punishment for an incestuous crime. The logic for this thinking is that Lot, his son, did commit such a misdeed, although unwittingly, and he must therefore have been following in the footsteps of his father. Another view is that Haran was punished for the anticipated crime of his son.[9] What emerges from these obvious rationalizations is a highly disguised sibling rivalry on the part of Abraham toward his brother, expressed in the need to denigrate the latter.

Psychologically it would be valid to assume that this rivalry had its roots in relation to the mother. As the youngest of the three brothers, Haran may have occupied a special position in her affections, thus stimulating Abraham's feelings of jealousy and abandonment. The biblical narrative even deprives Haran of the comfort of his mother at the hour of his death. It says that *Haran died in the presence of his father* (11:28). What could be the purpose of such a statement? It seems to emphasize the absence of the mother, to point out her non-existence at this crucial time. Whether she was already dead or not, ambivalent feelings toward her may here be expressed in identification with the dying brother. At this critical period he is abandoned by the unfeeling mother, even as Abraham may have felt himself to be. That identifications can be conflicting and contradictory is an aspect of unconscious life.

It is not the intent here to attribute to Abraham the actual content of these legends which may have evolved at a much later time. The feelings and motivations that prompted them may be in response to the underlying attitudes hidden in the biblical text. Legends and myths arise in the popular mind in unconscious identification with the hero.

We now come to the relationship between Abraham and his wife, Sarah. In contrast to the theoretic lowliness of the position of women in that era, Sarah was clearly a highly influential figure in the life of Abraham. Yet her background is almost as much of a mystery as that of the Patriarch's mother. The text says, "And Abram and Nahor took them wives; and the name of Abram's wife was Sarai; and the name of Nahor's wife, Milcah, the daughter of Haran, the father of Milcah, and the father of Iscah (11:29)."

There are two puzzling details about this verse. Milcah is identified twice, first as the daughter of Haran, who is then described again as her father. In contrast, Sarah's parentage is not mentioned at all but in the place where it would be expected, an unfamiliar name, *Iscah* is brought in, one that never occurs again in the Scriptures. Moreover, if Milcah and Iscah are both the daughters of Haran, why the repetition of the phrase, *the father of?* A more recent translation of this literature does simplify the wording by reducing it to "the father of Milcah and Iscah."[10]

Talmudic scholars, sensitive to every incongruity in the holy text, do identify *Iscah* with Sarah in one of their alternative explanations. The most plausible reason given is that the name is suggestive of the word meaning *princess* and is thus another form of *Sarah* in the Hebrew.[11] The explanation concerning Sarah's identity most generally accepted among Talmudic scholars is the one offered by Abraham himself later in the story. He says of her, "And moreover, she is indeed my sister, the daughter of my father, but not of my mother; and so she became my wife (20:12)." This statement was made in an effort to extenuate himself for posing as Sarah's brother during their sojourns in Egypt and Gerar.[12]

Some rabbinic opinion, uneasy about the incestuous aspect of this relationship, pointed out that the word *daughter* in the Bible was also used to describe a *granddaughter* suggesting that Sarah may indeed have been Abraham's niece. But his own words seem clear and forthright, though offered in expiation of his conduct. However, even as a half-sister, Sarah would be equally related to Haran and thus would have *belonged* to both the father and the younger brother.

On a reality level, marriages of half-siblings were not contrary to the law and custom of those times.[13] Psychologically, things may have been otherwise. The obscurity in the text regarding Sarah's parentage may indicate an effort to deny feelings of guilt in the marital relationship on the part of Abraham. In a more than usual sense, he may have been experienced his wife unconsciously as an incestuous object. These dynamics play a role in his behavior as will be seen shortly.

Abraham and his people migrate southward into Canaan. The first specific locality mentioned is the town of Shechem, which is a considerable distance from Haran. The text says:

And Abram passed through the land unto the place of Shechem, unto the terebinth of Moreh. And the Canaanite was then in the land. And the Lord appeared unto Abram, and said, Unto thy seed will I give this land; and there builded he an altar unto the Lord, who appeared unto him (12:6–7).

The rather laconic statement, "And the Canaanite was then in the land," appears unrelated in the context. It was well-known that the Canaanites were in the territory through which Abraham was passing.[14] Why then was it necessary to refer to this fact? The irrelevance of this detail points to its possible significance in terms of unconscious content, as we shall see.[15]

Shechem was the largest town of the area, well-fortified, and dominating the road which ran northward and southward, from Syria to Egypt. The *terebinth of Moreh,* "the oak of teaching," was at that very site, probably a sacred spot tended by priests, where oracles were revealed. Symbolically, the mother-city was guarded by the father-oak, a kind of divinity.

The reminder about the presence of the Canaanites may indicate that Abraham became uneasy when reaching this town whose inhabitants might prove to be unfriendly. Since it was not unusual for nomadic groups to wander through the countryside in the sparse areas between towns and since the text gives no indication that the inhabitants of Shechem showed hostility toward Abraham, one can assume that factors within the Patriarch himself must have stirred up his anxiety. The symbolic value of a land and a city as representative of the mother seems to have had more than usual significance for the biblical Hebrews. If this was so, then Abraham's *passage* through Canaan and his arrival at Shechem involved an unconscious *taking possession* of the mother and may have aroused feelings of uneasiness. The directly expressed prediction that *his seed* would inherit the land, strengthens the unconscious oedipal connotations. Guilt feelings in relation to Sarah, who belonged to *the father,* may also have been activated by his trespassing through the land, also the domain of *the father.* If, indeed, the fantasy was to take possession of the land, including the city, a wish safely displaced to the future, Abraham would feel guilty at this aggressive thought and expect retaliation. He there-fore needed, not only God's promise as a form of reassurance but his protective presence, for God also *appears* to him. The confus-ing word, *then,* may unconsciously express a contrast in time with the future, when the fantasy of Abraham would be fulfilled and the Canaanite would *no longer* be in the land.

Abraham continues his journey southward. Then we are told that there is famine in the land and he seeks refuge in Egypt. One wonders why the Patriarch fled so quickly from the country to which God had directed him. The Bible does not enlighten us on this point, merely making the factual statement, "And there was a famine in the land; and Abram went down into Egypt to sojourn there; for the famine was sore in the land (12:10)." Some rabbinic sources however rebuke him for his seeming lack of faith at this time.[16] Drought and the consequent famine were generally interpreted as signs of Divine displeasure. Abraham's anxiety must have increased in spite of God's reassurance and he hastily leaves.

But the Patriarch is also uneasy about entering Egypt, as manifested by a rather curious incident that then takes place. He anticipates that his wife, because of her great beauty, will be ap-propriated for the Pharaoh's harem. In that event, he assumes, his own life would be in danger. Abraham therefore pleads with Sarah to pose as his sister. He presents the picture of a man in a state of anxiety.

> And it came to pass, when he was come near to enter into Egypt, that he said unto Sarai his wife: "Behold now, I know that thou art a fair woman to look upon. And it will come to pass, when the Egyptians shall see thee, that they will say: This is his wife; and they will kill me, but thee they will keep alive. Say, I pray thee, thou art my sister; that it may be well with me for thy sake, and that my soul may live because of thee (12:11–13)."

His fears are realized and Sarah is taken from him. However, through God's intervention a plague falls upon the house of

Pharaoh, Sarah's true identity is revealed and the might and power of the Hebrew God are so impressed upon the monarch that he returns Sarah to her husband. Later on, a similar incident is repeated in almost identical fashion in the kingdom of Gerar, a locality which lay between Canaan and Egypt.

The same weakening of his defenses and sublimations that caused Abraham to abandon the *Promised Land* may also have been the basis of his anxiety on entering Egypt and Gerar, territories of the powerful father-kings. Abraham was then ready to surrender the *forbidden* woman in order to save himself from death, a fantasied death which is here a derivative of castration anxiety, the punishment for oedipal misconduct. For, indeed, the incidents both in Egypt and Gerar, with their strangely repetitive pattern and the fact that Abraham anticipated them before they occurred, have a decidedly unrealistic aspect. They are more understandable as fantasies stemming from anxiety based on unconscious factors as referred to above. In real situations, as will be seen later, Abraham clearly shows himself to be a man of courage.

Moreover, the outcome in both incidents adds to the fantasy quality. The two rulers not only return his wife but also enrich him with gifts, thus acknowledging that his God is greater than theirs, even as his God was better than Terah's. In this rather ambiguous father-son contest, Araham comes out victorious. He is submissive to the earthly father to a degree that could be considered masochistic, but is saved by the Heavenly One.[17] Furthermore, the kingly father figures are threatened with the plague, or death, classical punishment for incestuous wishes. This detail may express another projection on the part of Abraham himself. It is they who are guilty of such wishes and worthy of punishment, not he.

Many of Abraham's problems and conflicts center around the father-son nucleus. He remains childless for many years in spite of God's repeated promise that a son would be born to carry on the father's mission. The very fact of Abraham's long years of childlessness could have had a psychogenic significance. If Sarah was a mother surrogate, then the sexual relationship with her would be impaired and the emotional reasons for childlessness explained.

God's promise to him is of a very grandiose nature. His descendants were to be as numberless as the sand of the sea and the stars in the heavens. Does not the comparison itself betray ambivalence by bringing together the most lowly substance with the most elevated? The very nature of this promise in its limitless abundance may contain an unconscious reversal of the real wish —a fantasy that he might never have a competitor in the form of a son and thus never be displaced. Moreover, his own ambivalence as a son gave him good reason to fear retaliation from one of his own.

It is made abundantly clear that Abraham's dearest wish was to have an heir of his own flesh who would carry on his great task. We cannot doubt that this desire was profoundly real. That it contained ambivalent features, largely unconscious, attests only to Abraham's essential humanness. What, then, was his actual behavior to three son figures?

The first of these was Lot, the son of his deceased brother Haran. Since Abraham had been childless for many years, Lot seemed the most likely person to become his heir. And indeed he took Lot with him from the town of Haran and they dwelt in Canaan together. But on the first occasion of a conflict, Abraham suggests that Lot should leave him. It will be recalled, in this familiar episode, that ". . . there was a strife between the herdsmen of Abram's cattle and the herdsmen of Lot's cattle," because the flocks belonging to the two men were so large, the land could not produce sustenance for them all.

> And Abram said unto Lot: "Let there be no strife, I pray thee, between me and thee, and between my herdsmen and thy herdsmen; for we are brethren. Is not the whole land before thee? separate thyself, I pray thee, from me; if thou wilt take the left hand, then I will go to the right; or if thou take the right hand, then I will go to the left (13:8–10)."

Lot chooses the well-watered plain of the Jordan, to the east, and settles in the ill-fated town of Sodom. Abraham remains in Canaan.

This story is uniformly pointed to as significant of Abraham's love of peace. It is also used to indicate the Patriarch's generosity since he allowed Lot to have the first choice of territory for his flocks. Another explanation for this action is that Abraham did not wish to arouse the hostility of the Canaanites by taking up so much of the pasturage for both his own herds and those of Lot. Rabbinic sources, moreover, declare that Lot, being an idol-worshipper, was not worthy of filling the role destined for Abraham's son.

The fact remains, however, that Abraham, quite readily and without any evident regret, sends away the man who stood in a son relationship to him, even though there was as yet no other to fill that important role. While there seems to be some reality basis for this act, it can be better understood on the level of unconscious motivation. Abraham may have felt threatened by the idea of an heir who would one day take his place. It might be argued that this separation from Lot indicated rather Abraham's faith in God, who had promised him a son of his own. But even belief in such a promise would not necessitate separation from Lot, especially his removal to such a distant point.

In the actual sequence of events as described in the Bible, the promise of a son occurs immediately *after* Lot departs.

And the Lord said unto Abraham, after that Lot was separated from him: "Lift up thine eyes, and look from the place where thou art, northward and southward and eastward and westward; for all the land which thou seest, to thee will I give it, and to thy seed for ever (13:14-15)."

These words sound like an effort at reassurance. Abraham's hostility toward a son is here acted out in reality by sending Lot away, while his positive wishes in this direction find expression in the hope of a fulfillment safely put off to the future. In the meantime, he remains the sole important figure in relation to God, to Sarah, and to his people. It might be recalled at this point that

Lot was related to Sarah, not only by her marriage to Abraham, but through actual blood ties. He may have represented a younger sibling rival for the love of the mother, thus bringing about a repetition of an earlier trauma.

A situation occurs in which Abraham shows the positive aspects of his feelings for Lot, together with a sense of responsibility for this member of his family. Word reaches him that Lot, among others, had been taken captive during a war upon Sodom and Gemorrah. Abraham at once rallies his men about him and they pursue the enemy for a considerable distance to the north. They win a victory and free the prisoners, also recovering the rich spoils of war that had been captured. When the king of Sodom gratefully offers him a reward Abraham refuses to take "even so much as a shoe-latchet." To do so would lessen the virtue of his act in the eyes of God. This is clearly a deed that had to be done for its own sake.

But the reward which Abraham refuses from the king comes instead from the Heavenly Father. For it is immediately after the rescue of Lot that God reveals himself once more to the Patriarch, saying,

> "Fear not, Abram, I am thy shield, thy reward shall be exceeding great." And Abram said: O Lord God what wilt Thou give me, seeing I go hence childless, and he that shall be possessor of my house is Eliezer of Damascus (15:1–2)?"

God reassures Abraham, telling him that his heir would be a son of his own. Why does Abraham need reassurance at this point? What is it that he fears? The Patriarch has just fulfilled a valorous deed by saving Lot and the other prisoners of war. He has obeyed the edict of his conscience by not accepting any reward for his heroic achievement in battle. Why is it that God appears to him in a vision *now* and repeats his promise of a son and heir?

The last time an event of such magnitude took place was also after a separation from Lot. Then too God had promised Abraham a son. In a sense, the Patriarch was suffering from a kind of separation anxiety, the fear associated with the loss of a potential heir. This repetitive sequence of events seems to indicate how

strong were the undercurrents of Abraham's feelings, both positive and negative, toward the man who stood in a son relationship
to him. The act of saving Lot must have evoked Abraham's
warmer feelings toward his kinsman. One whom we aid becomes
closer to us. Then the Patriarch had to part from Lot once more,
leaving him in Sodom. He was reminded now that only his chief
steward, not even a blood relative, might be the only one left as
his heir. Abraham's fear on this occasion clearly concerned his
childlessness, an apprehension compounded by guilt for his own
role in separating from Lot.

There are indications, however, that this mood of anxiety
also involved ambivalence. Related to the fear of *not* having a son
may have been the opposite fear, that of *having* one. A rabbinic
legend brings out this conflict with remarkable intuitiveness, although also in hidden form. It says that God appeared to him
at this time in order to comfort the Patriarch for the blood he
had been forced to shed in the preceding battle. It seems that
Abraham had strong moral principles against this kind of violence. God then assures him that among his descendants there
would also be pious men who, like himself, would be a shield to
their generation. On this occasion, God offers him a rare privilege,
the right to ask for anything he wishes.

How does Abraham utilize this opportunity? He replies,

"O Lord of the world, if in time to come, my descendants
should provoke thy wrath, *it were better that I remained
childless*. Lot, for the sake of whom I journed as far as
Damascus, where God was my protection, would be well
pleased to be my heir. Moreover, I have read in the stars,
'Abraham, thou will beget no chilren.' Wherepon God raised
Abraham above the vault of the skies, and He said, 'Thou
art a prophet, not an astrologer.' "[18] (*italics added*)

This legend deals subtly with several aspects of Abraham's
human frailties, showing the tendency both to expose and defend
this revered personality. Why was Abraham so acutely sensitive
to the shedding of blood, even for the commendable purpose of
saving his nephew? Such an attitude can be understood as a re-

action formation, a defense against the opposite kind of feeling, that of aggression. Moreover, why is Abraham so submissive and self-defeating when he has an opportunity of assuring himself of an heir merely by stating his wish? That this desire was uppermost in his mind is evident by the fact that he voices it in a negative form, asking God *not* to grant him what he most wants. His rationalization, the fear of God's possible displeasure which might be brought about by Abraham's descendants, is exactly the opposite of what God has just told him—that there would be pious people among these descendants, who would also be a shield to their generation. Perhaps Abraham is not too pleased with this prophecy about others, unconsciously, a son, who might take his place in God's love. He is now ready to settle for Lot as an heir. There was little danger that his nephew could compete with him in righteousness.

God does not accept Abraham's submissive attitude. There is a touch of mild reproof in his reply, "Thou art a prophet, not an astrologer." Abraham's ambivalent feelings are brought out in this brief story. He tries to defeat himself by renouncing what at the same time he wants most.

One wonders, however, if even this compounded fear, that of *not* having a son and of *having* one, explains fully the intensity of Abraham's anxiety as it is reflected in the quality of God's reassurance. The words, "Fear not, Abram, I am thy shield," would be appropriate only in a situation where there was a sense of imminent danger.

The Patriarch had just returned from warring against kings in order to rescue Lot and his companions. He defeated the once-powerful *fathers,* depriving them of *sons* and the spoils of war, an action which must have required great courage and resolution. Abraham's whole psychic tendency was to work out conflicts along the lines of sublimation and compromise. But his strong sense of reality is evident here. The situation demanded immediate action and he responded to the need. However, the psychological aftermath was another matter. Abraham's anxiety must have been aroused by his daring in being so aggressive with father figures. God's communication to him at this time dealt not only with the theme of an heir, stimulated by the separation from Lot, but also served as a reassurance of protection from the fantasied punitive retaliation of the father against whom he had been so hostile. Both aspects are contained in the brief opening words, "Fear not, Abram, I am thy shield, thy reward shall be exceeding great."

But Abraham's mood fluctuates. Told to look up at the heavens and see the stars, the Patriarch is promised that his seed would be as numberless. The Bible then says, "And he believed in the Lord; and He counted it to him for righteousness." The very fact, however, that this expression of trust was necessary indicates that *disbelief* had been a possible alternative. And, indeed, an attitude of doubt comes out in the very next verse. God says to him, "I am the Lord who brought thee out of Ur of the Chaldees, to give thee this land to inherit." And he said: "O Lord God, whereby shall I know that I shall inherit it (15:4–8)?"

One wonders, first of all, why God suddenly introduces himself as if it were the beginning of the theophany and not a continuation of the preceding verses in which God had promised Abraham an heir of his own. Also, why does God now present himself as the Deity who brought Abraham out of Ur of the Chaldees? For the call from God had come to Abraham in Haran.

What can be the meaning of this rather strange sequence? We shall try to understand it as a projection of Abraham's fantasy. He dared to have faith in God and to hope for a son. But this trust in a father image may immediately have evoked conflicting emotions stemming from the unconscious, which were further stimulated by the second promise God made involving the inheritance of the land, with its underlying significance of forbidden oedipal content. Abraham's anxiety increases. He sees God suddenly in relation to his father Terah, who actually did bring him forth from Ur, thus *taking him away* from his native land, symbolically, the mother. Distrust and ambivalence toward the earthly father are momentarily displaced to the Heavenly One.

God responds to this situation by instructing Abraham to prepare for the ritual known as the *covenant of the pieces*. This mystical experience is discussed by the writer in a separate study.[19] The ceremonial, probably based on an ancient custom, involved

the dividing of certain animals into halves and the passing between the pieces of the covenanting parties, indicating the concepts of both separation and union, of threat and promise, depending on how faithfully the covenant would be kept.[20] The
biblical account concerning Abraham is a variation of this custom
but takes on a character of its own.

An untoward incident, clearly not a part of the ritual, occurs
after Abraham has prepared the animals and is awaiting the
expected revelation. The Bible says, "And the birds of prey came
down upon the carcasses, and Abraham drove them away (15:11)."
Such a happening could not have been very meaningful in itself.
Unless it had some significance in this context it would hardly
have been recorded. The very casualness and brevity with which
this detail is mentioned leads one to suspect that it has unconscious
connotations. So might an important element in a dream be
innocuously presented.

The birds of prey swooping down over the bloody parts of the
freshly-slain animals must have been an added factor in building
up within Abraham a mood of apprehension and anxiety. He
may already have identified himself unconsciously with the sacrificial animals on the one hand, and at the same time, experienced
aggression and guilt in the slaying of these creatures which probably had totemic significance. Abraham could thus have reacted
to the birds of prey with an unconscious infantile fantasy relating to the preoedipal mother, the fear of being eaten. The vulture
was a maternal deity of the ancient Egyptians with special significance as a phallic mother. Regressive castration fears may have
been evoked in Abraham as a consequence of the anxious ex-
pectancy with which he must have awaited the coming of God.

The act of driving off the birds of prey, in addition to its
reality aspect, may also have signified an effort on the part of
Abraham's ego to ward off the approaching experience of submission to a great and mysterious Power. But the defense does
not succeed. The Bible goes on to say:

And it came to pass, that, when the sun was going down, a
deep sleep fell upon Abram; and lo, a dread, even a great

darkness, fell upon him. And He said unto Abram: 'Know of a surety that thy seed shall be a stranger in a land that is not theirs, and shall serve them; and they shall afflict them four hundred years; and also that nation, whom they serve, will I judge; and afterward shall they come out with great substance. But thou shalt go to thy fathers in peace; thou shalt be buried in a good old age. . . . And it came to pass, that, when the sun went down and there was thick darkness, behold a smoking furnace, and a flaming torch that passed between these pieces. In that day the Lord made a covenant with Abram, saying, 'Unto thy seed have I given this land, from the river of Egypt unto the great river, the river Euphrates . . . (15:12–18).'

Here we see again the backward and forward surge of negative and positive feelings. The seed of Abraham must be punished and purified before they win the land of Canaan. We can understand this prophecy as a projection of Abraham's own feelings toward his heirs. It may also represent his identification with hostile sons and the consequent guilt and need for punishment, here safely displaced to his progeny.

The smoking furnace and the flame that pass between the pieces must indeed symbolize the Divinity. This mystical power is incorporated by the parts of the animals and thus renews the bond of unity between this symbolic representation of Abraham and the God with whom he covenants. Physically inert and passive, the Patriarch allows himself to be possessed by the Spirit, thus showing his trust in God.

The profound affects associated with the theophany are clearly conveyed in the biblical narrative. *Dread,* in the sense of awe and fear, are feelings also experienced toward the oedipal father. In the graphic description, ". . . lo, a dread, even a great darkness fell upon him," the words *dread* and *darkness* are used as equivalent terms. One gets the impression that the affect of dread and darkness is felt here as a palpable *thing* having a physical, or material quality, which *falls* upon Abraham. This psychic drama occurs at a time when the setting sun enfolds the earth in the obscurity of night. We see here again Abraham's tendency to respond with strong emotions to cosmic forces and to project his feelings upon them.

It is an interesting anomaly that the sun, symbol of the mighty father and source of all light, now disappears, leaving a great darkness. So might the intrapsychic image of the father return in sleep and dreams. The darkness may also symbolize a defense against the forbidden voyeurism toward the father and the fear of being seen by him.

The fact, however, that Abraham allowed himself to sink into this trance-like state indicates that the positive elements in the situation outweighed the negative. A man of strong will, he nevertheless gives himself over to this experience with a trust that is greater than his fears. The feelings of dread that pass over him recall the religious emotion described by Rudolf Otto in what he calls the *mysterium tremendum*. He says,

> The daemonic-divine object may appear to the mind an object of horror and dread, but at the same time it is no less something that allures with a potent charm, and the creature, who trembles before it, utterly cowed and cast down, has always at the same time the impulse to turn to it, nay, even to make it somehow his own.[21]

How does the concept of *covenant* enter into the biblical episode under discussion here? Perhaps it might be well to emphasize that the idea of covenant at that time expressed not only a specific agreement between two parties but also a relationship in a more general sense, indicating that the two now had a special bond between them.

The experience begins with Abraham's demand for proof that God would fulfill his promise regarding the inheritance of the land of Canaan. How does God proceed to convince the Patriarch? The first step has to be taken by Abraham himself. He is told to prepare the sacrificial victims in accordance with God's specific instructions. Abraham therefore must have enough trust in God to carry out the command. So the process starts with an act of obedience, indicative of Abraham's basic confidence. The performance of sacrifice in itself always connotes the idea of atonement and thus relieves guilt. Abraham himself, lying upon the ground and falling into a deep sleep, expresses profoundly both trust and submission to him whose revelation he awaits.

Evidently words alone had not been convincing enough. God had uttered verbal assurance and a promise earlier. What more did the Patriarch need and want? He must have desired to *experience the very Presence of God* in a convincing and dramatic fashion. After Abraham's preparation of the sacrifice, his atonement and submission, God takes the active role, passing between the pieces. Thus he accepts the offering and renews the bond between himself and the Patriarch. The covenant consists, first, in Abraham's willingness to obey, to atone, and to submit. God's share is to convince Abraham that the Deity is there and present, therefore his words have authority.

The story about Abraham's hospitality, when he entertains angels unawares, is one of the best-beloved about the Patriarch. It presents a vivid picture of nomadic, pastoral life in one of its most appealing aspects. Hospitality was akin to the saving of life, for a wandering stranger not only found himself without food and water, but was a likely object of suspicion and hostility. But once he has been welcomed into the encampment and partaken of food, he is immune to aggression. Hospitality was therefore regarded as a great virtue.

There is however an element of urgency about the manner in which Abraham performs his duty of hospitality. It is the difference between enjoying the performance of a good deed and the anxious zeal with which it is carried out. The text says:

> And the Lord appeared unto him by the terebinths of Mamre, as he sat in the tent door in the heat of the day; and he lifted up his eyes and looked, and lo, three men stood over against him; and when he saw them, he ran to meet them from the tent door, and bowed down to the earth, and said, "My Lord, if now I have found favor in thy sight, pass not away, I pray thee, from thy servant. Let now a little water be fetched, and wash your feet, and rest yourselves under a tree. And I will fetch a morsel of bread, and stay ye your heart; after that ye

shall pass on; forasmuch as ye are come to your servant."
And they said, "So do, as thou hast said." And Abraham hastened into the tent unto Sarah, and said: "Make ready
quickly three measures of fine meal, knead it, and make
cakes." And Abraham ran unto the herd, and fetched a calf
tender and good, and gave it unto the servant; and he hastened
to dress it. And he took curd, and milk, and the calf which he
had dressed, and set it before them; and he stood by them
under the tree, and they did eat (18:1–8).

Talmudic interpretation connects this episode in time sequence with the one at the close of the preceding chapter. That
event deals with the circumcision of Abraham as a sign of his
covenant with God, in relation to the promise of a son and heir.
Thus, although it is the heat of the day and Abraham is an old
man in a state of convalescence, he *runs* to meet his guests, *bows
down, hastens,* orders Sarah to make bread *quickly, runs* unto the
herd to select a calf himself, and *serves* his guests.

The zeal to do a good deed cannot in itself explain the pitch
of excitement within Abraham which this narrative conveys. The
Patriarch, it seems, was in a state of inner tension and anxiety.
His perceptive powers also may have been affected by this mood
for he does not seem to know clearly what is going on. The
biblical verses quoted above contain elements of confusion, not
only about the identity of the guests but also in regard to their
number and the manner in which he becomes aware of their presence. First we are told clearly that it is the Lord himself who
appeared to him. But in the very same sentence, Abraham looks
up and sees *three men.* There is also a conflicting picture of their
physical proximity to him. One moment we are told that "three
men stood over against him;" in the next instant he is running to
meet them, so they must have been a short distance away.[22]

Abraham may indeed have been in a difficult interim period
at this time. The influence of the circumcision experience, with
its accompanying affects, would still have been upon him. Moreover, not one, but two portentous events loomed before him, a
prophecy of good and one of evil. The coming of a son had been
promised. But Abraham must also have known the predictions of

doom that were then hanging over the cities of Sodom and Gemorrah, the territory where Lot and his family lived.

Both these events, in fact, are closely associated with the visit of the strangers to Abraham. For it was after the Patriarch performed his kindly act toward the three strangers that the prophetic promise of a son was again made to him.

It is on this same occasion that the famous scene takes place in which Abraham bargains with God in an effort to save the wicked cities of Sodom and Gemorrah from destruction. Two of his three heavenly visitors move on to Sodom to carry out their mission there. The third, evidently God himself, tarries a bit. He decides to take Abraham into his confidence about the impending doom hanging over the cities of the Plain and says to him, "I will go down now and see whether they have done altogether according to the cry of it, which is come unto Me; and if not, I will know." Before meting out such dread punishment, God decides to investigate the situation himself. Abraham then lingers before the Lord and dares to argue the matter with him, saying, "Wilt thou indeed sweep away the righteous with the wicked? . . . Shall not the Judge of all the earth do justly (18:23–25)?" He asks God if he would spare the cities should fifty righteous men be found there. Encouraged when God agrees, Abraham keeps decreasing the number on whom the fate of the cities should depend until he succeeds in reducing the number to ten.

Psychoanalytically, this dramatic little dialogue could be explained as a projection of what was going on within Abraham, the conflict with his own superego. Lot and his family lived in Sodom, and their fate also was involved if these cities were destroyed. Abraham had been instrumental in sending Lot into this city of depravity where even hospitality was a crime. The Patriarch himself had just practiced this virtue and had been rewarded with the promise of a son. His feelings of guilt toward Lot may easily have been stirred by this double stimulus, and a wish aroused to save him from the doom that threatened the city. The sequence of events must have some significance—the hospitality, the promise of a son, and immediately after, the discussion of Sodom and its imminent destruction. Might not Abraham's plea for the cities have been in the service of guilt feelings, therefore taking on an unusual intensity of righteousness? Abraham pleads for all the people, thereby disguising the identity of the one in the many, a mechanism commonly found in dreams.

The unusual and rather charming anthropomorphic quality of God in this scene conveys the feeling that Abraham is standing before his personified conscience. The doubt which God expressed about what was going on in Sodom may have been the doubt in Abraham's own heart about the justice of his behavior toward Lot.

Commentators have been inclined to eulogize this episode as marking the high point of nobility and righteousness in the character of Abraham. Yet this favored son of God is here more righteous than God himself, even as he was superior to his earthly father. He may thus not only be compensating for guilt feelings toward Lot, but also expressing some unconscious hostility toward God, the Father. The mechanism of displacement may be involved here. It is not he who wishes to put Lot out of the way, but God, and moreover, without just cause. So Abraham reverses the roles, as he did with Terah, and becomes father toward God, gently reproving him. Abraham thus removes the cloak of perfection from God and dons it himself. He overcomes the Father in the very act of becoming like him. At the moment when he is altruistically pleading for others, his own narcissism, here expressed as a need for self-righteousness, stands clearly revealed. Only on such unconscious defensive motivation can the behavior of Abraham be understood here. For nowhere else is there any indication that his concept of God could be described as anything less than perfect.

The interpretation that conflict about his nephew is the chief determining element in this scene is strengthened by the fact that during the events that follow in Sodom, Lot is quite openly the central figure. We hear no more about the number of righteous men or the lack of them in the city. Only Lot and his family seem to be involved.

A series of events now take place, the meaning of which

is most puzzling. Two of the three angels that had visited Abraham proceed to Sodom. They meet Lot at the open space near the gates of the city and reluctantly allow themselves to be persuaded by him to take shelter in his home for the night.

A mob surrounds Lot's house and demands that he surrender the strangers to them for the laws of Sodom forbid hospitality. Lot resorts to a rather drastic measure to appease the hostile crowd. He faces the mob and implores the people to take his two virgin daughters instead and do with them what they will, but to spare his guests, to whom he owes the duty of protection. Lot is saved from this dramatic sacrifice when the angels open the door of the house, draw him inside, and at the same time cause blindness among the people outside so that they cannot find the door.

Let us consider this puzzling episode, which is so full of unreality, as stemming from the unconscious of Lot, who here plays the role of hero. Blindness may express castration, the punishment for incest. But it was the multitude who was thus afflicted so that they could not *find the door,* symbolically, could not violate the daughters of Lot. We can assume that a displacement has occurred here. It must have been Lot himself who was thus tempted. And indeed it was he who offered his daughters as a substitute. Both the wish and the penalty are displaced to the angry mob. The good strangers inside the house protect him from the bad strangers outside, in a dramatic symbolization of the good, internalized object, the superego, fighting off the evil, projected id impulses.

The next day, again with the help of the angels, Lot and his two daughters escape the destruction that takes place in the city, but his wife looks behind her and is turned into a pillar of salt.

Biblical commentators say that Lot was saved, not for any virtue of his own, but for the sake of Abraham. And indeed, apart from his relationship to Abraham, Lot has little significance. On what basis, then, did this myth develop and why was it considered important enough to be included in the sacred text?

If Lot was saved because of Abraham, then the other events in the story must also have some connection with him. The entire myth might be understood as a fantasy that developed in identification with the thoughts and feelings of Abraham as he contemplated the possible fate of his nephew. It was an answer to the problem of what happened to the cities and to Lot after Abraham's dramatic bargaining with God.

There is considerable evidence that the cities of the Plain were actually destroyed by earthquake in biblical times. The fate of Lot therefore was one to tempt the imagination of men. The ambivalent attitude toward him concealed in the myth might indeed be Abraham's own. The line of association does, in fact, proceed directly from Abraham to Lot as two of the angels leave the former and move at once to the latter.

The ambivalence referred to finds expression in several ways. Lot is allowed to practice hospitality, the virtue which Abraham himself esteems so highly. But this virtue is offset by the price Lot was willing to pay for it—the degradation of his daughters. We know that even in those days the violation of a virgin was considered a heinous offense. When Jacob's daughter, Dinah, was violated by a prince of Shechem, his act was not forgiven though he fell in love with the girl and wanted to marry her, offering rich gifts for her hand. The whole town suffered a cruel punishment at the hands of Dinah's brothers.

In the other instance of ambivalence, Lot is saved from destruction but the hostility is displaced to his wife, a person of whom we know practically nothing, so she can hardly in herself have earned such a punishment. Ernest Jones has explained the unconscious meaning of salt in mythology as a symbol for semen.[23] Thus the pillar of salt into which the unfortunate woman is transformed is a phallic symbol both in form and content. The hostility toward Lot is expressed in symbolic masculine form, an immobilized phallus. The punishment may be for *looking* while the city, a mother symbol, is being despoiled.

The theme of incest between Lot and his two daughters, warded off in the earlier incident, does come openly to the surface, in a dramatic return of the repressed. After their escape from the destroyed city, the father and daughters dwell in a cave together. The young women express a fear that the rest of humanity has been destroyed and that the human race is in danger of extinction. In order to avoid this calamity they decide they must bring forth children. They give their father strong wine and on successive nights each of them lies with him and conceives.

Symbolically, we might say, it is the son who returns to the cave, the womb of the mother, in an effort to deny that the whole world, again, the mother, was destroyed. The two daughters may represent both daughter and mother, separate yet one in the unconscious.

Lot may be considered in this myth as symbolizing an aspect of Abraham himself. The episode may indicate the high point of his own oedipal conflict, also in the form of a reversal. Unconsciously, it was not the daughters who wished to violate the father, but the son, Lot, representing a repressed part of Abraham himself, who wanted to commit incest with the mother. The abhorred but unconsciously desired act is not only displaced to Lot but as a further defense, makes him an unwilling and unwitting victim.

It is interesting to note that while biblical commentators have little that is good to say of Lot, the Bible itself nowhere states that he was unworthy as a person, nor do his deeds actually condemn him as such. For the most part, the character of Lot has been built up on inference through the work of interpreters. It seems likely that they were influenced by unconscious indentification with Abraham's own ambivalence and wished to justify the latter's conduct.

The story of Abraham and his first-born son, Ishmael, shows a continuation of the pattern of ambivalence in Abraham toward an heir. Ishmael is the offspring of Hagar, the Egyptian handmaiden of his wife Sarah. In accordance with the law and custom of those days, Sarah offered Hagar to her husband to make up for her own barrenness. In the conflict of jealousy that arose between the two women after Hagar conceived, the latter, we are told, despised her mistress and Sarah complained bitterly to her husband.

Abraham told her to deal with Hagar as seemed suitable to

her. This was also according to the law of those days as set forth
in the Code of Hammurabi, which stated that a concubine could
again be reduced to the status of a servant.[24,25] Sarah treated her
handmaid so harshly that Hagar fled into the wilderness. There
an angel appeared and told her to return to Sarah, comforting her
with the prophecy that she would bear a son who would be the
father of a multitude of people.

The tension between the two women continued and grew
more acute after Sarah herself gave birth to Isaac. On the occasion when the child's weaning was being celebrated by a feast,
Sarah saw the son of Hagar *making sport,* or *mocking,* or perhaps,
more innocently, just *playing,* depending on how the rather ambiguous Hebrew term is translated. It may be that the very sight
of Ishmael, here contemptuously referred to as the *son of Hagar,
the Egyptian,* was enough to arouse Sarah's anger and anxiety on
this important day in her own child's life. "Wherefore she said
unto Abraham, Cast out this bondwoman and her son: for the son
of this bondwoman shall not be heir with my son, even with
Isaac (21:10)."

We are told that such a thing was *very grievous* in the eyes of
Abraham but God himself urged him to do what Sarah said, for
his descendants were indeed to come from Isaac. As for Ishmael,
God promised to make a great nation from him also. So Hagar
and Ishmael are sent forth into the desert with some bread and a
bottle of water. They lose their way in the wilderness and would
have perished had not God sent an angel to rescue them, according to the story.

Beneath the manifest content of this episode, other motivations can be discerned. Abraham sends his own son and the
woman who bore him, into the desert to face a possible death.
The Bible, with its rather unusual protectiveness where the problem of Abraham's righteousness is concerned, absolves him from
guilt by projecting the responsibility to God. Commentators emphasize that Abraham acquiesed to this deed in order to maintain
peace in the household, pointing out that he was known as a man
who loved peace. But surely Abraham was not such a weakling,
nor was he so afraid of Sarah, that he could not have settled this

problem without resorting to so drastic a measure. In a large nomadic encampment people can live together without seeing each other for days at a time.

Abraham's act can only be understood as an aggressive one, an attitude manifested on two occasions: first, when he allowed Hagar, who was already bearing his child, to be mistreated by Sarah, and second, when he actually sent her and his son away into the wilderness.

Rabbinic tales try to make amends for this behavior. They tell how Abraham yearned for his son and visited Ishmael in the desert when the latter was a grown man. Abraham does not find Ishmael at home but his wife is in the tent. She does not know Abraham's identity and fails to observe the most common laws of hospitality. Moreover, she is harshly mistreating her children. Abraham leaves a cryptic message with her to convey to Ishmael, advising him to put away the tent-pin which he had there and put another in its stead. Ishmael understood. He divorced his wife and got another.

In this legend, Abraham tries to correct a situation where a home is marred by an undutiful wife and mother. May this not be an effort on the part of the commentators to justify Abraham's own conduct to an *undutiful* woman?

The birth of Isaac, the fulfillment of God's promise, is something of a miracle. It occurs when Abraham is a hundred years old and his wife, Sarah, ninety. The child is born a year after God establishes his covenant with Abraham through the rite of circumcision.

It cannot be accidental that it was *after* the birth of Ishmael, the son which the Egyptian bondwoman, Hagar, bore to Abraham, that God establishes this covenant with the Patriarch. Isaac therefore was the first child born after the rite had been performed. He was the destined heir, the one who was to succeed and displace the father. If we accept the common psychoanalytic significance of circumcision as a symbolic partial castration, the penalty for incestuous wishes, it is understandable why the ritual should have preceded the birth of Isaac rather than that of

Ishmael.[26] Hagar was an Egyptian, a stranger, with whom incestuous bonds would be remote. Sarah was not only the desired
woman, the beloved wife, but she was also a kinswoman and
therefore much more likely to be an unconsciously forbidden
object. The price of a son from her would more clearly involve
the submissive act toward the father which circumcision implies.

We shall not enter here into the problem of why this rite has
retained such a strong hold in Jewish life throughout the ages
and the needs it must continue to serve. Briefly, circumcision de-
notes acceptance into the Hebrew fold. It expresses a permissive
attitude toward adult sexuality in return for acceptance of God's
Law and obedience to his morality.

The biblical injunction for the circumcision rite directs that
it be performed upon every male Hebrew child when he is eight
days old. Among other peoples this ceremony is usually carried
out between the period of puberty and marriage. Transposing it
to infancy can be understood psychologically as a defense against
its association with incest wishes. The rite becomes instead a
token of the covenant by which God promised Abraham and his
seed the privileges of adult sexuality.[27] He was to become the
father of a multitude of nations. The threat is thus transformed
into a promise. The very token which unconsciously expressed
castration becomes the symbol of the opposite—fertility, the command to be fruitful and multiply.

The next important event in the life of Abraham is the
dramatic incident when he is called upon by God to sacrifice
Isaac, the long-awaited only son of his union with Sarah, the son
who was to be his heir, and through whom God's promise to him
was to be fulfilled. Here we have a high point of drama and near-
tragedy, the culmination of Abraham's lifetime of ambivalence
toward a son. It is significant that this story occupies a place of
special importance in biblical literature and has been an engross-
ing subject in the Talmud and in the work of commentators
throughout the centuries.

Everywhere the courage of Abraham and his unfaltering faith
in God is extolled because he showed such readiness to carry out

this supreme act of sacrifice. But nowhere except in psycho-analytic writings is this act described in its true significance. As the time drew near for the son to displace the father, a powerful struggle of conflicting feelings within Abraham must have brought about the crisis which reached its peak in the near-sacrifice of Isaac. The *call* from God to sacrifice the ambivalently loved and hated son must also have involved repressed feelings of hostility toward the Father who ostensibly made this demand upon him. Such a deed would unconsciously have been an act of aggression toward God himself by frustrating the entire grand de-sign for which Abraham had been called in the first place. The man who, according to rabbinic tradition had been the first to comprehend God as the Creator of the universe, was now about to commit him to an act of annihilation.

Abraham must have felt as if he were about to give up his own life. And indeed, psychoanalytically, an identification with his son, the intended victim, must have been one of the circum-stances which made it possible for Abraham to submit to this command from God. The unconscious turning of the aggression against himself, the masochistic fantasy in which he became the victim, may have taken place. The sacrifice would then have been in the service of both feelings, aggression and the accompanying need for punishment. In unconscious fantasy, the son may some-times be experienced as the grandfather, the return of the father's father in the son.[28] If so, he would be an object of both intensified love and hate.

The biblical narrative of this event (22:1–19) is characterized by a remarkable lack of affect, even in this literature of restraint. There is not a single word which betrays feelings of any kind. This experience was probably the most profound, the most mov-ing, the most significant of the Patriarch's life. Artists and writers have reenacted the scene with the fullness of emotion that it must inevitably call forth in the human heart. Yet the story in the Bible consists of a series of factual statements.

The contrast between the content and the form serves to heighten the dramatic quality. But this masterpiece of literary understatement cannot have been produced consciously for this effect. The complete draining of emotion from the story of Isaac's near-sacrifice is psychologically sound. It expresses Abraham's mental state. This is how one feels at a moment of incalculable sorrow, of a tragedy, the full import of which cannot yet be faced. The suppression of feeling was Abraham's defense in an unbearable situation. It represented a temporary flight from reality such as one sees in people who are in a state of emotional shock.

Whatever unconscious factors may have entered into the kind of experience Abraham went through on Mount Moriah, one important thing stands out clearly. The occasion must have been a conflict of almost unbearable intensity. In this struggle, love and the sense of reality, which can only be founded on love, triumphed. In that blinding moment of anguish, Abraham must have realized that the God he worshipped was a God of love, who did not demand this cruel deed from him. This is indeed the lesson he taught his people and the world. But the insight came as a result of his own inner struggle, and we can today understand better the specific nature of that struggle as we probe more fully into the complexities of the human psyche.

It was significant for the development of Judaism that the sacrifice of Isaac was averted and that Abraham's healthy ego triumphed over the eruption of the sadistic superego. Freedom from guilt could not be won through self-castration as an act of submission to the Father, but on a reality level, through the overcoming of ambivalence. Abraham's positive feelings, his genuine love for Isaac, gained the ascendancy. Love overcame guilt and fear, decreasing the amount of his narcissism. Thus one can say with Freud that psychoanalysis shows man to be not only less moral than was formerly thought, but also more moral.

The biblical narratives about Abraham can be understood as a kind of psychological documentary of his life. They deal with his struggles to grow in emotional and spiritual maturity. His problems mainly involve the basic relationships of family life, where man's most intense emotions are rooted. By overcoming the inner conflicts of jealousy and competitiveness, with their accompanying aggression and fear, the positive feelings of warmth and cooperation were able to find expression.

From the extended family characteristic of the Patriarchal Era developed the clan, the tribe, and the nation. So Abraham, who conquered hostility through the ideal of a just and loving God, became the psychological model as a father for a whole people, whose religious goals could be expressed in strivings similar to his own.

The life of Abraham gives indications of the relationship between man's intrapsychic struggle and the development of an ethical social system based on religion. Freud has stated that cultural progress grows out of instinctual renunciation.[29] In the significant areas of Abraham's conflicts with his ambivalent feelings, the positive elements won over the hostile ones, thus leading to a sense of wholeness, or *oneness* within himself, the reflection of a unified superego. This process makes possible a greater sense of unity with others. Thus the capacity grew within Abraham for a closer union, not only with his family and his tribe, but in his feelings toward other peoples, as expressed in the ideal of being the father of a multitude of nations and a blessing to all the earth. This feeling of oneness in regard to the self and to humanity is a condition to a sense of Oneness about God as the projected Superego.

Abraham typifies in the life of an individual a process that, to a certain extent, is similar to the experiences of a whole people. Freud says,

> It can be maintained that the community, too, develops a superego, under whose influence cultural evolution proceeds. . . . The superego of any given epoch of civilization originates in the same way as that of the individual; it is based on the impression left behind them by great leading personalities, men of outstanding force of mind, men in whom some one human tendency has developed in unusual strength and purity. . . .[30]

Two Episodes
in the Life of Jacob

 CHAPTER TWO

Two EPISODES in the life of Jacob, both of dramatic intensity, are particularly meaningful from a psychoanalytic viewpoint. Around the story of these experiences his entire life history can be understood. One of them is Jacob's dream on the night he flees from home after deceiving his father Isaac and stealing the blessing that belonged to his brother Esau. The other is his mysterious encounter twenty years later, on his way back to Canaan, when a stranger comes out of the night and wrestles with him.[1]

It is significant that among the ancient forefathers of the Hebrews it was Jacob, later known as Israel, who gave his name to his descendants. Jacob possessed the qualities that make for survival. The theme of his life pattern could be summed up in the word, *striving*.

Jacob's struggle for existence began within the womb, which

he had to share with his twin brother, Esau. The conflict was so intense that Rebekah, the mother, wondered that she could remain alive. She asked God the meaning of her ordeal and he replied:

> "Two nations are in thy womb,
>   And two peoples shall be separated from thy bowels;
>   And the one people shall be stronger than the other people;
>   And the elder shall serve the younger (25:23)."*

The sibling rivalry thus began in the prenatal state. Esau, ruddy and covered with hair, was born first. Jacob followed, his hand grasping Esau's heel, as if expressing protest at his brother's precedence. The name *Jacob*, meaning *one who takes by the heel,* or *supplants,* is symbolic of the relationship between the two which was to play such an important role in his life.

At this point, let us consider briefly Jacob's parentage. His father was Isaac, son of Abraham. The most important story in the Bible about Isaac is one in which he plays a passive role. Abraham shows his willingness to sacrifice this only son to God, as an act of piety, and Isaac evidently acquieses without a struggle. According to the story, only God himself saves the youth, already bound to the sacrificial pyre.

This dramatic event epitomized Isaac's position in the family. He was born when his parents were of advanced age. He was the answer to Abraham's prayers and a reward for his virtues. Isaac thus belonged to Abraham in a special sense, being God's gift to him. What God gave, Abraham showed his willingness to return in the form of obedience to the Divine Will. Thus Isaac never really had a life of his own. He stood forever in the shadow of those two great fathers, Abraham and God.

Isaac's mother, Sarah, was a woman of strong and forceful personality. She was the beloved wife of Abraham's youth. She had left the comforts of her native land to share the hardships of a semi-nomadic existence at the side of her husband. To safe-

---

* All biblical quotations and references in this chapter, unless otherwise noted, are from Genesis.

guard the rights of her beloved son, Sarah went to the extreme measure of having her handmaid, Hagar, and the child this woman had born to Abraham, driven from the camp.

The only son of an overly-protective mother and a powerful father who *walked with God*, Isaac's psychic destiny was not hard to foretell. The highly traumatic experience he endured must also have had an ineradicable influence upon his character. He remained a nonentity, completely overshadowed by his parents. Indeed, so little was there to tell about him that the compilers of the Bible, as if in an effort to cover up this painful deficiency, relate a few events regarding him that are repetitions of what happened to Abraham, and give him a few of the virtues that clung so abundantly to his father's name.

After the death of his mother, Isaac found a new mother figure in his wife, Rebekah. She was chosen for him by the wise steward of his father's house, presumably Eliezer.

In the familiar story of the meeting at the well, Rebekah superbly passes the test of character put to her by the trusted envoy of Abraham, who had traveled a long distance to find a wife for Isaac from among the Patriarch's own people. Following a prayer for guidance, the steward approaches Rebekah with the words, "Give me to drink, I pray thee, a little water of thy pitcher. And she said: "Drink, my lord"; and she hastened, and let down her pitcher upon her hand, and gave him drink." Then follow the words immortalized in this charming episode when the young woman, "who was very fair to look upon," added, "I will draw for thy camels also until they have done drinking (24:17–19)."

Rebekah not only showed kindness but also strength and courage. She willingly left home for a strange land to meet and marry Isaac. The Bible says, "And Isaac brought her into his mother Sarah's tent, and took Rebekah, and she became his wife; and he loved her. And Isaac was comforted after his mother's death (24:67)."

There is no doubt about the contrasting characters of the twin sons which Rebekah and Isaac brought into the world, or the nature of the family relationships. In a few biblical sentences the picture is drawn. ". . . Esau was a cunning hunter, a man of the field; and Jacob was a quiet man, dwelling in tents. Now Isaac loved Esau, because he did eat of his venison; and Rebekah loved Jacob (25:27–28)."

The weak, overprotected, and traumatized Isaac, fixated to an oral level, loved Esau, who brought him choice foods. He favored the strong, virile son, who typified the ego ideal he himself had not attained. Rebekah loved in greater measure the son who represented the intellectual and spiritual aspects of life. As a member of the household of Abraham after her marriage, Rebekah was available to the influence which emanated from that great personality. Midrashic literature stated that Abraham favored Jacob, regarding him as superior to Esau and the one destined to become the leader of the tribe.[2]

Let us consider more fully the impact upon Jacob's development of the important personalities in his life. It was fortunate for him that the weakness of Isaac was compensated for in large measure by the stature of his grandfather, Abraham. The latter became an ego ideal, a model sustained and nurtured with the support of Rebekah.

Although the same age as Jacob, Esau was so different in physical build and character qualities that he could easily have played the role of an older brother. His position as the first-born and as Isaac's favorite gave him a special importance in the family. It is likely that the more aggressive aspects of Esau's personality may have furthered the development of reactive, defensive traits in Jacob. He had to devise patterns of behavior to deal realistically with the physically stronger brother who gave way readily to his emotions. Jacob therefore learned to meet physical strength with mental cunning, a pattern which he seems to have retained for a large part of his life.

Although Jacob and Esau were non-identical twins, so different in fact that they could be called *antithetical,* the reality of their twinship must have had some effect upon their development and relationship to each other. We will assume that Rachel nursed both her babies. Since she favored the smaller, physically weaker child, Jacob must have been given preference at his mother's breast, again supplanting Esau, who probably had to wait until his brother was fed. Children were not weaned until they were two or three years old, perhaps even longer, so this experience of oral frustration, if our assumption is correct, was a long one for Esau.[3] It may have had something to do with his inability to tolerate oral tensions later on, as manifested in the episode we shall soon consider. Or, if a wet-nurse was utilized for Esau, which is also a possibility, his experience of *mothering* would have been different than his brother's.

Jacob, on the other hand, by enjoying oral gratification through this long nursing period, may have been helped to move forward in his emotional growth at a more rapid pace. But it is also possible that Jacob suffered from guilt feelings at being the object of his mother's preference. If so, his fears of Esau's real or fantasied reprisal would be strengthened, especially since his twin brother was constitutionally a larger and stronger child.[4]

The rivalry with Esau for the mother, as well as the realistic need to share her, must have had its impact upon the oedipal pattern too. It could have increased competitive wishes but also the capacity for renunciation. The fear of Esau, moreover, may have become blended later with the dread of the oedipal father, thus endowing the internalized images of both figures with a greater degree of aggression. There can be no doubt that Jacob's experience as a twin-sibling, with its confusing concepts of rights and privileges, must have had an effect upon the development of his character.

The relationship with his mother was also, very likely, a complicated one for Jacob. Her strong personality, with its tendency to direct and control, might have made him into a weak, submissive person. And indeed he is described as a "quiet man, dwelling in tents," that is, close to home and mother. But there are indications that Rebekah's strength had a predominantly ego quality which could therefore be directed toward conscious, realistic aims and be capable of genuine object love. Otherwise Jacob himself would have lacked the courage to strive and to grow. Her feelings for him, while too supportive, perhaps, tended to foster self-confidence.

The fact however that the mother was a stronger personality

than the father certainly must have made Jacob's masculine development more complex. In his case, it was the maternal figure rather than the paternal one who represented the reality principle in life. The youth's struggle for maturity was therefore particularly difficult, for separation from his mother involved a renunciation of the pleasure principle without the support of a strong father figure. The energy for this act had to come through the formation of an ego ideal, probably influenced by the personality of Abraham, but mediated through the mother. It would not be surprising if a large measure of dependency on a strong mother figure remained and had to be resolved gradually as part of his continuing struggle for growth.

The first significant act of Jacob's life recorded in the Bible is the well-known transaction by which he obtained the coveted birthright from Esau. This right brought with it leadership of the tribe and a double share of the father's wealth.[5] It was a large prize yet Esau surrendered it readily to satisfy an immediate bodily need. Coming in from the field, faint with hunger and tempted by the aroma of the freshly-cooked pot of red lentils which Jacob had just prepared, he yielded to the other's proposal that he barter his birthright for the food, rationalizing thus, "Behold, I am at the point to die; and what profit shall the birthright do to me (25:29–32)?" This physically strong man resembled his weak father in his oral fixation. He could not resist the pleasure of immediate gratification for the sake of a greater postponed good, thus indicating his infantile stage of emotional development and a lack of capacity for assuming the spiritual leadership of the tribe. The only moral evaluation which the Bible makes of this barter is contained in the words, "So Esau despised his birthright."

The responsibility for Jacob's behavior was projected onto Destiny herself at the very beginning of Jacob's life. It was prophesied that he would rule over his brother. But Jacob has been generally condemned for this act. The basic moral code of the Judeo-Christian world, more strict than the Bible itself, from which it derives, blamed him for taking advantage of another's weakness.[6, 7] In the biblical story, however, it was Esau, surrendering his birthright for a paltry gratification of the flesh, who is censured.

Jacob's second aggression against Esau was stealing the blessing of the first-born by deceiving Isaac, then ill and blind. This was indeed a planned act of out-and-out deceit, involving a wrong against the father as well as the brother.

The familiar story of this household drama, told with vivid detail, is fraught with strong emotions. Isaac is old and his vision dimmed. He calls Esau, his first-born son, and tells him to take his bow and arrow, go out into the field and find venison " '. . . and make me savoury food, such as I love, and bring it to me, that I may eat; that my soul may bless thee before I die.' "

Rebekah overhears her husband and reports the matter to Jacob. She suggests a plan to have him impersonate Esau and receive the blessing in his stead. The only objection Jacob offers is his fear of discovery, saying

> "Behold, Esau my brother is a hairy man, and I am a smooth man. My father peradventure will feel me, and I shall seem to him as a mocker; and I shall bring a curse upon me and not a blessing." And his mother said unto him: "Upon me be thy curse, my son; only hearken to my voice . . . (27:11–13)."

Jacob was thus placed in the dilemma of disobeying his mother or deceiving his father. He chose the latter which was, of course, more in accordance with his wishes.

At Rebekah's instruction, he brings in two kids from the flock and his mother prepares a stew. Rebekah then takes the finest garments of Esau and clothes Jacob in them. Upon his hands and neck she puts the skin of the kids and then gives him the food she had made.

Jacob goes to his father and pretends to be Esau. Isaac is puzzled and expresses his bewilderment in the well-known words, "The voice is the voice of Jacob, but the hands are the hands of Esau." Nevertheless, he is evidently persuaded and bestows upon Jacob the blessing of the first-born.

No sooner has the youth left than Esau arrives from the hunt.

When he too brings in the food he prepared, Isaac is taken aback
and "trembles very exceedingly." He breaks the bad news to Esau,
saying, " 'Thy brother came with guile and hath taken away thy
blessing.' " In the course of this emotional scene, Esau cried out
movingly, "Hast thou but one blessing, my father? bless me, even
me also, O my father. And Esau lifted up his voice and wept
(27:34–38)."

Isaac, however, cannot undo the blessing which has already
been given. He blesses Esau too, but utters the words as if he were
indeed only a mouthpiece for Destiny:

> "Behold, of the fat places of the earth shall be thy dwelling,
> And of the dew of heaven from above.
> And by the sword shalt thou live, and thou shalt serve
>   thy brother;
> And it shall come to pass when thou shalt break loose,
> That thou shalt shake his yoke from off thy neck (27:39–40)."

Esau is filled with hatred for Jacob and vows to kill him as
soon as Isaac dies. Rebekah, alarmed, conveys this intent to Jacob,
bidding him flee for safety. He is to go to her brother Laban in
Haran and "tarry with him a few days," until his brother's anger
passes.

While we can read the imperative of history and of destiny in
the act of deception carried out by Rebekah and Jacob, our feelings of compassion go out to Esau, so cruelly betrayed. This situation was quite different from the selling of the birthright, where
Esau was given a choice, and where he voluntarily yielded his
rights in order to satisfy a physical appetite.

There is a puzzling aspect in the enormous difference with
which Esau tossed aside his birthright on that earlier occasion and
the poignancy of his grief when he learned that Jacob had stolen
the blessing of the first-born from him. It is possible that in the
earlier instance, Esau did not take the transaction seriously. He
was dealing with a brother, one physically weaker than himself.
He may not have had the intent to keep his vow. This interpretation can only be conjectural, of course. But there is no doubt that

the blessing from a father in the latter days of his life was a significant event, fraught with meaning for the future.[8, 9]

We see clearly in this account the impartiality of the biblical narrators in portraying character. Jacob and Rebekah are openly presented in an unfavorable light while Esau and Isaac, the victims of an unjust and hurtful experience, evoke our sympathy. At the same time, the Bible does not moralize or point out that Jacob would have to change and grow through struggle, as he actually does, before becoming a fitting leader of a people with a spiritual mission.

The basic material of the above episode was, of course, necessary for the development of the biblical theme. It explains how Jacob entered into his inheritance despite the odds of not having been born first, and why he was given the name *Jacob,* "one who supplants."

This act by which a younger brother overcomes an older one has a familiar folktale quality. It represents a wish fulfillment on the part of a weaker sibling. That which was ordained by nature, by the order in which the twins were born, is reversed. This gesture of rebellion is one with which many people can secretly identify and therefore the more strongly deprecate.

Another aspect of this story gives us pause. The text of this rather lengthy episode is unusually free of any obscurity in contrast to many other portions of the Bible, especially where character traits of heroes are involved. There are no ambiguities or undercurrents of disguised meanings. An unexpected conclusion can be drawn from this fact. In spite of all the moral indignation that Jacob's behavior has evoked through the years, it is possible that biblical censorship found nothing here that had to be hidden or suppressed. The storyteller could therefore give full expression to his sense of the dramatic. The narrative is clearly a tale of deceit and is presented as such. The tone of the story indicates disapproval of Jacob's behavior. But the openness with which the act of an important personality is here depicted seems to suggest that the morality of those days did not place such misconduct in the category of unforgivable deeds. This episode has probably been subject to misinterpretation when evaluated by the moral tenets of our own era, a view also held by a number of biblical commentators.

Jacob's flight from home marked an important step forward in his development. The dream which he had at this turning-point in his life occurred during that first night, when he was in the desolate countryside. His head rested upon a stone and his only source of comfort was the brightly-lighted sky above him, which shone with the peculiar brilliance and nearness characteristic of a semi-tropical land. Jacob was alone with his thoughts and feelings after that eventful day.

Let us try to empathize with him. The youth did not know when he would see his home and his beloved mother again. He probably was filled with guilt and fear because of the deed he had committed. How could he make good the wrong he had done? Atonement could be achieved by utilizing the blessing for the greater good of his people rather than for his own selfish gain. In this way alone would his act of aggression and deceit be justified, or even annulled.

These must have been Jacob's thoughts, these his resolutions on that lonely night. It was around his plans and purposes for the future that Jacob gathered courage. He had truly left home and mother behind him, in a psychological as well as a physical sense.

And then came the dream. Jacob saw a ladder reaching from earth to heaven, with angels ascending and descending upon it. God stood beside him and spoke, telling him that he would be the leader of a great people and inherit the land of Canaan.

The desired justification for his wrongdoing thus finds expression in the dream. It was God's will that he, Jacob, rather than Esau, should be the leader of the tribe. In confirmation of this, God blesses him. This blessing, freely given by the Heavenly Father, strengthened, or even took precedence over the blessing he received under such different conditions from his earthly parent. It was, in a sense, absolution for his guilt, which he so greatly needed at that moment.

What other aspects relating to his situation does the dream

express? There is the sexual symbol of the ladder connecting heaven and earth (father and mother). In stealing the blessing from Isaac, Jacob was making himself the potential head of the household, thus, in his unconscious, also putting himself in his father's place in relation to the mother, thereby reactivating an infantile oedipal wish. The intrapsychic tension evoked by this situation may explain the degree of terror in which Jacob fled from home and the urgency with which his mother, probably also suffering from unconscious guilt feelings of a similar kind, hastened his departure.

The unconscious conflict and Jacob's efforts to deal with it come out in the dream. Upon the ladder, framework of the earlier oedipal structure, appear the angels. These winged figures seem particularly suitable to express both phallic wishes and the renunciation of such wishes. The juxtaposition of the two elements in the dream, the background of the ladder and the angels in the foreground, moving upon this structure, might well symbolize Jacob's newly strengthened desire to give up infantile incestuous longings, symbolized by the ladder, and utilize this energy for superego gains, as represented by the angels. The same concept is expressed when the Heavenly Father in the dream takes the place of the earthly one in Jacob's life.

An aspect of wish-fulfillment may also be seen in the dream. The physical separation from his mother, especially under the circumstances which caused him to leave home, strengthened his psychological independence, making it possible for Jacob not only to renounce childish wishes but to allow himself the hope of adult satisfactions. The dream expresses this through the sanctioning, or blessing by the Father of sexual union between a man and a woman, as symbolized by the ladder between heaven and earth. We see here the use of condensation of meanings, a characteristic of dream formation.

The ladder as a sexual symbol is very similar in meaning to a bridge which, in dreams, may also indicate a transition in the life situation of the dreamer.[10] The use of the ladder symbolism may therefore have this further meaning, for the dream certainly occurs at an important period of change in Jacob's life.

The youth's mood upon awakening is one of reverence and awe. But the vow which he makes to accept the Lord as his God is not made in a spirit of fear and submission, but rather on the basis of a comradely partnership and with a sense of social and spiritual responsibility. If God will do his share, will be with him and protect him, then Jacob will accept him as God. Thus he established a new identification with an Idealized Father Image, a step made possible by leaving home and mother. In giving up a larger amount of his incestuous wishes and in overcoming more of his aggressiveness to the father, he also gives up more of his fear.

It is interesting that Jacob's attitude toward God is typical of the Jewish tradition. It does not represent a complete surrender to an Authoritarian Father, but a willing acceptance of responsibility in return for the promise of mature satisfaction.

As a part of his covenant with God, Jacob asks that he may return to his father's house in peace. With the further development of the superego and the renunciation of oedipal wishes, came the desire for atonement of the aggression against the father and a more peaceful relationship with him.

A second explanation about Jacob's leaving for Haran is given in the chapter immediately following the episode under discussion. He is sent by Isaac himself, under the influence of Rebekah, to seek a wife among his own people. The reason given is that the parents want to avoid his following in the footsteps of Esau, who had married two Canaanitish girls, regarding whom the text says, "And they were a bitterness of spirit unto Isaac and to Rebekah."

Higher Criticism is of the opinion that this second account is an interpolation of a later date. However, the two stories have an understandable sequence in the unconscious even though on the surface they seem to contradict each other. The aggression against Isaac which Jacob had committed, involved, as we have seen, an acting out in fantasy of oedipal wishes. It was therefore imperative that Jacob should get himself a wife. In both accounts, it is Rebekah who instigates Jacob's departure from home. The second explanation for his leaving points more clearly to her own emotional involvement, although of an unconscious nature, and the wish to rectify the situation.

Rather than interpret this *second episode* on a literal basis, it seems more likely that the explanation it contains was used, perhaps initially by Rebekah and then accepted by Isaac as his own, to explain Jacob's absence which had already taken place as related earlier. It would have provided a rationalization for their son's precipitate flight.

Jacob's first experience on reaching the town where Laban dwelt was his romantic encounter with Rachel at the well and his *love at first sight*. Thus he acts promptly upon the inner awareness of his emotional readiness for adulthood manifested in the dream.

Theodor Reik points out that Jacob's falling in love with a girl at the well in the same town where his mother's fate was decided in a similar situation may have been no accident, but was more likely a need to repeat a relationship that had an incestuous basis.[11] While this factor may have been present, the differences are also significant. Rebekah was chosen by the steward of Abraham's household rather than by Isaac himself. She was selected for her kindly, maternal qualities. It was she who had to take the initiative in going to meet her future husband.

Jacob's first meeting with Rachel is in an active, masculine role. He helps her by moving away the heavy stone that covered the well and by watering her sheep. Moreover, he reproves the lazy shepherds who are lolling around. It is not Rachel's maternal character but her feminine charms that captivate him. Here is indeed a picture of an energetic young man, ready to meet the realities of work and love. The "quiet man dwelling in tents" has become a purposeful and active personality. This change was made possible through the maturation that comes with the acceptance of moral and social responsibilities and the overcoming of oedipal conflicts.

Jacob is welcomed by Laban, his mother's brother, and enters into the life of the household, working as a shepherd. After a month has passed Laban asks him what his wages should be.

Jacob, who is in love with Rachel but lacks the money customary for the bride-price, replies that he will work seven years for the hand of Rachel. Laban answers, "It is better that I give her to thee, than that I should give her to another man; abide with me (29:19)."

After this period of service is over, Jacob asks for his bride. A wedding feast is celebrated and in the night, a woman, probably heavily veiled, is brought into the nuptial chamber. But in the light of the morning, Jacob discovers that he had been deceived. Instead of the beautiful and beloved Rachel, the woman beside him was her older sister, Leah, described in the narrative as having *weak eyes*. The disappointed lover reproaches his uncle for this breach of faith and Laban replies,

> "It is not so done in our place, to give the younger before the first-born. Fulfill the week of this one, and we will give thee the other also for the service which thou shalt serve with me yet seven other years." And Jacob did so, and fulfilled her week; and he gave him Rachel his daughter to wife (29:26–28).

One wonders if the memory of his own act of deceit, when he took Esau's place with his father, helped Jacob to bear the disappointment of being the deceived instead of the deceiver. No doubt the fact that he had to wait only one week longer for Rachel made the situation easier to endure.

Jacob spent twenty years of his life in the household of Laban. It was a period of growth, marked by industry in his work as a shepherd and increasing maturity in the roles of husband and father.

The relationship between Jacob and his father-in-law was a strongly competitive one. The younger man complained bitterly to his wives that Laban had changed his wages ten times. Thereafter Jacob makes a bargain with Laban asking that his payment should consist of that portion of the flocks characterized by certain markings and coloring. Jacob then utilized special methods of cattlebreeding based on the folk beliefs of those days. The plan prospers and Jacob finds himself the possessor of a goodly share of the flocks. Again he has manifested the quality of assuming the initiative for his own destiny rather than being a passive instrument of fate.   7 4 - 8 7

Jacob's growing prosperity creates unbearable tension between himself and the sons of Laban. Their hostility is also reflected in the darkening countenance of the father-in-law. At this point, God instructs Jacob to return to his own land, a directive which seems to echo the call of his own heart.

Again Jacob behaves in a fashion typical for him. Instead of announcing his intention openly to Laban and leaving in a dignified way befitting the head of a large household, he conspires secretly with his wives and departs stealthily from the home where he had lived for so many years. This need to repeat an early way of behaving should become clearer when considered from a psychoanalytic viewpoint. The same unconscious factors that prompted the earlier flight from Isaac and Esau must have had a share in this one. Let us, however, review the reality factors first.

Jacob might actually have been deterred from his purpose had he told Laban of his plans. But on the other hand Laban and his sons had no rational basis for stopping him or taking by force that which he had legally acquired. And there is no proof that they would have behaved violently toward a man so closely tied to them in kinship. Laban's behavior when he pursues Jacob and makes peace with him confirms this. And where was Jacob's faith in God at this point? Was is not at God's command that he was returning to Canaan? We must conclude that unconscious, irrational factors connected with the earlier experience had a part in his unseemly flight.

It is on the journey back to his old home, on the bank of the Jabbok River, that Jacob undergoes the second emotional crisis with which we are chiefly concerned. What was his situation at the time? He was, of course, anticipating with apprehension the meeting with Esau. Jacob had carried out elaborate plans to appease his brother by sending messengers ahead with herds of cattle as gifts. These were to be presented together with obsequious greetings. And now Jacob had his answer. Esau was on the way to meet him with four hundred men.

Jacob was in mortal terror. He separated his household into two camps so that if Esau fell upon one part and destroyed it, the other might still be saved. Then Jacob sent everyone ahead of him across the river while he remained behind. He must have felt a great need to be alone on this fateful night, perhaps the last one of his life. Having done all he humanly could to avert disaster, Jacob could now give himself up to the inner meaning of this crisis in his life.

It seems inevitable that his thoughts should have turned to another night, twenty years earlier, when he left the beloved land to which he was now returning. There was a remarkable similarity between the two situations. Again he had deceived a father, leaving home without his knowledge and consent. Again he had left behind him angry brothers who felt that he had enriched himself at their expense. And this time he actually possessed the women of the household, Laban's daughters, one of them the beloved Rachel, who might easily have represented a mother surrogate to the unconscious.

A sense of the uncanny must indeed have pervaded the soul of Jacob as he camped alone in the desolate night. He must have known that feeling described by Freud as *déjà vu*, "I have experienced this before," as the emotions of that earlier occasion, rising from repression, came upon him.

What takes place during this eventful night? The Bible story is a dramatic one. "And Jacob was left alone; and there wrestled a man with him until the breaking of the day (32:25)." This *man*, held by tradition to be an angel, or God himself, injures Jacob in the hollow of his thigh after a contest which is described with such ambiguity that it is unclear, at first, who prevails against whom. At the end, Jacob seems to have power over the stranger, who wishes to leave, saying, "Let me go, for the day breaketh." Jacob refuses to allow his adversary to depart until the latter has blessed him. The mysterious visitant then asks Jacob his name, and on being told, replies,

> "Thy name shall be called no more Jacob, but Israel; for thou hast striven with God and with men, and hast pre-

vailed." ... And he blessed him there. And Jacob called the name of the place Peniel: "for I have seen God face to face, and (yet) my life is preserved (32:27–31)."

Many biblical commentators of the past have been inclined to regard this episode as a dream. And indeed this seems a logical explanation considering the state of mind in which Jacob lay down to sleep on that troubled night. How did he deal with the problem in this dream, as we shall assume his experience to be? He is attacked by a *man*, as he expected to be attacked by Esau on the morrow. The explicit use of this word in the Bible where the concept, *angel,* is certainly a common one, must have some significance. Yet in the latter part of the dream the visitor behaves as a heavenly apparition and is accepted as such by Jacob.

We shall begin by assuming that this figure is a composite one to the unconscious of the dreamer, a mechanism characteristic of this state of mental functioning. The fear of Esau provided the immediate stimulus for the dream. On one level, therefore, Jacob was preparing himself for the ordeal which he expected to face the next day. Wrestling with the stranger was a way of trying to achieve mastery of a coming trauma and a present overwhelming fear. But Jacob must also have been anticipating such a situation, with repressed anxiety, for the past twenty years. These feelings would now be reactivated and increase his apprehension.

However, the stranger with whom he struggled must signify even more. The fear of Esau was closely tied up with guilt feelings toward Isaac, his father, whom he had wronged at the same time. Both of these earlier aggressions were associated in Jacob's unconscious with oedipal strivings, together with the guilt and anxiety such wishes aroused. There was a further reason for the reactivation of these feelings. Jacob was returning home to fulfill his birthright. This time, if God's promise was to be realized, he would soon take the place of his father as leader of the tribe in the Promised Land. To the unconscious, this may also have meant to possess the mother. The figure in the dream therefore would represent the angry father of the childhood oedipal conflict, who had come to punish him. It would also symbolize the more mature aspects of the internalized father, who appears in the form of a heavenly visitant, representing his projected superego, the Deity Himself.

But the wrestling in the dream not only signified the wish to protect himself against the aggression of others. On a deeper level, the need was for protection against his own feelings of a similar nature. The stranger with whom the dreamer struggles so desperately must therefore also stand for Jacob's own id strivings, the personification of his incestuous and aggressive impulses. The mysterious figure thus represents both elements of a conflict —the dangerous forces of the id and the strength of the superego. Therefore he is both man and angel at the same time. Even as within himself Jacob experiences the battle between different aspects of his personality, so the figure with whom he struggles is a mirror-like reflection of the self, with the forces of good and evil engaged in dramatic intrapsychic conflict. *Jacob was wrestling with his own projected image of himself.*

A further meaning of Jacob's uncanny guest may be to regard him as a symbol of Death. The situation fittingly calls for such a condensation. Death and a father image were certainly associated in Jacob's mind that night. To the unconscious, death is the punishment for aggression against the father.

What are some of the other elements in the dream? There is a curious ambiguity about the antecedents of the pronouns in the biblical description. "And when he saw that he prevailed not against him, he touched the hollow of his thigh; and the hollow of Jacob's thigh was strained as he wrestled with him (32:25–27)." The words have a truly dream-like fluidity which seems to confirm the fact that the dreamer is himself playing several roles. On the one hand, he wishes to overcome his fear of the angry father and to subdue and conquer him. On the other hand, he is afraid of his own id impulses and longs for approval and support from the superego.

Only if Jacob can renew his identification with God will he have the courage to meet the angry father-brother figure that awaits him and to lessen the anxiety caused by guilt feelings.

Such an identification must be achieved through the further subjugation of instinctual forces—hate, aggression, and incestuous wishes. How does this take place in the dream? At first it is not clear who injures whom. But if both combatants are one, and if each symbolizes two aspects of the dreamer's personality, then the confusion about who hurt whom is understandable. Moreover, the self is in a state of intrapsychic struggle, with the outcome still a matter of uncertainty. Then a resolution comes about. Jacob is injured in the hollow of his thigh, an obvious displacement for the phallus.

Out of this conflict of the night, out of fear of the avenging father, out of Jacob's sense of guilt and wrongdoing, comes a solution—not complete submission to the father nor the crime of overcoming him. Jacob yields to a partial castration, and by thus appeasing his guilt, is able to overcome his fear. It is his pattern of behavior to meet conflict with active mastery and with compromise, showing the tendency to struggle and the will to survive. Actually, the dream portrays with dramatic condensation how castration anxiety brings about the renunciation of instinctual wishes and the strengthening of the superego, a process which, in Jacob's case, seems to have been renewed and deepened at periods of emotional crises in his life. The sublimation of a part of his instinctual forces was a necessary step to becoming head of his people. Free from fear, and with a new feeling of kinship toward his brother, Jacob could meet him on the morrow with a *conquering love.*

The mystery of why it is the heavenly messenger who pleads to be released from the power of Jacob, the one who has suffered the injury, is intriguing. The stranger cries out, "Let me go, for the day breaketh," words which might indeed come from a ghostly apparition who dreads the light of day. If this element of the composite figure in the dream represents the father of the childhood oedipal conflict, then his ghostly nature, as a figment of the unconscious, is psychologically clear, and he would vanish in the light of day, as does a troubled dream.

But together with this reassuring thought, the dreamer has another source of comfort. In the dream he has made a further renunciation of his regressive oedipal wishes; now he need no longer fear the ghost of his father but can even win love and a blessing from his former rival. And so he demands the blessing as a reward, and the stranger, who came as a *man,* now speaks as the *angel,* or God himself. Jacob's injury of the flesh becomes synonymous with his victory of the spirit.

The change of name, which the form of the blessing takes, expresses this re-born Jacob. The bestowal of a new name had many meanings in the thought of antiquity. One of them indicated a significant change in status. Thus, a new name was given as part of puberty rites and, in some lands, at the time a man became a father. Jacob's change of name at this period of his life may well signify his new role as father of the children of Israel, spiritual head of the tribe. *Isra-el,* "one who prevails with God," is his new name, and it befitted the personality of the man who had the capacity to meet conflict and crises with striving, especially in the direction toward a more mature self.

The rabbis have long interpreted Jacob's wrestling with the stranger as a battle between the two natures within Jacob, so that this psychoanalytic interpretation serves rather as a confirmation, or a different approach, leading to the same conclusion.

One further point in this content should claim our attention. The children of Israel are prohibited from eating the *hollow of the thigh* of animals, corresponding to the part of the body where Jacob was injured. Theodor Reik believes that we have here a relic of an ancient totemistic legend really belonging to a possible earlier version of Jacob's wrestling match in which it is he who injures a deified father. This association with the prehistoric crime of the primal horde, although deeply unconscious, would, according to him, explain the prohibition of eating the injured portion of the father.[12]

Another meaning can be drawn from this ancient prohibition. In the episode as described, Jacob himself is clearly identified with the animal, the injured portion of which is prohibited as food. Jacob thus becomes the symbol of the sacrificial *son,* who yields up a part of himself to the father. And indeed his father Isaac almost became such a sacrifice.

Among many ancient peoples the first-born son belonged to the gods even to the point of being offered up to them. In the biblical tradition the first-born male was also claimed by God in a special sense. "Sanctify unto Me all the first-born, whatsoever openeth the womb among the children of Israel, both of man and of beast, it is mine (Exod. 13:2)." Here too, an identification is made between the son and the sacrificial animal. The first-born sons were assigned to priestly service and the first-born animals were offered as sacrifices. Later, the tribe of Levi took over the duties of such sons but even to this day, in Jewish families, a special ceremony (*Pidyon Ha-ben*) is conducted in which the father pays a small sum of money to free his first-born son from the ancient obligation of priestly service.

Psychoanalytically, this position of the oldest male can be considered as stemming from the ambivalent feelings of the father toward the son who is destined to displace him. Moreover, this displacement occurs, not only in the future but also in the present, for the child becomes the object of the woman's care and ministrations which hitherto has belonged solely to the man himself. The sacrifice of the son, or its symbolic substitute, represents a synthesis of two opposing forces, similar to that of the totemistic meal. It involves hostility to the son but is expressed in the loving form of a religious rite. It is also an act of appeasement to a father image by one who remembers his own hostility as a son. The *hollow of the thigh,* symbol of the power to create, gives man a God-like quality. It thus belongs to God and becomes a token sacrifice.

Let us consider now a brief comparison of the two dreams of Jacob, separated from each other by twenty years. On both occasions, a renunciation of instinctual wishes is involved, leading to a strengthening of the dreamer's identification with God and the receiving of a blessing from the Deity. In the first dream, angels appear upon the ladder. In the second, the stranger behaves as a heavenly visitant, thus confirming that to the unconscious of Jacob the angel represented a projected superego.

At the time of the first dream, Jacob had escaped from the

scene of actual danger. He could therefore turn his thoughts to the problem of atonement by resolving to direct his energies along more acceptable pathways. On the second occasion, Jacob was facing what he believed to be mortal danger. His anxiety on a reality basis was therefore considerably greater. This anxiety finds a needed outlet by placing the dreamer in a very active role, that of wrestling. And because the danger is great, the price he is willing to pay for absolution and compromise is higher than in the first dream.

The different character of the two dreams may be attributed, in part, to the different stages of development in the life of the dreamer. The youthful Jacob faced the problem of repressing his incestuous wishes and re-directing his sexuality into socially permitted channels. Hence the emphasis in the first dream is upon the ladder, the angels, and the new relationship with God. But the more mature Jacob, who has come to enter into his inheritance, to assume the role of leadership, faced more directly the problem of his aggressiveness and the projected fears of his own hostility in relation to Esau and Isaac. This is adequately expressed by the physical combat with the stranger. It is only when the son is stronger than the father that he shows his readiness to become head of the tribe. This, together with the power to sublimate part of his strength for social and spiritual goals, is a necessary development for leadership.

This thought might be further developed by comparing the names of the two places where Jacob underwent his mystic experiences. The first was called *Bethel,* "House of God" and the second, *Peniel,* "Face of God." The earlier oedipal experience involved leaving the house of his father, i.e., the mother. He found a substitute relationship in a new, spiritualized identification with the Father-God. Later, an older Jacob struggled to renew this identification with God as a necessary condition for spiritual leadership. By surrendering a portion of his physical self, and with it, more of his narcissism, he seeks to achieve a greater capacity for sublimation as symbolized by the *Face of God.* The displacement from below upward, characteristic of dreams, may indicate Jacob's wish for greater spiritual strength at this time.

Several other incidents connected with Jacob's return journey lend themselves to interesting speculations. He re-visits Bethel and worships there, after exhorting his household to put away any strange gods that they had brought with them from their former homes. This is done in response to God's express command to return to Bethel and worship the God " 'Who appeared unto thee when thou didst flee from the face of Esau, thy brother,' and Jacob built an altar there and called the place *El-bethel,* the 'God of Bethel' (35:7)." Immediately after this, the biblical story records an event that seems strangely unrelated to the context. We are told that Deborah, the nurse of Rebekah, died there and was buried under an oak, which was then called the *oak of weeping.*

No previous mention had been made of Deborah's leaving with Jacob upon his trip to Haran twenty years earlier. She had departed from Haran with Rebekah at the time of the latter's betrothal to Isaac and no reason is given for assuming that she ever left her mistress again, Why, then, this isolated and unexplained statement about Deborah's death at Bethel? Commentators say that this is interpolated material, not a part of the main narrative. If so, one wonders why it was put into precisely this place? At the locale where Jacob first experienced God, while fleeing from Esau, Deborah, a mother figure so closely associated with Rebekah all of Jacob's life, dies, and is buried under an oak tree. Is this not a dream-like presentation of the oedipal conflict and its solution? Jacob is here repeating, on his return trip, his original experience at Bethel. In a reconciliation with the spiritual Father, he repeats once more his renunciation of the mother, who is then buried beneath an oak tree, a father symbol. Good reason then for calling it *the oak of weeping.*

It is significant, also, that shortly after this event occurs, Jacob suffers a real tragedy, an actual giving up, when Rachel, his beloved wife, dies on the journey, following the birth of her second son, Benjamin. Although a small tomb marks the supposed site of Rachel's burial, its real location is unknown. The fact that her death is related at this particular time may indicate that Jacob must make this further sacrifice of his still active oedipal wishes before he can return and face his father. Thus the death of Deborah may be a kind of preparation, or foreshadowing of the other tragedy, the death of Rachel. It might have been intended to serve as a propiatory gesture to ward off the greater sacrifice, but failed in this purpose. The statement about Deborah's death, therefore, although an anachronism on a reality level, may have the deeper logic of the unconscious.

Even in the tragic event of Rachel's death, Jacob's capacity to make the best of a situation, to strive and to endure, can be seen. Rachel called her son Ben-oni, *son of my sorrow,* but his father changed it to Benjamin, *son of my right hand.*

The Personality
of Joseph

 CHAPTER THREE

AMONG THE biblical heroes of ancient Israel, the personality of Joseph, son of Jacob, stands out as one of particular interest and appeal. Why should this be so? Joseph does not have the impressive, somewhat daemonic power of Abraham and Jacob, men who stood in terrifying intimacy to God himself. Nor does he have the romantic aura of such figures as David and Solomon, the kingly heroes of Israel in the days of its greatness.

What, then, is the basis for the universality of response that Joseph has evoked in so many people throughout the centuries? Is his just another "success" story of a country boy who made good? This element certainly adds to the appeal but would hardly be a sufficient explanation of such long-term popularity. It must be that Joseph, because of his very human qualities, offers many opportunities for identifications. The conflicts that he goes through and the feelings he experiences touch upon familiar

areas in many people's lives. It should be interesting to see if
the study of Joseph will determine whether he actually has psychological validity as a real person. To what extent did Joseph's
behavior stem logically from his character? How much of his
personality can be understood in terms of the early influences of
his life?

Joseph was next to the youngest of Jacob's thirteen children,
his eleventh son. He was, however, the first-born child of Rachel,
who was Jacob's beloved. Joseph occupied a favored position with
both his parents, a fact which must have had a deep influence
upon his character development and life experiences.

At the time when Joseph was born, Jacob had reached a
period in his life which, we can assume, had a certain mellowed
maturity. He must have achieved at least a partial resolution of
his sibling rivalry with Esau and of the oedipal conflict with his
father Isaac, as witnessed by the reconciliation with them. Jacob's
position of power as Patriarch and the father of many sons must
also have had a maturing effect upon his personality. That he
loved Joseph deeply and preferred him above the others is an
important but self-evident aspect of our story.

What about Rachel, Joseph's mother? What sort of person
was she? We meet her first as a shepherdess of her father's sheep.
Thus, she is leading an active, outdoor life, facing responsibilities
and the natural hardships of such a task. Although girls did
occasionally perform work of this kind, it was generally considered a man's job.

Jacob's first meeting with Rachel was at the well, where she
came to water her flock. He rolled away the heavy stone which
covered the well and helped her with her task. One must assume
that Rachel was generally able to protect herself from undesirable advances or teasing behavior of the rough shepherds whom
she customarily met at the well. That unpleasant incidents did
occur in such settings is indicated by the experience of a group
of shepherd girls at another time and place. They were the
daughters of Jethro, whom Moses helped to protect from unruly
shepherds when he came upon them in the desert on his flight
from Egypt.

Rachel presents herself, therefore, as a sturdy and independent young woman. That she was not lacking in feminine charm and beauty is well attested by Jacob's immediate attraction to her.

Another instance which shows Rachel's resourcefulness and lack of timidity is revealed in the incident of the teraphim many years later. When Jacob, with his wives and children, fled from the home of his father-in-law, Laban, taking with them all their flocks and possessions, Rachel also took the small household gods which belonged to her father. The significance attached to these teraphim had long been unclear. Archaeological findings of ancient Hurrian law now indicate that they were usually in the possession of the head of the house, and may have signified the right of title to a chief share in the inheritance. Rachel may therefore have wished to obtain them for Jacob.[1] These small figures may also have been important to her as a kind of good luck symbol, a connecting link between the old home she was leaving and the new land to which she was going.

Laban pursued the party in great anger at their leaving him so unceremoniously. The loss of his gods must have added to his resentment and he accused Jacob of stealing them. Jacob, who was unaware of Rachel's deed, protested, and allowed Laban to search the encampment. Rachel hid the teraphim in the saddlebag of a camel and sat down upon the saddle, which was standing within the tent. She asked her father to excuse her from rising as "the manner of woman was upon her." Rachel thus showed herself to be quick-witted and daring. Like Laban, she was not averse to resorting to deception when it suited her needs. We have no indication however, that such behavior was typical.

Rachel's older sister, Leah, became Jacob's first wife in consequence of Laban's trickery. We can sympathize with Jacob as, in the morning after the nuptial night, he beheld the face of the weak-eyed Leah instead of the beloved and beautiful Rachel. He had worked seven years in payment for his bride, only to be thus deceived. Jacob married Rachel a week later and worked seven years longer to pay for her. Fourteen years is a long time to work for a wife and is a tribute to Jacob's love for Rachel.

It is understandable that the relationship between the two

sister-wives should have its difficulties. The competitive spirit was strong and manifested itself chiefly in the desire of each to produce as many sons as possible and thus prove herself a successful wife. In this contest, Leah is triumphant. After she has given birth to four sons and Rachel is still barren, the latter cries out to Jacob in despair, "Give me children or else I die." Jacob replies with understandable anger, which must also have contained elements of pain and disappointment. "Am I in God's stead who had withheld from thee the fruit of the womb?"

In her frustration, Rachel presents her handmaid, Bilhah, to her husband as a substitute, and thus gets two sons by proxy, Dan and Naphtali.

The competitive spirit between the two wives continues, and when Leah notes that she is no longer conceiving, she gives her own handmaid, Zilpah, to her husband. The concubine gives Jacob two more sons, Gad and Asher.

Leah's first-born son, Reuben, must have entered into the spirit of this contest. During the wheat harvest he went out into the field and found mandrakes, which he presented to his mother. It was believed that this plant had the magical property of inducing conception. Rachel pleads with Leah for some of the mandrakes and the latter drives a bargain with her sister. Rachel may have the mandrakes if she will send Jacob to sleep with Leah that evening. This incident indicates the acceptance of both wives of the fact that Jacob belonged to Rachel by virtue of his love for her. In this form of partiality Jacob may have been violating the rights of co-wives for an equal share in cohabitation with the husband.[2]

Rachel's long period of barrenness may have had a psychogenic basis. Rebekah, Jacob's mother, came from the same family as Rachel, being Laban's sister. The two women resembled each other in character and perhaps in looks. Rachel may therefore have been a mother surrogate to Jacob's unconscious, a factor which would help to explain his *love at first sight*. Rachel was the first woman Jacob met after he left his home and mother in a period of psychological stress. The Bible says that he asked for Rachel's hand in marriage almost immediately and offered to work for her seven years since he lacked the money to pay the bride-price as was customary in those days.

We are told that the seven years seemed but a few days, so great was Jacob's love for her. This seems a little hard to understand. In the face of such great love, seven years would more likely seem an almost interminable time for a passionate young lover. But if Jacob was still to some degree under the influence of an oedipal attachment to his mother, and Rachel was a mother figure, then he would be in no haste for a mature sexual expression of his love. He would be content to enjoy a prolonged romantic courtship.

After Leah had given birth to seven children, six sons and a daughter, and her handmaid, Zilpah, two sons, and Rachel's handmaid, Bilhah, two sons, Rachel had her first child. Joseph was born in the seventh year of her marriage. One can imagine the joy of both parents over this long-awaited event. It is not surprising that Joseph became the favorite son of his father as well as the deeply-cherished child of his mother.

As Rachel's only son for a number of years, Joseph had no sibling rival for his mother's affections. Actually, he never knew such rivalry even at a later age, for Rachel died when his younger brother Benjamin was born. His feelings for this brother, who was six years younger, were very tender, as later events indicate.

During the semi-nomadic period of the family's existence, each wife had her own quarters, where she lived with her children. Such quarters consisted of a separate tent for each wife. It was divided into two parts with one section reserved for Jacob. He lived in the tent of the favorite wife most of the time.

Under this type of family structure, Joseph had a favored place. The home of his mother must have provided an atmosphere much more relaxed and free from tension than the living quarters of Leah, which were full of noisy siblings. Little time was actually spent within the tent but it provided a place of quiet and refuge for the young Joseph and opportunities for a closer and warmer relationship with his father. Rachel herself, as a secure and loved wife, must have had more spontaneous and unconflictful affection to bestow upon her son, whereas

Leah, who felt herself hated, may have become embittered and hostile to some degree and thus less able to give her children a full measure of love.

Joseph's unrivaled possession of the mother as far as siblings were concerned and his father's favoritism must have given strong support to his ego development. As Freud once said, in relation to himself, "A man who has been the indisputable favorite of his mother keeps for life the feeling of a conqueror, that confidence of success that often induces real success."[3] A fulfilling experience of having been loved, cherished, and preferred by both parents must certainly have had a large share in the courage and confidence with which Joseph faced the ordeals and tribulations of his later life.

Joseph's childhood and youth were certainly not free from problems, as the biblical story makes clear. His favored position must have aroused envy and hatred among his brothers from earliest years. It seems likely that Joseph was exposed not only to the jealousy of Leah's sons, but of Leah also. The competitive spirit between Rachel and Leah must have strengthened the normal rivalry among the siblings. The children of the rival wife, forming a more or less consolidated group, would have found Joseph a convenient object for their hostility. Their feelings would have gathered intensity through indentification with their mother's jealousy and her inferior position in Jacob's love.

There was another factor which increased the enmity that Joseph aroused. He was endowed with qualities which made him genuinely superior to his brothers. We are told that he was "of beautiful form and fair to look upon." He certainly had exceptionally high intelligence, judging by his later achievements. Thus he stood out among his brothers, more handsome, more gently nurtured, and probably more intelligent, as well as more favored by the father.

Joseph must have been quite vulnerable to the hostility of his brothers because of his youth and aloneness. One of the most difficult situations to endure is to be one against many, particularly in relation to one's peers. Joseph was in this position among his brothers for a long time.

To be both superior and vulnerable is a fateful combination. The first factor arouses envy and the second makes it easy and satisfying for the envious to express their resentment through aggression. A certain type of competitive envy is one of the most common of human emotions, so much a part of human nature that Freud regards it as normal rather than neurotic. In fact, he looks with some suspicion upon those individuals who show a striking lack of such a feeling under provocative conditions. Joseph's presence must have served as a constant reminder to his brothers of his natural superiority and favored place in the family. Joseph therefore may have innocently contained within himself the factors which served constantly to ignite the hatred and aggression of his brothers.

The sheer force of the numbers arrayed against him must have increased Joseph's feelings of insecurity and fear. Some of his older brothers may also have represented threatening father figures to him, perhaps in the oedipal situation. Actually, Reuben, the oldest, acted out such a role when he had a clandestine sexual relationship with Bilhah, Jacob's concubine, who had served as a proxy to Jacob for Rachel herself.[4] The fact that this occurred after the death of Rachel, when Bilhah probably acted as a mother substitute to Joseph, must have had a strong impact upon him. Perhaps it is not entirely accidental that it was Reuben who tried to save Joseph when the latter was threatened with death by his brothers at the time they sold him into slavery. Having displaced Jacob as the father on one occasion by possessing his concubine, Reuben may have identified with Jacob also in developing a special fatherly protectiveness toward the young boy.

Joseph must have felt the loss of his mother keenly. He was probably only about six years old at the time. For Joseph was born in the fourteenth year of Jacob's sojourn with Laban, and the birth of his brother Benjamin, which was the cause of Rachel's death, occurred on the journey back to Canaan, six years later. After this event, Joseph had only his father to look to for love and support. There was also the young Benjamin, who may have played an important role in Joseph's development by providing him with an additional object for his love, helping to develop feelings of tenderness and protectiveness.

Jacob must have been aware of the difficult position in which Joseph found himself and thus increased his own protective love. He gave Joseph the extra moral support needed to endure the hostile feelings of his older brothers, but by so doing, also fanned the flames of their anger.

Jacob is often criticized for showing so openly his preference for Joseph and thus stimulating jealousy and hate among his other children. Jacob may have had a close identification with Joseph and given him the love that he himself would have liked to receive from his own father, who favored Esau. Jacob's predilection for a *younger son* must have remained with him all his life. In his old age, when he traveled down to Egypt to see Joseph again and met Joseph's children also, he bestowed the greater blessing upon the younger son, Ephraim.

On a reality basis, however, it was considered customary for the head of a large family to have a favorite son. This role was generally occupied by the eldest male child of the favorite wife, which was Joseph's position. It was also the custom to present such a child with special gifts.

The well-known incident in which Jacob bestows upon Joseph a coat of many colors, evidently a garment much finer than any of his brothers possessed, raised their anger to such a pitch that "they could not speak peaceably unto him." Regardless of the custom of the times, their reaction is indeed humanly understandable.

We are told that as a youth of seventeen, Joseph fed the flock with the sons of Bilhah and the sons of Zilpah, children of his father's concubines. Biblical commentary indicates that the sons of Leah showed contempt for Joseph by not associating with him. It may be, however, that Jacob thought it safer to put him with the sons of the concubines who would have more fear and respect for Joseph and would therefore be less likely to do him harm.

Joseph's behavior toward his brothers while in the field seems far from commendable. The Bible, with its customary frankness, says that Joseph brought evil reports of his brothers to his father. Here the youth was acting in that most unadmirable of roles—a tale-bearer. What these reports were, we are not told. It seems likely that they included accounts of mistreatment and hostility toward himself. It may well be that Joseph needed the support and comfort of his father on a reality basis in the difficulties that faced him.

What other indications do we have of the way that Joseph actually conducted himself toward his brothers? There was evidently a certain arrogance in his manner which must have served to irritate them considerably. This arrogance is clearly seen in his attitude while relating his dreams to them, as well as in the content of the dreams themselves. There is nothing cringing or submissive about the way he says to them:

> "Hear, I pray you, this dream which I have dreamed: for behold we were binding sheaves in the field, and lo, my sheaf arose and also stood upright; and behold, your sheaves came round about and bowed to my sheaf." And his brethren said to him, "Shalt thou indeed reign over us?" And they hated him yet the more for his dreams and for his words. And he dreamed yet another dream, and told it to his brethren, and said, "Behold, I have dreamed yet another dream: and behold, the sun and the moon, and eleven stars bowed down to me." And he told it to his father and to his brethren; and his father rebuked him, and said unto him: "What is this dream that thou has dreamed. Shall I and thy mother and thy brethren indeed come to bow down to thee to the earth?" And his brethren envied him; but his father kept the saying in his mind (37:6–11).*

The manifest content of these dreams seems clear enough. They are child-like in their simple allegorical meaning. But the unconscious purpose of the dreams can be understood when they are seen not only as the ambitions of an adolescent youth in a competitive struggle with his brothers, but also as a defense against anxiety in relation to these hostile siblings. Not only is

* All biblical quotations and references in this chapter, unless otherwise noted, are from Genesis.

Joseph unafraid of his brothers, the dream says reassuringly; they are actually submissive to him. These two aspects are brought out interestingly in the wording, "Lo, my sheaf arose and also stood upright; and behold, your sheaves came round about and bowed down to my sheaf." The first action is one of Joseph's own power, expressed in symbolic terms of sexual potency. Joseph is as powerful as his older and stronger brothers, for his sheaf *also* arose and stood upright. But not only is Joseph strong and powerful; he controls and rules over his brothers, who are submissive to him.

In the second dream, Joseph includes the parental figures too, images which certainly had not been threatening to him on a reality basis. In fact, Rachel was probably no longer alive at this time. Including her in the dream may have contained a further element of denial and wishfulfillment. Not only was his mother still alive but she was subject to his control. Thus Joseph may have been expressing how great was his need to be powerful— so powerful that he could even rule over father and mother. The dreams may therefore indicate how strong were his repressed feelings of fear and insecurity and his consequent need for defense against the awareness of such painful feelings, together with a wish for mastery of the situation. His arrogant manner may also have been largely defensive in its purpose, serving to conceal his feelings of weakness not only from his brothers but from his own consciousness.

As could be expected, the brothers reacted with anger and hostility to this presumptuous attitude, saying to him, " 'Shalt thou indeed reign over us? Or shalt thou indeed have dominion over us?' And they hated him yet the more for his dreams and for his words (37:8)."

This expression of hatred and resentment came after Joseph's first dream and yet it did not deter him later from telling them the second one. What was Joseph trying to prove here? That he could withstand the hostility of his brothers? Perhaps that was his need. He had to overcome his fear of them and to compensate by dreams of conquest in the future.

His brothers must have reacted not only to the content of the dreams, which actually have a kind of defiant, childish quality, but also to the temerity with which this next to the youngest son of Jacob stood up to them. After the second dream, Jacob himself rebukes Joseph, saying, "What is this dream that thou hast dreamed? Shall I and thy mother and thy brethren indeed come to bow down to thee to the earth (37:10)?" One gets the feeling, however, that Jacob's rebuke was more for the sake of family discipline than because of any real annoyance on his part, for he "kept the saying in his mind" but "the brothers envied him." That the brothers could feel envy in response to a dream also indicates the significance that dreams were thought to have in those days as a source of prophetic revelation.

The climax of the brothers' hostility to Joseph is reached in the fateful episode that leads to his being sold as a slave. Joseph is sent by his father to find out if all was well with his brothers and the flocks. They had been away for some time, pasturing the sheep at a considerable distance from the home site. It is possible that Joseph was not sent with them originally because their absence was to be a prolonged one. However, when Jacob became anxious over the delayed return, he sent Joseph to look for them.

One may wonder why Joseph set out on this rather arduous journey wearing his beautiful coat of many colors. The youth must have possessed a simpler garment more suited to his task. Why then did he choose to flaunt this coat before the hostile eyes of his brothers at a time when he was far from the safety of his father's house?

If Joseph was afraid of his brothers, he may have worn the coat as a form of reassurance for himself and as a warning to his brothers that he was *cloaked* with his father's love and they should therefore not dare to molest him. Moreover, in donning the robe associated with Jacob, the youth *became* the father, thus assuming the omnipotence and invulnerablity accompanying this role. Certainly Joseph would not have wished to arouse his brothers' jealous hate at a time when he was in such a defenseless position. It is also likely that he was not fully aware of the intensity of this hatred. But unconsciously he must have known.

The fact that he put himself into such an exposed position indicates a repression of this awareness. It is a characteristic of defensive behavior that it often misjudges reality.

The appearance of Joseph, who had been spared the hardships of a long sojourn in the fields, appearing now in his fine raiment and probably covering his uneasiness with an arrogant manner, must have aroused the brothers' hostility to a high pitch. Even the sight of him in the distance stirred them to angry mutterings. "Behold, this dreamer cometh. Come now, therefore, and let us slay him and cast him into one of the pits, and we will say: An evil beast hath devoured him; and we shall see what will become of his dreams (37:19–20)."

Reuben, the oldest, dissuades them from acting out this wish and they compromise by stripping him of his coat and casting him into a dry pit.

There is a vast distance between the wish to kill and the actual performance of such a deed. Reuben's suggestion did not meet with opposition. But the wish to get rid of Joseph must have been very strong and the temptation to do so while they were far from Jacob's presence must have strengthened their determination. They act readily, therefore, upon Judah's suggestion to sell him as a slave to a passing caravan which was on its way to Egypt.

The brothers bring Joseph's coat, dipped in the blood of a goat, to their father and allow him to draw his own conclusions that an evil beast has *without doubt* torn his son to pieces and devoured him. The distraught father is overcome with grief and refuses to be comforted, declaring that he would go down to the grave mourning for Joseph.

It seems rather puzzling that Jacob does not even seem to suspect any possible violence on the part of his sons toward Joseph, although he knew of their enmity. Perhaps he felt that they were not really capable of such a crime. But factors of a more unconscious nature may have been involved. In such a deeply traumatic situation, it is likely that defensive aspects of a regressive nature will appear. If Jacob had a strong sense of identification with Joseph, as we have assumed, then the apparent violent death of this beloved figure would have the emotional impact of a partial annihilation of the self, perhaps a self-castration. The consequent hostility and rage which such feelings would evoke toward his sons might have been too overwhelming for the father. The sons were guilty, at the very least, of having left Joseph unprotected, of having allowed harm to come to their brother. They therefore must have appeared in Jacob's eyes as the actual murderers of Joseph.

This intolerable thought may have made it necessary for Jacob to repress immediately any suspicion of possible violence on the part of his sons, or even to utter one word of blame against them. The immediacy with which Jacob drew the conclusion which his sons had hoped for, not even asking for an explanation or expressing one word of reproach against any of them, points to a strong need for denial and repression on the part of the father.

All his life Jacob must have carried with him some element of dread that his own brother Esau might do him harm, perhaps to the point of killing him. In later years, this fear must have been more or less successfully repressed. The violent death which Joseph appeared to have suffered may have reactivated Jacob's own apprehension regarding Esau. To have suspected his sons, to have questioned them, to have uttered even one word of blame, would have allowed these feelings to come more readily to the surface. Jacob would then have been forced to face a similar fear in regard to his sons. If they were capable of killing Joseph, might they not be capable of killing him too?

Jacob's anxiety would thus have had several sources—his own identification with Joseph, the identification of his other sons with Esau, and the realistic father-sons relationship with its inherent ambivalence. Might not the sons of a patriarchal family, under stress, revert to a situation resembling the primal horde, with its repetition of the unmentionable crime?

Only on the basis of such unconscious factors can Jacob's prompt reaction to the sight of Joseph's bloody coat be understood. What parent normally would not respond with anger and reproach to an older sibling who has allowed a younger one to come to harm? What parent normally would not demand a rehearsal of the scene in which the injury has occurred and point out how greater care on the part of the other might have averted the disaster?

The tendency for discharge of emotions by blaming others is a very human one. That Jacob did not do so cannot be attributed to saintliness on his part or a regard for the feelings of his sons. His reaction can be seen as one of appeasement. He quickly absolves them of any blame. This pattern is similar to his appeasing tendencies with Esau. Thus he is able to strengthen the repression of his own hostility and to ward off the anger of those he feared. At once however this warded-off anger is turned against himself. Jacob declares that he will never recover from this sorrow and will carry his grief with him to the grave. The self-punishment accomplishes two needed ends—an outlet for the anger through self-aggression and a punishment of his sons by arousing their guilt.

Another factor in Jacob's reaction to Joseph's apparent death may be involved. It is possible that some element of ambivalence may have been present even in the relationship to the beloved son. Wherever there is strong identification, some repressed hostility must be indicated, for when one person unconsciously thinks of himself as occupying the role of another, he tends to obliterate that person. Jacob may have envied Joseph the position of being a favored son. Joseph did not have to struggle to be accepted by the father, as Jacob himself had to do. Moreover, it was Joseph with whom Jacob had to share Rachel's love. However, this ambivalence toward Joseph, a pattern from which very few human relationships are entirely free, must have played a minor role in Jacob's reactions at this time. The love he bore this son evidently had many positive aspects.

Jacob's feelings toward his other sons in regard to this tragic event come out much more clearly in later years, on the occasion when they have to travel down to Egypt to buy grain, because of the famine in Canaan. A full account of this adventure will be presented shortly, but the relevant point here is the attitude of the father when Benjamin, his youngest son, is required to accompany the brothers on their second journey into Egypt. This is a condition made by Joseph, now Viceroy of Egypt, who had recognized his kinsmen on the first trip but himself remained unknown to them. Simeon, the second oldest of the group, had, in fact, been retained there as a hostage.

At first Jacob refuses to let Benjamin go. He cries out, "Me have ye bereaved of my children; Joseph is not and Simeon is not, and ye will take Benjamin away; upon me are all these things come (42:36)."

Now the truth comes out. It is the brothers of Joseph who have caused the father's loss. If he blames them even for Simeon's absence, how much more would he hold them guilty for what he thought had happened to Joseph. As he makes the accusation, Jacob again emphasizes his own suffering. Reuben, the oldest son, tries to reassure him about the safe return of Benjamin, saying, "Thou shalt slay my two sons if I bring him not to thee; deliver him into my hand and I will bring him back to thee." But Jacob's distrust and fear are too great. He answers, "My son shall not go down with you; for his brother is dead, and he only is left; if harm befall him by the way in which ye go, then will ye bring my gray hairs with sorrow to the grave (42:37–38)."

Reuben's suggestion that the lives of his own sons should be forfeit if any harm comes to Benjamin indicates his acceptance of the *lex talionis* principle in this situation. If he failed, even inadvertently, in his duty to take care of the younger brother, then he would consider such severe punishment justified. True, these words were spoken in an effort to reassure and persuade the anxious old father, and there must have been little doubt in Reuben's mind that such a penalty would never have been exacted. Indeed, legend says that Jacob replied, "Are not your sons my sons also?"

But the very utterance of such a pledge indicates the degree to which the sons of Jacob must have been held responsible in the heart of the old man for the grievous loss he had suffered.

The harsh reality of the continued famine forced Jacob to change his mind and let Benjamin go. Again, as in the case of Joseph's time of danger, it is Judah who seconds Reuben in expressing feelings of responsibility for the safety of Benjamin. He declares, "I will be surety for him; of my hands shalt thou require him; if I bring him not unto thee, and set him before thee, then let me bear the blame forever (43:9)."

We see Jacob again yielding to a stark reality. Again we see him using the old art of appeasement. He instructs his sons to prepare choice gifts and to bring double the amount of money needed to pay for the grain, in an effort to find favor with the powerful Prime Minister of Egypt. Thus, in this aftermath of the famine, the full story of Jacob's reaction to the earlier loss of Joseph can be more clearly understood.

Let us return now to Joseph himself. The sudden violent change in his life situation was indeed a challenge to his ego strength. The daring and cruelty of his brothers in treating him so harshly must have had a tremendous impact upon the youth. No longer could he repress awareness of their aggression, brutality, and hatred toward him. His father's protection was no longer available. He was alone in the world for the first time in his life, in the hands of strangers, an object for the slave market of Egypt.

The journey from Dothan to Egypt took a number of days. The youth had an opportunity to gather his inner resources and prepare himself for what might be awaiting him.

Joseph's experiences in Egypt indicate clearly that he responded to this new situation with strength and resolution, even under the most trying circumstances. His Egyptian master, Potiphar, an officer in the household of Pharaoh, was so impressed with Joseph's abilities that he appointed the Hebrew slave overseer of his household and left its management entirely in his hands. We are told that the affairs of Potiphar, both in the house and in the field, prospered exceedingly under Joseph's able management. Thus the young man faced the first crucial test of his new life. He was able to meet a sudden harsh ordeal, the separation from a loved parent and a familiar way of life, and the change to a position of slavery in a strange land.

That Joseph was able to make this adaptation and to do so

with phenomenal success indicates a strong ego. Joseph had faith in himself and was not overwhelmed by his new circumstances, painful though they must have been at first. The child who had been accepted and loved by both his parents had developed enough inner strength to meet the challenge of his young adulthood. The adolescent dreams of superiority were an indication of the will to overcome and to triumph over obstacles. At that time, the obstacles had been his brothers. Now there were other battles to fight, and Joseph could use satisfying means in reality rather than in dreams.

On another level, he must also have been struggling to overcome his brothers again. They had placed him in this new situation in an effort to defeat him. There was no sign of masochism in Joseph. He had a healthy wish to succeed and perhaps to discomfort those who wanted to destroy him. Joseph, the dreamer, was also a man of action.

The famous episode with Potiphar's wife revealed Joseph's basic integrity. He not only had a strong ego but a well-formed superego. Joseph refused to yield to the woman's importunities to be her lover, explaining that his duty was to the master who had placed him in a position of trust. Potiphar, who had befriended him and made him a favorite, must also have been a father figure to the youth. Potiphar's wife, therefore, would be doubly forbidden, not only out of loyalty to the master but because she too was probably a parental figure. In connection with this situation, Joseph may have had some memories of the wrath that was aroused in Jacob when Reuben slept with Bilhah, his father's concubine. At any rate, Joseph was able to resist this sexual temptation. Even more ego strength must have been needed to face the threatening consequences of his non-cooperation, for he must have known that he would arouse the woman's anger and enmity by daring to refuse her favors. Her approach to him was in the form of a command, ordering him to do her bidding. When he refused, she became even more aggressive, catching hold of his garment and repeating her order, "Lie with me." She was treating him as a servant. Joseph's refusal on a high moral and religious plane must have intensified her anger and need for revenge. He, a Hebrew slave, was putting her to shame, not only by a sexual rejection but by revealing more nobility of character than she, an Egyptian noblewoman, possessed. She punished him by a neat reversal of the situation, charging him with the deed which she herself had wished to commit.

There is no indication in the story that the Hebrew overseer was even subtly provocative to the wife of Potiphar. Indeed, one may wonder why Joseph was seemingly so impervious to the charms of the great lady. Was this indifference and avoidance in the nature of a defense? Joseph's high moral attitude, his undeviating loyalty to Potiphar, who entrusted everything to his care, may indicate a certain amount of reaction formation to feelings of desire and guilt. Such a defense on behalf of the superego would tend to strengthen character.

That Joseph's fate was not even worse when the spurned lady bitterly accused him before her husband of trying to attack her sexually is significant of the true regard in which Potiphar held him. The officer of Pharoah must also have undertsood something of his wife's true character and therefore acted with leniency toward him. Had Potiphar really believed Joseph guilty of a wanton attack upon her, the sentence would have been death for the presumptuous slave.

Joseph was removed from his position and thrown into prison. Again he was hurled from the top to the bottom of the ladder. Again he was a seemingly innocent victim of other people's baser impulses. The two factors that served to arouse his brothers' hatred may have operated here too. Joseph was genuinely superior and at the same time in a vulnerable position. It may well be that Potiphar's wife was not only attracted by the handsome youth but also irritated by his manner, which may have expressed the defensive arrogance retained from earlier years. This quality, which would convey to others a narcissistic over-evaluation of himself and a subtle rejection of others, would certainly tend to elicit envy and hatred.

Joseph, in prison, once more shows an acceptance of a difficult situation and makes efforts to improve it. Once more, he wins the favor of his superior and is given special tasks and privileges.

Here again Joseph shows faith in a father figure. He feels himself capable of winning approval by practicing the virtues of hard work and loyalty. It may be too that Joseph unconsciously experienced his fall from grace as deserved punishment for wishes of a forbidden kind. Thus he may have been stimulated to regain the favor of the father which he had so recently forfeited.

The next change in Joseph's life situation was brought about by his interest in dreams. He who had dreams of his own was also gifted in understanding the dreams of others. Two other prisoners, the baker and the butler, officers of Pharoah, are troubled by the dreams they have one night. Joseph acts as interpreter and his predictions promptly come to pass. The butler is restored to his position in the palace and the baker is hanged.

Although Joseph implores the butler to remember him, the latter fails to do so until Pharoah himself has a dream which baffles the wise men of his court. Then the butler recalls Joseph, who had interpreted his own dream so successfully. The Hebrew slave is removed from his dungeon and hastily prepared for his appearance at court.

> And Pharoah spoke unto Joseph: "In my dream, behold, I stood upon the brink of the river. And behold, there came up out of the river seven kine, fat fleshed and well-favored; and they fed in the reed-grass. And, behold, seven other kine came up after them, poor and very ill-favored, such as I never saw in all the land of Egypt for badness. And the lean and ill-favored kine did eat up the first seven fat kine. And when they had eaten them up, it could not be known that they had eaten them, but they were still ill-favored as at the beginning. So I awoke. And I saw in my dream, and, behold, seven ears came up on one stalk, full and good. And, behold, seven ears, withered, thin, and blasted with the east wind, sprung up after them. And the thin ears swallowed up the seven good ears. And I told it unto the magicians; but there was none that could declare it to me (41:17–24)."

Joseph's interpretation of the dreams, that Egypt would enjoy seven years of plenty, followed in turn by seven lean years, makes a profound impression upon Pharaoh. Moreover, the young

Hebrew immediately presents a plan for dealing with the situation. Grain is to be stored throughout the land during the period of plentiful harvest to provide for the years of famine. Again, Joseph the dreamer shows himself to be also a man of action. He is given the task of carrying out this program and is made second in power to Pharaoh himself.

We might digress here briefly to observe that the dreams of all three Egyptians, those of the two officers in prison which Joseph had interpreted earlier, and the dreams of Pharaoh himself, deal with problems on an oral level. The butler dreams of pressing juice from the fruit of the vine into Pharaoh's cup and presenting it to his master. His wish, ostensibly, is to be once more the good, nourishing mother. The baker dreams of carrying baked goods for Paraoh, but birds come and eat the food from the basket which is perched upon the baker's head. The officer is thus the object of oral aggression. His dream may express a fear resulting from his own projected hostile wishes. His punishment is death, as the dream symbolically foretells.

In Pharaoh's dreams the devouring cows and ears of corn may symbolize the Egyptian concept of the primitive cannibalistic mother who consumes her young, an image still found in the unconscious fantasy of children and in dreams. We have a hint here that in this land where all nourishment depends upon the Nile, the alternately giving and withholding mother, oral problems may retain their importance psychologically to a greater degree than customary.

Joseph becomes the good father of Egypt by providing food. His success is phenomenal. Again he uses his very real abilities and his capacity for hard work to consolidate his position. His achievements therefore cannot be said to be based on fortuitous circumstances alone. For the rest of his life, Joseph remains in Pharaoh's favor. This is no small accomplishment when one considers how fickle were the moods of those mighty potentates.

The story of Joseph's personal life in Egypt is treated in the most meager fashion. We are told that Pharaoh selected a wife for him in the person of Asenath, daughter of Poti-phera, priest of On. Tradition says that this Poti-phera and Potiphar, Joseph's first master, were one and the same. Other legends declare that Asenath was actually the daughter of Dinah, Joseph's half-sister, born of her violent union with the prince of Shechem. She was spirited away to Egypt and adopted by the priest of On. The motive for this latter myth was evidently to give Asenath a Hebrew mother.

Two sons are born to him as a result of this marriage. Their names are significant and give one of the few indications about Joseph's emotional state in the land of Egypt. The first-born was called *Manasseh*, which means "making to forget," for Joseph explained, "God hath made me forget all my toil, and all my father's house." The second was named *Ephraim*, "to be fruitful," "for God hath made me fruitful in the land of my affliction (41:51–52)."

Here we have it, then. Through the names he gave his sons, Joseph reveals some of his innermost feelings. The declaration that God had made him forget his suffering and "all his father's house," may indeed express the solace he found in his sons. But it says also that he had never forgotten the traumatic experiences he had endured, nor the ties to his home and family. Egypt, the land of his triumph, is at the same time the "land of his affliction."

The story of Joseph's reunion with his brothers in Egypt can be regarded as the high point of his life history; it was the vindication and the triumph of his whole existence, containing within it the full complex of his sibling rivalry and its resolution.

There is severe drought in Canaan, even as in Egypt, during those predicted lean years. But because of Joseph's wise administration of the task entrusted to him, Egypt does not lack for food.

Jacob sends his ten sons down to the land of the Nile to buy grain for the family, keeping Benjamin, the youngest, at home. The men are recognized by Joseph as they bow before him, but they are not aware of his identity. He accuses them of being spies. They protest their innocence, declaring that they are twelve brothers, the sons of one man in the land of Canaan. The youngest was with the father, and "one is not." Joseph demands that they prove their story by bringing Benjamin down to Egypt.

The tone of this reunion can best be appreciated through the perspective of Joseph's youthful dream of conquest in which the entire family, including the parents, bowed down to him. The similarity and the difference between those dreams and the later events will be significant for our understanding of Joseph.

As with so many of the biblical narratives, the story can be understood on two levels. Except for a few details that seem puzzling, and which we will consider later, the events as described could actually have taken place. They have a reality aspect. We know that in periods of famine the Hebrew shepherds of Canaan did go down to Egypt to buy grain. We know that a group of them remained there.

But this particular story of the reunion in Egypt has a quality so dramatic, so perfect in its storytelling pattern as it rises through a series of events to a climactic end, that the role of the story-teller must here be given special consideration. It is a storyteller who is wholly in tune with his hero and his theme. It may be that the biblical story represents an artistic reformulation of actual happenings.

Let us consider it first from the aspect of a reality situation. Joseph's reaction when his brothers were brought before him on their first visit is one of understandable anger. He spoke roughly, pretending not to know them. Being able to carry out such a pretense until the moment he deemed suitable to reveal himself is an example of self-control. His rough treatment probably expressed some of his real feelings and as such was a healthy acknowledgment of his resentment.

When Joseph takes his brothers into custody on the charge that they are spies, he learns inadvertently that they are suffering from a sense of guilt because of their treatment of him long ago, and that they regard their present plight as a just punishment for this sin. His strategy of forcing them to bring Benjamin with them on their next trip serves both the purpose of satisfying his tender longing to see his younger brother again and also of testing the others to see if they have really mended their ways. Would they have more regard for Benjamin than they once had for him?

But other aspects of this demand reveal its ambivalent nature.

We learn in a later scene that Judah at this time explained to Joseph how difficult it would be for the father to part with this youngest son, what sorrow it would cause the already sorrowing Jacob. Joseph evidently was not responsive to this plea. Nor does he consider the anxiety such a trip would involve for Benjamin himself. It seems that the emotional investment in this plan was too great for Joseph to relinquish it. In this matter he could not behave with a rational consideration even for the feelings of those he loved. His first impulse is to keep all the brothers as hostages in Egypt, with the exception of one, who is to return to Canaan and bring back Benjamin. We see here how deeply involved Joseph becomes in this situation. He changes the plan, however, and lets the brothers return, keeping only one as hostage. He chooses Simeon, the second oldest, instead of Reuben, because the latter had interceded for him at the crucial period when he was sold into slavery.

We are not told directly the reason for this change of plan but it becomes clear in the words which Joseph speaks to his brothers after he has held them as prisoners for three days. He says,

> "Do this and live; for I fear God: If ye be upright men, let one of your brethren be bound in your prison-house; but go ye, carry corn for the famine of your houses; and bring your youngest brother unto me; so shall your words be verified, and ye shall not die (42:18-20)."

He could not let his people in Canaan starve while he acted out his need to punish. Joseph had a superego; *he feared God.*

The second meeting with the brothers shows Joseph's tender feelings in the ascendancy. When he beholds Benjamin, he is moved to tears. But he controls his emotions until he can go into a separate chamber and weep unobserved. Then he washes his face and returns. This is a moving example of Joseph's spontaneous tenderness. There must have been a strong impulse to reveal himself to his brothers at this time. What a fitting retribution for his suffering at their hands! His dream had literally become true and they were now bowing humbly before him.

But Joseph could wait for his moment of triumph. Perhaps he

no longer had so strong a need for the acknowledgment of his superior position and strength. If so, this would be proof that his adolescent dreams were largely defensive rather than narcissistic. As suggested earlier, they had been prompted more by feelings of insecurity than exaggerated self-love.

Joseph treats his brothers well, serving them a generous repast as guests in his own home, giving them gifts of clothing, and filling their sacks with grain.

The severest ordeal to which Joseph subjects them is described in the well-known incident of the silver goblet which he causes to be placed into Benjamin's sack of grain. The brothers are overtaken on their homeward journey, accused of stealing this object, and brought back before Joseph.

One wonders what moved Joseph to choose this particular item for his purpose. The cup may here symbolize the mother's breast, or the mother herself, whom Joseph and Benjamin shared.[5] In this episode an element of ambivalence may be detected in Joseph's feelings for Benjamin. For in reality this incident must have caused the younger brother considerable fear and anguish. But positive aspects are also involved here. Through the symbolism of the mother whom they once had in common, Joseph brings Benjamin back to him, and in due time, accepts him lovingly.

This bit of behavior may be a reenactment of an old conflict. In a sense, Benjamin had truly deprived him of his mother, for she died at his birth. Perhaps, at that time, as a defensive reaction to his deep sense of loss and its accompanying hostility, the young Joseph adopted a protective, nurturing mother role toward the infant brother. Such a development would help to explain Joseph's deep tenderness and affection for Benjamin.

In describing the stolen object, Joseph's steward says, "Is not this it in which my lord drinketh, and whereby he indeed divineth?" Is it possible that there is a relationship between these two functions which the cup serves? Symbolically, one can say that the breast which once fed him also made him powerful. The nursing period goes back to the time when the infant feels himself a part of the omnipotent parent. The flight of time involved in foretelling the future may really represent a wishful return to the past, when the child truly felt omnipotent and omniscient, for he possessed what must have seemed to him like the limitless source of all good—the mother's breast.

There is a puzzling detail in this incident of the stolen cup and its consequences. The brothers are overtaken by the steward of Joseph, who subjects them to the unjust accusation and the humiliating search. The Hebrew shepherds know the danger they will face if they return under the cloud of this apparent theft. There is no indication in the narrative that the steward is accompanied by any other servants. The scene takes place on the road, a short distance from the city. What could have prevented the brothers from ignoring the orders of this one man? They could easily have thrust him aside and continued on their way.

The unrealistic aspect of this submissiveness indicates an element of fantasy in this part of the story. It may be an expression of Joseph's youthful dream—to conquer his brothers single-handed. And, in fact, one of the few displays of narcissistic pride in which Joseph indulges, comes when the brothers return and stand ignominiously before him. He says to them, ". . . know ye not that such a man as I would indeed divine (44:15)?" This little scene is reminiscent of an earlier one, when Joseph arrogantly tells his brothers his dreams of future greatness and power in which they would submit to him. The steward in the later incident may well represent Joseph himself, and therefore he is alone.

The brothers might have abandoned Benjamin to his fate and continued on their way. Indeed, they were given every opportunity to do so. Joseph's steward declared, "He with whom it is found shall be my bondman; and ye shall be blameless." But all the brothers returned with him and appeared before Joseph once more.

The great man of Egypt reproaches them for what they have done, but when Judah says despairingly that they will all be his bondmen, Joseph replies, "Far be it from me that I should do so;

the man in whose hand the goblet is found, he shall be my bond-man; but as for you, get you up in peace unto your father (44:17)."

The Viceroy's decision to keep Benjamin as a slave and Judah's dramatic intercession for the younger man lead to the climax of the story. Judah concludes with the words, "Now therefore, let thy servant, I pray thee, abide instead of the lad a bondman to my lord; and let the lad go up with his brethren. For how shall I go up to my father, if the lad be not with me? Lest I look upon the evil that shall come on my father (44:33-34)."

Joseph is deeply moved by this plea and can no longer restrain himself. Still, before giving free expression to his emotions, he orders the servants to leave the room. "And he wept aloud; and the Egyptians heard, and the house of Pharaoh heard." The control of this strong man finally broke in the grip of a powerful emotion. Not in a mood of narcissistic triumph, but in an outburst of love and longing does Joseph finally reveal himself to his brothers. Thus he indicates the loneliness and homesickness that he must have endured during those many years in an alien land. His first words to his brothers are, "I am Joseph—doth my father yet live?"

His immediate concern was for the beloved parent of his childhood. Even though he had several previous reports that Jacob was alive, he asked it now, not as the Viceroy of Egypt inquiring about a stranger and therefore not sure of receiving a truthful answer, but as a son seeking his father.

The sudden dramatic revelation frightens the brothers and immobilizes them. They are unable to answer. Then Joseph shows his true compassion, speaking with a moving simplicity and drawing them closer to him with the words:

"Come near me, I pray you," And they came near. And he said, "I am Joseph, your brother, whom ye sold into Egypt. And now be not grieved, nor angry with yourselves, that ye sold me hither; for God did send me before you to preserve life. For these two years hath the famine been in the land; and there are yet five years, in which there shall be neither plowing nor harvest. . . . So now it was not you that sent me

hither but God; and He has made me a father to Pharaoh,
and lord of all his house, and ruler over all the land of
Egypt (45:4–8)."

Only after he has sustained and comforted them with an obvious rationalization does he allow himself a few words of gratification regarding his high office. If one can detect a note of triumph over the brothers, it is one so humanly understandable
that its absence would have made Joseph a less believable person.
Again, when he tells them of his plans to bring them all to Egypt
does he permit himself the satisfaction of saying, "And ye shall
tell my father of all my glory in Egypt and all that ye have seen,"
adding immediately, "and ye shall haste and bring my father
hither," as if his glory might be a further inducement to bring
Jacob on the long journey from Canaan to Egypt (45:13). One
gets the impression here, not of a need to extol himself before
the aged and sorrowing father, but rather to give him cause for
rejoicing at the earliest possible moment that the son he thought
lost was not only alive but had achieved success and greatness.

It is interesting at this point to note that when Jacob hears all
this marvelous tale about Joseph and the high estate he has attained, the father's response is simple and to the point. He says,
"It is enough; Joseph my son is alive; I will go and see him
before I die." It was Joseph his son he yearned for, not the
Viceroy of Egypt.

Joseph kisses and embraces all his brothers, weeping as he
does so. His reunion with Benjamin is especially tender. Joseph's
feelings are evidently contagious, for even Pharaoh and his household are drawn into the mood of this drama. He encourages and
supports Joseph in the plan of sending for the entire tribe of
Israel and settling them in Egypt.

This story of Joseph's reunion with his brothers contains
several elements that are puzzling from the viewpoint of reality.
First, Benjamin is spoken of as if he were still a young boy, a *lad*.
Yet he certainly must have been a grown man by this time. The
Bible tells us that Joseph was thirty years old when he was ap-

pointed to his high office. He would now be close to forty, and Benjamin, about six years younger. The reference to Benjamin as a *lad* may indicate a strong identification on the part of Joseph with his younger brother in this episode. He therefore sees him in the image of his own youthful self. The traumatic situation of the past, when he himself was at the mercy of his brothers, is repeated, but this time the outcome is happily different.

Another significant detail is the *loud voice* with which Joseph weeps when he finally yields to his feelings. Interestingly, he had tried to ward off this very situation. Repeatedly he restrained his tears, once going into a separate chamber to weep and again by sending the servants out of the room at the moment when he revealed himself. But the very urgency of his need to conceal was evidently a defense against the fear of his own intense feelings. But the long-repressed emotions had to come out. There is convincing proof here too of the pain and anguish, the sense of loneliness that Joseph must have suffered, not only in Egypt, but during the years of his youth, when his brothers rejected him.

The strength of feeling with which Joseph draws his brothers to him is expressive of how he must have longed to be close to them in those far-off days. He had repressed this need and wish at that time. Instead, the defensive pride and arrogance which further alienated them had taken its place. Now, in contrast to the *secret* longing, comes the *loud* noise of his weeping. A repression is suddenly lifted. Only when he is in reality stronger than they are can he give up his defenses and allow his warm feelings to come out. Joseph uses his position of power to give expression to his love and to protect and care for those dependent upon him.

Midrashic literature tries to find an explanation of why Joseph did not try to establish contact with his family long before the appearance of his brothers in Egypt. Psychologically the answer seems clear. He could not return to the brothers who had so cruelly rejected him. It was they who had to come to him. Only when he was beyond their power to do him injury, only when he stood above them in prestige and strength, could he accept them with the magnanimity and compassion that they had failed to show him.

Yet Joseph's need for love and acceptance from his brothers was greater than his wish to triumph over them. In the light of that which man strives for can he be understood. Joseph's basic goal was the attainment of love.

One of the signs of true maturity that Joseph revealed during his sojourn in Egypt was his acceptance of himself. Although he was an alien in the land and thus looked down upon by the Egyptians, Joseph's sense of self-esteem evidently remained high. He made no attempt to conceal his background or to change his religion. When his brothers appear in their rough shepherd clothes, Joseph reveals no sense of shame or inferiority, even though herdsmen were regarded as an inferior caste in Egypt. He claims them lovingly as his brothers and makes arrangements for all of the family to come to Egypt and settle there, even securing the cooperation of Pharaoh in this project. When Jacob arrives, Joseph hastens to meet him. He even arranges an audience with Pharaoh for Jacob and five of the brothers. The white-haired Jacob, at the venerable age of a hundred and thirty, speaks to Pharaoh with dignity, and the mighty ruler of Egypt bows his head to receive the blessing of the Patriarch of Israel.

Such inner security and self-acceptance on the part of Joseph must be attributed, in part, to his relationship with Jacob. When Joseph was so abruptly separated from his father, the youth brought with him an internalized image of a strong, kindly, protective parent, the influence of a matured and spiritualized Jacob. The latter had to go through considerable struggle in his own lifetime to achieve this state, for he himself had to overcome the handicap of a weak father figure.

The Bible dwells at length upon Jacob's relationship with God and the promises that are held out to him if he proves himself worthy. Jacob strives to achieve this goal. In contrast, there is very little in the story of Joseph about any struggle between himself and God. He accepted God as he accepted his father, with faith and trust. On entering Egypt and on subsequent occasions, Joseph makes the simple, quiet assertion that God was with him. When he is called upon to interpret Pharaoh's dream,

Joseph says confidently, "God will give Pharaoh an answer of peace."

A large part of Joseph's strength came from this aspect of inner harmony, his trust in a beneficent God who was always with him. Perhaps nothing attests more fully to the high degree of maturity which Jacob finally reached in his later years than this influence which his own personality made possible in his beloved son.

Joseph's maturity is once more manifested after the death of his father, when his brothers, still suffering from guilt and insecurity, fear that Joseph might now take a belated revenge. They plead again for his forgiveness, saying that this was Jacob's wish. Joseph's eyes fill with tears as he replies, "Fear not; for am I in the place of God!" The Talmud comments that Joseph wept at this point because his brothers showed their distrust of him and must have felt that he hated them.[6] This is an astute observation and one must conclude that they were unable to understand his capacity to forgive and to love.

Joseph's strong sense of self-identity is brought out clearly at the time of his death, when his last request is that his bones should eventually be brought to Canaan and buried there with his fathers.

The personality of Joseph is characteristic of the son and the brother rather than that of the father figure, even though he was "father to Pharaoh and all the land of Egypt." The *fathers* of Israel are Abraham, Isaac, and Jacob. Joseph is not included among them. The conflicts of the first three Patriarchs were centered in the father-son relationship, hence in their efforts to achieve a more idealistic identification with God. In regard to Joseph, the problem of sibling rivalry was paramount. Perhaps that is another reason why Joseph is so humanly understandable. The conflict with siblings does not have the same kind of repressive, utterly forbidden quality that the oedipal struggle does. But as a source of poignancy and pain, this area of human relationship has perhaps been underestimated in comparison with the problems of the child-parent situation.

Joseph tended to live harmoniously with father figures. For this reason there are some who question Joseph's masculine attributes. But there is no indication in the biblical narrative that Joseph was submissive and fearful in relation to these figures. Rather he earned their confidence and approval by his real efforts, ability, and trustworthiness.

But there are areas of Joseph's personality which this study professedly leaves unexplored. What was the relationship between Joseph's oedipal conflict and his sibling rivalry? To what extent did he try to resolve the one through the other? Did his faith in the father contain an element of denial in regard to ambivalent feelings and a consequent reaction-formation? Did Joseph *have* to have faith in a father figure?

Perhaps it is because he did not go through the soul-searching experience of revolt and conciliation with the father that Joseph did not attain the impressive patriarchal qualities of Abraham and Jacob.

In one important situation, Joseph even loses out as a son. His name is not immortalized among the twelve tribes of Israel. Jacob promises him a double share of inheritance and calls two of the tribes after the sons of Joseph—Ephraim and Manasseh. But the name of Joseph himself loses this form of perpetuation. Thus Jacob ostensibly gives his most beloved son a double portion, but in reality deprives him of his inheritance. Joseph is conquered and swallowed up by his sons, who take his place. Some ambivalence on the part of Jacob might be involved here.

When Joseph brings the two boys to him for a blessing, Jacob exclaims, "... And now thy two sons, who were born unto thee in the land of Egypt before I came unto thee into Egypt, are mine; Ephraim and Manasseh, even as Reuben and Simeon, shall be mine. And thy issue, that thou begettest after them, shall be thine; they shall be called after the name of their brethren in their inheritance (48:5–6)." Jacob here puts the two sons of Joseph in the same category as his own sons, distinguishing between these first two children of Joseph and others that he might later have. One gets a feeling that he is almost taking them away from Joseph.

To the distress of the father, the younger son is given preference in the blessing bestowed by Jacob. In this, one of the last
acts of his life, Jacob ignores Joseph's wishes and feelings, reverting to his own favoritism for a younger son. In a sense, he elim-
inates Joseph and puts the two youths in their father's place. This
action may be the response of the aged father to a son who has
dared to rise above him in power and status. Thus, in his relationship to Israel, Joseph remains a son rather than the father of
a tribe.

This ambivalence in Jacob must have had a corresponding
note in Joseph himself. But the need to repress the hostility and
to atone for the guilt is in line with the slowly crystallizing
Hebraic tradition. Joseph honors his father in death as in life,
undertaking, in person, the long funeral journey to Canaan.
Jacob is interred in the Cave of Machpelah, to rest with his
fathers. The son returns to Egypt.

The character of Joseph, seen in terms of his early environment and later patterns of behavior, seems to have definite
psychological unity. Whether this effect was brought about because the Joseph stories have a historical basis or because they
are the product of a people who had a strong intuitive understanding of human motivation and conduct is difficult to say.
Perhaps both factors were involved.

A Character Study
of Samuel

 CHAPTER FOUR

SAMUEL APPEARS upon the scene of biblical history in an epoch quite removed both in time and circumstance from the one with which we have thus far been concerned. Abraham, Jacob, and Joseph, for all their human qualities, stand in a kind of roseate glow cast upon them by the pristine charm of the Patriarchal Era. The beginnings of an unfolding, whether of individual or group life, has a particularly romantic aura of its own.

It was different in the days of Samuel. Israel had a longer history behind it now. The time was roughly about the middle of the eleventh century B.C.E. The Hebrews had known slavery in Egypt, the never-to-be-forgotten escape to freedom, the exaltation at Mount Sinai, the imprint of the leadership of Moses, the weariness of desert life, the crossing of the Jordan, and the slow conquest of the Promised Land. And yet, in the somewhat problematic chronology of biblical times, the period from the days of Moses to the time of Samuel was only about two hundred years.[1]

The heroic days of Joshua were followed by a long period of intermittent warfare and settlement upon the land. During those years the leaders in Israel were people who arose spontaneously to meet some special challenge, usually during the crises of war. The source of their power and authority however was always religious and their rise to leadership was generally in response to a *call* from God. They were known as *judges,* a term which had a wider connotation in those days than in our own. Although chiefly military leaders, they served as arbiters in internal matters as well and generally also led in the performance of communal religious rites.

At the time of Samuel, the period of the judges was drawing to a close. The tribes of Israel were now living in fairly compact groups, separated only by natural barriers and some areas of Canaanite strongholds which had never been subdued.

The most threatening enemy at this time came from another source. A warlike people, the Philistines, coming from somewhere in the general area of the Aegean, had settled along the seacoast. They were established chiefly in five cities, each with its own ruler but united in a kind of confederacy. The Philistines had more sophisticated weapons than Israel. The Bible describes their use of iron chariots. They would make forays into the hill-country, where most of the Israelites were settled and at various times subdued certain tribes, subjecting the people to oppressive taxation and laws. This was the situation at the period with which we are now concerned.

Samuel is known as a transition figure, the last of the judges and the first of the prophets. He sat in judgment among the people, he aroused them to military action in times of danger, he served as head priest in religious functions. It was he who established the Monarchy and crowned the first two kings, Saul and David. All these services Samuel could perform because he was known and accepted as a seer and a prophet, who communicated the will of God to the people.

The character of Samuel offers special opportunity for a study in the psychology of leadership. His figure stands out with a kind of solitary impressiveness during this period of ancient Israel which served as an interlude between the days of the Judges and the time of the Monarchy.

There are two images of Samuel that tend to linger in the popular mind. One is that of the child in the Temple, under the tutelage of the old priest, Eli, and the awe-inspiring event that took place there, of being *called* by God. The other image is probably that of an old man with a long grey beard, stern and uncompromising in the fulfillment of his various duties. The vigorous man of middle years would be absent from these recollections. Perhaps the life story of this personality may explain this rather curious vacuum which has its source in the biblical narrative itself.

While he did not attain the heights of prophetic genius reached by some of those who came after him, Samuel filled a role which was uniquely his own. Serving a people who led a simple agricultural life, he faced problems and tasks different from the later prophets of a more urban culture. He acted as a unifying force during an era when his people was being seriously threatened by the conquering and oppressive Philistines, with the considerable danger that the Hebrew nation might disintegrate into separate tribal groups, each with its individual and probably transitory history. Through his moral leadership, Samuel helped to avert this disaster. Historians say that while Moses formed the Hebrews into a people, it was Samuel who helped to maintain and strengthen the unity so essential to its survival.

Samuel seems to have been a man peculiarly shaped both by his time and personal history for the role he was to play. We shall try to evaluate the influences that helped to form this leader and, in turn, to understand his own later significance for the group.

The biblical story of Samuel's life begins, significantly, with his parentage and the environmental factors that were involved. The account of his birth sounds like an idyllic folktale, a rather interesting variation of the myth of the birth of a hero. It is also understandable however from a reality aspect. In terms of

Samuel's personality development, the narrative is psychologically meaningful. And indeed myth itself does not spring out of thin air but has a psychic reality of its own. In the Bible, particularly, stories of the birth of heroes generally have an underlying coherence with the life of the individual concerned.

The biblical account is about a woman, Hannah, who had no children. Her disappointment was the more keenly felt because there was a rival wife in this non-monogamous family. Peninnah was successful where Hannah had failed, being the mother of numerous offspring. The situation was further troubled because the measure of a wife's success was largely on the basis of her child-bearing abilities. Sterility was regarded not only as a social stigma but as valid grounds for divorce.

However, of the two wives, Hannah was the more beloved by Elkanah, the husband. On the occasion of the yearly pilgrimage to the sanctuary at Shiloh, where the family regularly came to make its sacrifice, he showed his love for Hannah in a special way. Peninnah and each of her children received from him a portion of the sacrificial meal, but to Hannah he gave a double portion. This evidently aroused Peninnah's jealousy for we are told that immediately after this, Hannah's rival "vexed her sore to make her fret, because the Lord has shut up her womb." This situation repeated itself year after year, on the same occasion.

At one of these times, Hannah was so vexed, she could not eat. Then Elkanah comforted her with tender words, saying, "Hannah, why weepest thou? And why is thy heart grieved? Am I not better to thee than ten sons (1:8)?"*

After this, Hannah entered the Temple and prayed to God for a son, vowing that if her wish were granted, she would dedicate him to God's service for all his life.

A curious incident now took place. Eli, the old priest, sitting at the doorpost of the Temple, observed Hannah's somewhat unusual behavior. He noted the lengthy time she remained at her

* Biblical quotations and references in this chapter, unless otherwise noted, are from First Samuel.

prayers, the evident intensity of her emotions, and the fact that although her lips moved, no sound came forth. He concluded that she was drunk and reprimanded her. Hannah explained quite humbly that it was not so, that she was a woman of sorrowful spirit who had poured out her soul before the Lord. The priest then gave her his blessing.

Eli's misjudgment of Hannah's behavior is interesting. Biblical commentators point out that this incident indicates that Eli must have been of a suspicious and distrustful nature. While this inference may be correct, one wonders if there might not have been some basis for the impression which Eli formed of her as she prayed before the Ark. Perhaps there was something in Hannah's mood that was neither truly reverent nor prayerful. She entered the Temple to make her request of God shortly after Peninnah had *sorely vexed her*. She had refused to eat, so deeply was she disturbed. Vexation is a feeling that involves both anger and sorrow. Refusal to eat is a sign of hostility and protest against a parental figure. In this instance, it was the sacrificial meal of which Hannah refused to partake. This amounted to an angry rejection of God, the Father, who had denied her a child. It was also a rejection of her husband, although he had shown his love by giving her a double portion.

Hannah's mood, therefore, when entering the Temple to pray for a child, must have been a mingled one in which anger played a large role. Indeed, when Eli rebukes her for being drunk and she denies this, she explains, "Out of the abundance of my complaint and my vexation have I spoken . . ."

One wonders why Hannah did not follow the usual custom of praying aloud. It was chiefly the fact that her lips moved soundlessly that aroused Eli's suspicion. Secrecy may have been a motive here, for she did not reveal even to Eli the nature of her fervent plea. The Bible says, "She was in bitterness of soul—— and she prayed unto the Lord and wept sore." The contrast between this agitated behavior and the silently moving lips must indeed have seemed incongruous to the observing priest.

Hannah may have silenced her lips quite consciously and

with some effort, since doing so was out of keeping both with custom and the intensity of her feelings. Her evidently strong wish for secrecy may have been a desire to spare herself any further humiliation, should her request not be granted. We can assume that strong narcissistic needs, dependency on others for feelings of self-esteem and the accompanying vulnerability, were involved in Hannah's attitudes towards her barrenness. Her prolonged stay before the Ark indicates the degree of effort she must have put into her plea. This element is most obvious in the bargain she makes with God. If he will only fulfill her wish, the child would be returned to him for a lifetime of service. In effect, she would then be vindicated as a wife and God would gain a servant.

For Hannah, the birth of Samuel meant an answer to her prayer. She did not return to Shiloh again until the child was weaned. This was a matter of several years, for in those days children were not weaned until they were two to three years of age, or even longer.

Hannah's refusal to accompany Elkanah on the yearly trip to the sanctuary during the years of Samuel's infancy seems a little puzzling. The distance from Ramah, the village where the family lived, to Shiloh, was only about twelve miles. She could have taken the child with her and traveled in a cart or on a donkey. Nothing is said about the possible hardships of such a journey. Some biblical commentators infer that Hannah remained at home so that she would be able to spend as much time as possible with the child before she had to give him up. But if Samuel had not yet been weaned, she would have had to take him with her anyhow.

Hannah's own words give a clearer indication of the reason. The Bible says, "But Hannah went not up; for she said unto her husband, 'Until the child be weaned, when I will bring him, that he may appear before the Lord and there abide forever (1:22).' "

It seems likely that not until she could present her child to Eli as the dramatic fulfillment of her prayer, the triumphant denouément to the little scene in the Temple, did Hannah wish to appear before Eli again. Samuel was to be the joyful vindication, not only in the eyes of a rival Peninnah, but also before Eli, who had so cruelly misjudged her.

And indeed Hannah makes the most of the situation when the great moment finally arrives. After the appropriate sacrifice is made, the child is brought before Eli and Hannah says, "Oh, my lord, as thy soul liveth, my lord, I am the woman that stood by thee here, praying unto the Lord. For this child I prayed; and the Lord hath granted me my petition which I asked of him; therefore I also have lent him to the Lord; as long as he liveth he is lent to the Lord (1:26–27)."

Then Hannah prays to God. This time her prayer is quite in contrast to the silence of her earlier plea. She expresses her exultation in a ringing hymn of praise and thanksgiving that declares loudly her triumph over her enemies and her sense of identification with an omnipotent God, who is clearly on her side (2:1–10).

Some biblical critics believe that this hymn was written at a much later date but was placed here because it seemed to fit the occasion so well. Since controversy covers so much of the field of biblical criticism, we shall enter into this problem only to the extent of agreeing that the song does indeed seem to express Hannah's feelings in a way that is harmonious with what we have seen of her character.

There is not a single word in the text to indicate feelings of sorrow or loss as the woman leaves her child in the Temple with Eli. One must indeed wonder how real Hannah's love for Samuel could have been. She brought him into the world and suckled him with the sole intention of returning him to God, whose gift he was. The boy could not have had much meaning to her as a separate person. More likely he was unconsciously perceived as an extension of herself, a part she was sacrificing to the God who had saved her from feelings of humiliation and defeat.

Hannah thus reveals her character with impressive clarity in the brief space that is devoted to her. She is a woman with a large amount of narcissim, whose exaggerated need for self-esteem had been wounded by her barrenness. Had she been a more feminine woman, her natural wish for a child would have expressed itself with more of longing than of rage, and she would not have been so willing to surrender the child as a form of sacrifice.

When her injured self-love is repaired by the birth of Samuel and her atonement for unconscious feelings of aggression and guilt is accomplished by keeping her promise to God, Hannah's tensions are evidently released. She is then able to function more naturally as a woman and to produce a number of other children.

However, the mother's attitude toward this first child must have conveyed itself to him in countless non-verbal as well as verbal communications. These must have expressed not only a self-involved treasuring but also a reactive process of readiness to give him up in accordance with superego demands, which would prevent a true development of object love. One can imagine the woman's frequent admonition to the small boy that he was promised to God and could not misbehave as other children did. He was a *holy* child, set apart from the world around him.

The only indication of Hannah's tender feelings for the young Samuel is the statement that she brought him each year a linen robe which she made herself. The annual bestowal of this gift has the quality of a ritual. The garment which Hannah made must have represented the mother herself to Samuel. Perhaps it symbolized the tie which bound him to the rejecting parent for whose tenderness he must have longed in vain throughout his life. As we shall see, the wish and need for the woman became deeply repressed in Samuel and found expression in a reactive rebellion against her. But he who must revolt against the mother does not really give her up.

In contrast to Hannah, Elkanah, the father, seems to have been a man of warm emotions. He comforts his wife with loving words when she is unhappy. He lets her have her way when she does not wish to accompany him to Shiloh before the child is weaned. Elkanah's mildness and warmth, therefore, may have had an alleviating effect upon Samuel's early environment. The fact, however, that the mother and father roles were, in a sense, reversed, could not have been without effect upon the child's development.

Elkanah was evidently in complete agreement with Hannah's plan of giving up the boy to God's service. Whether his acquiescent attitude came out of his own convictions, stemming from his obviously religious frame of mind, or whether it was a sign of passive yielding to Hannah's will, there is little way of knowing. A suspicion that some element of the latter might have been involved arises on the basis that narcissistic women, whose erotic feelings are centered largely in themselves, tend to choose passive husbands and vice versa[2] Samuel may therefore have had a rather passive and submissive father as a model for identification in the first few years of his life.

. To the modern reader of the biblical story, it must seem rather impractical as well as psychologically undesirable to leave a child of two or three to do service in the Temple. At this age he would certainly be much more of a burden than a help. But if he was brought there in the nature of a sacrifice, as we assume, then the actual consequences would be less important than the unconscious meanings of the act to those who thus surrendered him. Perhaps, also, the importance of early training in terms of environmental influence might have been a determining factor.

Samuel himself could have experienced this separation from his parents only as an abandonment and his emotional development must have been deeply influenced by it. The fact that it took place shortly after his weaning would have greatly increased the trauma. Soon after losing the breast, he also lost the mother.

One wonders if this experience may be related to the fact that there is hardly any reference to women in Samuel's life history. The whole area of women and sexuality seems to have undergone a severe repression, as we shall note in more detail later.

The father figure was evidently replaced by Eli, with whom a close identification must have followed, and through Eli, with the God he represented. The boy's character development, therefore, would have been along the lines of submission and obedience to God, the need for sacrifice to him, and at the same time, a deep sense of personal destiny. This pattern was a continuation of the attitudes with which his parents had presumably surrounded him from the time he was born.

Samuel had to learn unquestioning obedience to the ritual of the Temple, and how to place duty to God above the gratification of instinctual desires. But it was largely a discipline which was sanctioned from within, for Samuel seems to have accepted wholeheartedly the goals which were set for him. This harmony between ego and superego ideals may have been one of the main sources of his strength.[3] The three important adults in Samuel's early environment all concurred in an implicit acceptance of what his life was to be. He was trained for his career in much the same way that a small child in a royal family is brought up from earliest days for a life of special duty and special privilege.

This kind of training, which is based on empathic acceptance of values and standards, of that which is implicit rather than expressed, has tremendous efficacy because it meets with so little inner resistance.

The next incident which the Bible records of Samuel's youthful days at Shiloh is that of his mystic experience when God reveals himself to him for the first time.

There are dramatic and moving elements in the familiar narrative of Samuel's call to service. The boy, sleeping in the Temple, hears a voice calling to him out of the night. He thinks it is Eli, the priest, summoning him. The youth runs to Eli, who is probably lying in an adjoining alcove, and says,

> "Here am I; for thou didst call me." And he said: "I called not; lie down again." And the Lord called yet again Samuel. And Samuel arose and went to Eli, and said: "Here am I; for thou didst call me." And he answered: "I called not, my son; lie down again." Now Samuel did not yet know the Lord, neither was the word of the Lord yet revealed unto him. And the Lord called Samuel again the third time. And he arose and went to Eli, and said: "Here am I; for thou didst call me." And Eli perceived that the Lord was calling the child. Therefore Eli said unto Samuel: "Go, lie down;

and it shall be, if thou be called, that thou shalt say, 'Speak, Lord; for Thy servant heareth (3:3–9).' "

What could have been the nature of Samuel's experience, psychologically speaking? Arlow describes it as an hallucinatory one, similar to those of other prophets who felt themselves summoned to God's service.[4] It is, however, in the specific aspects of this event that we may hope to find a fuller understanding of Samuel as an individual. The *call* came to him at a youthful age, very likely the period of puberty. Also, there was another human being closely involved, the personality of Eli, the priest.

Indeed the content of the message Samuel received was one in which Eli played an important role. The narrative says,

> So Samuel went and lay down in his place. And the Lord came, and stood, and called as at other times: "Samuel, Samuel." Then Samuel said: "Speak; for Thy servant heareth." And the Lord said to Samuel: "Behold, I will do a thing in Israel, at which both the ears of every one that heareth it shall tingle. In that day I will perform against Eli all that I have spoken concerning his house, from the beginning even unto the end. For I have told him that I will judge his house for ever, for the iniquity, in that he knew that his sons did bring a curse upon themselves, and he rebuked them not. And therefore I have sworn unto the house of Eli, that the iniquity of Eli's house shall not be expiated with sacrifice nor offering for ever (3:9–14)."

This is rather strange content for a young boy's first experience of being called to God's service. It deals with the condemnation of others. Samuel's own selection as priest and prophet is not actually voiced in this communication. It seems to follow by inference. The very fact that God reveals himself to him is an acceptance in deed rather than in word. Only a prophet of God receives his revelations. The import of this experience is emphasized by the explanation, "And the word of the Lord was precious in those days; there was no frequent vision."

Now, strangely enough, the communication made to Samuel is almost identical with an earlier *message* of which Eli himself was the recipient. We are told that Eli is visited by a *man of God* who predicts that the priest's two sons, who have been behaving wickedly, would not succeed their father in the priesthood but would be cut off in the prime of life. Eli, moreover, is censured for his leniency in that he saw his sons doing evil and "rebuked them not." He is told that God has chosen another as his faithful priest. Who could this other be but Samuel, whom Eli must have loved as the worthy son who did not disappoint him.

There were no outstanding seers or prophets at this time. Who then would have dared to reproach the head priest? We must assume that this *man of God* was Eli's own superego, which perhaps revealed itself to the old man in a dream or hallucinatory experience. It bears evidence of his own clear inner decision of the painful course he had to take in rejecting his own sons, and his sense of guilt regarding them. The pain is alleviated by projecting this decision on God and receiving it from a mysterious messenger.

It is immediately following this event that Samuel receives his *call*. The message, as we have seen, also consists of God's angry repudiation of Eli's sons and the dread punishment that will be meted out to them. Again the old priest is referred to in censorious terms because he failed in his responsibility by not properly discipling his sons.

Thus, both in content and time sequence, the experiences of Eli and Samuel seem to have a direct relationship to each other. The old priest whose "eyes have begun to wax dim," and the ambitious young novice, ready to enter upon his spiritual inheritance, were psychologically prepared to communicate with one another on this important issue. These circumstances, together with the manner in which Samuel's *call* is narrated, as well as its unusual message for a theophany, suggests that some special kind of communication, perhaps on a different level of consciousness, was taking place between Eli and Samuel.

It is interesting to speculate about the nature of this psychic communication. Perhaps it was the outgrowth of a deep empathic understanding between the two that had developed during their close relationship of many years.[5]

There seems to be no doubt in Samuel's mind that it is Eli who is calling him. He responds, not with a question, "Did you call?" but with the statement, "Here am I; for thou didst call me." Nor is Eli's answer merely a reply in the negative. He instructs the boy to "lie down again." Why was this directive necessary? Samuel would naturally return to his bed at this point. It seems that Eli was impelled to make sure that the boy would do so. Perhaps the impending communication, of which Eli himself was not conscious at this moment, could only take place when both the persons involved were lying prone upon their beds, in the silence of the night, probably in the eerie glow of an oil lamp. And indeed we are specifically informed that Samuel returned to his bed.

Since Eli had *received* the message first, the *call* must have emanated from him and found a quick but uneasy reception in the all-too-ready adolescent. It was, in fact, Eli who perceived that "the Lord was calling the child" and who then prepared him for the experience.

The repetition of the call, which came three times, the exact duplication of the wording, the similarity of Eli's response, all add a kind of hypnotic quality to the situation. One difference in the wording may be meaningful. When Eli instructs the boy how to respond, he tells him to say, "Speak, Lord, for thy servant heareth." But Samuel actually answers, "Speak, for Thy servant heareth," thus omitting the word *Lord*. Did the youth still unconsciously, and perhaps intuitively, feel that it was Eli who was communicating with him?

The text makes a point of saying that Samuel did not yet know the Lord; this was to be the first revelation. How then was the boy to distinguish the voice of God from the voice of Eli? Arlow comments, in his study, that because Samuel thought the voice he heard was Eli's, the old priest was the "hallucinatory God." Certainly God and the father-image are closely associated in the unconscious. How much more significant would such a connection be in the case of Samuel, to whom Eli had been both mother and father, as well as priest!

There is evidence of guilt feelings on the part of both Eli

and Samuel because the election of the youth as spiritual heir involved the rejecting of Eli's own sons and a prophecy of their death. Evidently it was no small matter to predict the disinheritance and removal from high office of the sons of a priestly family. The fact that this would be accomplished through their untimely death greatly increases the tensions. These ominous events are revealed to the youthful Samuel with the dramatic introductory words, "Behold, I will do a thing in Israel at which both the ears of every one that heareth it shall tingle (3:11)."

It is no wonder that this decision had to come from God himself. It is also understandable that in Samuel's *vision* the explicit mention of himself as the chosen one could not find a place, for his selection was associated with the destruction of his competitors. We are told that Samuel "feared to tell Eli the vision," and did so only upon urging. The latter once more alleviates his own pain by replying "It is the Lord; let Him do what seemeth Him good."

Thus, Eli communicates his decision to Samuel on the level of unconscious awareness and Samuel then re-communicates to Eli what the old priest had conveyed to him in the first place.

It seems likely that Samuel was endowed with a particularly psychic sensitivity from earliest days. His whole life tended toward the development of such a quality. Samuel spent his youthful years ministering in the Temple instead of participating in the usual carefree play or physical tasks on the farm that the average boy was heir to. The rigidity with which ceremonial in the Temple had to be carried out, the boy's sense of closeness to God at an early age, which may have become a substitute for the normal libidinal ties of family life, must have helped to develop in Samuel a readiness for the kind of psychic response that was involved in the experience under consideration.

The youth's call to God's service, coming as it probably did, at the age of puberty, can be understood as a special kind of initiation to adulthood. The emphasis here however is not upon the sanction for mature sexuality but on a strengthened relationship to the Father-God and to the people of Israel.

Freud has explained that the formation of each individual's

ego ideal, which he uses here as synonymous with the superego, is based largely on the image of the idealized father of one's childhood and the values he represented. He says, "In so far as it is a substitute for the longing for a father, it contains the germ from which all religions have evolved." He goes on to say, "Social feelings rest on the foundation of identification with others, on the basis of an ego ideal in common with them."[6]

Samuel's ties with Eli created the environment that is psychologically understandable for this kind of development. The libido that normally would have been invested in heterosexual objects would be largely deflected to other pathways and functions through identification with the old priest and the common ego ideal they shared in the God they served and worshipped together.[7, 8]

The personality of Eli must have had an important impact in other ways as well upon the young boy placed in his care at such a tender age. We do not know much about Eli. His own sons were grossly rebellious toward him. They were guilty of such extremes of misconduct as committing acts of sexual impropriety with women at the doors of the Temple, probably in imitation of the cult of sacred prostitution practiced by the Canaanites. They also transgressed customary behavior by forcing worshippers to yield up a larger share of the sacrificial meat than was due to the priests. Such flagrant defiance of the religious prohibitions of Israel must have been related to their deep resentment against the father-priest and a wish to hurt and humiliate him.

One can infer that Eli was responsible to some degree for such feelings in his sons. His leniency toward them may have been a defense against his own awareness of guilt in his role as a father. It is likely that he was better able to bestow more tender feelings upon the young Samuel than he could give his own children, with whom he was probably involved in ambivalent attitudes.

Significantly, at a later date, Samuel's sons, too, failed to develop into worthy people and were unacceptable as successors to their father. This similarity of experience may point to common emotional problems in both these men. It may also indicate how closely Samuel identified with Eli, taking over important patterns of his character structure. It seems that men who stand in a special relationship to God have special problems in their roles as fathers and, one might add, as husbands.

The fact of Samuel's marriage and the name of his wife is omitted from the biblical account. The first indication of his married state is the reference to his sons. A complete omission of this kind is unusual even though the Bible tends to treat such matters casually, for the most part. We can assume that this area of Samuel's life was a conflictful one and therefore subject to repression.

Samuel's reputation as a prophet evidently became firmly established throughout all Israel while he was still a youth. The Bible says, "And Samuel grew, and the Lord was with him, and did let none of his words fall to the ground. And all Israel from Dan even to Beersheba knew that Samuel was established to be a prophet of the Lord (3:19–20)." The fact that the young novice began his prophetic career at an early age made him more vulnerable psychologically to the difficult situations associated with this role.

Samuel was about twenty-two when the most catastrophic event of his life and of his times occurred. Israel suffered a decisive defeat at the hands of the Philistines. In the last desperate battle, the Israelites resorted to an extreme measure. The Ark was taken from the Temple at Shiloh and brought into the battlefield, upheld by the two sons of Eli. The purpose of this strategy was to arouse terror in the hearts of the Philistines and to bolster the courage of the Israelites. But the plan backfired. The Philistines felt so threatened by the actual presence, as it seemed to them, of the terrifying God of the Hebrews that they fought with increased energy and resolution. The Hebrews were defeated and the Ark itself captured by the enemy.

The bad news was brought to Eli as he sat anxiously awaiting word of the outcome. When he heard that not only was the battle lost and his two sons killed, but the Ark itself taken, the old man must have lost consciousness. He fell off his seat, suffered a broken neck and died.

It seems very puzzling that not a single word is given about Samuel and how he reacted to these shocking events. At one blow he lost not only the man who had been his father, teacher, and priest, but also the sacred Ark which must have been more than a mere symbol to him. He had been brought up in its presence and for him it must have been the abode of God in a special sense. Moreover, Shiloh itself was evidently taken by the Philistines at this time and the sanctuary destroyed, as archaeological findings indicate. According to biblical chronology, twenty years pass before we hear of Samuel again.[9] This striking omission to any reference about the life of the chief personality of this period is certainly strange.

According to tradition, the first twenty-four chapters of the first book of *Samuel,* dealing with material up to the time of his death, were written by the prophet himself. If this is so, the long interval of silence could express Samuel's own denial and repression of a traumatic period in his life. He may have been so overwhelmed by the great disaster that he wished to draw an amnestic veil over the years that followed. Even if these chapters should represent a composite authorship, the same psychological mechanisms could still be involved. For the writers of the biblical text, the years of humiliating subjection to the Philistine overlords that followed the military defeat would have been a painful period to deal with, both in itself and in empathy with the feelings of Samuel.

The prophet must indeed have felt that God had deserted him, together with his people, who had been given over to the enemy. He was the servant of a rejected people, a factor which would greatly increase his own feelings of rejection. The first great abandonment of his life had been by his parents. The defeat of his people and its consequences was the second severe trauma and must have affected him profoundly.

The conquest of territory by the Philistines could also have symbolized to Samuel the seizure of *the mother* by the enemy. It was his duty to protect the mother and to keep her safe from hostile forces. In this task he had failed. He was therefore no longer a hero but resembled more the abandoned child of his early life.

It is interesting that after these events Samuel made Ramah his chief abode. He returned to the home of his infancy. Was he perhaps seeking that bit of earth, *the mother,* where he had once known the warmth and security of a nursling?

The same tendency of repressive silence that hangs over this period is seen in relation to the Ark and to the Temple at Shiloh. The destruction of the latter is not even mentioned in *Samuel.* There is a later reference to a place called *Nob,* where the priests then had a house. As for the Ark, it was returned to the Hebrews by the Philistines after an outbreak of plagues in their cities was attributed to the presence of this *alien god.* The Ark was then set up in a new locale, within a private home, under a special guardianship appointed for its care.

Samuel's story is resumed almost as if there had been no lapse of many years. Only the rather wistful statement is made that the time was long, since the Ark abode in Kiriath-jearim, its new home, and "all the house of Israel yearned after the Lord." Samuel responds to this call. He tells the people to put away their false gods and return to the Lord and he would pray for them. Thus Samuel ties up the threads of his broken life at the very point where they had come apart. He leads his people back to God, and in doing so, finds again the reason for his own existence. This return may represent the successful *working through* of his traumatic experience.

While the Hebrews are gathered at Mizpah for prayer and sacrifice, the Philistines move against them once more, probably assuming that they have come together for militant purposes. Then Samuel prays to God for his people and, we are told, the Lord answered him, causing a great storm which unnerved the Philistines so that they fled before the pursuing and attacking Israelites. After this event, "the Philistines were subdued and they came no more within the border of Israel; and the hand of the Lord was against the Philistines all the days of Samuel."

The victory is clearly attributed to Samuel's intercession with God. We must assume that the earlier defeat was just as clearly, although silently, also associated with the young prophet whose renown was then widespread throughout the land but whose power had seemingly failed at a crucial time.

After the triumphant resumption of his spiritual leadership, Samuel became known as the *great interceder.* He continued to serve as judge and priest for the people, making his rounds among them. He would perform the sacrifice upon a hilltop and join the community elders for the sacrificial meal.

That the old wounds left their scars, however, is indicated by the fact that Samuel never had the Temple rebuilt or the Ark restored to its rightful place. There is not even a reference in the biblical text to the consideration of such a possibility. One must wonder why.

By renouncing both Temple and Ark Samuel may unconsciously have expressed the feelings of rejection he must have experienced, first from his parents and then from the Deity. The favored child of God, known to all Israel as the Lord's appointed prophet, had been too suddenly hurled from his narcissistic security, the youthful confidence in his own powers. Added to this personal involvement must have been a feeling that perhaps the people also did not wish to be reminded of their humiliation by worshipping before the very Ark whose presence on the battlefield had been without avail.

The latter part of Samuel's life is associated with the first two kings of Israel, Saul and David, in the time of the Monarchy. This new development in the history of Israel begins in a dramatic fashion. The elders, representatives of the people, come to Samuel at Ramah and request that he select a king to rule over them. They point out that he is old and his sons are not worthy to succeed him. Samuel was probably over seventy then.

This request threw Samuel into a state of conflict. He must

have experienced it as another great abandonment. True, as they indicated, he was now an old man. Israel was in need of a young and vigorous personality who could unite the tribes and lead them in war. Their independence and actual possession of the land could only be kept secure by military strength. The request made by the elders therefore had a sound realistic basis. What they were asking for was a certain separation of church and state, a temporal leader in addition to their religious one.

Samuel's first reaction is one of displeasure at this request. He turns to God for guidance. The response of the Deity on this occasion is a rather curious one.

> And the Lord said unto Samuel: "Hearken unto the voice of the people in all that they say unto thee; for they have not rejected thee, but they have rejected me, that I should not be king over them . . . they have forsaken Me, and served other gods, so do they also unto thee. Now therefore hearken unto their voice; howbeit thou shalt earnestly forewarn them, and shall declare unto them the manner of the king that shall reign over them."
>
> And Samuel told all the words of the Lord unto the people that asked of him a king. And he said: "This will be the manner of the king that shall reign over you: he will take your sons, and appoint them unto him, for his chariots and to be his horsemen; and they shall run before his chariots.
>
> And he will appoint them unto him for captains of thousands, and captains of fifties; and to plow his ground, and to reap his harvest, and to make his instruments of war, and the instruments of his chariots. And he will take your daughters to be perfumers, and to be cooks, and to be bakers. And he will take your fields, and your vineyards, and your olive-yards, even the best of them, and give them to his servants. And he will take your men-servants, and your maid-servants, and your goodliest young men, and your asses, and put them to his work. He will take the tenth of your flocks; and ye shall be his servants. And ye shall cry out in that day because of your king whom ye shall have chosen you; and the Lord will not answer you in that day." But the

people refused to hearken unto the voice of Samuel; and they said: "Nay; but there shall be a king over us; that we also may be like the other nations; and that our king may judge us, and go out before us, and fight our battles." And Samuel heard all the words of the people, and he spoke them in the ears of the Lord. And the Lord said to Samuel: "Hearken unto their voice and make them a king. (8:7-22)."

In God's reply we have a projection of Samuel's own feelings which reveal a striking quality of ambivalence. Samuel reluctantly accepts the realistic need of the times for a military and political leader, yet his sense of self-importance in relation to his people must have suffered a cruel blow. We have here a significant example however of the prophet's struggle against this narcissistic trait and how he rises above it in action if not in feelings. Perhaps the reality factors were too strong to be ignored. But Samuel could have retired in a mood of anger and disillusionment, leaving the people to determine their own destiny. Instead, he deals with his sense of hurt by projecting it upon God. It was the Lord himself whom they were rejecting. Here Samuel's identification with God is so encompassing that even the Deity is pictured as having ambivalent attitudes towards a kingship for Israel.

The relationship depicted between Samuel and God throughout this crisis conveys a feeling of special intimacy. "And Samuel heard all the words of the people and he spoke them into the ear of the Lord." The prophet is here truly the mediator between the people and God, almost as though he were the only source of knowledge available to God himself concerning what the people said. The grandiosity implied here can be understood as compensatory for Samuel's sense of wounded self-esteem.

Higher Criticism generally tended to see this vivid description regarding the evils of kingly rule as an interpolation of a later date. But other scholarly opinion holds that both positive and negative attitudes toward a monarchy more likely reflected the actual period involved.[10] Psychologically, it is understandable that Samuel himself would have had ambivalent feelings about it. Together with his sense of personal rejection must have been the fact which he could no longer keep from awareness, of his sons' unworthiness and his own failure as a father. The sons of Samuel, like those of Eli, were corruptible, in contrast to their fathers. Eli's leniency must have been true of Samuel also. He made his sons judges although he must have known that they would not be able to fulfill their duties meritoriously because of their moral weakness of character. In the moving speech which Samuel makes to the people on the occasion when Saul is anointed king, Samuel not only talks about his own services to the people but mentions his sons, saying, "And behold, my sons are with you." Thus he ignores the fact that the people had rejected his sons and he puts them forward again as if they were an important contribution which he was making.

If, as evidence indicates, Samuel's attitude towards his sons was ambivalent, then his leniency regarding their behavior can be understood on the basis of guilt feelings and the need to repress these. Severity would have involved a recognition of the moral turpitude on the part of his offspring, thus emphasizing his own failure as a father.

It is another man's son whom Samuel must anoint as the first king of Israel. The quality of the first encounter between Samuel and Saul is strikingly expressive of the personality of the aging priest. We are told that God had revealed to Samuel the day before the full details of Saul's coming, informing him that this young man was to be the Lord's anointed. Samuel was therefore ready to receive him. His need to be fully prepared for this event by advance information from God may reflect his own insecurity in regard to this first step in his displacement. The tone of the divine revelation is one of directness and intimacy, as of two close friends communicating with each other. God says, "Tomorrow about this time I will send thee a man out of the land of Benjamin, and thou shalt anoint him to be prince over My people Israel, and he shall save My people out of the hand of the Philistines; for I have looked upon My people, because their cry is come unto Me." The specific role that Saul is to play as military leader is here clearly defined.

The simplicity of God's message to Samuel and the manner

in which the latter informs Saul of his destiny show a considerable contrast. The unsuspecting hero of the litttle drama about to unfold, accompanied by a servant, is in the quest of his father's strayed donkeys. The two men, finding themselves at the town where Samuel resided, plan to utilize the priest's reputation as a seer and inquire of him where the donkeys might be found. Samuel himself meets them at the gates of the city, saying,

> "I am the seer; go up before me unto the high place; for ye shall eat with me today; and in the morning I will let thee go, and will tell thee all that is in thy heart. And as for thine asses that were lost three days ago, set not thy mind on them; for they are found. And on whom is all the desire of Israel? Is it not on thee, and on all thy father's house?" . . . And Samuel took Saul and his servant, and brought them into the chamber, and made them sit in the chiefest place among them that were bidden, who were about thirty persons. And Samuel said unto the cook: "Bring the portion which I gave thee, of which I said unto thee: Set it by thee." And the cook took up the thigh, and that which was upon it, and set it before Saul. And Samuel said: "Behold that which hath been reserved! set it before thee and eat; because unto the appointed time hath it been kept for thee, for I said: I have invited the people." So Saul did eat with Samuel that day. And when they were come down from the high place into the city, he spoke with Saul upon the housetop. And they arose early; and it came to pass about the break of day, that Samuel called to Saul on the housetop, saying: "Up, that I may send thee away." And Saul arose, and they went out both of them, he and Samuel, abroad. As they were going down at the end of the city, Samuel said to Saul: "Bid the servant pass on before us—and he passed on—but stand thou still at this time, that I may cause thee to hear the word of God."
>
> Then Samuel took the vial of oil, and poured it upon his head, and kissed him, and said: "Is it not that the Lord hath anointed thee to be prince over His inheritance (9:19–10:1)?"

Samuel then displays his powers as a clairvoyant, telling Saul of a series of incidents that would occur as he proceeded upon his homeward journey. The Bible then says, "And it was so, that when he turned his back to go from Samuel, God gave him another heart; and all those signs came to pass that day."

The tone pervading this narration is one that emphasizes the importance of Samuel himself. It is he, the powerful leader, *the man of God*, who with dramatic suddenness, without any initial preparation for Saul of what is to happen, elevates the unknown son of a farmer to the high position of the Lord's anointed.

The abruptness with which Samuel initially presents himself to Saul as the man of power and reveals to the bewildered stranger the high destiny in store for him has a dramatic quality. Its unconscious purpose may have been to overwhelm the younger man and place him at once psychologically under Samuel's influence. The words, "And I will tell thee all that is in thy heart," emphasizes his prophetic ability. The magical words spoken by Samuel, "On whom is all the desire of Israel? Is it not on thee and on all thy father's house?" have a seductive quality. They must have had a powerful impact upon the unsophisticated Saul, bringing forth the only verbal response recorded of him in this entire story. The Bible says, "And Saul answered and said: Am not I a Benjamite, of the smallest of the tribes of Israel? and my family the least of all the families of the tribe of Benjamin? wherefore then speakest thou to me after this manner?"

The actual anointment the next day was followed by the suggestion that Saul would become another man when he met a band of prophets on the journey home, and he would prophecy among them.

A word of explanation about these young, roving men of God whom Saul does indeed encounter is in place here. They are first mentioned during the days of Samuel. It is assumed that he helped to organize and foster these groups of young people who wandered about the country with their musical instruments, small harps, timbrels, and pipes, singing and prophesying. Their purpose evidently was to arouse the religious spirit among the people, to induce backsliders to give up their false gods and return to the God of Israel. They performed a function similar to the religious revivalists at the gospel prayer meetings in our own time.

Samuel seems to have been peculiarly fitted to evoke this type of mystic, emotional upsurge of religious feeling in these young men, many of whom may have been his pupils and devotees. This same power, in greater measure, Samuel must have exerted upon Saul, with the expectation, consciously or unconsciously, of making him into a puppet king, whose spiritual strength and grace were to come from Samuel himself.

While ostensibly the selection of Saul was made by God, psychologically we must view this choice as an act of Samuel's, in response to the obligation he had undertaken. Indeed, the old priest behaves throughout in the *grand manner,* making it clear in every word and gesture that it is indeed he who is thus omnipotently creating a king out of a simple peasant.

What underlying psychodynamics might have prompted Samuel to make this particular choice? A tall, handsome stranger suddenly appears at the gates of the city. Samuel is on his way to the hilltop to partake of the sacrificial meal when he comes face to face with Saul. His first response must have been an intuitive one that here was a man truly fit for a king. His youth and physique would fit him for military leadership and place him in a role as non-competitive as possible with Samuel himself.

The fact that Saul was a stranger must have added a certain mystique to his appearance. Samuel himself was delivered into the hands of a stranger as a child. He too was chosen above Eli's own sons. *The stranger* is a defense against *the father,* or *the son,* with whom one is tied in unconscious, forbidden fantasies. Coming from the tribe of Benjamin, the smallest and therefore least significant numerically, and being the son of a simple agricultural family, must also have made Saul less threatening to Samuel.

Probably the most significant factor that influenced Samuel's choice was the unconscious one of narcissistic identification. Saul must have represented the priest's own idealized self, or ego ideal, on a physical basis. The younger man may have reminded Samuel of how he once looked himself or of how he had wanted to look.[11]

Saul proves his fitness for the role assigned to him. When the city of Jabesh-Gilead, east of the Jordan, is besieged and its inhabitants threatened, Saul arouses the people to take military action and leads them against the enemy. The details of this exploit will be treated more fully in the next chapter, which deals with the story of Saul. It is after this demonstration of his prowess that Saul is publicly anointed as king.

On this occasion also Samuel relinquishes his position as sole leader and bestows the power of ruler upon another. That this moment was a poignant one in Samuel's life is revealed in the speech he makes to his people. His appeal to them strikes one as very moving, yet oddly irrelevant. He says, in part,

> "Here I am; witness against me before the Lord, and before His anointed; whose ox have I taken? Or whom have I defrauded? Or whom have I oppressed? Or of whose hand have I taken a ransom to blind mine eyes therewith? And I will restore it to you." And they said: "Thou has not defrauded us, nor oppressed us, neither hast thou taken aught of any man's hand (12:3–4)."

Why does Samuel feel this need to protest his incorruptibility? No one had accused him of such misdeeds. It must have been the request for a king that carried with it, for Samuel, the connotation of his own unworthiness. When a person is displaced it must be because he is unworthy, according to the unconscious pattern of thinking and feeling. Did this not happen with the sons of Eli and with Samuel's own sons? In fact, the very deeds from which he seeks vindication are the kind of which his sons were actually guilty. Might there have been some degree of identification with his sons and therefore with their feelings of guilt and of rejection? If so, he would need the reassurance of his people that they were not rejecting him and did not consider him unfit for office.[12]

But Samuel was evidently not content with the warm and immediate vindication offered by his people. He was not really ready to relinquish any part of his power. If he was not guilty of wrongdoing, then they must retain him as the leader. On this occasion when a king was anointed, he would show the people who the real source of power still was—himself. As is customary in biblical narrative, the marvelous goodness of God is rehearsed before the people at crucial moments of their history and all that he did for them in the past is recounted. This ritual Samuel now performs, using the occasion to identify himself once more with the power of God. He reinforces his position as representative of the Lord by an impressive demonstration of his might. Samuel calls upon God to send thunder and rain in the midst of the harvest season, when rain is unusual. This was to be a sign from heaven of God's disapproval because the people had asked for a king. The thunder and rain came, and "all the people greatly feared the Lord and Samuel." Then Samuel became magnanimous and reassured them, saying that he would not cease to pray to the Lord for them. Thus he made clear that he was retaining power as their spiritual leader, both over them and over their king.

The conflict with Saul that came later is thus clearly foreshadowed. It seemed almost certain from the start, judging by Samuel's attitude. He seemed to be waiting only for the first false move on Saul's part so that he could demonstrate to the people and to the king how wicked they had been in displacing him. Saul's doom was pronounced even at the time of his anointment.

The details of this conflict between Samuel and Saul will be considered in connection with a study of the latter, in order to avoid repetition of similar content. Briefly, Saul disobeys Samuel twice and thus incurs a severe rejection by the religious leader. Then, we are told, the word of the Lord came to Samuel saying that God was sorry he had chosen Saul to be king because of his disobedience. "And it grieved Samuel; and he cried unto the Lord all night," the Bible goes on to say. Samuel therefore did show signs of conflict about Saul. His repudiation of the young man he himself had anointed had its element of pain for Samuel. Perhaps this was a narcissistic hurt for he had erred in his estimate of Saul, no doubt thinking that the king would be completely subservient to his will. Perhapse it was also a disappointment in his own projected ego ideal, which Saul may have represented.

After his second and final rejection of Saul, Samuel never sees the king again. Although Saul continues as ruler of Israel, he does so without the blessing and friendship of the old priest. At God's behest, Samuel goes to the town of Bethlehem and there secretly anoints the youngest son of the household of Jesse. It is David, destined for an eventful life and a glorious history. Thus, in secrecy, the man who will one day displace Saul is chosen.

Samuel does not actually see that day arrive. He dies while David is still an outlaw, hiding from the wrath of Saul, whom he had offended by his own brilliant achievements in war. Samuel's death is recorded with a brevity that seems rather anticlimactic. The Bible says, "And Samuel died; and all Israel gathered themselves together and lamented him, and buried him in his house at Ramah." The next sentence resumes the story of David's activities, which had thus been briefly interrupted.

However, the element of the dramatic is not omitted from the figure of Samuel even after his death. It is in harmony with his character that reality factors regarding him should take second place to the mysterious influence he seemed to have exercised upon men. We hear of Samuel again in connection with the event leading to Saul's tragic death.

It is the eve before a great battle with the Philistines on Mount Gilboa. The situation looks unfavorable for the Hebrew soldiers. Saul, still suffering from the pain of abandonment by Samuel, and full of gloomy foreboding, pays a secret visit to a medium, the woman of Endor. He pleads with her to bring up the spirit of Samuel and learn from him the outcome of the battle that lies ahead. In the dramatic scene that follows, the prophet rebukes Saul for *disquieting* him in this fashion. He reminds the king that God has rejected him and foretells the defeat of the Israelites on the morrow. He also predicts the death of Saul and his sons in the struggle.

Thus, the man who had once given Saul a *changed heart*, abandoned the king he had created. It is possible that in the fighting on Mount Gilboa the next day, Samuel's strong, suggestive influence may have had a part in the king's death, for Saul actually kills himself, falling upon his own sword.

In retrospect, let us see what the elements in Samuel's upbringing were that prepared him so successfully for his role. From earliest days he was *set apart* for a special task which he himself accepted. What he wished to be, and what he was able to become, were in harmony with each other for the most part. When this kind of inner relationship failed, Samuel seemed to respond as to a traumatic rejection on an intrapsychic level, bringing about a depression. Such situations represented a conflict between his ego and his ego ideal.[13]

Thus, the character structure of Samuel emerges with striking psychological consistency. The degree of narcissism in his make-up was an essential quality for his role as leader. The feelings of omnipotence which often accompany the narcissistic personality helps to attract and hold large masses of people. It exerts a kind of fascinating effect upon his followers. They wish to share in his omnipotence as they once longed to be protected by the powerful father in their childhood days.[14]

Samuel must have possessed this magnetic quality to a considerable degree. His influence both over the individual and the group had an arresting, almost magical quality, probably stemming from the firm conviction that he spoke the word of God.

We have seen how Samuel's whole life history prepared him psychically for the type of leadership he exerted. The fact that he did not have the normal experience of growing up within a family circle probably helped to develop him as a leader. Freud points out that the absence of close personal ties strengthens the capacity for group ties. He says, ". . . in the great artificial groups, the church and the army, there is no room for woman as a sexual object."[15]

Through his identification with God, Samuel also became identified with his people, and had a sense of responsibility toward them. He was the instrument through which they heard the word of the Lord.

Samuel's relatedness to the people was also strengthened by his role as a priest. He performed the ritual of the sacrifice in a community setting and participated in the communal meal that followed. Through this function his position as a leader was continually renewed, for he served as the good father who becomes united with his children in the common worship of an Idealized Father.

These repeated acts of sacrifice which he performed may also have served as an outlet for his aggressive impulses as well as for the appeasement of guilt. For such is indeed the double nature of sacrifice. There is aggression involved in the killing of the sacrificial animal, the significance of which Freud has explained in relation to the totemic meal. There is appeasement of guilt in the atonement which the sacrifice represents as an act of worship.[16, 17]

Samuel's capacity and opportunity to function in the role of leader helped him to utilize constructively a large part of his narcissistic and latent homosexual libido. It is from these sources that much of the psychic energy for the formation and mainte-nance of the ego ideal is drawn. Samuel must have derived strength and satisfaction from the ability, for the most part, to live up to the high standards of his ego ideal, or conscience. Under the circumstances here described, Samuel was able to per-form most of the time without undue neurotic consequences in the form of symptoms.

With the exception of the years for which we have no record, Samuel evidently maintained the acknowledged prestige and esteem as the chief religious leader of Israel during his lifetime. The position which he continued to hold was a sure sign that Samuel was able to serve his people genuinely as an effective moral force.

Saul,
the Tragic King

 CHAPTER FIVE

SAUL, THE first king of ancient Israel, is often described as a tragic figure. Classically, the essence of tragedy is a blind and futile struggle against one's destiny. Psychoanalytically, it can be understood as the struggle with unconscious conflicts. In this sense the word fittingly describes the subject of this study.

The personality of Saul is therefore of special interest, for this king of antiquity is clearly portrayed as suffering from an emotional malady, or, in the graphic terminology of the Bible, as being possessed by an *evil spirit*. The purpose of this study is to present a developmental picture of Saul's history and his patterns of behavior to see if there is a psychological consistency in the biblical material concerning him, and to discern, if possible, the specific nature of his conflicts.

The first monarch of ancient Israel appears upon the scene of Hebrew history in the unassuming role of a farmer's son, who together with a servant is engaged in looking for his father's strayed donkeys. The impression one gets from this situation is that Saul is still quite a young man and, as such, logically subject to parental guidance and control. The Bible, in fact, calls him *young and goodly*. Yet Saul at this time was already the father of a number of children, according to the more convincing of the two possible interpretations of available chronological data.[1] His son Jonathan was evidently old enough to serve as a soldier of unusual courage and strategy only two years later (13:2).* Saul therefore must have been a man who had reached the prime of life when we first meet him on his quest for the lost donkeys.

The question that occurs is why Saul, the son of a prosperous farmer, should have been sent upon this rather menial errand. It is true that donkeys were valuable animals. Moreover, in those times even men of substance occupied themselves with the ordinary tasks of their day. But a duty such as this one would seem more suited to a younger man, like Jonathan. Nor is there any doubt whether Saul undertook this obligation of his own free will or was commissioned to do so by his father. The Bible says clearly that Saul was sent by his father upon this mission. Perhaps it is not without significance that Saul's introduction to history is in this role of carrying out a task given to him by his father, as we shall see.

As Saul and the servant wander farther and farther from home in their unsuccessful search, Saul becomes uneasy and says, "Come and let us return; lest my father leave caring for the asses, and becomes anxious concerning us."

The servant replies that they are now in the vicinity of the city where Samuel is residing and suggests that they consult him regarding the whereabouts of the lost animals. Saul's first reaction to this is that they do not have a present to bring the man of God. The servant says that he has a small silver coin which he will use for this purpose and the two proceed to the city gates.

In this brief introductory episode, we see Saul yielding twice to suggestions that come from others, first, his father, and then,

*All biblical quotations and references in this chapter, unless otherwise noted, are from First Samuel.

the servant. We also see him expressing concern twice about the expectations of a father figure, first, that his father would be expecting them home, and second, that Samuel would expect a gift. It is interesting that the servant has a small silver coin with him but the son of the master does not, thus placing Saul in a position of dependency toward the servant. In fact, when he comments upon his father's anxiety about their absence, Saul puts the servant upon the same level as himself, using the pronoun *us*.

This first view of Saul also suggests a certain incongruity between his physical appearance and his demeanor. We are told that "there was not among the children of Israel a goodlier person than he; from his shoulders and upward he was higher than any of the people." Yet he gives the impression of being modest and unassuming to the point of timidity.

Samuel met the two men within the city gates as if he were expecting them. Without any preliminaries, Saul was invited to be the seer's guest at the sacrificial meal that was about to take place on the hilltop. He was assured that his father's donkeys had been found. Samuel then acclaimed him as the future king of Israel.

Saul was evidently completely unprepared psychologically for this *moment of destiny*. Again, there is an impression of the incongruous in the situation of this princely-looking man, engaged in looking for his father's donkeys, being met by Samuel and elevated at once to a place of high honor. It has a folktale atmosphere of a prince in disguise. But such a person must generally perform some act of unusual merit before the kingdom is bestowed upon him. In Saul's case, the prize was given first and the act of merit had to come later.

Samuel's own reasons for this choice are discussed in the previous chapter. Briefly, he wanted a man who could be a warrior-king but at the same time someone of a submissive and dependent nature, who would offer as little competition as possible to his own power. Perhaps he recognized these qualities at once in a person of Saul's position who was occupied in hunting for his father's lost donkeys.

After the communal feast, Saul was brought to Samuel's house to spend the night. The prophet talked with his guest as they sat upon the house-top in the cool of the evening. Nothing is said of the content of this talk but we can assume that in the course of it, the relationship between the two was more firmly established. Saul must have known of Samuel before but evidently had not met the spiritual leader of Israel in person, for when they first saw each other, Saul did not recognize him.

The next day at sunrise Samuel called Saul, who slept in the guest-chamber on the roof, and accompanied him to the edge of the city. The servant was sent ahead and Samuel secretly anointed Saul king of Israel, pouring a vial of oil over his head and kissing him. Samuel then told Saul of several episodes that would take place on his way home, thus demonstrating his clairvoyant powers.

As Samuel predicted, Saul met a band of prophets coming down from the hill, playing upon their musical instruments and chanting their prophecies. Then "the spirit of the Lord came mightily upon him and he prophesied among them." Saul thus identified himself with the followers of Samuel. That this role was a completely new one for him is made clear by the reaction of the people, who said to one another, "What is this that is come unto the son of Kish? Is Saul also among the prophets?" It seems clear that Saul became a changed man during the period of less than a day that he spent with Samuel. We are, in fact, told that after Saul's anointment by the priest, "God gave him another heart."

What information, if any, does the Bible give regarding Saul's parentage? His father, Kish, is described as a "mighty man of valour." In biblical parlance, this may indicate social prestige rather than physical prowess. Kish was a wealthy farmer and probably regarded as a pillar of society. Except for the one descriptive phrase, which occurs at the very beginning of Saul's history, little more is known about Kish. There is no reference to Saul's mother, not even her name being mentioned.

When Saul returned home, he evidently did not reveal his secret anointment to anyone. Of his public selection as king, the Bible gives two varying accounts. Some biblical critics attribute these seemingly contradictory versions to the work of different editors. However, the traditional point of view that both events occurred as described does not seem to lack either realistic or psychological validity.

In the first account, Samuel calls a national assembly for the purpose of selecting a king. But before the actual choice is made, he expresses his displeasure for the second time at their request for a ruler, saying that this amounted to a rejection of God himself. This was hardly an auspicious way in which to present a future king, and indicates Samuel's reluctance to carry out the will of the people. It presages his ambivalence to the person who is to fill the role. As for the new ruler himself, he was being invited to enter upon his kingdom with feelings of guilt, as a representative of something *bad* that the people had asked of God.

The method that was used to select a king was the casting of lots. The choice fell upon Saul but when they looked for him, he could not be found. With God's help they find him hiding among the baggage. This baggage probably consisted of the saddles and saddle-bags left at one part of the assembly grounds by those who had journeyed to the meeting. Saul evidently found himself unable to face this sudden publicity and had sought refuge there. He was brought forth from his hiding-place and received by the people, who shouted, "Long live the king." We are told, however, that "certain base fellows said: 'How shall this man save us?' And they despised him, and brought him no present. But he was as one that held his peace (10:27)."

Perhaps it is not too surprising that Saul was overwhelmed when called upon to take his place as king. Being anointed secretly by Samuel was one thing. Standing up before all the people as their king was another matter, particularly after the doubtful approval of such a figure by the priestly leader himself. Samuel's introduction of Saul was not characterized by effusiveness. He said simply, "See ye whom the Lord hath chosen that there is none like him among all the people?" He was referring to the fact that Saul stood head and shoulders higher than any of the others. This, then, was his major claim to the kingship, a claim which the spiritual head of Israel found it easiest to accept. Saul returned to his father's farm and continued to live as he had before, except that he now had a small group of retainers with him.

What must have been Saul's thoughts and fantasies as he worked quietly on the farm? No doubt he was wondering when and how his first call to duty would come and if he would be able to meet the challenge. His title to the kingship could have no real meaning until he had proved himself. Saul thus had an opportunity to prepare in fantasy for what might lie before him.

When the call came, it was indeed a dramatic and urgent one. Kinsmen from the city of Jabesh-Gilead, east of the Jordan, were besieged by the Ammonites, a neighboring people. The imperiled city tried to make terms with the leader, Nabash, but he agreed to do so only on the condition that the right eye of every inhabitant of the city be put out, so that it might be a "reproach upon all Israel." The elders of the city asked for seven days respite so that they might send for help throughout the borders of Israel. Nabash agreed, evidently convinced that such assistance would not be forthcoming.

This message was not even brought directly to Saul, so little was he as yet regarded in the role of leader. But as he was guiding the oxen out of the field after the day's plowing, Saul heard the loud weeping of those who had just received the news. When he learned about the terms of Nabash, we are told that

> . . . his anger was greatly kindled. And he took his yoke of oxen, and cut them in pieces, and sent them throughout all the borders of Israel by the hand of messengers, saying, "Whosoever cometh not forth after Saul and after Samuel, so shall it be done unto his oxen." And the dread of the Lord fell on the people and they came out as one man (11:6-7).

Saul and his army completely routed the Ammonites and saved the people of Jabesh-Gilead. The new ruler had proved his worth as a warrior-king. This victory was the first important move on the part of the Hebrew tribes in this period of history to test their strength, and it stimulated them to the task of regaining the freedom they had lost to the oppressive Philistines, their most powerful foe.

What aspects of Saul's personality does this quick and dramatic response reveal? The man who hid shyly behind the baggage when he was elected king, now becomes a leader of men. He arouses his people to action on behalf of a distant city at a time when lethargy and discouragement tended to separate the tribes from one another. The very boldness of his gesture in sacrificing a valuable pair of oxen, and the imperative quality of his command must have stimulated a responsive boldness in his followers. Here was a man who must be in deadly earnest about his mission. Such a person could be trusted as a leader. This factor, together with the brutal nature of the threat which Nabash had employed, prompted the Hebrews to unprecedented action. It is noteworthy that the intensity of Saul's response to the challenge is in sharp contrast to the modesty and self-effacement with which he had been living since his election.

One wonders why Saul chose the killing of the oxen as a method of stirring up the people. Evidently he was a man of impulsive behavior. The oxen were close at hand when the message for help reached him. Moreover, one reason the people were indifferent to calls from other tribes was that they did not wish to leave their farm work undone while they went off to war. Saul had to show them they could not plow their fields in peace while their kinsmen were in danger. The act was also expressive of his own readiness to give up the life of the famer for that of the soldier-king.

We may detect further meanings in this symbolic gesture. The oxen, which actually belonged to Kish, may have represented an extension of the father himself. In killing the oxen, Saul might have acted out the conquest of the father who kept him tied to the plow. In addition, these animals may have represented an aspect of Saul's own personality. Oxen are submissive, castrated males who plow the soil in dull routine. By slaying them, Saul may have been overcoming the submissive element in his own personality and rebelling triumphantly against the father, with whom his relationship must have been an ambivalent one. Saul could free himself from the control of Kish, however, only under the influence of a more powerful parental figure, that of Samuel.

After the successful display of his leadership, Saul is publicly anointed king by Samuel. In his earlier election there was no ceremony of anointment. This latter occasion could be understood as the inauguration, the official beginning of his rule. As described in the study about Samuel, this event was used largely by the priest to concentrate attention upon himself and to demonstrate the power he still exercised. He again reproached the people for their wickedness in asking for a king. Not a word of praise or encouragement is extended to Saul from the man who had chosen him. He is exhorted to fear the Lord and to obey his commandments.

The people however express their loyalty to Saul and threaten with death those who had questioned his rule. Saul intercedes for them and the occasion closes on a note of general amicability.

After a period of only two years came the inevitable split between Samuel and Saul. It occurred when Saul intruded into an area which Samuel considered his own—the religious leadership.

Israel was now engaged in a more organized effort, under the leadership of Saul, to defeat the Philistines. The army was encamped at Gilgal, awaiting Samuel's arrival, so that he might perform a sacrifice before the men went into battle. Saul waited the seven days requested by the prophet but the latter did not appear.

In the meantime, the military situation was rapidly deteriorating. Saul's men, frightened by the large hordes of the enemy that were massing against them, were deserting. Finally, on the seventh day, the distraught and impatient king decided to perform the sacrifice himself. No sooner had he completed this act than Samuel arrived. Saul's excuses were in vain. The king was sternly rebuked for his disobedience and told that his kingdom would be taken from him. God would find another to fill his place.

Biblical commentary tends toward the explanation that it was not in the actual performance of the religious ritual that Saul erred, but in the fact that he had failed in a test situation by not obeying Samuel. While it was true that laymen could perform sacrifices themselves, it was customary to have a priest do so when a whole community was involved. This was one of Samuel's chief duties on his circuit tours. On this particular occasion, when the divided powers between church and state were being put to the first test, it must have been of special importance to Samuel that he himself should perform the sacrifice before that important body, the army. He could ill tolerate Saul's usurpation on this occasion. Saul had not only been disobedient but had shown a lack of faith in the man of God, whose prophetic powers supposedly should have been a guiding influence in the military action. Saul thus put his own judgment above that of the leading priest and prophet of Israel. He was again defying the father.

After Saul's unhappy experience with Samuel, the very next military undertaking is initiated by Jonathan, his son, in a spectacular fashion. He and his armour-bearer climb the heights of a rocky plateau at Michmas, where the Philistines are encamped, and boldly attack, killing about twenty men, according to the biblical account. This fierce assault within a small area of land upon the edge of the precipice may have started a landslide, for we are told that an earthquake followed, adding to the terror and confusion among the Philistines. Across the valley, the watchmen of Saul on the heights of Gibeah, see the tumult in the ranks of the enemy. Saul learns that Jonathan and his armour-bearer are not in the camp and makes the correct surmise about what is going on. He and his army hastily move into the battle area and Israel wins a great victory that day.

It is during the course of this long and strenuous day of fighting that Saul again behaves in a rash and impulsive fashion. He imposes a vow upon the people, forbidding them to eat any food until evening as a form of sacrifice to insure God's favor in the outcome of the battle. Jonathan does not hear his father's injunction and when the army enters a forest and the youth sees some honey upon the ground, he extends his rod and lifts some of the honey to his mouth. One of the men then tells him of the ban his father had placed upon eating that day.

Jonathan's reaction was not one of horror or regret although the breaking of the ban carried a curse with it. He expressed a criticism of his father for increasing the hardships which the army had to endure, pointing out that the men would have had more strength with which to win a greater victory had they been permitted to take nourishment.

In the evening, when the battle had been won, the people were faint with hunger. They seized eagerly upon the spoils, slaying the cattle upon the ground without following the prescribed ritual of ridding the animals of their blood. Again Saul shows his concern for religious law and directs the people to slaughter the animals upon a rock. This is the second time within one day that Saul imposes regulations of a religious nature upon the people. Then he proceeds to build an altar to God. The Bible makes a point of stating that it was the first altar Saul built to the Lord.

The king must have been as a driven man that day. He was not content with the victory and with building an altar. He suggested that the battle be continued that night and the fighting go on until morning so that not a man of the enemy would be left. Again the men agree obediently to his wishes, saying, "Do whatsoever seemeth good unto thee." But a priest interposes, suggesting that they consult God first. We are told that God did not respond to Saul's prayer that day. The conclusion the king drew from this was that someone had sinned and God was displeased. Saul then called the chiefs together and questioned them regarding the conduct of their men, declaring that even if it were his own son who was at fault, he would have to die. We are told that "there was not a man among all the people that answered him."

Why should Saul have named Jonathan as the possible sinner? We have no indication that he knew anything about the latter's innocent violation of the ban earlier that day. Was the king only trying to prove to his men that even if someone dear to him was involved, he would still carry out his duty to God as he saw it?

There is something in the way Saul expresses himself that indicates real hostility when he declares, ". . . though it (the sin) be in Jonathan my son, he shall surely die (14:39)." When the chiefs do not reply to his questioning, Saul's next move hardly seems open to any other interpretation than that of deadly anger against his son. Instead of calling for a general casting of lots to

discover the culprit, as was customary, Saul asks that all the men
of Israel be on one side while he and Jonathan are on the other
side, with the choice to be made between these two sides. The
father here clearly and unequivocally accuses the son and demands
his punishment even before the casting of the lots takes place. We
have the impression that Jonathan's sin was committed even before he violated the ban; that the more recent violation was only
being used as a substitute for a greater sin of which he had been
guilty.

The lots are cast and Jonathan is revealed as the wrong-doer.
Saul asks him what he has done and the youth replies that he
tasted a little honey. He makes no excuses and asks for no mercy,
saying only, "Here I am; I will die." Saul was evidently ready to
carry out the punishment, for he repeats his earlier declaration,
saying ". . . thou shalt surely die, Jonathan." But the people intervene and save the hero of the day.

On what basis did the people dare to contradict the wishes of
their king? All that day they had obediently followed his rather
arbitrary orders, saying only, "Do what seemeth good unto thee."
But now they act vigorously against his judgment. Their reason-
ing is given in their answer to Saul, when they declare. "Shall
Jonathan die, who hath wrought this great salvation in Israel? Far
from it; as the Lord liveth, there shall not one hair of his head
fall to the ground; for he hath wrought with God this day
(14:45)."

This was indeed the very reason Saul must have felt the need
to punish Jonathan. Let us recall the earlier events of the day.
Jonathan suddenly takes the initiative from his father by secretly
embarking on a military exploit of his own, thus providing the
stimulus for a victory that is decisive for the Hebrews.

What must have been Saul's feelings as he learns of the
excitement in the Philistine camp and then finds out that Jonathan had departed from Gibeah! His son had acted without con-
sulting him. Jonathan had stolen the show and made himself the
hero of the day. Coming as this did, after Saul's rejection by
Samuel at Gilgal, the king's vulnerability to being displaced must
have been considerably increased.

While the biblical account says nothing of Saul's reaction to all this, his behavior during that entire day can be seen as a response to feelings of hurt, anger, and guilt. The vow of fasting which he imposed upon the army may have represented not only a way of propitiating God but also unconsciously, of punishing the people for accepting Jonathan as a hero. Actually, fasting upon a day of battle was not a customary procedure.

Some may wonder if Saul expressed willingness to sacrifice Jonathan with the hope that the people would intervene, as they actually did, and thus absolve him from this painful duty. But there is nothing in the account to justify such an interpretation. On the contrary, Saul's whole demeanor that day was one of a man possessed. His need for a further outlet of his aggressive energies is indicated by his wish to prolong the battle during the night. His expressed desire not to leave one man alive may have represented an effort to displace his hostility from Jonathan to the enemy.

This zeal for fighting was in decided contrast to Saul's earlier attitude at Gibeah before Jonathan took over the initiative for the battle at Michmas. We are told that "Saul tarried in the uttermost part of Gibeah under the pomegranate tree . . ." One definitely gets the impression here of delayed action. Perhaps the king's zest for battle had been lessened and his confidence in victory decreased after he had incurred Samuel's displeasure at Gilgal. Anyhow, while he tarried with his chosen group of six hundred men, and the enemy waited in the camp on the hilltop across the valley, many of Saul's army drifted away to hide in the hills of Ephraim. Jonathan must have grown increasingly impatient and finally determined on action of his own.

Saul's wish to prolong the battle during the night may also have expressed a need to regain his rightful role as the one who initiates a battle and directs it. These unworthy personal motives may have been sensed by the priest, who interposes with the suggestion that God's will be determined in this matter. It is then that Saul is forced to face the conflict between himself and Jonathan, which is the real issue involved.

It is interesting that when Jonathan becomes the people's

hero, Saul takes on a role that is comparatively new for him. He becomes very concerned with securing God's favor for his people in this military campaign, imposing religious regulations of a rather severe nature and building his first altar to God. He climaxes this religious zeal by a willingness to sacrifice his son because of the latter's unwitting violation of the ban. These desperate efforts to appease the father seem to be parallel with the growing antagonism to his son. By sacrificing Jonathan at this time, he would be satisfying both impulses, his aggression and his guilt.

One gets the impression that Saul is behaving toward Jonathan as Samuel had earlier behaved toward the king himself. Just as the priest had punished Saul for taking the initiative at Gilgal, rejecting the king in the name of God, so Saul was ready to do with Jonathan. His religious fervor is also expressed by acting as a father-priest toward the people. It is possible that Samuel's rejection of him at Gilgal was followed by a period of depression during which he displayed the inactivity manifested at Gibeah. His increased religious zeal and his antagonism toward Jonathan, with whom he must also have identified as the *bad son,* is understandable psychoanalytically. Having lost Samuel as a "good object," he identified with him instead and became *a Samuel* to the projected image of himself in Jonathan.

However, Saul allows himself to be restrained by the people. He does not act out his aggressive impulses and we have no basis for believing that he would have done so under any circumstances. We know how wide is the gap between speech and action. His anger may have dissipated itself in the little scene of the casting of lots which he caused to be enacted, and the episode may have ended as he basically wanted it to.

It is interesting that he gave up his plan to pursue the Philistines further that night. He submits to the will of God, as revealed by the priest, as he had submitted to the will of the people. Thus Saul was able to overcome his impulse of murderous rage and allow his positive feelings for Jonathan and the more normal aspects of his superego to control his behavior.

After the successful battle at Michmas, Saul threw himself

with great energy into continuous warfare. We are told that ". . . he fought against all his enemies, on every side, against Moab, and against the children of Ammon, and against Edom, and against the kings of Zobah, and against the Philistines; and whithersoever he turned himself, he put them to the worse. And he did valiantly, and smote the Amalekites, and delivered Israel out of the hands of them that spoiled them (14:47-48)."

One might detect in this energetic and continuous warfare an effort on the part of Saul to externalize his own conflict and to ward off his depression by expressing his hostility in socially approved ways. He may also have learned the danger of inertia, for it allowed others to take over the leadership.

After this period of zealous war-making, Saul's second clash with Samuel occurs and this experience is evidently another turning point in his life. Saul again disobeys an injunction of the head priest and is again rejected by Samuel.

Higher Criticism theorizes that actually only one such incident took place and that the two accounts are from different sources, giving the impression of two separate incidents. For our purpose, however, all of the material has equal psychological validity and we will accept the biblical account as presented.

Samuel commands Saul to make war upon the Amalekites, the most ruthless foes of Israel, who almost wiped out the Israelite tribes in the desert of Sinai when they were fleeing from slavery in Egypt. Saul is adjured to carry out the dreaded *herem* against these people. This meant that every living thing, men, women, children, and animals, were to be utterly destroyed as an offering to God. This primitive procedure was not the usual method of warfare but was performed in certain instances by all the peoples of that area in those times.[2] Scholarly opinion differs about the degree to which the Israelites carried out the *herem* in their conquest of the Canaanites.[3, 4]

We will not enter here into the question of what prompted Samuel to impose such a duty upon Saul on that particular occasion. It is our purpose, rather, to see what its consequences were for the king. Saul first took the precaution of warning the friendly tribe of Kenites, who lived among the Amalekites, to depart from them, in order not to share the same fate. Then the Hebrews made war upon their foes, winning a decisive victory. However, Saul and his men spared the life of Agag, the king, and saved the best of the sheep and oxen.

Samuel learned of Saul's disobedience and, greatly perturbed, set out to confront the king. Saul must indeed have been very fearful of the consequences of his act. He meets Samuel at a short distance from the camp and attempts to beguile him with the greeting, "Blessed be thou of the Lord; I have performed the commandment of the Lord."

Samuel answers sternly, "What meaneth then this bleating of the sheep in mine ears, and the lowing of the oxen which I hear?"

Saul tries to exonerate himself, saying that it was the people who took the animals as spoils for the purpose of sacrificing them to God. Such intent, incidentally, was not indicated earlier when the action took place. Samuel thunders in reply, "Behold, to obey is better than to sacrifice; and to hearken than the fat of rams. For rebellion is as the sin of witchcraft, and stubbornness is as idolatry and teraphim."

It is interesting that Samuel puts the sin of rebellion and stubbornness in the same category as witchcraft and idolatry. To rebel against Samuel was to show a lack of faith in the God he represented. Such an attitude was equivalent to belief in magic and false gods.

Saul then confesses that he has sinned and admits that it was because he feared the people that he followed their wishes. Samuel must have understood well Saul's low sense of self-esteem, for in his denunciation of the king he cries out, "Though thou be little in thine own sight, art thou not head of the tribes of Israel?" Saul pleads for Samuel's pardon but the priest sternly repudiates him saying, "Because thou hast rejected the word of the Lord, He hath also rejected thee from being king."

As Samuel turns to go away, Saul seizes the priest's robe as if to detain him. It must have been a desperate gesture for it was strong enough actually to tear the garment, or perhaps a decorative strip of cloth hanging from the waist. Another interpretation of the unclear text is that it was Samuel who seized hold of Saul's robe and tore it, in order to express symbolically what he then said to Saul, "The Lord hath rent the kingdom of Israel from thee this day, and hath given it to a neighbor of thine, that is better than thou."

This rending of the garment can be seen as a symbolic castration. Perhaps the very ambiguity of whose garment was torn points to a mutual castration. Saul had reduced Samuel to impotence by disobeying him, and the priest, in turn, punished the king by rending the kingdom from him.

The distraught ruler pleads with Samuel to return with him to the camp and perform the sacrifice so that the king of Israel might save face. Samuel finally yields to this plea. Afterwards, the priest commands that Agag be brought before him. Then, in the sight of all the soldiers, Samuel himself hews Agag to death with his sword.

One wonders if Agag served here as the image of the disobedient king of Israel himself, whom the angry priest thus violently destroyed. Samuel then returns to his home in Ramah. He never meets Saul face to face again.

Samuel's rejection of the king was a private matter between the two and did not affect Saul's position on a reality level. The priest did not have power to make and unmake kings at his will. The psychological impact, however, of what had occurred was overwhelming for Saul. Of what good was the kingship if God, through Samuel, had rejected him, and moreover, had taken away the royal prerogative from his descendants?

Immediately after this, we are told that "the spirit of the Lord had departed from Saul, and an evil spirit from the Lord terrified him." It is clear that the same power which had favored him was now punishing him. This is a good description of how Saul's ambivalent relationship with Samuel gave way and led to his illness, feelings of depression and persecution.

Why did Saul disobey Samuel's command to carry out the *herem* against the Amalekites? Samuel intuitively describes his act as one of rebellion. Saul evidently had a need to rebel against a father figure. We know that psychologically submission and rebellion go hand in hand. Saul's relationship to his own father seemed to be of this character and he transferred these feelings to Samuel. Probably this transference took on an even more intense character because Saul became so clearly an object of Samuel's influence, a puppet king, the man to whom God gave a *changed heart* as soon as he was anointed by the priest. Such a degree of submission to a figure as dominating as Samuel may have been very threatening to Saul's ego. The strength that he received from the priest must have been illusory, accentuated by Samuel's magnetic power. The healthy aspects of the king's personality would tend to rebel against this threat to its integrity. This factor, together with the aggression that always accompanies submission, made it inevitable that Saul should defy Samuel.

The form that this defiance took is also significant. He spared the life of Agag, the king. Saul's act of mercy must have been made on the basis of identification. He treated Agag as he himself would have wished to be treated in a similar situation. As for saving the best of the animals, Saul may indeed have listened to the voice of the people. The Hebrews, themselves a pastoral and agricultural people, evidently found it difficult to destroy these innocent and realistically valuable creatures. The hatred which could have helped them enforce the religious dictum against the Amalekites, a people who had been so implacably hostile to their own, could not apply to the animals.

Saul must have spoken truly when he told Samuel that he feared the people and therefore obeyed their wishes. To some degree, this fear had a reality basis. The Hebrews were a democratic nation with a representative government of elders. The people were truly the power behind the throne. But Saul was their accepted king, their leader in victorious battle, and it was customary for them to obey him. Saul's fear therefore must also have contained some unrealistic elements, reflecting his own insecurity. If he was able to rebel against Samuel, might not his people, *his sons,* be capable of rebelling against him? He thus projected his own hostility upon the people and feared them.

Immediately after Samuel's second and more vigorous rejection, Saul succumbs to his emotional malady. He is now truly a sick and melancholy king. The *evil spirit* that haunted him was the incorporated image of a sadistic, rejecting father, probably made more terrifying through Saul's distorted projections which preceded the incorporation.[5] It is also likely that physiological factors of his age made the trauma of approaching displacement particularly hard to endure.[6]

It is during this period of his illness that David enters upon the scene of Saul's life and becomes the central figure around which the king's emotional conflict rages.

According to some biblical commentators, there are two accounts in the Bible of the first meeting between Saul and David. However, as heretofore, we shall follow the sequence of events as they occur in the text and try to see their psychological significance.

Saul's first encounter with David takes place when the king's retainers suggest that someone be found who could play upon the harp and thus soothe the troubled spirits of the king. David is selected for this purpose. We are told that when the youth stood before Saul, the king loved him greatly and made David his armour-bearer. Thereafter, whenever Saul was troubled by his *evil spirit* the young man played for him and the king found relief.

David is brought before the king in a new role when the youth offers to fight the giant Philistine, Goliath, who has tauntingly challenged the Hebrews as the opposing armies faced each other on opposite hills across a valley. Saul tries to clothe David with his own suit of armour, probably the only one of its kind in the Hebrew camp. But David finds that he is hampered by this apparel and takes it off, explaining that he is not accustomed to it. Then, as the well-known story relates, David selects five smooth stones out of the brook, puts them in his shepherd's bag, and with his sling in his hand, goes out to meet Goliath. David slays the contemptuous challenger of the Hebrews by hurling a stone into the giant's forehead.

It is after this exploit that the king seems not to know David and asks the captain of his host,

"Abner, whose son is this youth?" And Abner said: "As thy soul liveth, O king, I cannot tell." And the king said: "Inquire thou whose son the stripling is." And as David returned from the slaughter of the Philistine, Abner took him and brought him before Saul with the head of the Philistine in his hand. And Saul said to him: "Whose son art thou, thou young man?" And David answered: "I am the son of thy servant Jesse the Bethlemite (17:55–58)."

Some commentators think that the king's question refers to David's lineage rather than to the identity of the youth himself. The fact that David answers by describing himself as the son of Jesse without even giving his own first name seems to confirm this interpretation. He assumes that the king already knows him from his earlier role. Why however should Saul suddenly be interested in David's lineage if he has met the youth before? This wish to know more about him is understandable. David is suddenly a hero. The memory of another occasion when a youth suddenly became popular in the eyes of the people must have recurred to the king. This time it is not Jonathan, the son of Saul, who has thus displaced him. Whose son, then, is this young man?

The fact that Jonathan is somehow psychologically involved is strengthened by what happens next. As David replied to Saul, making the simple statement of his identity, it is *Jonathan* who responds. The text says,

And it came to pass when he (David) had made an end of speaking unto Saul, that the soul of *Jonathan* was knit with the soul of David, and Jonathan loved him as his own soul. And Saul took him that day and would let him go no more to his father's house. Then Jonathan made a covenant with David, because he loved him as his own soul. And Jonathan stripped himself of the robe that was upon him and gave it to David, and his apparel, even to his sword and his girdle (18:1–4). (*italics added*)

Why does Jonathan respond so intensely to David even before Saul has had an opportunity to answer the youth's modest announcement about his family background? The very wording of the text has an odd quality here because of the sudden intrusion of Jonathan into a situation where David and Saul were communicating.

This intrusion of Jonathan makes necessary and justifies a digression in the continuity of our own commentary. We must pause in the study of the relationship of Saul and David and ask ourselves, "What is Jonathan doing here? Why has he suddenly appeared upon the scene?"

Why indeed should the son of the king respond in this enthusiastic manner to the youthful hero of the day, at the very moment when the latter is being viewed favorably by Saul? This incident recalls a somewhat similar situation described by Freud, when a young man falls in love with another youth at the very time when the latter is being regarded approvingly by the first boy's mother.[7]

It seems likely that Jonathan was reacting to David on the basis of narcissistic identification. *He loved David as he wanted his father to love him.* The very expression, "his soul was knit with the soul of David" is a wonderfully apt description of this process.

It is not difficult to conjecture what must have preceded Jonathan's emotional reaction. He must have experienced a brief period of intense jealousy when David appeared before the opposing armies as the youthful champion of Israel and performed the valiant deed of the hero. Was this not an achievement that belonged more appropriately to the son of the king rather than to an unknown shepherd youth? But evidently Jonathan could not permit such feelings to reach awareness and had to defend himself against them.

As in the process described by Freud, the feelings of jealousy, rivalry, and aggression must have been repressed, and the rival became a love object.[8] In this *altruistic surrender* Jonathan actually strips himself of his clothes and puts them on David, including even his sword. Jonathan thus withdraws from the competition but enjoys fulfillment in fantasy through the close bond he establishes with David.[9]

The problem remains of why Jonathan did not allow himself to maintain his normal role. Why, in fact, had he not answered the challenge of Goliath himself? Certainly it was not for lack of physical courage. Some other factor must have restrained him. Jonathan's earlier experience with his father at Michmas must have had a shattering effect upon the youth. He had shown spectacular initiative and courage and it is reasonable to suppose that he expected glowing praise and expressions of love from his father as a reward. Instead, Saul singled him out as a culprit and sinner before the entire army, expressing the intent to take his life.

It is interesting to speculate what Jonathan's motivations may have been in taking the initiative from his father at Michmas, the act which we regard as stimulating Saul's hostility. Actually, this was the second time that Jonathan behaved in this fashion. Shortly after Saul was anointed king at Gilgal, it was Jonathan who initiated the war for liberation against the Philistines by boldly attacking the enemy garrison in his own town of Gibeah. Saul came to his support by *sounding the horn* throughout all Israel, summoning the men to war. There is no indication of how Saul reacted to this first incident in which Jonathan acted as *agent provocateur.*

It seems likely that Jonathan's behavior on a conscious level was prompted largely by a wish to win his father's approval and love rather than to outshine him. Sensitivity and the need for love are more apparent in Jonathan's personality than ambitious or aggressive wishes. The longing for his father's love may have been so great that Jonathan was willing to overcome his feelings of jealousy toward David and, instead, to identify with him, thus vicariously enjoying Saul's favor. The immediacy and fervor with which he bestows his apparel and sword upon the other youth indicate an over-compensatory reaction of a defensive nature, as we have noted. Jonathan's insecurity in his relationship with Saul must have had its roots in an unconscious awareness of his father's ambivalence toward him, and of his own reactive hostility, which had to be covered and atoned for by so many defensive maneuvers.

In addition to this excessive need for love, Jonathan may have been reacting *headily* to his father's sudden elevation to royalty.

If he was insecure, Jonathan may have tried to overcome this feeling by sharing in his father's newly-acquired power. Perhaps it was this stimulus that enabled him to undertake two projects against the Philistines, so daring that they could not have been the premeditated acts of maturity. Only the unconscious fantasy of sharing omnipotently in the powers of a father-king might have prompted Jonathan to such daring. We get a suggestion of this aspect on the occasion when he reveals to his armour-bearer the intention to climb the crag of Michmas and attack the enemy. As a rationalization of this unrealistic endeavor, he says, ". . . there is no restraint to the Lord to save by many or by few." The power of God, symbolic of the father, and vice versa, was the strength on which Jonathan depended.

Another aspect of Jonathan's personality, however, is revealed by his ability to criticize his father for imposing a vow of fasting upon the men during a day of battle. Perhaps the fact that he had already proven his worth made it possible for him to do this.

It is significant that Jonathan did not plead with his father for his life when accused of breaking the ban. This behavior suggests that the son must have been overcome with hurt pride and a sense of deep injustice. His immediate compliance was a masochistic expression of hatred against Saul, for by allowing himself to be killed, Jonathan would also be deeply injuring his father.

Jonathan's tendency to overly-strong identification comes out clearly in his love for David, as we have seen. Just as he shared exultantly in his father's newly-gained power, so he became one with David in the moment when the latter was the object of his father's approval.

Jonathan's relationship to David is further revealed in the poignant scene that takes place later in the story, when David pleads with Jonathan to help him escape from the jealous wrath of Saul. Jonathan not only gives this help but assumes that David will ultimately be victorious and win the kingship. He, in turn, begs David to show him kindness when that day comes, and to spare his household also. It seems a little unrealistic at this moment when it is David who is in danger of his life and dependent on the good will of Jonathan, that the latter should be the one who pleads for clemency from David.

Jonathan had evidently not only renounced his faith in his father but was also freely yielding up his own rights to the throne by acknowledging David as the successful rival. We see here again Jonathan's tendency to relinquish his own role. The young man's loyalty to David and the defiance of his father indicate the more open break-through of Jonathan's hostile feelings toward Saul. His surrender to David may have been prompted not only by narcissistic identification but as a further expression of a sadomasochistic tendency, to hurt his father by hurting himself. And indeed it became one of Saul's deepest sources of distress that Jonathan so readily gave precedence to David, even to the point of yielding the kingdom to him.

It is significant of the great change in Saul that he did not himself accept the scornful challenge of Goliath. Where now was the spirit of the man who had impetuously carved up his pair of oxen and impelled the people to follow him all the way across the Jordan to save their brethren? Where was the zealous warrior who had defeated Israel's enemies on all sides?

It is possible that Goliath may have represented more than a challenge to physical combat as far as Saul was concerned. The taunting giant may have appeared to the sick king as the very embodiment of the sadistic, destroying father, the evil spirit which tormented him. Had Saul been able to externalize his conflict at this time, had he gone out to meet Goliath and conquered him, the king might have regained his emotional health. But this he evidently was not able to do. The man who felt rejected and abandoned by God, the *Good Father,* and who could not overcome the introjected *bad father,* was not able to meet the terrifying monster in an actual contest.

All we are told about Saul's reaction to David immediately after the latter's victory is that "he would let him go no more to his father's house." This was in line with Saul's policy stated at the very beginning of his reign, that ". . . when Saul saw any mighty man or any valiant man, he took him."

In the first account of how Saul and David meet, however, when the youth stands before him as a minstrel, Saul's reaction is expressed with much more warmth, for we are told that "Saul loved him greatly." His affection was for the skilful player on the harp, but for the hero who slays Goliath, there is only the statement that implies further need for his services.

As David goes on to greater exploits, he becomes increasingly popular among the people. Then there occurs the famous incident when the army is marching home from a victorious battle and the women come out to greet the returning heroes with song and dance. And they chant, "Saul hath slain his thousands, and David his ten thousands." This becomes a turning point in the relationship between Saul and David. We are told that "Saul was very wroth, and this saying displeased him. And Saul said, 'All he lacketh is the kingdom!' And Saul eyed David from that day and forward." This is an apt description of a paranoid reaction, expressing Saul's jealousy, suspicion, and rage.

The very next morning after this incident Saul was again suffering from an onset of his *evil spirit,* and "he raved in the midst of the house." This is the first time that behavior of this type is ascribed to him. The sequence of events is clearly delineated. Saul was hurt by the greater acclaim shown to David by the women. This led to a depression and to *raving,* aggression expressed on an uncontrolled verbal, or oral, level.

The secondary role given to Saul by the women of Israel must have been experienced as a rejection by the mother. This trauma would be especially painful after Saul's repudiation by Samuel, the father-priest.

David tries to calm the king by playing on the harp, but the very sight of this man drives Saul into such fury that he throws his spear at him twice. The depression thus gives way to murderous rage when David stands before him. The same pattern of feeling, although in milder and more repressed form, must have animated Saul when Jonathan became the people's hero during the battle of Michmas. Saul was indeed sensitive to being displaced.

David avoids the hurled spear both times. This double escape must have seemed like an act of Providence, for the text says, "And Saul was afraid of David, because the Lord was with him, and was departed from Saul."

How did it happen that David escaped as he did? Saul must have been a skilful warrier and adept at throwing a spear. David was occupied in playing upon the harp and therefore should have been an easy target. But perhaps the youth, aware of the disordered mind of the king, was on guard. Certainly the second time he must have been prepared, having experienced the hostility of the man before whom he stood.

However, it may also be true that Saul unconsciously did not really wish to kill David. If the youth was a son figure, then Saul would also have positive feelings toward him. Just as the king had allowed himself to be dissuaded from killing Jonathan at Michmas, so now he may have avoided actually hitting David with the spear, thus compromising with the aggression that demanded an outlet.

The feeling that God was with David must also have been a deterrent to the impulse to kill. For if God favored Saul's rival, then to slay him would be to incite the wrath of God upon the king's own head. Saul had feelings both of fear and awe toward David, as the text clearly states. It is likely that these attitudes were already operative before he threw the spear. If so, it would be a half-hearted gesture, expressing his own self-doubt as well as his ambivalence.

If Saul's hostility toward David had been only on the basis of a competitive jealousy he could have gone out and tried to be more successful than the latter. As king, Saul was in the superior position. He was a brave and able soldier. Why, then, was Saul unable to compete with David on a reality level?

Saul must have been living in fearful expectation of being overthrown by a competitor, an outcome clearly predicted by Samuel. Since the king's own anointment had been a secret one, he could assume that his rival would also be chosen in the same fashion. Saul would therefore have no actual way of knowing who would displace him.

David's brilliant achievements in war must already have marked him in Saul's eyes as the potential successor to the throne, the *unknown neighbor* of whom Samuel had spoken. Perhaps he recognized in David's bearing the confidence of a man who has been divinely appointed to a mission, one who had a silent pact with Destiny, such as Saul himself had known. He and David would thus share a relationship with Samuel, an unspoken common experience which may have been understood by both of them on a level of non-verbal communication.

Another factor may also have been involved. When David first appears upon the scene as potential hero and volunteers to fight Goliath, Saul attempts to clothe the youth in his own armor, as we have seen. While this solicitude may have expressed only a normal concern for David's safety, Saul's quick response to someone about to perform a heroic act of leadership bears further scrutiny. Might not his gesture indicate an immediate identification with David, who at that moment may have represented Saul's old, warlike self? The depressed king, seeing before him a replica of his pastoral youth might have sought to escape from his dilemma by *becoming* David. Saul's failure to strike the youth with his hurled spear may thus have had the additional motive of sparing an object of narcissistic identification.

Saul's situation at this time was indeed a pitiable one. In reality, he had proven himself a successful soldier-king, accomplishing the purpose for which he had been chosen. As far as the people knew, Saul was the only elected and anointed king of Israel. There is no indication that they were thinking in terms of a successor. And if they were, then Jonathan, the brave and popular young warrior, would be the logical heir to the throne. The shepherd youth's anointment by Samuel was evidently not known to the people. Nor did David in any way contrive against Saul.

However, to get rid of his threatening rival now becomes a kind of obsession with Saul, and his efforts in this direction form the basis for a number of dramatic episodes. His first plan, oddly enough, is to give his elder daughter, Merab, to David for a wife.

Ostensibly, this is to serve as a stimulus to the young warrior to continue fighting the Philistines. The hope on Saul's part is that David would be killed in the process. The king's motivation is expressed quite openly. "For Saul said, 'Let not my hand be upon him, but let the hand of the Philistines be upon him (18:17).' "

The plan apparently involved a complete disregard for his daughter's feelings in the situation. Evidently Saul could not go through with it as far as Merab was concerned. We are told quite without explanation that at the time when Merab was to have been given to David, she was wed to another.

Then Saul learns that his younger daughter, Michal, loves David, and the king decides to give her to him, ". . . that she may be a snare to him, and that the hand of the Philistines may be against him." When informed of Saul's plan, David modestly protests his poverty and humble estate. The king then lets it be known indirectly that the only dowry he desired from David was a hundred foreskins of slain Philistines.

This episode is certainly puzzling. It has the character of a fairy tale where the suitor for the king's daughter must first prove his worth by an accomplishment of unusual courage. As Otto Rank points out, this serves the purpose of providing the father with an outlet for his jealousy and aggression toward the man who takes his daughter from him. It also creates a situation where a number of young rivals are usually killed in the attempt to win the prize.[10]

In the fairy tale the father's hostile motive is unconscious. But Saul not only takes the initiative by offering his daughter to the prospective bridegroom but is clearly aware of his unworthy purpose. Involved in this situation is also an unconscious hostility toward the woman as evidenced by a king whose mother and wife are not even mentioned in the biblical narrative. However, beyond a lack of regard for his daughter, the plan may unconsciously express a masochistic submission to David. A motive, openly acknowledged to oneself, of a kind that is usually repressed, often conceals a more secret one. Saul's proposal to make David his son-in-law follows immediately upon the statement that ". . . he stood in awe of him (18:15)." The king may have felt a need to placate his rival, fearing from this son figure the hostility which he must have anticipated from Jonathan, toward whom he had actually shown aggression. Saul therefore may have wished to appease David by offering him the hand of Michal. We are told that it *pleased* the king to learn of his daughter's love for the man he now hated. Evidently Michal's attachment made it easier for Saul to carry out his plans.

There are aspects about this episode that give it an air of unreality. No indication is given that David had shown any reluctance in fighting the Philistines even without the offer of a reward. At the time that Goliath challenged the Israelites, David heard that the successful opponent would win riches, honor, and the hand of the king's daughter. But such a promise and its fulfillment are never mentioned again. It is not known who started this rumour among the people but the source may have been the same from which this later part of the narrative stemmed, that is, the fantasy of the king himself. For indeed the more bizarre elements in the story may have been only a product of Saul's heightened imagination and not taken place at all in reality. And although the impression is given that David was expected to perform the feat singlehanded, the text states that ". . . he and his men slew of the Philistines two hundred men (18:27)." So the task, after all, was not so impossible.

It was in the nature of the grim trophies that Saul demanded where the element of the fantastic can be suspected. It symbolically equates death with castration. The conclusion can be drawn that his wish to castrate David himself is here displaced to the Philistines.

The ritual of circumcision is understood psychoanalytically as a symbolic, partial castration offered in submission to God for the privilege of adult sexuality.[11] By asking for a hundred foreskins, Saul may have been indulging in a fantasy of being God-like, an attitude which would compensate for his real feelings of fear and submissiveness. But even in those primitive times, feelings and wishes of such a nature, in all probability, could only be entertained in fantasy. The story foreshadows Saul's later behavior when he is involved in a continual struggle with David, seeking to destroy him but always being frustrated in these attempts.

Saul's attitude toward this marriage is clearly shown later in the narrative. When David at last flees into exile from the wrath of the king, the latter gives Michal in marriage to another, even though she was David's lawful wife. Not until David himself becomes the ruler does he reclaim her.

As David's success and popularity continue to increase, Saul's desperation also must have grown. He now speaks openly to Jonathan and his retainers, suggesting that they should slay David. Jonathan pleadingly intervenes. Saul then reveals the more positive side of his ambivalent feelings and his easy suggestibility. He responds to Jonathan's moving plea that David has done no wrong and has served all Israel well; why should Saul shed innocent blood and bring sin upon himself? Saul then declares that David would not be put to death, and the young man continues to serve in the presence of the king as before. The ease with which Saul is dissuaded from his hostile purpose may indicate further his involvement on the basis of narcissistic identification.

But the old pattern repeats itself. A war breaks out again, David once more becomes a hero in battle, and again the *evil spirit* falls upon Saul. Once more David plays upon the harp to soothe the king and, as before, Saul hurls his spear at him. Now David accepts the fact that his life is in danger and he must flee from Saul.

Evidently the youth has sensed the situation correctly, for this time Saul takes more direct and daring steps to slay him. He does this now, not in a mood of uncontrollable rage, but with a definite plan which indicates that his purpose is more firm and his compunction less. He sends messengers to wait outside David's house and kill him in the morning when he comes out. It seems that Michal gets wind of this and tells David that he must escape that very night. She lets him down through the window and he flees to Samuel at Ramah. Michal then cleverly misleads Saul's messengers, who now seek him openly. She tells them David is sick and points to a covered figure lying on the bed, where she had placed a teraphim, or household god.

Saul seemingly remains indomitable in his intent and sends the men again, saying, "Bring him up to me in the bed, that I may slay him." He is not satisfied now to have his men kill David, but wishes to do so with his own hands. We see here how Saul's obsession grows steadily in strength, over-ruling the deterring elements in his behavior more and more. Nevertheless, he still manages to fail in his purpose, as he probably unconsciously intends.

Saul receives word that David is with Samuel at Ramah, and the king sends messengers to bring him back. We now have another of the dramatic episodes that enhance the story of this life and death pursuit. Saul's men come upon Samuel standing at the head of a band of prophets and prophesying. We are told that the spirit of God came upon the messengers and they too prophesied. Saul learns of this and sends another group of men. The same thing occurs three times. It is clear that Saul's messengers are reluctant to fulfill their task. Saul then goes himself. But he also yields to the magnetic influence of Samuel's prayers and joins the band of prophets. The king's reaction is even more pronounced. He remains in a trance-like state all day. The intensity of his response may indicate the strength both of his hostile wishes and his consequent guilt as evoked by the presence of Samuel.

David comes back from Ramah and when Saul is free from the mystical influence of Samuel, his old rage against his rival returns. This time he spurns Jonathan's further pleas and demands that David be brought before him and put to death. Jonathan warns David, who leaves hastily, knowing that this time he must depart forever from the presence of Saul.

Shortly after this, an episode is related which depicts Saul as the perpetrator of a most bloody and brutal act. He hears that David has found temporary respite in the house of the priests at Nob. There the head priest gave him bread and also the sword of Goliath, for David had left in haste and was weaponless.

This news infuriated Saul. We are told that he summoned

all the priests of Nob before him and then ordered his men to murder them in cold blood. His horrified guards refused to obey. Saul then turned to the chief of his herdsmen, Doeg, the Edomite. It was he who had first brought word to Saul of David's being helped by the priest. Doeg had no compunctions about carrying out Saul's command and murdered all eighty-five of the priests. The entire city of Nob was then put to the sword by this same bloody stranger who, we are told, killed all the inhabitants, including women and children. Even the animals were slain. Only one man, a son of the head priest, escaped and fled to David for refuge.

This is the story as the Bible tells it. Aspects of it sound incredible and may represent a myth-like exaggeration of the facts. It seems unlikely that the priests would passively allow themselves to be slaughtered by one man, or that Saul's retainers would permit this horrible deed to be perpetrated before their very eyes. Nor does it seem reasonable that one man could wipe out an entire community all by himself.

This story may serve the purpose of expressing symbolically the intensity of Saul's rage against the father-priest and his wish to kill him. In this episode, he kills the father over and over again. Saul's hatred against Samuel, whom the priests must have represented, was stirred up by the king's rivalry with David, who may have played the role of a younger sibling here. Saul could not tolerate a situation in which his rival received protection from a father figure who had treated the king so differently. The slaughter of the entire town may express hatred of the mother and of the people of Israel, by whom the king also felt rejected. The *Edomite*, as Doeg was known, means *the bloody one,* and refers to a native of Edom, a people whose legendary ancestor was Esau, a man who *lived by the sword.* Doeg may here personify the castrating, evil aspect of the personality, which in turn fears retaliation.

The above interpretation regarding the episode of the priests does not imply that the murder of one or more of them might not have taken place but it indicates that this fact, or fantasy, may have been used to express what was going on unconsciously in Saul's mind and in the fantasy of the people concerning him. On a reality basis, this act was not in harmony with Saul's personality. The man who fell in a trance-like state when he heard Samuel prophesying, and who had such difficulty in carrying out his hostile wishes toward even one person, must have had a good deal of repressed aggression but would hardly be able to act it out in the fashion described.

David is now an outlaw in the wild terrain of the southern Judean hills. Many followers join him there, especially those who had cause for discontent in the social system of that day.

The king is driven by his obsessive zeal into this remote territory to seek out David for the purpose of taking his life. Several dramatic events are recorded in which the situation is reversed. For it is Saul who inadvertently falls into the hands of David but the king is spared by the very person whose life he seeks. In the first episode, Saul enters a cave for a period of respite. It happens that David and his men are sitting in the deep interior of the same cave. David comes up to the unsuspecting king and cuts off a piece of his robe with a sword. He is then filled with remorse at having performed this indignity against the Lord's anointed, and forbids his men to harm him.

When Saul goes on his way, David follows and calls after him, holding up the fragment of robe. He points out that Saul's life was in the hands of the man he sought to kill. David then makes a moving plea to the king to stop pursuing him. Saul is overcome with emotion and weeps aloud, admitting that David has returned good for evil. He now acknowledges his belief that David will surely inherit the kingdom.

But in spite of Saul's apparent change of heart, David knew better than to take the word of his ambivalent king at its face value. Saul returns home and David remains in his mountain stronghold.

During these events Samuel dies. Some time evidently passes before the old obsession takes hold of Saul again. It is probably stimulated when some men of southern Judea report to the king that David is hiding in their home territory. Saul resumes the chase. But it is David who invades the camp of the pursuing party at night and comes upon the figure of the sleeping king. He removes Saul's sword and the cruse of water at his side. Then he withdraws to a nearby hill and shouts loudly to Abner, captain of the guard, taunting him for not keeping better watch over the king. He holds up his trophies to prove that the king's life had been in his hands. Again David movingly pleads that he has done no evil yet he had been driven out and hunted and not permitted to live among his own people. According to David's complaint, leaving the land of Israel also meant being driven away from the presence of the Lord, as if Saul were saying to him, "Go, serve other gods."

Once more Saul weeps and admits his wrongdoing, crying out, "I have sinned; return, my son David; for I will no more do thee harm, because my life was precious in thine eyes this day; behold, I have played the fool and erred exceedingly (26:19–21)."

But David knows that he will never be safe in the presence of the emotionally unstable king and therefore decides to seek refuge in the territory of the enemy. He secures political asylum from Achish, Philistine king of the city of Gath, and lives in the southern city of Ziglak.

After this, Saul's pursuit of David ends. Realistically, Saul could have followed David into Philistine territory, especially since the fugitive was in a city set apart for him and his followers. The target was clear and defined. It is doubtful whether Achish would have gone to the measure of supporting David in a war against Saul.

Why, then, did the king of Israel abandon his quarry at this point? David must have guessed correctly that only by leaving the land and the people of Israel would he have any real rest from the mad pursuit of Saul. Actually, Ziglak was no farther away geographically than other areas of southern Judea which David had frequented. On an unconscious level, however, by quitting the homeland, David was giving up not only the realities of his land and his people, but the symbolic values for which they stood, the mother and sons for whose love he was a rival. He was also leaving *the presence of the Lord,* and therefore was no longer a threatening competitor to Saul for God's favor.

No doubt, also, the incidents in which David spared Saul's life must have had a profound effect upon the king. David had proven his moral superiority over Saul, who must have been overwhelmed anew by his guilt feelings. Moreover, Saul may have experienced what David did to him on both occasions as partial castrations, warnings of what might happen.

The cutting of the king's robe in the first episode and the removal of his sword and cruse of water in the second, have symbolic significance. The first incident may also have re-activated the earlier experience with Samuel, when the rending of a garment, too, was involved.

The last event in the troubled life of Saul is the dramatic episode that ends in his death. The Philistines are gathered for an all-out attack against the Israelites. When Saul beholds the mighty host of the enemy he is greatly afraid. This is a different Saul from the one who had waged war with such zealous fury.

It seems odd that the account of this battle is prefaced by the statement that Samuel was dead and all Israel lamented him. We had been told earlier about Samuel's death. What, then, was the meaning of this somewhat redundant statement at this point? Psychologically, it might indicate that Saul felt Samuel's absence and abandonment with particular intensity at this crucial moment. This interpretation gains emphasis from the statement that immediately follows, which explains that the king had forbidden the practice of necromancy, the calling up of ghosts or familiar spirits. When Saul was filled with fear and trembling at the sight of the enemy, he tried to inquire of God regarding the outcome of the battle. But God failed to reveal himself to the terrified king. Saul then makes his famous visit to the woman at Endor who, according to the story, brings up the spirit of Samuel for him.

Saul must have had a strong intuitive feeling of what his fate would be in the coming battle and was making a last desperate effort to get a reprieve from the main source of authority in his life—Samuel. He thus refused to accept the finality of Samuel's death, and in spite of his own edict against necromancy, uses this method in his hour of need.

The consequences are inevitable. The spirit of Samuel sternly reproaches him, saying, "Why hast thou disquieted me, to bring me up?" He then prophesies the defeat of Israel and the death in battle of Saul and his sons. Saul falls in a faint upon the floor of the hut. He is restored by the ministrations of the woman who, in a touching scene of motherly concern, kills her fatted calf and bakes bread so that she may feed the king, who has not eaten all that day.

Thus Saul's effort to win forgiveness from the introjected father, externalized in the spirit of Samuel, fails. Actually, Saul fails to forgive himself. His outward channel of aggression in the pursuit of David being closed, Saul yields to his depression. His death on Mt. Gilboa is literally a suicide. The Israelites are over-whelmingly defeated and Saul is relentlessly pursued by enemy archers. We are told that "he was in great anguish by reason of the archers." This anguish must have been mental for there is no statement to the effect that he had actually been wounded. The pursuing archers may have represented vividly the furious father. Saul asks his armour-bearer to kill him, pleading as an excuse that the enemy would do so and then expose him to humil-iation. The armour-bearer refuses and Saul then falls upon his own sword.

Three of Saul's sons are slain in the battle, Jonathan among them. He is finally united with his father in death. Perhaps his longing for the father, together with his sense of guilt, motivated this conclusion.

The Philistines do as Saul feared. They behead the king and hang his body and those of his sons on the city wall of Bethshan, a half-Canaanite town that had probably quickly surrendered to the Philistines. When news of this reaches the city of Jabesh-Gilead, the men of that town make a midnight march to Beth-shan, take down the bodies of Saul and his sons, and bury them with honor in their own land. Thus the people who had been the first to be delivered by Saul in the early days of his rule were the ones who rescued his body from the mockery of his enemies.

Saul had gone into the battle of Mt. Gilboa fully convinced of its outcome. In this last gesture, he did not try to flee from fate. The troubled king of Israel, after a long struggle, submitted to his tragic destiny.

Let us now try to summarize briefly the picture Saul presents in terms of his personality structure and pathology. Saul gives the impression of having been a rather lonely person, suffering from feelings of isolation and withdrawal. There is no indication that he had a particularly close relationship with anyone although he not only had a wife but also a concubine, Rizpah. His personal life with them is never mentioned. Two of the children most involved in his history, Jonathan and Michal, definitely take sides with David, against their father.

Although the people give evidence of loyalty and obedience to Saul for the most part, there is no indication of a strong emotional attachment to him. On several occasions they differ with him and show preference for Jonathan and David. We have seen, too, that Saul feared the people, so his feelings toward them must have been ambivalent. He seemed to inspire neither great friendship nor great emnity. Even in the case of David, the object of so much hostility, little is told of the younger man's real feelings toward Saul. He respected his king for the most part and on occasion pleaded with him for mercy and justice. But neither love nor hate are expressed in David's attitudes toward Saul.

It seems that Saul responded strongly to situations which activated the intrapsychic conflict in a fashion common to a reactive depression. His rage, too, seemed to be in response to definite stimuli and usually followed the period of depression, both being set off by different aspects of the same traumatic experience. Thus, the depressions were responses to instances of rejection or abandonment. When these were also associated with a rival who threatened to displace him and who received the narcissistic supplies such as the love and esteem of others, of which he himself was so badly in need, the depression was followed by rage and aggression against the rival.

Saul could be described as a personality with paranoid trends, a situation which provided a vulnerable background for the depression. The conflict with Samuel was the struggle with a father figure in which the theme of submission and rebellion, with its accompanying undertones of mutual castrative tendencies and defenses against such feelings, played a large role. Saul's long contest with David exemplifies these patterns of behavior, with a reversal of roles for the most part, Saul now being the father.

The repression of sexuality in his social milieu gave an added intensity to the problem of latent homosexuality and its defenses. Saul's pursuit of David, particularly after the latter fled into outlawry, also had a decidedly obsessive-compulsive character. It is common for depression to be associated with symptoms of this type.[12]

Let us try to see more specifically what this pursuit meant for Saul. If the need to do away with his rival had been paramount, the king could have accomplished this aim easily on many occasions. He could have sent a posse into the hills with instructions to find David and kill him forthwith. The fact that Saul had to engage in this activity himself and to fail in it repeatedly shows that the pursuit in itself must have been very important to the king. It is not hard to see why. The conflict with David allowed Saul to externalize his intrapsychic conflict, providing the stimulus for turning the aggression outward, away from his own ego. An important part of therapy in depression is to find a channelized outlet for the introverted aggression. This purpose David served for Saul.

It is likely that on one level Saul first indentified with David, as indicated earlier, then projected part of his own ego upon the latter. He could then pursue David with the same sadistic fury which he himself experienced as the target of the punishing, introjected Samuel.

Saul's low sense of self-esteem must have been related to a castration complex. The fear that his kingdom would be taken away from him would assume a greater intensity because of un-conscious castration anxiety. This fear was based on an actual threat by a powerful father figure, and Saul had to cope with an actual rival who represented the instrument through whom this dreaded eventuality was to take place.

This leads one to conjecture what Saul's emotional fate might have been if destiny had not called him to the kingship. It is likely that he might then have escaped without a major break-down. But when the submissive son, ambivalently related to the father, is suddenly chosen by Samuel and given the recognition he must have longed for all his life, something new is added. For a brief period his ego is flooded with unaccustomed strength. He experiences the fulfillment of unconscious infantile wishes in a way that is beyond the scope of reality for most people in a similar psychological situation. His dreams literally come true. The powerful father accepts him and endows him with a God-like omnipotence. At this point Saul may truly have been over-come by *hybris*, a sense of self-confidence so strong that one feels like a god and is therefore immune to the consequences of his behavior. Saul must have experienced this sense of immunity or he would not have dared to ignore Samuel's behests and to dis-obey his commands. That the son of a farmer, humbly carrying out his father's orders, could reach this point of self-assertion, indicates an unrealistic sense of power. A more reality-minded person would have recognized that Samuel's possible disapproval was not a matter to be treated lightly.

That Saul's new strength was a vulnerable one is shown by the way it yielded quickly to the trauma of Samuel's rejection. The feelings of omnipotence must have suffered a severe collapse and led to a sharp decline in his sense of self-esteem, a process characteristic of depression. The sudden coming to reality of repressed wishes to replace the father must have made Saul more fearful that he would suffer the same fate. In fact, he invited this fate by his behavior toward Samuel so we must infer that strong guilt feelings played a role in his masochistic tendencies.

Saul could not solve his problem of jealousy and rivalry in the simple and primitive fashion that Cain did with Abel. The king had to cope with a moral system, both external and internalized. The fact that he did not kill David but only pursued him, and that he eventually paid with his death as self-inflicted punishment for his aggressive wishes, shows that morality was a potent force in his world of three thousand years ago.

On a reality level, Saul fulfilled the purpose for which Samuel selected him, strengthening the unity of the Hebrew tribes and establishing the monarchy on a sound basis by defeating the enemies of Israel. His personal life might have been a happier one had he not been called to this difficult position of the kingship. But though we see him as a tragic figure, Saul nevertheless has real stature as a historic leader of ancient Israel who served his people well.

David, the
Charismatic Leader

 CHAPTER SIX

THE PERSONALITY of David highlights Jewish history with an aura of glory that has not dimmed through the ages. This king of biblical days is not only the hero of a great past; he is also associated with the fantasy of an even greater future. For according to tradition, it is from the house of David that the messiah is to come.[1]

This messianic link with David's name can be understood as a longing for his return. The period of his rule had become an unforgettable memory in the long annals of a people.

And indeed David accomplished much. He provided security for his country, defeating its enemies and extending its boundaries. In his time, the children of Israel, so recently a group of loosely-connected tribes, were molded into a monarchy that had a respected place among the nations. It is not surprising that

David became the *glorious father* of Jewish tradition, the symbol of strength and power, a king who ruled his people with righteousness and justice. He was truly a charismatic leader, endowed with the capacity to evoke enthusiasm and support among his subjects.

The character of this man presents interesting contrasts and some intriguing problems. A great king and a fearless warrior, David was at the same time a weak, indulgent father, who almost lost his throne to his own son. Strong and often ruthless in battle, David was also capable of gentle and tender emotions and is beloved in Jewish legend as the *sweet singer of Zion*. He had the capacity to arouse strong feelings in many people, both men and women. He was the object of loyalty and love, of envy and hatred. We shall attempt here some understanding of the inner workings of this colorful personality of biblical days, who left such a strong imprint upon the hearts and minds of men for three thousand years.

The Anointment

It is interesting to compare David's introduction to biblical history with that of Saul. Both appear in relation to Samuel and his anoinment of them as future kings of Israel. In the case of Saul, it is he who comes to Samuel, although unwittingly, while the seer is quite prepared to recognize and receive him. With regard to David, however, it is Samuel who travels to the youth's home but does not know exactly who the nominee for the kingship will be. Samuel is told only that one of the sons of Jesse has been chosen by God for this role.

The difference can be seen as significant in the later relationship of the two men with Samuel. The priest chooses Saul and tries to make of him a puppet-king, as we have seen. By the time he is called upon to anoint the second ruler of Israel, Samuel has evidently learned to relinquish some of his need to control. He comes to Bethlehem to seek the king and humbly awaits guidance from God until the very moment of his choice.

Perhaps the most dramatic element in the story is the fact

that David was not even present when Samuel began to appraise the sons of Jesse. Seven passed before him and failed to meet the test. Samuel then asked the father if he had any other sons, and Jesse replied, "There remaineth yet the youngest, and behold, he keepeth the sheep." He is sent for and we are told that when he stands before Samuel, God says to the prophet, "Arise, anoint him; for this is he (16:11)."*

The young man who stood before Samuel was certainly different in personality from Saul. It may be that Samuel, disillusioned by Saul's disobedience, no longer looked for a man who would be submissive to his will, but rather for one who could meet the reality of a king who was already on the throne. Nor does he choose David for his impressive physical appearance, as had occurred in the case of Saul. Interestingly, Samuel is about to repeat this pattern. When he looked upon Eliab, the eldest, and saw his stature and comeliness, the prophet thought,

> "Surely the Lord's anointed is before Him." But the Lord said unto Samuel: "Look not on his countenance, or on the height of his stature; because I have rejected him; for it is not as man seeth; for man looketh on the outward appearance, but the Lord looketh on the heart (16:7)."

Although David was not chosen for his physical beauty, he was richly endowed by nature in this regard, for the Bible says of him, "Now he was ruddy and withal of beautiful eyes, and goodly to look upon." There must have been something in David's bearing and in the expression of his face that impressed itself upon the shrewd mind of Samuel and made him conclude, "This is the man."

It is interesting that the anointment of David was not followed by a demonstration of Samuel's clairvoyant power, as in the situation with Saul. Nor did it have the secrecy of a private interpersonal relationship, with the stronger libidinal tendencies that would then have been evoked. We are told that "Samuel

* Biblical quotations and references in this chapter are from First Samuel, Chapters 16–31; Second Samuel; First Kings, Chapters 12:11. Chapter and verse, when standing alone, refer to First Samuel.

anointed him in the midst of his brethren . . . and the spirit of
the Lord came mightily upon David from that day forward."

Another detail is of interest here. For the anointment of
Saul a *cruse* of oil was used, while for David, the oil was contained in a *horn*. Legend says that the cruse signified a limited
vessel, indicating Saul's shortened reign, while the horn was indicative of an overflowing quality which was suggestive of the
lengthy period during which the dynasty of David would rule.[2]

Psychoanalytically, the cruse is symbolic of a passive-feminine
receptacle and may suggest Saul's submissive attitude toward
Samuel, while the horn suggests David's stronger masculinity.

In the Home of His Youth

What do we know of David's early life, of his actual role
in the family, and the nature of his relationship with his parents
and siblings? The biblical material about this part of his history
is scant but meaningful. It can be inferred that Jesse thought so
little of his youngest son that he did not even consider his
presence necessary on the occasion when the religious leader of
Israel was present although Samuel had asked him to bring *his*
sons.

The only other occasion describing a direct interaction between Jesse and David is when the father bids him bring supplies
to his three brothers who are soldiers in Saul's army. Here again
the father commands and the son obeys. The text says, "And
David rose up early in the morning, and left the sheep with a
keeper, and took and went, as Jesse had commanded him."

There is no expression of warmth or affection between the
two. The fact that such feelings are not mentioned may not be
proof of their absence. However, the tendency of the biblical
narrative is to emphasize loving relationships between father and
son, where such exists, as in the case of Jacob and Joseph, and
to treat ambivalence by repression or indirection. The text provides more basis for assuming neglect or indifference on Jesse's
part than an affectionate attitude toward his youngest son.

Evidently popular fantasy responded to the suggestion contained in the biblical narrative of David's Cinderella-like role in the family. According to one of the many post-biblical legends that cluster around the personality of David, he is represented, not as the youngest son, but rather as the least esteemed.

One version explaining this despised position in the family is that he was born out of wedlock. The story is that Jesse was in love with a slave girl of his household and planned a secret meeting with her. But the wife of Jesse, knowing of his passion, disguised herself as the other woman and met her husband at the trysting-place in the girl's stead. David was the result of this union. However, in order to spare her husband the knowledge of the deception practiced upon him, the wife did not reveal the truth of David's legitimacy until the time of his anointment by Samuel.

Another version of the myth is that David was of such unusual coloring, having red hair and a fair skin, that his brothers suspected the mother of adultery. They wanted to kill both the woman and her child, but Jesse restrained them. The brothers agreed to spare the two on condition that David should occupy the position of a slave. It was for this reason that he served as a shepherd until he was twenty-eight, the time of his anointment according to this legend.[3] Thus in one form of the myth it is the father who is guilty of an attempted sexual misdemeanor, while in the second story, the mother herself is under suspicion.

The absurd and exaggerated elements in the above legends did not deter the mythmakers. Hyperbole in extra-biblical fantasies may have provided an outlet for the restraint generally practiced in the biblical literature itself. But like all legendary material, the stories contain inner truths.[4]

What light can the psychoanalytic approach throw upon the meaning of these myths of the birth of a hero? They sound like variations of the so-called *family romance*.[5] The latter is a typical fantasy of youth in which the young daydreamer imagines himself the secret offspring of one or both parents other than his own. In the usual fantasy of this type the child seeks a more exalted parentage than his real ones. One may wonder then what might have motivated a form of the myth in which the status of the child is affected unfavorably by appearing to lower the rank of the mother to that of a slave girl or degrading her sexually? It might be well to repeat here Otto Rank's view that the myth arises through identification with the hero.[6] These legends regarding David can be understood as reflecting his own state of mind empathically perceived by those among whom these tales developed.

The feeling of being unloved and under-estimated by his father and brothers finds a kind of masochistic expression and justification in the fantasies. David could tolerate this belittling however since he knew that the truth would emerge and his triumph be all the greater. Moreover, the legends provided an outlet for ambivalent feelings, especially toward the father, who is pictured as having uncontrollable sexual passions of which David is the innocent victim.

The variation of the myth, in which the mother herself is suspect, may express the intense sibling jealousy which David evidently aroused. The brothers not only hated him, but also their mother, who brought this youngest, rather unnecessary son, into a family where there were already a sufficient number of male offspring.

The stories indicate David's lack of security with any member of his family and his efforts in fantasy to seek solutions to this problem along different lines. Both myths may deal with David's wish to explain his role in the family, not on the realistic basis of his being the youngest and therefore the one most naturally subject to the menial duties of the household, but as the innocent object of the baser impulses in other members of the family.

The fairy tale element of the youngest or most despised child overcoming all obstacles to attain fame and fortune is a familiar theme. It is easily understood as the daydream of achieving mastery and conquest in the struggle of life. The child with many siblings who are bigger and stronger than he, may have special motivation in dreaming of overcoming these rivals. The more lowly the fantasied position of the hero, the greater is the pleasure derived from the final triumph. We see here a certain analogy with the situation of Joseph and his many older brothers.

The only direct interaction portrayed in the Bible between David and any of his siblings occurs when the youth fulfills his father's injunction to bring food to the three members of the family who are serving in Saul's army. David leaves his supplies with the keeper of the baggage and runs to the area where the men are gathered. It is then that he witnesses Goliath's taunting challenge to the Hebrews that they should find themselves a man to come out and fight him. It is a challenge the Philistine giant has delivered each day for forty days.

David learns from the men around him that there will be a great reward for the brave man who is willing to meet this idolatrous braggart. The king will grant him great riches and the hand of the princess. He inquires for confirmation of this report, which is probably mere rumor, and the people assure him it is true. Eliab, his oldest brother, hears this verbal exchange and turns angrily upon David with the words, "Why art thou come down? and with whom hast thou left those few sheep in the wilderness? I know thy presumptiousness, and the naughtiness of thy heart; for thou are come down that thou mightest see the battle (17:28)."

Eliab evidently does not yet know the real reason for the youth's presence and may have thought that he came empty-handed, a situation which would have added to his annoyance. It seems that, with characteristic youthful impetuosity, David was more eager to see wat was going on at the battlefront than to deliver the supplies in person to his brothers.

He responds to Eliab's rebuke in an offhand way, saying, "What have I done now? Was it not but a word?" However, he does not allow himself to be swerved from his purpose and immediately repeats his query to someone else concerning the reward for fighting Goliath. We see here a capacity for self-assertion but at the same time an appeasing and respectful attitude to one who must have been a father figure.

Since this exchange of words between Eliab and David is the only one recorded, it is difficult to interpret its true singnficance in terms of the basic relationship between the oldest and the youngest sons of Jesse. Several attitudes, however, are implicit in the words of Eliab. They are a reprimand for neglect of duty and they put David clearly in the category of the youngster whose only possible interest in the challenge of Goliath was to "see the battle." Yet the word *presumptiousness* implies more than that and indicates Eliab's feelings of rivalry with David. While reluctant to recognize that his youngest brother is now a potential soldier himself, Eliab correctly interprets David's deeper interest than that of an onlooker. It is this fact which must have aroused Eliab's anger. He wanted to reduce David to the position of shepherd-boy. It seems highly possible that a special antagonism existed between the oldest and the youngest sons of Jesse, strengthened at this time by David's selection and anointment by Samuel, while Eliab had been specifically rejected.

Both oldest and youngest sons held positions of particular importance in the family hierarchy of that day. We know that while primogeniture was the traditional form of inheritance, the opposite of this, ultimo-geniture, often found expression.[7]

There are other indications later in his life that David's relationship with his brothers could not have been a close and loving one. It is certainly striking that none of them are ever mentioned as participating in his long and glorious career, with the exception of a brief reference to Elihu, in *First Chronicles*. He is named there as one of a long list of officials and is described as *one of the brethren of David* (27:18). The fact that otherwise the brothers are never referred to could not have been mere chance, for the enumeration of those who served the king in many different capacities forms impressive lists in the biblical narrative. One wonders if this surprising lack of reference to them during David's lengthy reign may be based upon the possibility that they were all considerably older than he. However, the eldest, Eliab, was still young enough to be a soldier in Saul's army at the time when David himself was old enough to challenge Goliath. We must conclude that other factors were involved.

There are many occasions when conflict between brothers and rivalry among them is recounted in the Bible. Why then is this subject so carefully avoided in the case of David? We must assume that this area is one of special sensitivity for him and that the omission represents a repression, a technique which we have observed before in these biblical studies.

If there was a lack of friendly feeling between David and his brothers, how can we explain the fact that at a later period, when he was an outlaw from the court of Saul, they joined him in the wilderness of Judea? Interestingly, only the bare statement is made that ". . . his brethren and all his father's house heard of it, and they went down thither to him." Since they are not mentioned in any of the exploits of this period, we do not know whether they remained with him or only came for a brief stay, possibly because they feared Saul's vengeance might reach out to them too. If this was so, and they had to give up their homes and expose themselves and their families to the uncertainties and discomforts of living in an outlaw band, any latent hostility they may have had toward David would be aroused by this situation and they would have resented him even more.

There is nothing in the biblical text about David's mother. We can only make assumptions about his relationship with her on the basis of certain elements in his life history as his story unfolds. But certain inferences can be drawn now.

It seems reasonable to suppose that David's ego strength was based, in part, on an experience of loving acceptance by his mother. Without such support it is doubtful whether he could have developed the courage and confidence necessary to face a Goliath or to become the warrior leader of his people. The name *David* means *beloved* or *darling*. The significance of names was emphasized in those days more than in our own.[8] Someone therefore must have welcomed this child with tenderness. There seems more basis for thinking it was the mother rather than the father. Generally it was the mother's privilege to name the baby.

We might even boldly conjecture at this point that Jesse's attitude of indifference toward David may have been a reaction to the mother's love. Freud has suggested that the youngest son in the family group occupies a special position, often being the particular object of the mother's affection and the father's jealousy, the one, also, who is most likely to displace the father, both because of his protected position and the age difference.[9]

Another woman of David's family is mentioned a number of times in a curiously indirect fashion. This is Zeruiah, ostensibly David's half-sister. Zeruiah is the mother of David's nephews, Joab, Abishai, and Asahel, of whom the first two especially play so large a role in his career. They are constantly addressed by David as "ye sons of Zeruiah," but little information is given about her. This mode of address was not customary and probably had some special meaning for David. In those times people were known only by their first names except when it was necessary to establish their identity. They were then referred to in relation to the father, not the mother. The tone of rebuke and repudiation which always accompanied the oft-repeated expression, "What have I to do with you, ye sons of Zeruiah," may have applied to the mother as well as to the sons. The implication may have been that if the sons were bad, it was because they were the offspring of their mother. This form of address may also have had the unconscious purpose of depriving them of a father, making them illegitimate, as legend had made David himself. Thus he would be expressing hostility toward a mother figure. And indeed Zeruiah must have been considerably older than David, since her sons are his close contemporaries.

The Battle with Goliath

The next important events in the life of David are his meeting with King Saul and his battle with the Philistine giant, Goliath. David first appears before Saul in the role of the skilled player upon the harp, who comforts the melancholy king. Later he becomes the challenger of Goliath. When Saul expresses apprehension about the young man's ability to meet the seasoned warrior in single combat, David reassures the king. There is an ingenuous quality in the way the youth describes how he was accustomed to defending his sheep from marauding animals such as the lion and the bear, killing them with his bare hands. One wonders why David did not use his sling in such situations, a tool with which he was very adept, as we know. It certainly would have been a more realistic approach. It seems more logical to assume that such deeds were fantasies and that David imagined himself saying these rather boastful words to the king rather than actually doing so.

It is interesting to consider the content of this fantasy. Psychoanalytically, the intruding lion or bear could represent the threatening father. We know how often similar fantasies occupy the minds of little boys in the oedipal period, and how the overcoming of such dangers represents the imaginary, heroic conquest of the father.

The need to free himself from the father and to function as an independent human being may be seen in David's refusal to use the personal armour and sword of the king, which Saul offered him. David may have wished to be unhampered, not only by the oversized, heavy accoutrements of metal, but by the feeling of strong identification with Saul that might have accompanied the wearing of the king's apparel.

The young shepherd however quickly and repeatedly expressed the feeling that his strength and confidence came from faith in God, declaring, "The Lord that delivered me out of the paw of the lion and out of the paw of the bear, He will deliver me out of the hand of this Philistine (17:37)." He approaches Goliath with the words, "Thou comest to me with a sword, and with a spear, and with a javelin; but I come to thee in the name of the Lord of hosts, the God of the armies of Israel, whom thou hast taunted." He concludes with the confident pronouncement, ". . . for the battle is the Lord's and he will give you into our hand (17:45)." The use of the plural pronoun emphasizes that he was fighting as a representative of Israel rather than as a hero in his own right, just as he was entering the combat in the Name of God rather than for his own glory.

David's need to repress more narcissistic motives of self-glorification is of interest here. That such motives did exist, as they would for any healthy personality, were indicated earlier when he inquired what the rewards for such a conquest would be. But David's zeal to fight and destroy this enemy of his people must have been stimulated also by an unconscious need to over-come the projected hostile father. However, he was able to ac-complish this act of aggression only by idealizing his motive and fighting in behalf of the *Good Father* and his people, Israel.

Only by viewing David's first great conquest from the aspect of its possible psychoanalytic significance can we try to get some meaning from several puzzling and rather confused statements in the biblical text dealing with this incident. In fact, certain ob-scurities of the text throughout the narratives concerned with the story of David are of special interest from a psychological viewpoint. They are of frequent occurrence and their analysis discloses a significant relationship between the content and the form. In situations where subject matter of a conflictful or em-barrassing nature is involved, the meaning of the text becomes confused, vague, or metaphorical, at times characterized by a curious *non-sequitor* quality. We have noted this aspect of the biblical literature in the earlier studies presented here, but the narratives of David reveal it with particular significance.

Returning to the specific situation under discussion, the Bible relates that David hurled a stone from his sling which struck the Philistine in the forehead and killed him. Since the enemy was already dead, what was David's need to run forward, draw the giant's sword from its sheath and cut off Goliath's head? Such a triumphant gesture of victory when dealing with an enemy chief-tan was not unusual in those days. But when this gruesome act is carried out by a ruddy-cheeked shepherd boy, fresh from his father's farm, it seems to take on an added emphasis. It is clearly an act of symbolic castration.

Such an interpretation would help to clarify the puzzling statement that David took the head of Goliath and brought it to Jerusalem. Now this city was still a Canaanite stronghold, in the hands of the Jebusites. It is difficult to accept on a reality level that David left the scene of conquest and traveled over fifteen miles to bring the bloody trophy to a fortified hostile town. Furthermore, we are informed almost immediately after this, that Abner, the captain of Saul's guard, brought David, holding the head of the Philistine in his hand, into the presence of the king. Even as traditions from different sources, they must still have some meaning.

Perhaps this interesting contradiction can be understood on a symbolic level since it really makes no sense otherwise. Let us assume that the statement of David's bringing the head to Jerusalem represents a *wish* rather than an actual deed. The youthful hero would have liked to present the symbol of his triumph to the mother. The significance of a city as a mother symbol is utilized a number of times in the narratives about David, as we shall see later. Jerusalem is still a captive city, held by an alien, or hostile father. David kills the *bad* father, Goliath, and lays the sign of his triumph in the lap of the mother, as if to promise that she would one day be freed, a feat which he actually accomplishes when he becomes king.

It is not hard to imagine that the fortress of the Jebusites, this city pituresquely but forbiddingly situated on the mountain tops, so near to his own Bethlehem, may have aroused the youth's imagination as he tended his sheep on the hillsides. Perhaps he dreamed of some day conquering this fortress for Israel. If Goliath represented the evil father, then the Jebusites, who also defied the *Living God* must have been in the same category. The oedipal implications of this gesture seem clear. David wanted to overcome the bad father and *rescue* the mother. Not only a city but the entire land of Israel must have become a mother symbol for David. And he did indeed spend a large part of his life rescuing this mother-land from the enemy.

What might be the meaning of the seemingly contradictory detail, his coming to Saul with the head of the giant? This does not appear to have been a voluntary act. The text says, "And as David returned from the slaughter of the Philistine, Abner took him, and brought him before Saul with the head of the Philistine in his hand."

David here brings the proof of his victory to the father instead of the mother, but does so under the force of circumstance.

This second account probably represents what actually took place. Symbolically, the oedipal wish for the mother gives way to a relationship with the father under the necessity of reality. Presenting the head to Saul, however, was not only an act of homage but one of triumph as well.

Another detail interests us here. We are informed that David put Goliath's armour into his own tent. He had refused such apparel from the good father, Saul. Surely the armour of Goliath would fit him even less than that of the king. Why then did he wish to keep the battle-dress of the champion? Having killed the wicked father, David may have wished to identify with his former strength, as represented by the armour, a concept having its roots in ideas of primitive magic.

It is also possible that David's refusal to wear Saul's armour was based on the unconscious feeling that to do so was equivalent to displacing Saul and thus annihilating him. This David could not do with a *good* father but had no such scruples concerning Goliath.

This story of the slaying of the Philistine giant, while it may well have a reality basis, can also be understood as a rather typical myth dealing with David's coming of age. Overcoming Goliath represents the successful test of David's manhood, similar to ordeals of puberty rites. The elaboration of reality to mythlike proportions is a familiar process.

The Period of Exile

After this victory, David leaves his father's home and becomes a member of the king's household. The growing tension which developed between David and Saul, as described in connection with a study of the latter, will be referred to here only as it touches upon the personality of David. He is clearly the object of the king's alternate moods of jealousy and rage on the one hand, and his consequent feelings of guilt, with efforts at restitution on the other. But can it truly be said that David was a completely passive object in this situation? The very fact that he remained upon the scene and continued to be successful in battle showed that he did not withdraw from competition with Saul even at the risk of the latter's displeasure.

But David was not happy about his struggle with Saul. He longed for a reconciliation and did not leave the court permanently until he was convinced that the king was determined to take his life.

David's feelings for Saul must have been complex, embodying elements of transference from his own father. His difficulty in perceiving the full extent of the king's hostility indicates a conflict here. David evidently wished to view Saul as a *good* father and therefore repressed some awareness of the reality situation. The intensity of his feeling is expressed in the plea he makes to Jonathan to intercede with Saul for him.

A significant aspect of David's attitude toward Saul comes out dramatically when the youth finally does flee from the king and lives as an outlaw in the wilderness of Judea. Saul pursues him with the intent to destroy this rival. But it is the king himself who is trapped by David, as will be recalled. On two occasions, the hunted outlaw spares his monarch's life, declaring that none should dare to harm the Lord's anointed. Father, king, God, these concepts must have been closely associated in David's mind and served to make Saul an object of reverence. On one of the times referred to above, David cries out to the contrite, departing ruler, "After whom is the king of Israel come out? . . . after a dead dog, after a flea (24:15)."

This self-belitting may indicate a momentary turning against himself of the aggression withheld from Saul. Though not a characteristic gesture, it gives a fleeting revelation of how the small child, the eighth son of Jesse, may have experienced the powerful father. It is significant, however, that these deprecatory comments about himself were made on an occasion when David was in a position of strength and behaving with magnanimity toward his rival. He was, in effect, saying that even *a dead dog, a flea,* could behave more generously than the king himself.

David's need to have faith in father figures is shown when he turns to such people for help. First there was Samuel himself to whom David fled when he first feared that his life was endangered by Saul's anger. On his next and final flight from the camp of Saul, David stopped at the village of Nob. There he received assistance from the head priest, Ahimelech, who met him in fear and trembling, wondering why this important figure from the court of Saul came alone, in need of food and a weapon. David withholds the truth, telling Ahimelech that he is on a secret mission for the king and that his followers are awaiting him at a certain destination. We do not know what prompted this falsification. David may have wished to protect the priest from conscious involvement. In accordance with his own standards of justice, he may have felt that Ahimelech could not be held liable if he aided an enemy of Saul unknowingly.

David asks the priest for a weapon and is told that the only one available is the sword of Goliath. It is wrapped in a cloth and hidden behind the ephod. If David wished that, he could take it. David answers, "There is none like that; give it me (21:10)."

Biblical commentators have been puzzled by an aspect of this situation as well they might be. What was the sword of Goliath doing in the house of the head priest? Why was it kept in this peculiar place?

Ephod is a word used somewhat ambiguously in the Bible. A number of references are made to its use as an article of clothing. Thus, the young Samuel was "girded with a linen ephod" (2:18) and David, in the days of his kingship, was so attired when he danced before the Ark (II,6:14). The priests of Nob wore linen ephods at the time of their brutal murder, by Doeg, the Edomite, according to the story (22:18). The most elaborate description of an ephod is found in *Exodus: 28*, where it is part of the costume of the high priest. There it is worn over a long robe, upon the upper part of the body, with the breastplate containing the twelve stones representing the twelve tribes of Israel, resting upon it. Concealed somewhere within the ephod were the Urim and Thummim, thus kept close to the heart of the wearer. These objects, probably small stones, were used by the priest for the casting of lots to determine the will of God on certain occasions, often in response to a request by the king to "bring the ephod." Another, seemingly unrelated usage of this term is in reference to a graven image used in cultic fertility rites, a Canaanite practice but occasionally indulged in by some of the people of Israel in early times (Judg. 17:5). There it expresses the primitive concept of phallic worship.

The sword of Goliath hidden behind the ephod, suggests symbolic meanings. Realistically there would be no reason for this object to be kept in such a sacred place. Interpreted as one might an element in a dream, the juxtaposition of the sword, a powerful phallic symbol, and the ephod, associated first with phallic worship and then with the attire of those consecrated to the worship of God, suggests a sublimation of sexual and aggressive energy, a process essential in the development of religion.

In relation to David, the sword behind the ephod recalls the mood and spirit of the young champion who slew the Philistine in the Name of the God of Israel, thus diverting his personal aggression to a greater cause.

At the time of the combat no mention was made regarding the disposal of the sword although we were told that David put the armour of Goliath into his tent. The omission of this significant detail in the text may represent a repression on the part of David. Perhaps he could not then have accepted the symbolic powerful phallus of the slain giant. Ostensibly he had accomplished his heroic deed for a higher motive than personal glory. To have taken the sword of Goliath for himself on this occasion would have been an act of blatant narcissism, an acting out of the very impulses which he had the greatest need to repress and to sublimate, his competitive, aggressive feelings toward a father figure.

We can assume too that he did not wish to give the sword to Saul, for this gesture might have implied a more submissive role than David could accept. The problem may have presented an insoluble dilemma and so was repressed. Commentators have suggested that the sword may have been given into the priest's keeping as a valuable memento of a victory that had been won in God's Name. Only after he had declared his independence from the father by leaving Saul, could David appropriate the sword that had belonged to a father figure.

The hiding of the weapon behind the ephod may symbolize David's attitude toward aggression. Such feelings could rightfully be employed only at the behest of the superego, as represented by the ephod in the house of a priest. Significantly, even though Ahimelech tells him to *take* the sword, David says, "*Give* it me."

Thus we find him at a crossroads in his life, alone, uncertain about the next step, but fortified by the sword of Goliath in his hand. It seems however that he was not altogether free of the need for protection by a father figure in this hour of crisis. The one he turns to now seems a rather bizarre choice. David flees to Achish, king of the Philistine city of Gath. When he appears at the palace gates he is immediately recognized by the guards, who exclaim, "Is not this David, the king of the land? Did they not sing one to another of him in dances, saying: 'Saul hath slain his thousands, And David his ten thousands (21:12)?'" Interestingly, they interpret this verse as a sign that David has already displaced Saul as king.

It is at this moment that David becomes "sore afraid of Achish, the king of Gath." One wonders what David had actually hoped for or expected. An unknown stranger without a following could only have been an object of suspicion and placed himself in danger. Yet upon being recognized, David was afraid to acknowledge his identity.

The question that intrigues us here is why David should have chosen an enemy of Israel for the purpose of refuge in the first place. We are not told what motives, thoughts, or feelings prompted this hurried, solitary flight to a hostile city. There is only the cryptic statement, "And David arose, and fled that day for fear of Saul, and went to Achish, the king of Gath." Was it perhaps his intention to become a soldier of fortune under the banner of the heathen king? If so, his fame as a warrior would have stood him in good stead. Yet it was at the very moment when his identity was revealed that he froze with fear.

The familiar words of acclaim with which he was greeted

were the cause of his anxiety. The text makes this plain. It says, "And David laid up these words in his heart, and was sore afraid of Achish, the king of Gath." But we are not enlightened as to why this form of greeting affected David as it did. These were indeed the very words which had once roused Saul's jealous rage. In this moment of insecurity, David may have feared a similar response from another hostile king and therefore was unable to declare his identity boldly as he may have planned to do.

In an effort to understand this situation more fully, let us return to the problem of what might have motivated David's flight to Gath. We will assume that unconscious forces played a role in this action. When David left the village of Nob, just north of Jerusalem, he had to decide where to seek safety from Saul's anger. The weapon he carried must have recalled vividly his first great triumph. On that occasion, at least in fantasy, David had turned to the mother-city, Jerusalem, with the head of Goliath in his hand. Now he turns to Gath, the home of Goliath, the mother-city of the Philistines, with the sword of the defeated champion in his hand. What were his thoughts, his feelings, at this moment?

One can only conjecture. In this hour of severe emotional stress was David returning in fantasy to an earlier period, the time of his first triumph? Was he now acting out compulsively what had before been only a fantasy—the wish to *take possession* of the city owned by the hostile father, with the very sword taken from the father? At the same time, in the ambivalent fashion of unconscious conflict, did he wish to offer himself as a soldier to the king, to fight for Achish as he had fought for Saul? In reality, had he not brought the head of the Philistine, under the direction of Abner, to Saul himself? Should he not now therefore present the sword of Goliath to Achish? Perhaps this latter act was to serve as atonement for the unconscious fantasy that must have preceded it.

David's final rejection by Saul may have aroused childhood feelings of terror and abandonment, increased no doubt by rage at the injustice he had suffered. David may have temporarily lost the capacity to think and behave rationally. When he is greeted at the palace, not only with the song associated with the trauma of

Saul's displeasure but is hailed as the king of Israel, which put him in the place of Saul, the status he so much wanted yet dreaded, David is overwhelmed with guilt and terror.

The Bible says that he feigned madness at this point, to get out of his dilemma. This was a condition which his mingled feelings may well have approximated at the moment.

It is both daring and difficult to fill in the meager outline of this episode in the text with the material as presented here, even though done conjecturally. However, the completed picture does fit psychologically into the framework, which becomes understandable on this basis. The adventure ends favorably for David. The annoyed Achish has him thrown out with the words, "Lo, when you see a man that is mad, wherefore do ye bring him to me? Do I lack madmen, that you have brought this fellow to play the madman in my presence? Shall this fellow come into my house (21:15–16)?"

The description of David's simulated insanity is interesting. The text says, ". . . he scrabbled on the doors of the gate, and let his spittle fall down upon his beard." Scratching on the gate and drooling describe the behavior of an infant who wants to be taken up by the mother and fed. Such a person is hardly a threat to another man. One might say that David was seeking to escape from an intended oedipal aggression by returning to infancy so that he could not be held responsible.

That Achish and the city of Gath had some special significance for David is clear, for he came back to this town at a later period when he had an established following. He was then received as an ally. That time, also, he came at a moment of despair, when the hope of finding escape from the pursuit of Saul was again at a low ebb.

On this latter occasion David suggested that he have his headquarters in Ziklag, a town to the south, adding, ". . . for why should thy servant dwell in the royal city with thee (27:5)?" To occupy a royal-city with a father-king may have been too threatening for the outlaw from the court of Saul.

David's behavior toward Achish at that time indicates clearly what his real feelings were. He and his men went out regularly on raids to the south, supposedly against tribes of his own people, thereby serving the Philistine lord. Actually, he made these forays against the enemies of Israel and went to the extreme measure of completely annihilating the communities involved so there would be no one left who could bring the true tidings to Achish.

On one occasion David was asked by Achish to participate in a campaign against Israel. The Hebrew's reply has a non-committal note as he accepts this invitation. He says, "Therefore shalt thou know what thy servant will do (28:2)." Fortunately the other Philistine lords object to David's presence and he is sent back to Ziklag. Some biblical commentators have speculated about what David would have done, had he been forced to take part in the actual fighting. There is every reason to believe that he would not have fought against his own people. We know in whose behalf he carried on those secret raids while living under the protection of Achish. It was not likely that he would suddenly change his tactics.

It is significant, however, that David allowed himself to get into this kind of situation. Unconsciously he may have invited it in some manner. One wonders if he had a need to ally himself with a father toward whom he could express ambivalent feelings, friendly on the surface but hostile in reality.

In the later days of David's rule as king of Israel, he actually did conquer the city of Gath itself. This event is recorded in the two separate narratives of the biblical text which deal with the period. In *First Chronicles,* the statement is made that "David took Gath and her towns out of the hand of the Philistines (18:1)."

Gath was literally known as the *mother-city.* Smaller communities surrounded her and were subject to her authority. One biblical commentary remarks in regard to this situation that "the metaphor of the 'mother-city' is employed there, for the word referring to the surrounding *towns* literally means *daughters.*"[10]

Second Samuel, which is regarded as the earlier and more authentic source for this period of history, refers to the same episode by stating, "And after this it came to pass, that David smote the Philistines, and subdued them; and David took *Metheg-ammah* out of the hand of the Philistines (8:1)."

The word, *Metheg-ammah,* is considered a corrupt form. It is not used at any other time. The name means *bridle of the mother* and is believed to refer to the mother-city, Gath.

The use of this unusual word in place of the commonly known name of the city is puzzling. It could be understood however as a further elaboration of the mother symbol, a disguise which would be needed if the statement means that David took the *bridle of the mother* out of the hand of the Philistines, that is, took possession of the oedipal mother.

There is considerable evidence therefore pointing to the fact that Gath had meaning for David on the level of unconscious content. It should not be surprising that in a culture such as that of the ancient Hebrews, where the oedipal conflict was so strongly repressed, material of this kind should "ooze out from every pore," as Freud describes the tendency of the repressed.

The years of David's outlawry are marked by dramatic adventures. His life and the lives of his followers are made uneasy by the sporadic pursuits of Saul. In the intervals, David helps to protect the property of Hebrew shepherds and farmers from marauding tribes. On occasion, he comes to the aid of a community threatened by the Philistines.

David could not have found this kind of existence a satisfying one, judging by the bitterness with which he reproached Saul at the time when the two are so dramatically brought together. This is the only occasion, however, when David allows himself expression of such feelings. Although his situation was not brought about through any wrongdoing on his part, David did not indulge in self-pity or declaim against the injustice he was suffering. One wonders what philosophy or fortitude of spirit enabled him to accept this hard life so realistically. Perhaps it was his faith that the destiny predicted for him by Samuel would surely come to pass.

David, as King and Father

The next important period in David's history is that of his kingship, a role which he held for forty years, according to the biblical chronology. It was ushered in by the death of Saul and his sons at Mount Gilboa, a tragedy which David laments in the beautiful and moving poem in *Second Samuel,* attributed to his authorship (1:17–27).

His first years of rule are over the southern tribes only, with headquarters at Hebron, while the son of Jonathan, Ish-boseth, maintains the northern kingdom with the help of Abner, the captain of his host.

After seven years both Abner and Ish-boseth suffer violent deaths. The northern kingdom is then offered to David by the elders of Israel. The twelve tribes are now united. From this point begins one of the brightest periods in Jewish history in terms of the unity, strength, and power of the monarchy. David captures Jerusalem and makes it his capital city. He drives out the Philistines, extends the boundaries of his kingdom, and makes the people of Israel into a strong nation.

This second ruler of Israel lived much more regally than his predecessor had done. David built himself a fine palace on the hilltop. He took unto himself more wives and concubines and became the father of many sons.

It is in his role as a father that David reveals the most conflictual aspect of his personality. His relationship to his sons is marked by indulgence to their wishes, a lack of restraining discipline, and a surprising unawareness of their real character qualities.

When Amnon, his oldest son, was pining away because of a secret desire for his half-sister, Tamar, David yielded to a plea that the lovely young girl should come to Amnon's apartment and prepare food to tempt his appetite. This seems like a harmless indulgence to a sick youth. Yet if David had known his son and understood the weakness of his character, he would not have exposed both his children to such a dangerous situation. It is true that the whole shocking plot of Tamar's rape was instigated by another. It was Jonadab, Amnon's friend and cousin, the son of David's brother, Shimeah, who suggested to the lovesick youth the scheme of getting Tamar to Amnon's quarters.

The story as told in the text is a moving one (II, 13:1–22).

As Amnon makes his intentions clear, Tamar pleads piteously that her brother should not do such a wanton deed. If only he would ask their father, the king would not withhold her from him. Evidently marriage between a brother and half-sister was possible, especially as a royal prerogative. But Amnon would not be deterred. He takes her by force.

What follows is of special psychological interest. The text says,

> Then Amnon hated her with exceeding great hatred; for the hatred wherewith he hated her was greater than the love wherewith he had loved her. And Amnon said unto her: "Arise, be gone." And she said unto him: "Not so, because this great wrong in putting me forth is worse than the other that thou didst unto me." But he would not hearken unto her. Then he called his servant that ministered unto him, and said: "Put now this woman out from me, and bolt the door after her." Now she had a garment of many colors upon her; for with such robes were the king's daughters that were virgins apparelled. And his servant brought her out and bolted the door after her. And Tamar put ashes on her head, and rent her garment of many colors that was on her: and she laid her hand on her head, and went her way, crying aloud as she went (II, 13:15–19).

Why should Amnon's love have turned to hatred so quickly? It must have been a hatred born of shame and guilt. Her very presence was no longer tolerable to him because it was her person that had tempted him, although innocently, to a deed which he himself must have despised. The hatred he felt against himself was defensively turned against her. The victim tends to become hateful in the eyes of the aggressor.

Her brother Absalom, whose full sister she is, meets her on the way and perceives at once what must have taken place. He comforts her and takes her to his home. The text says, "So Tamar remained desolate in her brother Absalom's house. But when king David heard of all these things, he was very wroth. And Absalom spoke unto Amnon neither good nor bad; for

Absalom hated Amnon, because he had forced his sister Tamar (II, 13:20–22)."

Although David was *very wroth,* there is no indication that he did anything either to punish Amnon or to force him to right matters through marriage. Evidently the alternative for her was a life of seclusion and loneliness. We never hear of her again.

It is significant that in this story of sexual misdemeanor, there are no obscurities or evasions in the free flow of the narrative. Indeed, the style lends itself to the mood of the content with great artistry. Amnon has obviously committed a serious wrong that meets with open disapproval and later punishment. No need for denial or repression is therefore necessary.

It seems strange that Tamar did not flee to David and pour out to him the story of the wrong she had suffered. Would not a father who had shown solicitude and kindliness for Amnon be responsive to such a wanton hurt as she had suffered? The fact that Tamar did not seek David out at once, that he apparently heard of her plight only indirectly, shows there was not a close relationship between them. It does not seem to have occurred to Tamar to ask her father for help. Neither does Absalom go to David with the story. He holds his peace. Clearly he feels that he must take vengeance into his own hands. His behavior here indicates that Absalom is one who can bide his time, a man who can contain both his temper and a grudge until the right moment is at hand.

It is interesting that when Absalom sees Tamar he knows exactly what has happened without being told. If Absalom knew Amnon so well, why was David so unaware of what might happen if he sent Tamar to minister to his oldest son?

This occurrence reveals clearly that all was not as it should be between David and his children. Amnon is weak and undisciplined; if he cannot have what he wants, he gives way to illness. He yields to temptation but does not have the strength of character to make amends. Tamar, after a brief effort, gives in to her fate. She does not have the courage to fight her battle.

Absalom shows a lack of confidence in his father and takes matters into his own hands. This violation of the king's daughter is the prelude to a discord that continues to be revealed in David's life as a father.

There are those who point out that Amnon did only as David himself had done when the latter took Bathsheba. The son merely followed the example of the father. Let us see if this particular analogy is very convincing.

Both acts do represent a yielding to sexual temptation in ways that involved the breaking of social and moral codes. But there were certain differences in terms of the interpersonal relationships. There is no clear indication that David had to use violence with Bathsheba. The text does say, "And David sent messengers and *took* her. But it adds, ". . . and she came in unto him and he lay with her; for she was purified from her uncleanness; and she returned unto her house (II, 11:4)." We get an impression here that Bathsheba acted on her own volition, once she was brought into the presence of David. The tone and description of this meeting is quite different from that of Amnon and Tamar. Certainly the subsequent fate of the two women was also very different.

Amnon's punishment came two years later. At the time of the sheepshearing, Absalom made a feast, some distance from Jerusalem, to which he invited all his brothers. He had to have David's permission for this event. Here the father does have considerable compunction about entrusting the wily Absalom with the safety of his brothers and tries to dissuade him from the plan. Absalom had politely worded the invitation to include the king himself but David withdraws, saying, "Nay, my son, let us not all go lest we be burdensome unto thee." Then Absalom specifically asks that Amnon be permitted to go, together with the others. David again tries to put him off, saying, "Why should he go with thee (II, 13:25–26)?" But the king evidently finds it hard to say *no* to any of his sons and allows himself to be persuaded.

When the unsuspecting Amnon was heavy with wine, the servants of Absalom fell upon him and killed him. The first wild rumours that reached the palace were that all the king's sons had been killed by Absalom. But Jonadab, David's nephew, reassured the anxious father, saying, "Let not my lord suppose that they have killed all the young men, the king's sons; for Amnon only is dead; for by the appointment of Absalom this hath been determined from the day that he forced his sister Tamar (II, 13:32)."

If Jonadab knew that this sequel to Amnon's deed was inevitable, why didn't David understand as much? His uneasiness at allowing Amnon to go to the feast attests to unconscious awareness on his part which, however, was unable to prevent a realistic handling of the situation. It may well be that David had to repress an awareness of hostility in his sons. He may have had a strong need not to see their potentiality for hatred and aggresiveness. This repression on David's part may have served as a defense against the awareness of his own hostility both as a father and a son.

As we have seen, David always longed for a loving and protective father. He had a need to seek out such figures and to deny the reality of aggression in father figures. If this was so, then his own ego ideal would demand that he himself be without hostility in this role. Such a defensive need may explain, in part, David's inability to be firm with his sons or to see in them what he dared not see within himself.

David's sensitivity to aggressiveness in the father-son relationship must have been a consequence of his childhood situation. As we have noted earlier, his relationship with Jesse is treated very meagerly in the biblical text. However, tradition does idealize Jesse considerably. He is known especially as a very righteous man. In our other studies we have observed that such righteousness is often expressive of a severe superego and is accompanied by ambivalence towards sons. Legend generally represents unconscious or symbolic aspects of personality, so we should not consider it insignificant that Jesse's righteousness is stressed in such stories regarding him.

It is likely that David did not dare to see or experience this hidden aggression in his father. We recall the youth's apparently contented acceptance of his boyhood duties and how he tried to be a good shepherd, protecting his charges from danger. It seems that even then he was acting out his idealized image of the good father and repressing any awareness of a possible lack of love in Jesse.

David's development in terms of physical courage and championship in war may have been determined in large part by his need to overcome the hidden feelings of inferiority brought about by a lowered sense of self-esteem resulting from this parental rejection. But his unconscious guilt in becoming greater than his father and all his older brothers must also have had a share in David's inability to deal firmly with his sons. Thus, his role of the permissive father was probably based in large measure upon an ambivalent relationship with his sons, growing out of his own ambivalence.

There are indications that David succeeded in bolstering his ego strength by identification with an Idealized Father, who was both loving and strong. That the king succeeded in life as brilliantly as he did might be explained not only on the basis of inherent capacities but also on the character of his defenses, which tended toward reaction formation and a considerable ability for sublimation.

However, David did suffer deeply from the consequences of his own shortcomings. Let us return to the event of Amnon's murder. Absalom did not dare to go back to Jerusalem after this act. He fled to the land of Geshur, whose king was his maternal grandfather.

The fact that Absalom fled is repeated three times, at the beginning of three short consecutive paragraphs. One wonders what the meaning of this repetition might be. It may indicate that this flight was more important to the king than the death of Amnon. And indeed we are clearly told that "the soul of king David failed with longing for Absalom; for he was comforted concerning Amnon, seeing he was dead (II, 13:39)." David was concerned with the living rather than with the dead. It is also quite likely that Absalom was closer to David's heart than Amnon had been. This would not be hard to understand.

Absalom was a man of great beauty, a point which the Bible stresses, declaring, "Now in all Israel there was none to be so much praised as Absalom for his beauty; from the sole of his foot even to the crown of his head there was no blemish in him (II, 14:25)," His famous hair, long and luxuriant, was one of his special attractions. But Absalom had more than beauty. He must have been a man of compelling strength and personality. While his character was far from commendable, he evidently had the power to influence many people and to acquire many followers.

Absalom remained in exile for three years. This must have been a sad period in David's life. What greater trauma can a father endure than the murder of one son by another? It is like having a part of one's self destroyed by another part.

David longed for Absalom but could not in all conscience bring him back. The fact that he missed him, however, is in itself significant. It indicates a forgiveness of the heart, if not of the mind, to express this dichotomy in popular terms.

It is Joab who comes to David's help in this plight. He was aware of the king's longing for his son and concocts a scheme to move David's heart to open forgiveness. The general found a *mother* and sent her to the king with a pitiful tale. She related how one of her sons had struck his brother and killed him. The family clan demanded that she turn the miscreant over to them for punishment by death. But the woman declared that losing her remaining son would only add to her bereavement for then none would be left to carry on the family name and heritage.

David was moved by her plea and declared that he would save her son. The woman then suggested that the king do the same in his own case and recall Absalom from exile. David at once suspected the source of this strategy. He yields and sends Joab to bring Absalom back. We see here how the *good mother* is used to intercede with the father for the fate of a son. This situation may not have been a new one in David's life.

However, the king still will not receive Absalom within the royal palace. They live in the same city for two years but do not meet. This situation is evidently very frustrating to Absalom. He sends for Joab and when the latter twice fails to heed his call, Absalom employs the drastic method of having his servants set fire to Joab's field of barley which is next to his own. Joab hurries over to find out the reason for the conflagration. We have an interesting glimpse here of the measures to which Absalom will resort in order to have his way.

The king's son complains to Joab that he would rather have remained in exile than to be in Jerusalem and not to be allowed to see the king face to face. So Joab goes to David again and arranges a meeting between them. Absalom bows low before the king and David kisses his son.

It is after this apparent reconciliation that Absalom begins to act out his rebellion against his father, culminating in his efforts to seize the throne. The prince tries to make an impression upon the people of Jerusalem by riding through the streets in a fine chariot drawn by horses, with fifty men running before him. Another of his devices was to get up early and stand by the side of the road leading to the gate of the palace. There he would intercept those who came from all parts of the land to seek the court of the king for the purpose of getting a judgment on their cases. Absalom would greet these Israelites warmly, inquire what tribe they belonged to, and assure them that if he were a judge he would do justice to their cause. He added however that it was too bad there was no one who would really listen to their complaint no matter how valid it might be. Then when the simple farmer or artisan would try to bow low before this gracious prince, Absalom would restrain him from the humble gesture and kiss him instead. In this way Absalom "stole the hearts of the men of Israel." We can see now why he was so eager to effect a reconciliation with the king. Otherwise he probably would have not been free to move about the city.

It seems strange that word of Absalom's activities did not reach David's ears. One can hardly steal away the hearts of many people in secrecy. It may be that David's attitude of not wishing to know prevented people from telling him. Or he may have dismissed the matter as of no importance.

Absalom's plan to usurp his father and seize the throne reached a full-sized rebellion. When the moment was ripe he asked David for permission to go to Hebron, his birthplace, and there fulfill a vow of sacrifice that he had made while in exile, should God ever bring him back to Jerusalem. The king immediately grants this reasonable and pious request, saying, "Go in peace."

Absalom had spies scattered throughout the land. At a given signal they were to announce that he had been anointed king in Hebron. Absalom also invited a large following from Jerusalem without disclosing his true purpose to many of them. Thus he depleted David's defensive strength in the city and at the same time added to his own force, for he no doubt hoped that many of these would follow him, once he had been declared king. Thus the revolt was on in full strength.

David's reaction to this event and his behavior during this entire period of trauma reveal important aspects of his personality. His first words on receiving news of the rebellion indicate a clear and unequivocal decision. He says, "Arise, and let us flee; for else none of us shall escape from Absalom; make speed to depart, lest he overtake us quickly, and bring down evil upon us, and smite the city with the edge of the sword (II, 15:14)."

This sounds like a panic reaction of a terrified man. He does not even pause to consult Joab, the captain of his host. This king of an empire which he had himself established, this experienced warrior, seemed to lose all courage in the present crisis. True, David was no longer young, but he had the doughty Joab and an army to defend the city. It was this same army which did defeat Absalom and his forces later. What the actual military situation was at the moment, how many men were available for defense at short notice, we are not told. Evidently this aspect was not important in David's decision or it would have been noted. The king's immediate impulse was to flee in order to save both himself and his beloved Jerusalem from bloodshed.

Part of this impulse to run away may have been based on the feeling that he did not know how much defection there was within the ranks. The walled city could easily be defended from an outside attack but there was no way of knowing how many within Jerusalem, and even within the palace itself were on Absalom's side. David evidently felt that he would be safer away from the city. Nor could he bear to see kinsmen shedding the blood of kinsmen within the streets of his beloved *city of peace*.

However, other factors of a more irrational nature must have influenced his decision. The king must have been overwhelmed with feelings of rejection when he heard the words of the messenger, "The hearts of the men of Israel are after Absalom (II, 15:13)." It was a betrayal of his deepest affections, his son and his people. This was a moment when David was too hurt to be able to fight back.

The note of urgency within him must have been so great that none tried to dissuade him. The text says, "And the king's servants said unto the king: 'Behold, thy servants are ready to do whatsoever my lord the king shall choose (II, 15:15).' "

David's first words to the effect that none would escape Absalom except by flight give a new and startling indication of the king's real awareness of the character of Absalom. In this moment of crisis, the king's repression in this area may have lifted suddenly and he must have seen Absalom's ruthless ambition clearly for the first time. But even this insight need not have been sufficient to create the mood of panic and submission which seemed to have seized the king. Let us look further.

Absalom was acting out the great crime of humanity. He was actually doing what others do only in fantasy and then repress. Here was a son who was trying to destroy and displace his father. This awful crime may have stirred up David's own repressed oedipal impulses along similar lines. The projection of these upon Absalom would have added to the king's apprehension. What Absalom was doing in reality, David must have struggled against doing even in fantasy all his life. Moreover, the guilt for these fantasied crimes must have weighed heavily upon the king. Unconsciously Absalom's revolt may have seemed like a justified punishment to David, who had dared to overcome such powerful fathers as Jesse and Saul and such powerful siblings as seven older brothers. Thus David's feelings of guilt must also have prepared the way for a masochistic submission to an unconscious need for punishment. The same feelings of guilt which kept David from an awareness of the true character of his sons, which prompted him to be an overly-indulgent father, may now have prevented him from fighting his own cause.

It may have been such oedipal factors which also added to the urgency with which he fled the mother-city, Jerusalem. He was no longer the king, the father, the possessor of the beloved woman. In what may have been a sudden reversal of the father-son role, identifications which must have long been shaky at best, David renounces his position in a gesture which seems truly bewildering on a conscious level.

We are told that he left his ten concubines behind him in the city *to keep the house*. This ambiguous expression may mean "to keep the household, or family" intact, while David was away. Did the king hope that the sight of his concubines would bring Absalom to his senses and remind him that he was in his father's house, whose women were the inviolate property of the king? If so, David was again using the comforting mechanism of denial by refusing to face the depravity of which Absalom was capable. On another level, David must have had an inner awareness of his son's potential for the disregard of moral standards. Leaving his concubines behind may have been another gesture of oedipal surrender to the conquering rival. He who overcomes the father is entitled to the females of the household. This act on David's part may thus indicate guilt and masochistic behavior. And indeed one of Absalom's first moves when he entered Jerusalem was to take possession of his father's concubines *in the sight of all Israel,* as a sign that he had dispossessed his father.

The story of David's flight from Jerusalem is a moving one. The text says,

> And David went up by the ascent of the mount of Olives, and wept as he went up; and he had his head covered, and went barefoot; and all the people that were with him covered every man his head, and they went up, weeping as they went up (II, 15:30).

David was leaving in grief rather than in anger.

A number of graphic experiences occurred on that sorrowful flight, lending further insight into David's character and the meaning that this event must have had for him. As if in miniature, one gets a glimpse here of the different emotions this man of many-sided personality inspired in others. First, there was the touching expression of loyalty on the part of Ittai, head of his bodyguard of six hundred men from Gath. David bids him return with his men to their own land for they are foreigners and not obligated to fight his battle when the outcome was so uncertain. But Ittai declares his undying devotion and refuses to leave. Then come the head priests and the Levites, carrying the Ark. David requests that they return the Ark to the city, saying that if God favored the king, he would bring David back to Jerusalem. If not, then he would have to endure what was in store for him. We see here how David places himself in the hands of God for judgment rather than relying on his own efforts. The crisis, then, is a spiritual one for David. At the same time, he does not altogether abandon realistic endeavors. He tells the two head priests to return to Jerusalem with their sons. The two younger men were to act as messengers and bring word to David of what was happening in the capital.

David clearly was not ready to give up entirely. Once he had left the city he seems to have rallied his inner resources to some degree. When told that one of his counsellors, Ahitophel, was among the conspirators, he cries out, "O Lord, I pray

Thee, turn the counsel of Ahitophel into foolishness (II, 15:31)."
At this point he meets one of his advisers, Hushai, who comes to
him with his coat torn and earth upon his head, as a mourner.
David tells him to return to Jerusalem and pretend to be on
the side of Absalom. He would then have an opportunity to
defeat the counsel of Ahitophel. Thus we see that David is still
able to think and to plan.

The situation of this sad pilgrimage is ripe for tragi-comedy.
It is used not only for the expression of pathos, of loyalty and
courage, but also by the self-seekers and the revilers. A person
by the name of Ziba appears, a servant of Mephi-boseth, the
son of Jonathan whom David had befriended. He comes with
donkeys laden with food and drink for the weary travelers.
When the king inquires for Mephi-boseth, the wily Ziba maligns
his master, reporting that the latter was tarrying in Jerusalem,
for he had declared, "Today will the house of Israel restore me
the kingdom of my father (II, 16:3)." David then grants to
Ziba all his master's lands and possessions.

Why is David so ready to believe this treachery on the
part of one who had sat at his table and been as one of his
own sons? If one son could betray, why not another? David
may not have been too averse to such deception on the part of a
grandson of Saul. The basis for such a conjecture is the fact
that when David learns what is apparently the truth, instead
of punishing Ziba for his offense, he merely divides the property
between the two and impatiently dismisses the whole matter.

The climax of David's fall from power is dramatized in another incident that occurs on this journey. As the procession
continued in a north-easterly direction toward the Jordan Valley
and the wilderness of Judea, a man named Shimei, of the house
of Saul, came toward them. He ran along a parallel ridge of
land and as he ran he shouted curses and cast stones at David
and his followers, crying

> "Begone, begone, thou man of blood, and base fellow; the
> Lord hath returned upon thee all the blood of the house of
> Saul, in whose stead thou has reigned; and the Lord hath
> delivered the kingdom into the hand of Absalom thy son;

and, behold, thou art taken in thine own mischief, because thou art a man of blood."

Then said Abishai the son of Zeruiah unto the king: "Why should this dead dog curse my lord the king? Let me go over, I pray thee, and take off his head." And the king said: "What have I to do with you, ye sons of Zeruiah? So let him curse, because the Lord hath said unto him: Curse David; who then shall say: Wherefore hast thou done so? And David said to Abishai and to all his servants: "Behold, my son, who came forth of my body, seeketh my life; how much more this Benjamite now? let him alone, and let him curse; for the Lord hath bidden him. It may be that the Lord will look on mine eye, and that the Lord will requite me good for his cursing of me this day (II, 16:7-12)."

Here David reveals clearly the depths of his masochistic guilt and the need for punishment. Shimei becomes the instrument of God's displeasure. Perhaps if David endures this punishment, if he pays through suffering, God will have mercy upon him.

When David and his party reach Mahanaim, a town east of the Jordan, they are met by friends and treated with hospitality and kindness. At this place of refuge David rests and organizes his forces. His foresight in sending Hushai back to Jerusalem to confound the counsels of Ahitophel works out in David's favor. Absalom chooses the plan of delayed action and thus provides time for the army of the king to prepare for battle.

David wishes to accompany his men to war but is dissuaded by them and remains within the walled city. As the company leaves David commands his three generals, Joab, Abishai, and Ittai, to deal gently with Absalom for his father's sake.

The graphic story of this battle in the forest and the fate that Absalom suffered is a well-known Sunday school narrative. The forces of David decisively defeated the army of Absalom. Then the son of the king chanced to ride into the presence of David's men. He was mounted on his mule and as the animal went under the thick boughs of a terebinth, probably an oak tree, his head with its heavy hair was caught in the branches.

The mule went on and the man was left hanging helplessly in the tree. One of David's men saw him and brought word of it to Joab. The general demanded why he did not kill Absalom, saying that the reward would have been ten pieces of silver. But the man declared that not for a thousand pieces of silver would he have put forth his hand against the king's son; for he had heard the king's charge that they were to deal gently with Absalom. Joab however, took three darts and shot them through the heart of Absalom. Then the men took down his body and buried him in a pit in the forest and piled a heap of stones over him.

Word of the victory is brought to David but his first reaction is to ask how it was with Absalom. His behavior on hearing the news is vividly described in the biblical narrative.

> . . . the king was much moved, and went up to the chamber over the gate, and as he went, thus he said, "O my son Absalom, my son, my son Absalom! would that I had died for thee, O Absalom, my son, my son!"
>
> And it was told Joab: "Behold, the king weepeth and mourneth for Absalom." And the victory that day was turned into mourning unto all the people; for the people heard say that day: "The king grieveth for his son." And the people got them by stealth that day into the city, as people that are ashamed steal away when they flee in battle. And the king covered his face, and the king cried with a loud voice, "O my son Absalom, O Absalom, my son, my son!"
>
> And Joab came into the house to the king and said: "Thou hast shamed this day the faces of all thy servants, who this day have saved thy life, and the lives of thy sons and of thy daughters, and the lives of thy wives, and the lives of thy concubines; in that thou lovest them that hate thee, and hatest them that love thee. For thou hast declared this day, that princes and servants are nought unto thee; for this day I perceive, that if Absalom had lived, and all we had died this day, then it had pleased thee well. Now therefore arise, go forth, and speak to the heart of thy servants; for I swear by the Lord, if thou go not forth, there will not tarry a man with thee this night; and that will be worse unto thee than all the

evil that hath befallen thee from thy youth until now." Then the king arose, and sat in the gate. And they told unto all the people, saying, "Behold, the king doth sit in the gate"; and all the people came before the king (II, 19:1–9).

Here we have the dramatic climax of David's relationship with his son Absalom. The expression of his grief reaches an intensity of emotion that is not equalled anywhere else in this man's rich and varied experience. This particular son must indeed have meant a great deal to David. For we recall that after the death of Amnon, David mourned but was soon comforted.

A father's grief over the death of a son is to be expected. And we cannot doubt that David, in large measure, had capacity for true object love. But the quality of his emotion, particularly under the circumstances, and in view of his tendency to accept death philosophically, indicates an element of over-reaction. It takes strong words on Joab's part to bring the grief-stricken king to his senses and force him to behave realistically.

It is interesting that David does not rebuke Joab for the latter's deliberate disobedience. Yet on other occasions David had not hesitated to repudiate acts by his general. David may have felt so overwhelmed by the finality of what had taken place and by the authoritative action of Joab that he could not express his anger. This unexpressed rage may have found an outlet in the intensity of his mourning, a masochistic turning of his aggression against himself.

What was the source of David's attachment for Absalom? The father did not doubt that this son would have killed him had the occasion arisen. Indeed, when Absalom plans the campaign, and Ahitophel counsels that David should be pursued at once and destroyed, Absalom quickly agrees. There seems to be no compunction about such a deed on his part. His change of plan occurs because he apparently is convinced that the counter-advice of Hushai for a delayed action would be more to his advantage.

David's mournful plaint, "Would that I had died for thee, O Absalom, my son," seems to denote a strong identification with the slain youth. A part of David really must have died that day.

On the basis of what we have seen of David's unconscious dynamics, we can guess at the significance which his son Absalom had for him. Here was a man of great strength and beauty, of resolute and ruthless character, who was able to carry out in bold action the unconscious fantasy of every man—to dispossess the father and take his place. Such a fantasy, as suggested before, must have been especially strong with David, but with him as with normal man everywhere, the superego was equally strong, and defensive measures, active. Absalom may have represented for David a projection of his own oedipal aggression, carrying out in action his unconscious wishes. It is known that delinquent children frequently act out the unconscious fantasies of their parents. David's grief therefore may have been intensified by guilt. He not only lost a portion of himself; he had unconsciously helped to bring about Absalom's fate by the nature of his relationship with his son. The latter's revolt and punishment was an accusation against David, proof of his failure as a father.

David's sense of guilt at becoming so much greater than his father and brothers, and in overcoming Saul and Jonathan, must have been reactivated by his strong identification with Absalom. Was he not as guilty as his son? Had he not usurped both Jesse and Saul? Had he not thus, in a sense, also been guilty of patricide?

If Absalom had succeeded in his revolt, David might have had a quieting of conscience. He might have experienced his defeat as a deserved punishment on a certain level. Instead, he was now the indirect cause of the downfall of another beloved person. Moreover, David again had to resume his role as king, a position which would more than ever evoke in him feelings of guilt, largely irrational though these might be.

The way in which Absalom met death is highly symbolic. He who wished to destroy the father is caught and held immovable in a tree, a father symbol. He is ensnared by his hair, a symbolic castration. He is slain by darts, which can be interpreted as a homosexual attack and castration, the number used, *three*, being of phallic significance. Thus the man who attacked his father was symbolically slain by the father, actually by a father figure, Joab.

It is interesting that even the burial of Absalom continues the symbolism of the oedipal crime and punishment. "And they took Absalom, and cast him into the great pit in the forest, and raised over him a very great heap of stones; and all Israel fled every one to his tent." The emphasis on the size of the pit below, and the heap of stones above is a significant detail which may symbolize his engulfment by the mother in a oedipal embrace, and at the same time, the return to the womb. The fact that "all Israel fled" indicates a mass emotion of horror and fear. On a reality basis, they had won a victory. Why then should they flee to their tents? The revolt and death of Absalom had a fearful meaning for every man.

A further interesting detail about Absalom is given here. We are told that he had earlier designated a certain pillar in a valley near Jerusalem to be known as Absalom's Pillar. It is almost as if he knew that he would have no other monument in remembrance of his name. There is such a monument today, although it is believed to be a Roman work. This graceful pillar in a valley just outside the *City of David* seems a fitting memorial for the tragedy of this son.

David's difficulties with his children did not end with the death of Absalom though that remained the great trauma of his fatherhood. Near the close of David's life, his son Adonijah repeats in feeble fashion the rebellion of Absalom. While the ailing king is on his death-bed, Adonijah gathers followers around him in a valley near Jerusalem and has himself proclaimed king. Adonijah's purpose is not to usurp David, but to claim the succession. However, David is spurred by Nathan, the prophet, and Bathsheba to assert himself in this matter and make good his promise that Solomon would reign after him. He gives orders that Solomon should be anointed and declared king. This is done and the shaky efforts of Adonijah come to naught.

In describing Adonijah's revolt, the Bible says of him, "Now Adonijah the son of Haggith exalted himself, saying: 'I will be king'; and he prepared him chariots and horsemen, and fifty men to run before him. And his father had not grieved him all his life in saying: 'Why hast thou do so (Kgs. I, 1:5–6)?' " David's failure to discipline his sons is here plainly stated.

It is interesting to consider in what areas of human experience David allowed himself the fullest expression of feelings. Nothing is recorded regarding his relationship with women that rises to the intensity of emotion expressed in his grief at the death of Absalom. Another episode of deep feeling is the occasion when David is faced with the illness and subsequent death of his first child with Bathsheba. He lies upon the earth, fasting and praying for seven days.

The very first poignant expression of sorrow and loss that we get from David is the unforgettable lament when he hears of the death of Saul and Jonathan in the battle of Mount Gilboa. In it, he declares that Jonathan's love for him was "passing the love of women."

Some critics have interpreted this passage as suggesting a lack of masculinity in David. Others, however, point out that such a form of expression was common in those days. The latter view certainly seems more convincing, for David would not, even indirectly, cast aspersions on his own masculine traits.

Actually, at no other time does David express strong affection for Jonathan. It is the latter who felt that "his soul was knit with the soul of David." The son of Jesse asks for Jonathan's protection on the occasions of Saul's anger, and in return makes a vow of friendship, which he keeps. But the David and Jonathan theme seems to have been much overplayed as far as David's involvement was concerned.

David's song of lamentation may have contained an additional *motif*. The death of both a father and son at the same time, as in the case of Saul and Jonathan, must have touched deep chords in David. His strong identification with both these roles and his ambivalent feelings in both must have increased his longing to find harmony in such relationships. This feeling is beautifully expressed in the line, "In their lives, even in their death, they were not divided." This, we know, is an idealization, for there was considerable friction between Saul and Jonathan during their lifetime.

We can conclude that it is in the father-son relationship that David's deepest feelings were involved.

David's Relationship with Women

A man's attitudes to father figures and sons can be more fully understood only in the light of his relationships to women. David's experiences in this area are indeed colorful. There is basis for suspecting however that a good deal of embellishment around this theme has gone on in the fantasies of a romantic-hungry world. Even those who know little else of this biblical hero remember him as the lover of Bathsheba in what is frequently regarded as one of the great love stories of the Bible.

Actually, David's love life is portrayed in the biblical narrative with the constraint of expression and omission of detail characteristic of this body of literature. However, compared to the paucity of information about the sexual life of other biblical heroes, the accounts of David's romances can be considered generous indeed. It is clear that his repressions in this area were far less than those of Samuel and Saul.

David had at least six wives and ten concubines. This picture does not fit in with the usual reserve in regard to sexuality characteristic of this period in Israel, although it was common enough among the potentates of neighboring states. David thus set a new model for sexual expansiveness, an example which his son Solomon followed to a degree which became legendary.

One might ponder the significance of David's sexual relationships to at least sixteen women. It seems clear that his tender and sexual feelings were not fused to any great degree. Many of the women, particularly the concubines, must have been merely sexual objects. The fact that David left these ten concubines behind in Jerusalem when he abandoned the city in the time of Absalom's rebellion points to a lack of regard for them. It might be reasoned that he wished to protect them from the hardships of this hazardous flight. But the text does not indicate such a motive.

There are only three women in David's life whose story finds its way into the biblical narrative. These are Michal, Abigail, and Bathsheba. It will be interesting to see what roles they played and whether there was any similarity of pattern in David's relationship with them.

Michal made known her affections for the youthful David at the court of her father so that word of it reached Saul. Later, she showed her loyalty and concern for her husband by helping him escape from the king's wrath, when Saul sought his life. Nowhere, however, is there any overt expression of David's love for this first wife. When he fled from the court as an outlaw, she was taken from him and given to another. One of David's first acts when he became king was to reclaim Michal. Whether this was done because of his affection for her or to right a wrong done to both, we have no way of knowing.

Another of the few occasions in which Michal plays a role is the time when an irreparable break occurs in her relationship with David. Regardless of his degree of affection for her, Michal's opinion of him was evidently important to the king's self-esteem, and he could not tolerate an injury to his pride which she delivered. It was the time when the Ark was brought to its new resting place in Jerusalem. David, in a frenzy of joy dances before the Ark, "girded with a linen ephod." Michal watches the performance from a window of the palace and despises the king in her heart for what she regards as undignified behavior.

David comes in from the great public festival, his heart full of rejoicing. He had completed sacrifices to God and blessed all the people. He had dispensed bread and cake to every man and woman in the multitude. Now he was about to bless his own household. It was at this moment that Michal came to greet him and to utter her words of bitterness and reproach, saying, "How did the king of Israel get him honor today, who uncovered himself today in the eyes of the handmaids of his servants, as one of the vain fellows shamelessly uncovereth himself (II, 6:20)!''

These words must have struck like a blast of cold air upon David in his mood of joyous exaltation. She had turned his public worship of God into a shameful thing. She had made him into a clown cavorting before the women instead of a king humbly and joyously doing honor to his God. David answers her with anger and cold hatred, rejecting her permanently as a sexual partner and declaring that she would never bear him a child.

One wonders why Michal reacted so strongly to the sight of David dancing in the street before the Ark. Surely he must have been in a company of priests and other dignitaries. One could venture the guess that unconscious factors played a role in Michal's feelings on this occasion. David's joyous submission before God, as expressed in his worshipful dance, must have involved some sublimation of his instinctual feelings. Michal may have responded to this factor and felt rejected. He was choosing God in preference to herself. Significantly, her accusation was that he was abasing himself sexually by *uncovering himself*. This is generally regarded as a feminine mode of being seductive. Unconsciously Michal must have felt that by removing his usual royal vestures, David was relinquishing some of his masculinity, and this was an offense to her own ego. David's reaction to her rebuke was a logical one; he rejected her as a sexual partner since she had cast aspersions on his masculine role.

David had acquired this first wife by paying her father the bloody tribute of two hundred dead Philistines. He gains the second of the three women we are discussing by abstaining from *blood guiltiness*. It is Abigail who makes a conquest of her man by an appeal to several aspects of his personality. She uses her feminine charm and seductiveness, but most of all the womanly intuition that appeals to a man's ego, the area where the battle of conquest is often decided. Let us recall the story briefly.

At the time of their meeting, David was an outlaw, leading a kind of Robin Hood existence with his band of followers. The biblical narrative tells about a prosperous farmer and shepherd, one called Nabal who churlishly refused a request from David's men for bounty although the latter had often protected his flocks from marauding bands. David is filled with anger at this miserly man and resolves to punish him by an attack upon his premises. Abigail, the wife of Nabal, is a women of good understanding as well as beauty. She hastily formulates a plan for averting the coming disaster. Loading a generous supply of food and wine on donkeys, Abigail hastens to meet David. She apologizes humbly for her husband's foolish behavior and begs the outlaw leader to accept her offering. Abigail reminds David of the high office for which he was destined and pleads with him not to make himself unworthy in the eyes of God by shedding blood without cause.

David is moved by her charm and intelligence and yields to her plea. Shortly after this, Nabal learns of the danger that he had so narrowly escaped and dies of a stroke. David sends for Abigail and makes her his wife. Here was the good woman who had changed him from an angry outlaw, about to take vengeance into his own hands, into the anointed of the Lord, the future king of Israel.

Her swift acceptance of his marriage offer, her willingness to leave a prosperous home and farm to join this man who was still an outlaw and whose future was uncertain, seem to indicate that Abigail really did believe in David and wanted to go with him. Otherwise she might have used her considerable wit and talent for persuasion to extricate herself gracefully from this situation.

We hear no more about Abigail after her marriage with David. Perhaps we can assume that like the marriages in fairy tales they lived happily ever after. But this omission may have another significance. Abigail may have assumed a place that became of secondary importance in David's full and exciting life. She may have been neither a source of vexation and anger, as Michal became, nor an object of passion, as Bathsheba was, for a while at least. She was a womanly woman who could adjust her life to his needs. So at least one can safely conjecture.

Bathsheba, the third woman of the trio, was clearly the object of David's passion. He saw this beautiful woman rising from her bath and wanted her. This is actually the first time in David's history that we get an expression of his unqualified sexual attraction for a woman.

He aspired to Michal, for "it pleased him well to be the son-in-law of the king." He asked Abigail's hand in marriage, for she pleased him in terms of character qualities as well as feminine charm. But Bathsheba, seen first from a distance, was wholly a sexual object, at first.

One wonders, however, on what basis the world and Hollywood has built up the great romance of David and Bathsheba. What actually were the facts? They saw each other once, at David's behest, which Bathsheba may have interpreted as a command. Enough time elapsed for her to become aware of her pregnancy, which would have required a number of weeks at least. There could have been no doubt in Bathsheba's mind when she sent the brief message to David, "I am with child."

Did the king see her in the interim? As Maurice Samuel rightly points out in his delightful study of these three wives of David, if Bathsheba was seeing the king regularly, she would have had no need of sending this intimate message by anyone else. Such a communication, with its strong emotional significance between two people, is a moment to be shared by no other under normal circumstances.[11]

But the circumstances were far from normal, as we know. Bathsheba, who appears throughout in a passive role, quite different in this respect from Michal and Abigail, must have been in desperate straits. It was common knowledge that her husband had been away with the army for some time. The punishment for adultery was death by stoning. The woman's brief message to the king must have been a plea for help as well as a factual statement. It is revealing of Bathsheba's personality, however, that this plea was not more overtly made. Some women have the perhaps enviable talent of arousing in men the wish to help them. They do this, not by direct appeal, as Abigail did, but by presenting themselves in a silently helpless situation which puts the responsibility squarely upon the shoulders of the man. It is often the most irresistible kind of appeal.

On only two other occasions in the biblical story does Bathsheba again take the initiative. Yet both of these two times she is prompted to do so by others and so really acts only as a spokesman, in a sense. In the late days of David's rule, Nathan the prophet urgently requests Bathsheba to see the ailing king and ask him to make good his promise to her and put her son Solomon upon the throne. At this very time, Adonijah was arranging a *coup d'etat* and having himself declared king, not even waiting for David's death, which was then imminent. Bathsheba does as Nathan tells her and her request is granted. The weak court rebellion is put down and Solomon is declared king.

The second occasion of Bathsheba's initiative comes in response to a plea from Adonijah, who asks her to go to her son Solomon, now the ruling king, and request that David's last concubine, Abishag, be given to Adonijah. The concubine of a king is royal property, and in making this request, the hapless Adonijah was boldly and tactlessly indicating that he had not yet given up his ambitions for the throne. What prompted this senseless act on his part is hard to say. It was an avoidance of reality that cost him his life. Solomon, who had received his mother with warmth and graciousness, ordering a throne to be placed for her next to his own, and declaring that he surely would not deny any request she would make of him, goes into a rage and orders that Adonijah be seized immediately and put to death.

Why did Bathsheba not anticipate this result and try to dissuade Adonijah from such a course? Why did she act as the agent for him on this mission of death? We can only guess. Perhaps, on a deeply personal level, she would have liked to see her rival, Abishag, removed from the royal harem, for it must have been distasteful to think of this woman in a relationship both to David and to Solomon. And so wishful thinking took the place of a reality appraisal. Or perhaps she did not care what fate overtook Adonijah, the rival of her son. It may be, too, that she was just accustomed to doing what others asked her to do. Judging by the character of her son Solomon, who evidently denied himself little throughout his life, she may not have known how to say *no* to anyone.

However, the fact that Solomon honored and loved his mother, and that David selected her child from his numerous offspring as a successor to the throne, indicates that Bathsheba must also have had positive qualities. She was evidently able to arouse honor and respect as well as a protective love in both David and Solomon, and therefore must have been not only essentially feminine in her makeup but a person of real character as well.

One wonders what qualities in Bathsheba made it possible for her to have married a person like Uriah, a rigid, uncompromising man who did not dare to enjoy the pleasures of life. Perhaps the woman married him in passive obedience to her guardian's wish, even as she went in passive obedience to David's wish.

We have no indication anywhere in the story of a great and lasting passion between David and Bathsheba. The fact that it is not recorded does not mean that it could not have existed. The Bible puts no great emphasis upon romance for its own sake; its purpose is in another direction. The reality is, however, that David married Bathsheba because she was with child. If Uriah had gone to his home on that fateful night when David had him brought back on leave from the army for that very purpose, the love story of David and Bathsheba might never have been written.

It is significant that at a later date, during the revolt of Adonijah, Bathsheba did not even dare to enter the presence of the king without the encouragement of Nathan, although she must have known about this court intrigue. At that time, it was the young woman, Abishag, brought to the palace for the express purpose of warming and nurturing the old, sick David, who must have been more influential with him.

Perhaps the most obvious factor that points to the lack of

a lasting love relationship of great intensity between David and Bathsheba is the size of the king's harem. To use women mainly as sexual objects, without regard or affection for them as individuals, can have a dehumanizing effect upon the man as well. One may argue that this is an evaluation of our age projected into a period when such matters were looked upon very differently. We are, in fact, not judging but trying to understand the dynamics of David's personality. What inner needs did he have to exercise his royal prerogative in this expansive fashion? Was it because, as suggested before, David's tender and sexual feelings suffered from a certain degree of defusion so that he could not find a deep and lasting satisfaction in any of his relationships with women? Did he therefore try to make up in a variety of experience what was lacking in its quality? In the light of his ambivalence toward father figures, such a development seems likely. The lack of a strong, positive identification with the father makes a mature heterosexual development more difficult.

In each of the three love relationships under discussion, another man is somehow involved. In the case of Michal, there is Saul, with whom David is embroiled in a competitive life and death struggle of a very complicated kind. Abigail, too, is taken from a hostile father figure, who has refused David food. Nabal's death is actually a consequence of his conflict with David, for the pathologically stingy farmer has a stroke when he realizes how close he had been to David's punitive reprisal.

Bathsheba also becomes David's wife as a result of the unlovable behavior of her husband, the self-righteous Uriah, who refuses the pleasure of his bed while his fellow-soldiers are engaged in battle. As will be recalled, David then resorts to the device of sending him back to the war with a message to Joab requesting that Uriah be placed in the most exposed area of the battle, where he is slain. This is the sin for which David receives the stern rebuke of Nathan the prophet and is punished by losing his first child with Bathsheba, who is now his wife. It is the occasion, also, when God for the first time expresses his displeasure with the king.

It seems possible that David unconsciously took these women

away from a rival man, who was also a bad father. He overcame all three of these unfriendly father figures, practically causing the death of two.

David's sense of self-esteem depended not only on a loving acceptance from the good father but also on approval and admiration from the woman, particularly on the level of prowess in war. War and women must have been closely associated in the unconscious of David. One of the rewards promised for the defeat of Goliath was the hand of the king's daughter. As we have seen, David pays for Michal in bloody conquest of the enemy. He wins Abigail as a substitute for such conquest, and takes Bathsheba by subjecting her husband to death in battle. He almost loses two of his wives when the town of Ziklag is overcome by the enemy, and wins them back in another conflict.

"To the victor belongs the spoils," and women are part of the spoils. But to David, the woman is not only an object to be possessed; he wants her admiration as well. Conquest in war thus becomes a way of winning such approval. It is more understandable now why David's first *act* after defeating Goliath was to bring the head of the victim to Jerusalem, in a way of displaying his prowess to *the woman*.

It is when the women hail his victories in war, chanting, "Saul has slain his thousands, And David his ten thousands," that David's difficulties with Saul begin. It might well be that the youthful champion's reaction to this acclaim added to Saul's jealousy.

In the beautiful and moving lament which David composed on the occasion of the death of Saul and Jonathan during the battle on Mount Gilboa, the relationship between war and women is clearly brought out. The loss of these two great figures in battle is seen, not only as a cause for personal grief, but as a shameful defeat for those who have suffered death in battle. David cries poignantly, "How are the mighty fallen!/ Tell it not in Gath,/ Publish it not in the streets of Askelon,/ Lest the daughters of the Philistines rejoice,/ Lest the daughters of the uncircumcised triumph." Then he exhorts the women of his own people, "Ye daughters of Israel, weep over Saul,/ Who clothed you in scarlet, with other delights,/ Who put ornaments of gold upon your apparel." The lament concludes, "How are the mighty fallen, and the weapons of war perished! (Sam. II, 1:20–27)." Men are here metaphorically referred to as *weapons of war*. Thus manhood and victory in battle are synonymous and defeat is also a disgrace in the eyes of the women. The conquest by the man and the admiration of the woman are related in the unconscious.

We are assuming that there was a certain repression of feelings in David concerning the woman, a situation stemming from childhood traumas of the oedipal period. Such feelings would be of an ambivalent nature, the longing to *take possession* of the woman and also to be protected by her from the hostility of the father. There would be competitiveness toward the man in relation to the woman, originally the mother.

Are there any indications of the return of this repressed material? It can be discerned, considerably disguised, in David's attitude toward the *cities* he conquered or wished to conquer. A city is often used as a mother symbol in the unconscious. We have noted that certain cities and towns played this role for David.

That this usage was common in biblical times is revealed in the incident when Joab and his army pursue the traitor Sheba far up to the north of Israel, where he found refuge in a walled city. The pursuers batter at the walls, preparatory to taking the town. At this point a woman of the city calls to Joab and pleads with him to desist, crying, "Seekest thou to destroy a city and a mother in Israel (II, 21:19)?" The two words, *city* and *mother* are here used synonymously. The woman did indeed save the city through this appeal, and influenced the inhabitants to deliver the head of the traitor to Joab.

In connection with the village of Nob, home of the priesthood, another instance of a symbolic meaning of the town has been suggested earlier, explaining why this community, as a disloyal mother, became the object of King Saul's wrath. We have also noted the special importance that Gath seemed to have for David in terms of the unconscious. The town of Keilah may have served in a similar fashion. During his outlaw days, David saves this city from the Philistines but is himself close to being trapped in it by the betraying *fathers* of the community. They would have turned him over to the pursuing Saul, had David not been forewarned of this possibility by God.

Jerusalem, however, is the city chiefly associated with David. It is under David's command, in the early days of his kingship, that this fortress town is captured from the Canaanites and made into the great political and religious capital that united all Israel. Jerusalem, *city of peace,* is significantly known as the *City of David.*

The description of the biblical text regarding the taking of this city is quite confusing.

> And the king and his men went to Jerusalem against the Jebusites, the inhabitants of the land, who spoke unto David, saying: "Except thou take away the blind and the lame, thou shalt not come in hither"; thinking: "David cannot come in hither." Nevertheless David took the stronghold of Zion; the same is the city of David. And David said on that day: "Whosoever smiteth the Jebusites, and getteth up to the gutter and (taketh away) the lame and the blind, that are hated of David's soul—." Wherefore they say: "There are the blind and the lame; he cannot come into the house." And David dwelt in the stronghold, and called it the city of David (II, 5:6–9).

The implication of the corrupt text seems to be that the inhabitants felt so sure of themselves that they declared the city could be defended even by the blind and the lame. It was a challenge and a taunt.

A hypothesis to be considered here is that the corruption of the text at this point may express a psychological state within David himself. The text becomes faltering, confusing, and lacking in continuity, similar to the ways in which the *free associations* of an analysand break down when sensitive material is approached and resistance sets in for defensive purposes. The daring involved in the capture of Jerusalem, the mother city, and the intensity of the wish to carry out this deed, must have stirred David's fears on an unconscious level. It meant acting out the fantasy of forbidden oedipal wishes. The words, "there are the lame and the blind; he cannot come into the house," can be translated psycho-analytically into the thought, *one must not take possession of the mother or the punishment of castration, symbolically expressed as lameness or blindness, would be suffered.*

There are numerous legends associated with the capture of Jerusalem that confirm this interpretation. One of them says that this city remained so long in Canaanite hands because of an agreement made between Abraham and the children of Heth from whom the Hebrew chieftain bought the Cave of Machpelah as a burial ground for Sarah. The understanding was that the capital city of the Hittites was never to be forcibly taken from them. The legend states further that this agreement was engraved on a monument set up on a high tower within the city. There were two figures, one representing a blind man, Isaac, and the other, a lame man, Jacob. The Jebusites declared that before the city could be taken, this monument would have to be destroyed.[12] Thus came the boast that Jerusalem could be defended by the lame and the blind.

Here we have the story of a city that feels itself protected from attack because of a covenant with Abraham, father and patriarch. This covenant is engraved on a monument which is flanked by two castrated figures, Isaac and Jacob, the *sons* of Abraham. What can be the symbolic meaning?

Both Isaac and Jacob, at various times in their lives, had violated the incest taboo in their wishes and fantasies. That is, they had suffered from an oedipus complex and been afflicted, one with blindness and the other with lameness, unconsciously regarded as punishment for this sin. Their fate should be a warning to others to refrain from the same forbidden wishes. Only those who were not frightened by this portent of disaster, that is, those who did not suffer from castration anxiety or superego fears, could destroy the monument and take the city.

There are however some unexplained factors in this interpretation of the legend. We shall attempt further clarification. The protection of the *strange city* by a Hebrew, Abraham, occurs as part of the agreement resulting from the purchase of the Cave of

Machpelah from the Hittites. What could be the connection here? Actually, the Cave of Machpelah is far to the south, at Hebron. Actually, Jerusalem was the city of the Jebusites, not the Hittites, although the legend says the former were the descendants of the latter.

We may have significance by analogy in this story. The Cave of Machpelah, where Abraham buries his wife Sarah, is symbolic of the mother and the womb. It is *like* Jerusalem in that both are mother symbols and both originally belonged to strangers. Neither the cave nor the city, that is, the woman, should be taken by force from those to whom she belongs; for the woman is also the mother. The woman as *wife* can be acquired only by purchase within the framework of a contract. Abraham himself set the example for this procedure when he insisted on paying for the Cave of Machpelah although it was offered to him as a gift. Evident here is the power of the symbol, where *cave* and *city* represent the *woman,* who in turn, is often unconsciously confused in her roles as mother and wife, resulting from the unsuccessful solution of the oedipal conflict. The element that both the cave and the city are purchased from strangers in these legends is a defense against incestuous bonds.

Another legend says that Joab entered the city by placing a tall cypress tree near the wall. Then, while standing on David's head, Joab pulled the top of the tree toward him, grasping its tip. When the tree rebounded, Joab found himself on top of the wall. He entered the city and destroyed the monument referred to above. The tree, a phallic symbol, is used to enter the *city* and thus defy the oedipal taboo. Joab standing on David's head represents an extension of David himself, a part of him that is not egosyntonic and therefore displaced to the other. During their long relationship Joab gives the impression of serving this function for David a number of times, as we shall see later.

As is evident, legend was very busy in this field. Another story says that when David approached the city, one of the walls miraculously lowered itself so that he could enter the stronghold effortlessly. We are told that David did not wish to use force in capturing Jerusalem. He offered the Jebusites six hundred shekels for the city and bought it from them, receiving a bill of sale. It seems that tradition is eager to spare David the act of forcible invasion of this town, an attitude that can be understood only on the basis of the underlying meaning suggested here.

The city was evidently captured by a strategy. Perched high on hills which descended on three sides in the form of steep precipices, the fortress was impregnable to a frontal attack. The Israelite soldiers climbed up a rocky water tunnel that led from a spring outside the walls to the heart of Jerusalem. According to the version in *Chronicles,* David himself did not lead the attack. He declared that the one who would be the first to go up and smite the Jebusites would be appointed chief of the army. Joab answers this challenge and is rewarded accordingly. Actually, however, Joab seems to have been the military leader long before this.

Jerusalem becomes David's most beloved city. He longs to build a Temple there but is reluctantly deterred by Nathan the prophet, who said that God did not desire this from him. That great task was to be accomplished by his son Solomon.

It seems significant that Nathan's first response to David's plan of building a Temple was warmly receptive and approving. He says to the king, "Go, do all that is in thy heart; for the Lord is with thee." Later that same night, Nathan receives a message from God, quite lengthy and involved, but containing the idea that he did not wish a Temple from David. God goes to the trouble of explaining his reasons for this, saying that since the time he brought the children of Israel out of Egypt, he had walked in a tent and a tabernacle. The implication seems to be that God preferred the freedom of a portable house as in the days when Israel was a semi-nomadic people.

If this was so, why did he agree to a Temple that would be built by Solomon? Again, we must view these feelings as a projection and rationalization on the part of David himself. Legend indicates that David felt unworthy to build the Temple because he had shed so much blood. This incident may therefore reflect

David's own evaluation of himself, arrived at perhaps, with the help of the prophet, the king's true mentor, in a delayed reaction. This was so great a renunciation for David that the cause had to be projected to God and alleviated by a promise that the Davidic dynasty would continue for a long time to come. Yet there must have been another aspect to the conflict.

David seems to reveal a deep sense of guilt in this situation. We do not know, of course, the exact significance of what this project meant to him on an unconscious level. His wish to build this structure is associated with an awareness of the grandeur in living he has himself attained. The king exclaims, "See now, I dwell in a house of cedar, but the Ark of God dwelleth within curtains (II, 7:2)."

The implication is that the son again dares to be greater than the Father, a source of discomfort and guilt to David, as suggested before. Yet for this son to build a House for God may also have been experienced as a presumption. Ambivalence too may have played a part. The grandeur and permanence of a Temple, near the residence of the king, might have brought the Paternal Presence too close for reasons both of competition and guilt.

It is interesting that instead of accepting a house from David, God promises to build the king a house, in the sense of a dynasty. This reversal of the situation may have been more comfortable for David. The reason God gives for not wanting the king to build him a Temple is also rather intriguing. God wishes the situation to remain as it was in the past, when he had dwelt in tents among the children of Israel. Is it perhaps David himself who longs to maintain his earlier, more simple relationship to God that he had experienced in his own days as a wanderer and a dweller in tents?

The king however does have the privilege of building a new Tabernacle for the Ark and transporting that sacred object to the city of Jerusalem from the place where it had been housed in a private dwelling since the early days of Samuel. To this extent David succeeds in overcoming his ambivalence and making peace with the Father in an act of loving homage within the *City of Peace.*

David's Relationship with God

It has been noted in our earlier studies that the way each of the biblical personalities under discussion related to God was significant of his character structure. David offers some interesting contrasts to Saul in this respect. The first king of Israel must have experienced God as a much more distant and formidable Power than he appeared to David. In moments of crisis Saul feverishly built altars to God and tried to divine his will, not always with success. The figure of Samuel as well as his own personality stood between Saul and a more personal approach to God.

It was different with David. At the very beginning of his career, in his battle with Goliath, David confidently expresses the feeling that God is on his side and declares that he is fighting the Lord's battle.

On several occasions David speaks with God and seeks his advice in a much more informal fashion than Saul ever did. During his days as an outlaw he asks God on several occasions what course he should pursue. When he wished to help the people of Keilah, who were in danger of the Philistines, we are told that "David inquired of the Lord, saying: 'Shall I go and smite these Philistines?' And the Lord said unto David: 'Go and smite the Philistines, and save Keilah (I, 23:2).' " How simple and uncomplicated compared to several occasions when Saul tried so desperately through the help of priests and the casting of lots to determine God's will, also in a military situation. Again, when David heard that Saul was planning to trap him in that walled city, he once more inquired of God,

> "Will the men of Keilah deliver me up into his hand? will Saul come down as Thy servant hath heard? O Lord the God of Israel, I beseech Thee, tell Thy servant." And the Lord said: "He will come down." Then said David: "Will the men of Keilah deliver up me and my men into the hand of Saul?" And the Lord said: "They will deliver thee up." Then David and his men, who were about six hundred, arose and departed out of Keilah . . . (I, 23:11–13).

On this latter occasion David does employ the services of Abiathar the priest and the use of the ephod. Perhaps he does so at other times too and this procedure is taken for granted and therefore not mentioned in the text. But the tone of David's approach to God is, in general, more simple and trusting than Saul's.

After the death of Saul and his son Jonathan, "David inquired of the Lord, saying, 'Shall I go up into any of the cities of Judah?' And the Lord said unto him: 'Go up.' And David said: 'Whither shall I go up?' and he said: 'Unto Hebron.'" This conversation has a laconic quality. In such manner might a youth ask a wise and trusted father for direction. There is a brevity that bespeaks acceptance of each other in the roles of One who guides and the other who asks for guidance.

It was at Hebron that the men of Judah came to David and anointed him king over the southern tribes. On another occasion shortly after this event, the Philistines invaded the Valley of Rephaim. "And David inquired of the Lord, saying: 'Shall I go up against the Philistines? wilt Thou deliver them into my hand?' And the Lord said unto David: 'Go up; for I will certainly deliver the Philistines into thy hand (II, 5:19).'" When the enemy came up once more and spread themselves over the same valley, David again asked God what to do and this time the answer was somewhat different.

> And when David inquired of the Lord, He said: "Thou shalt not go up; make a circuit behind them, and come upon them over against the mulberry-trees. And it shall be, when thou hearest the sound of marching in the tops of the mulberry-trees, that then thou shalt bestir thyself; for then is the Lord gone out before thee to smite the host of the Philistines (II, 5:23-24)."

We have here an anthropomorphic concept of a personal God who closely directs David's military strategy. The militant father leads the way in the tops of the mulberry-trees, a phallic symbol. We see again how much David's warfare against the Philistines remains a *battle of the Lord*.

However it would not be correct to give the impression that

David constantly asked God for directions about what he should do, in military matters or otherwise. The instances quoted are among the few times that David seems to require specific advice and support.

Do these four occasions have anything in common? Two of the times involve the occupation of a city, Keilah and Hebron. The other two are associated with fighting the Philistines who have occupied a valley. A town and a valley are both female sexual symbols. Does David feel a special need to ask the Father's permission and support before he takes possession of such a symbolic locality? In view of the evidence, it seems so. When the Philistines are defeated in the Valley of Rephaim, David exclaims, "The Lord hath broken mine enemies before me like the breach of waters (II, 5:20)." This figure of speech, together with the concept of God riding in the tops of the mulberry-trees gives additional credence to this view. It is not hard to believe that in saving the towns and valleys of Israel from the enemy, David was unconsciously rescuing the mother from the aggressive sexual attacks of the bad fathers. But he dared to do so only with the support of the Good Father.

Nowhere in Saul's career do we get a moment of such intimacy with God as is revealed on the later occasion when David expresses his gratitude for the prophetic assurance that his dynasty would continue after him for many generations. The text says, "Then David the king went in, and sat before the Lord; and he said: 'Who am I, O Lord God, and what is my house that Thou has brought me thus far?' " He expresses the conviction that God has chosen the people and the land of Israel for a special purpose. The description of David coming in and sitting down before the Lord must refer to his entering the Tabernacle and sitting before the Ark.

In spite of its personal quality, however, David's attitude to God was always clearly that of the worshipper and the suppliant, who longed for God's love and protection, and who felt the need of confession and forgiveness. David's acceptance that God's love is contingent upon moral behavior, that he is the God of righteousness, who punishes and rewards in accordance with a moral law is consistently revealed. In subtle but inescapable ways, we see a progression from earlier times toward an ever stronger union of morality and religion. This unity finds particular expression in the personality of David. More than any of the leaders who preceded him, David showed the struggle between the temptation of wrongdoing and the desire to do good, in a way that is profoundly human. His relationship to God was that of a son who longs for a loving and trusted Father, One who would clearly be on his side and protect him from enemies. While it lacked the high idealism of the later prophets, David's attitude to God was one which is perhaps nearer to that of the average man. It may be the very quality of experiencing God according to the wishes, needs, and feelings of so many people that helps to make David such an enduring and beloved personality.

One of David's most significant acts as a theocratic king was to bring the Ark back into public religious life, a role it had lacked since the early days of Samuel.

The Ark was the most important religious symbol in the life of Israel. It recalled the covenant made with God through Moses at Mount Sinai. We have considered earlier the problem of why Samuel did not restore the Ark to its appropriate role in the religious ritual of the people. That Saul continued the pattern set by Samuel in ignoring the existence of the Ark is not surprising. Saul's personality was too rigid to allow creative thinking in this area of relationship to God, which was so conflictful for him at best.

It was different with David who, as we have observed, was much more free and warm in the expression of his religious feelings than Saul had been. The return of the Ark to Jerusalem was a matter of great personal importance to the king. Some historians describe this event as the calculated gesture of a shrewd ruler who wished to strengthen his capital city by making it the religious as well as the political center of the monarchy, thus uniting the northern and southern tribes more firmly. But the spirit of the text clearly belies this.

Let us try to explore psychoanalytically what this event may have meant to David on a deeply personal level, and the meaning of the dramatic incident that occurred on this occasion.

The Ark had to be transported from the small village of Kiriat-jearim, several miles from Jerusalem. The transfer of the sacred object was begun with due pomp and ceremony. It was carried in a new cart drawn by oxen. It was driven by two sons of Abinadab, more likely great grandsons, for several generations must have elapsed since the Ark was placed in the house of Abinadab after its return from the Philistines.

David, together with a joyous company playing upon musical instruments, preceded the cart. Suddenly tragedy intervened upon this happy scene. As they reached the threshing-floor of Nacon, the oxen stumbled. Uzzah, one of the two descendants of Abinadab, put out his hand to steady the Ark and keep it from falling. We are told that ". . . the anger of the Lord was kindled against Uzzah; and God smote him there for his error; and there he died by the Ark of God (II, 6:7)."

Considered from a psychological point of view, what could have caused the death of this man? It seems clear enough that he died of fright. We know from studies of primitive peoples that the breaking of a taboo can cause the death of the wrong-doer. It seems to occur as a kind of self-imposed punishment through auto-suggestion, brought about by fear. The instantaneous nature of Uzzah's death indicates an overwhelming intensity of reaction. The forbidden gesture may have caused an inhibition of impulses so great that life itself was stopped.

What could have been the nature of this terrible misdeed? We know that among neurotics the compulsive taboo of touching springs from deeper sources. It represents a forbidden impulse. Certainly on the surface Uzzah's gesture of saving the Ark from falling appears most commendable and the punishment he suffered, unjustified. But unconsciously this gesture may have had other meanings. When the oxen stumbled, Uzzah feared that the Ark would fall. The intensity of this fear may indicate the presence of an unconscious wish that some calamity would overtake this powerful father symbol.

All of his life Uzzah had dwelt in the presence of this dreaded and revered object. The Ark, of course, must have symbolized the earthly father as well as the Heavenly One, and thus became the representative of the oedipal conflict. His feelings toward the Ark may therefore have contained strong aggressive impulses. Uzzah may have put forth his hand, consciously to support the Ark but unconsciously, perhaps, with the hope of hurling it down. It must have been the unconscious awareness of his hostility and the realization that his forbidden wish was close to actuality that caused the immediate death by terror.

Are we not going pretty far afield, and with little evidence, the reader may ask at this point. Well, let us consider other factors in the situation. The oxen stumbled when they reached a threshing-floor. The threshing-floor, where grain is beaten, has sexual connotations. This must have been particularly true in ancient Israel, where *the land* played a role of special symbolic value in the lives of the people. It was truly the *mother-land,* as is well known. The Ark is a father symbol, probably signifying to many the very Presence of the Father himself.

If we assume a more than usual father-son ambivalence in a household which has been the dwelling-place of the Ark for many years, the symbolism of the cart containing the Ark and drawn by oxen, is intensified by the oxen stumbling against the threshing-floor or in sight of it. Uzzah's oedipal aggressive wishes may have been stimulated by this situation. His fear would have increased in proportion to this unconscious hostility. Had the Ark actually fallen on the ground, the worst would have happened, as far as Uzzah was concerned. As experienced in unconscious fantasy, his aggressive wishes would have been realized. Symbolically the father would have been humiliated and profaned. Uzzah's hasty and impulsive gesture was meant to avert this catastrophe. However, it may also have contained the double meaning so often found in the obsessive compulsive symptom, that of expressing an impulse and the defense against it, combined in one action.

The transporting of the Ark from Kiriat-jearim recalls the earlier event when the sacred relic was brought there. It will be recollected that the Ark had been captured in battle by the Philistines. Its presence in the Philistine cities had been accompanied by much misfortune among the inhabitants in the form of widespread illness. In accordance with the advice of their wise men, the Philistines put this dangerous object into a new cart drawn by cows, and sent it off in the direction of Hebrew territory. The cows came to the village of Beth-shemesh, where the men were busy harvesting the grain. They rejoiced to see the Ark and built an altar and made sacrifices. But calamity soon overcame them. The text says that God smote the men of Beth-shemesh who had gazed upon the Ark (6:19).

We see here some interesting similarities to the later event. The sin committed by the people of Beth-shemesh was *looking*. Psychoanalytically, scoptophilia and touching are closely related. Both are part of the fore-pleasure in the sexual act. Both are forbidden in situations where sexuality is forbidden. Both can express hostile as well as sexual impulses. As in the later situation, the Ark drawn in a cart, appears in a harvesting scene. This time the men look instead of touching; the number involved is much greater. It is so unrealistic for a village in ancient Israel that we can assume further symbolism is at work. We are told that God "smote of the people seventy men and fifty thousand men." Even the way of recording the number is unusual, first mentioning the *seventy* and then the *fifty thousand*. We know that numbers have mystical and magical meanings among ancient peoples, a form of superstition still prevalent among us today. The seventy men remind one that the Sanhedrin, the authoritative religious legal assembly of later Israel, was made up of that number. We can assume therefore that the *seventy* of Beth-shemesh stood for the elders of the town. The *fifty thousand* might have represented the ordinary citizens of the community. Both the elders and the people were punished for this sin of *looking*.

Interesting too is the name of the village where this dread incident occurred. *Bath-shemesh* means "House of the Sun." We have an overdetermination of meaning here. Men reap their wheat harvest in the valley of the *House of the Sun*. In this domain of the father, where the fruit of the earth is being gathered, they dare to gaze upon the Great Father symbol, a forbidden oedipal aggression.

Another element seems common to both occasions—the factor of surprise. The men of Beth-shemesh looked up from their work and beheld the cart containing its dread and precious object. They were taken by surprise and they *gazed*. So too was Uzzah surprised. The sudden lurch of the cart came unexpectedly. The man put out his hand on impulse and *touched*. Both acts involved uncontrollable behavior brought on by the unexpected.

From a psychoanalytic point of view, surprise may involve a return of the repressed. A situation which stimulates the release of repressed material may occasion surprise. This emotion is also related to oedipal feelings, which may be aroused more intensely by witnessing a primal scene. The child *surprises* the parents by intruding suddenly into the forbidden situation. He is himself startled and surprised by what he sees.

It may be that the suddenness of what occurred in both situations under discussion stimulated an expression of the forbidden impulses and caused the terror and guilt that led to such dreadful consequences. It is significant that on both occasions those who took over the care of the Ark after the catastrophe were not harmed but rather enjoyed special blessing. Perhaps the fact that these people came prepared for their task made it possible for them to perform it on an ego level. Their impulses were therefore under control and sublimation was more possible. The indication that the presence of the Ark brought good fortune may be understood as the reward for such sublimation.

The death of an unknown person by the name of Uzzah, who had not even been mentioned before, could not be significant in and of itself. It was the event that was important. This event must therefore have had a wider significance. Uzzah's act of sacrilege may well have been an expression of the people as a group. The sight of the Ark may have stirred up unconscious ambivalent feelings toward God. Some of these feelings may have been caused by guilt and fear because the Ark had been abandoned and neglected for so many years. The fact that it had been thus treated indicates in itself that this object inspired dread in its beholders.

David's reaction to the death of Uzzah was, as could be expected, a very personal one. However, its nature is rather puzzling. We are told that he was *displeased* with God. *Displeasure* seems a strange word to express a man's feelings towards God. It is an attitude of disapproval. David's sense of justice dares to find expression here even in his attitude toward God. His immediate identification with Uzzah may indicate strong defenses on his own part against the awareness of similar hostility within himself.

Indeed the king must have interpreted what happened as an expression of Divine displeasure against himself. And yet David was dancing and singing before the Ark with worshipful joy. Why then should this have happened? David's displeasure was followed quickly by fear. If the Ark was going to cause misfortune, perhaps it was better not to bring it within the city, so close to his own dwelling-place. David's lack of trust, so unusual for him, may point to feelings of ambivalence and guilt.

The Ark was placed once more within a private dwelling, the home of a Philistine from the city of Gath, Obed-Edom. Here is another mystery. Why should the Ark be put in a non-Israelitish dwelling? Perhaps this was to be a test. If the Ark brought good luck to a stranger, how much more would it do so to a Hebrew! Perhaps also the move was as unconscious rejection of the Ark, which had caused the death of an apparently innocent man.

The sacred object remained in the house of the Gittite for three months and, we are told, the family prospered. It does seem puzzling that a son of Abinadab, who had ministered to the Ark for so long, should be punished, while a stranger was blessed. However, perhaps it is not so illogical. A son may not take privileges in relation to a father, but a stranger may. We know that in dreams the father is frequently represented as a stranger, a form of disguise against incestuous or hostile wishes. After this good omen, David gathers courage and completes the transport of the Ark.

In bringing the Ark to Jerusalem, David was clearly fulfilling a wish that brought him great joy. Every child at some time in the early years of his life has a fantasy of separating mother and father so that he may himself have exclusive possession of one or the other, or of both. Guilt accompanies such a process. The intensity of feeling which David possessed both for the city of

Jerusalem and the Ark points to the strength of the unconscious factors involved. The king may now have been undoing the aggressive fantasies of his childhood in this act of true sublimation. He was re-uniting father and mother, expressing his joyful renunciation as he danced before the Father-God. In this sublimated form, he was able to keep close to him both parents, symbolized by the city and the Ark, a fulfillment which this eighth child in the family of Jesse had not been able to achieve in his childhood longings.

David also served Israel as a model and prototype for a new kind of religious expression. He established a new pattern of worship, not only by his organization of a more elaborate form of ritual, but by the way in which he personally expressed himself in prayer.

It is not without reason that tradition ascribes a large part of the book of *Psalms* to David and calls him the *sweet singer of Zion*. He led the way in expressing religious feeling with greater warmth and spontaneity. David thus gave the people a valuable form of self-expression that provided a source of comfort and an aid to sublimation. To a people who, in principle, rejected worship through concrete images, the process of verbalizing their religious feelings more fully was a step forward in emotional and moral growth.

We shall not enter here into the controversial problem of the extent to which David was the real author of the psalms called by his name. That he possessed poetic and musical ability from the time of his youth and was known for these achievements is attested by the fact that he was chosen to bring solace to the unhappy King Saul. The beautiful lament over the deaths of Saul and Jonathan, embodied in the narrative of the text in *Second Samuel*, is definitely attributed to David's authorship. If he was capable of writing poetry as superb as this, it is readily conceivable that he may have written others too which could also have been preserved. Writing was not an uncommon skill in his time.

The spirit in many of the psalms and the themes with which they deal closely resemble David's own attitudes to God. The concepts of God as the Protector, the Rock of Salvation, the

Source of righteousness, who punishes evil, rewards good, and forgives the repentant, which abound throughout the Psalms, are also expressed by David.

The king's genuine belief in Israel as the people chosen by God to be his own people and to promulgate his ideals indicate that David had a basic respect for his subjects and a sense of humility about his own role. The land too belonged to God and the people. These three elements, God, the people, and the land, formed an inherent unity, based on Divine purpose and plan. The king himself was but an instrument to help in carrying out this plan.

Such attitudes would tend to reduce the feelings of omnipotence and the strength of narcissistic wishes for glory that are the special pitfalls of kings. Thus in his role as religious leader, David had opportunities for creative self-expression which must have been helpful to him in coping with his own psychological problems.

David as a Leader

Let us now move to another aspect of the personality of David. He was a leader among men from the time of his youth when he slew the giant Philistine. How did he relate to others in this role of influence and power? How did he treat his soldiers, his friends, and his enemies?

David stimulated feelings of loyalty and love in many of his followers. This fact is so evident that we need not pursue it further. Let us rather try to see what qualities of his personality evoked this response. David seems to have had a strong sense of justice which prompted him to deal fairly with his men. An instance of this is revealed in a law he laid down regarding the division of the spoils of war.

At the time when David was an outlaw, living under the protection of Achish, his own headquarters, Ziglak, was raided and burned by hostile tribes from the south during David's absence. All the women and children were taken captive, including David's two wives, Ahinoam of Jezreel and Abigail of Carmel. Stirred up by anger and grief, the forces of David pursued the enemy and overcame them. The Hebrews recovered their beloved ones and their possessions. On the way to this battle, two hundred of David's soldiers had been too weary to proceed so David left them in charge of the baggage, some distance from the actual combat.

After the victory, the men who participated in the fighting wished to keep all the spoils for themselves, declaring that those who had not taken part in the battle should not receive any of the rewards. David answered,

> "Ye shall not do so, my brethren, with that which the Lord hath given unto us, Who hath preserved us, and delivered the troop that came against us into our hands. And who will hearken unto you in this matter? For as is the share of him that goeth down to the battle, so shall be the share of him that tarrieth by the baggage; they shall share alike." And it was so from that day forward, that he made it a statute and an ordinance for Israel unto this day (I, 30:23–25).

As a good leader, David first explains the reason for his act and then firmly declares his decision, taking full responsibility.

What was there in David's own background that might have prompted this strong sense of equality in dealing with his men? We recall that David was *left behind* on several occasions when he was living in his father's house. One of these was the time when Samuel came to perform the sacrifice and choose a successor to the throne. Again David was left behind to guard the sheep while three of his older brothers fought in the wars with Saul. One can imagine occasions when these brothers would return from a campaign proudly displaying their share of the spoils. How left out the young David must have felt then! But one does not need to look for such specific examples. We know psychoanalytically that the sense of justice in children is related to a strong wish that all brothers and sisters should be treated equally. Where the family is large, this need and wish for justice may become correspondingly strong, for the possibility of partiality is also greater.

David's sense of justice is revealed with dramatic consequences when the significance of his own conduct with Bathsheba is brought home to him. Nathan the Prophet tells the king the well-known parable of the rich man who took the only ewe lamb of a poor peasant in order to feed a guest. David's indignation is greatly kindled at the injustice of such behavior and he responds at once with the decision to punish the wicked man. Perhaps it was this same sense of justice that enabled the king to receive humbly the stern rebuke of the prophet expressed in the dramatic words, *Thou art the man.*

David's character qualities reveal a strong sense of loyalty, as we have seen, and an abhorrence for the betrayer. On the occasion of Saul's death in battle, a messenger who brought the news to David, boasted falsely that he himself had slain the defeated king. He hoped to be rewarded for this deed but David indignantly repudiated him and meted out the death penalty, for he had dared to kill the Lord's anointed. The same punishment was bestowed on the murderers of Ish-boseth, the son of Saul, ruler of the northern tribes. When these conspirators brought word of their deed to David, thinking to gain profit for it, he declared,

"As the Lord liveth, who hath redeemed my soul out of all adversity, when one told me, saying: Behold, Saul is dead, and he was in his own eyes as though he brought me good tidings, I took hold of him, and slew him in Ziklag, instead of giving him a reward for his tidings. How much more, when wicked men have slain a righteous person in his own house upon his bed, shall I not now require his blood of your hand, and take you away from this earth (II, 4:9–11)?"

David's feelings of indignation are understandable in both these instances. His many associations with the house of Saul could hardly leave him indifferent to the death of the two kings. Whether his anger was a bit too righteous and expressed a reaction formation to his hostility, we have no way of knowing. His response may also have been an effort to appease an unconscious sense of guilt at thus overcoming the father and the sibling. Both deaths did result in advantage to himself. However his manifest feelings and behavior were still an expression of nobler character than rejoicing at the destruction of his rivals.

It is also true that there were times when David displayed qualities which were in direct opposition to those we have just discussed. During his long career as a warrior, David was strikingly ruthless to his enemies on certain occasions. When such ruthlessness also takes on what seems like a rather bizarre quality, we may suspect unconscious influences at work in addition to the callousness of war.

During his conquests, David overcame Moab, a land on the eastern borders of the Dead Sea. After the victory he made the prisoners lie down on the ground in lines. Then he measured off two of these human lines and had the men put to death. Those in the third line were spared and became his servants.

What could be the meaning of this strange procedure, which evidently was not a customary one? David had some special associations with the people of Moab. His great grandmother, Ruth, was originally a Moabitess. When David had to flee from Saul and feared that the latter might take revenge upon his parents, the young man brought his father and mother to the king of Moab for safety.

There is no word in the text to indicate that the Moabite king was guilty of any unkindness to the parents of David. But interestingly legend in the rabbinic literature says that the king put Jesse and his wife to death.[13] It may well be that the purpose of this legend was to provide some justification for David's own later cruelty to the Moabites.

If Moab was associated with David's parents and earlier ancestry, the son may also unconsciously have expressed his hostility to parent figures and siblings by treating the Moabites with special cruelty. His arbitrary method of deciding who should live and who should die, by choosing two lines out of three, has a quality of omnipotence. David must unconsciously have been acting God-like in this situation. He may here have been asserting the power and the vengeance that the small child dreams of having toward the *giants* of his own family. It is now no longer they but he who has the power of deciding life and death. It is intersting that this account of the victory over Moab follows immedi-

y. It is true that he had a special grievance against the
er had shown to David. But the new king was persuaded by
s advisers that David's envoys were sent only for hostile reasons,
o spy out the city. So Hanun subjected them to humiliating treat-

long time. He then sends the following message to the king in
erusalem. "I have fought against Rabbah, yea, I have taken the
ity of waters. Now therefore gather the rest of the people
ogether, and encamp against the city, and take it; lest I take the

Then we are told that

David gathered all the people together, and went to Rabbah,
and fought against it, and took it. And he took the crown of
Malcam from off his head; and the weight thereof was a talent
of gold, and in it were precious stones; and it was set on David's
head. And he brought forth the spoil of the city, exceeding

And he brought forth the people that were therein, and
put them under saws, and under harrows of iron, and under
axes of iron, and made them pass through the brick-kiln; and
thus did he unto all the cities of the children of Amnon
(II, 12:29-31).

Why this contradiction of first Joab taking the city and then
David repeating this act, under the direction of Joab? David was
far from being a puppet king. Even later in his career, when
losing some of his vigor, David still wished to take an active part
in battle and several times had to be restrained from doing so.

Perhaps one should again look for other factors. Rabbah is referred to as the royal city, the *city of waters,* both names significant of the mother. Not too long ago, David had been the object of God's displeasure and punishment because of the affair with Bathsheba. Did he, therefore, require support from a father figure before he dared to invade the royal city? Did this act have to be a kind of formal gesture only, following the real invasion by Joab? We recall that it was Joab who was the first to enter another capital city, Jerusalem. There, also, David did not take the lead. But when the king does arrive upon the scene, at Rabbah, he goes through further motions of an ostentatious display of authority, removing the great crown from the head of Malcam, probably the figure of an idol (Milcom), the national deity of Ammon, and placing it upon his own head. His repressed hostility must have been increased at this time because of the loss of his son, which he perceived as a punishment from God. In spite of David's repentance for his behavior with Bathsheba, the hidden anger may have found displaced expression in unusual cruelty toward the children of Ammon, especially in the capital city.

David's Relationship with Joab

A study of David would be incomplete without a scrutiny of his relationship with Joab, the captain of his host, and Abishai, brother of Joab, both of them sons of his half-sister Zeruiah. Joab shows a rough but firm loyalty to David for most of their many years of association. However there are times when both Joab and Abishai show this loyalty by behaving toward others with such harshness and brutality that David loudly and strongly disclaims responsibility for their acts. One of his oft repeated phrases is, "What have I to do with you, ye sons of Zeruiah." Thus he repudiates their conduct and separates himself from them. This need to do so however may indicate how strong the tie between them really was, particularly with Joab.

Can this relationship be viewed only as the shared responsibility of a king and his general, or does Joab fulfill other needs of a more unconscious nature for the king? It seems that the latter is true. One gets the impression that Joab acts as a kind of *alter ego* for David, with the role of clearing the way for the fulfillment of the king's *real* wishes, often in contradiction to his *expressed* wishes. Joab thus performs for David the distasteful tasks which the king is not able to do for himself. The captain of the host often seemed to serve as the object for the projection of David's more unacceptable impulses of an aggressive and sexual nature. Thus he helped to save face for the king both in the eyes of the people and in terms of David's own superego. Let us see if the material supports such a construction.

We have recently referred to Joab's role in taking the cities of Jerusalem and Rabbah, where he acted as a kind of substitute for David. In the king's liaison with Bathsheba, it was Joab to whom David turned again for help, this time in the conspiracy for getting rid of Uriah. Thus Joab makes it possible for David to possess the woman openly, just as he facilitates his conquest of the cities. He gives David permission, as it were, to own the woman, symbolically the city. We have also seen how Joab fulfilled David's unspoken wishes in having Absalom recalled from exile.

There were times, however, when Joab acted in ways that were directly contrary to David's expressed desires and instructions. One of these was his murder of Abner, the captain of the host over the Northern tribes in the days when David ruled only over Judea. Joab had his own score to settle with Abner, who had killed Asahel, Joab's younger brother, in battle. A second time when Joab defied David was in the slaying of Amasa, another captain of the host, the military leader of Absalom's forces during the latter's rebellion. David had retained Amasa after the revolt was over. Both murders were committed by Joab, not only in cold blood, but in treachery, as he approached each of these men under the guise of friendship. Abner, who came to make peace with David in the early days at Hebron, was himself a betrayer. He had deserted Ish-boseth, the son of Saul, for purely personal reasons.

One wonders if David's need for appeasement or his sense of

guilt or both were so great that he not only forgave Amasa, the rebel captain of Absalom's army, but tried to put him in place of Joab himself. Complicated motives must have prompted such an act. Did he wish to placate the forces that had opposed him and thus retained the man who might achieve this for him? If so, it was certainly a gesture of weakness and would be recognized as such, not only by the previous followers of Absalom, but by David's own loyal soldiers. Was it prompted by a need to punish Joab for his most unforgivable deed, the murder of Absalom?

An unconscious influence which may have caused David to forgive Amasa and place him in an important position may have been an identification of Amasa with Absalom. He forgave Amasa as he longed to forgive and be reunited with his erring son.

But can one say that in slaying Abner and Amasa, Joab was fighting only his own cause? The fact that Joab dispatched them relieved David of having to deal with men who were traitors at heart and who must have been personally obnoxious to him. Again, Joab carried out what must have been real but unrecognized wishes of his king. By betraying the betrayers, Joab may have served his David again.

What about Joab's slaying of Absalom? This deed represented the epitome of Joab's disobedience of David's direct commands. It was an act which no other would have dared to commit and one which moved the king, as we have seen, to expressions of deep mourning. Was there anything in this deed which could be in harmony with our thesis that Joab tended to carry out the real though unconscious wishes of the king? If David was so strongly identified with his son, then the feeling must have been an ambivalent one, for this kind of identification carries with it the wish to displace the other. David's warmth and love for Absalom were conscious, his hatred was unconscious.

Such ambivalence toward a son was unacceptable to David's superego, which evidently was strongly molded on the ego ideal of being a loving father. But Absalom had been guilty of the most extreme hostility that a son can have, not only the wish but the act of trying to displace the father. David's repressed feelings toward him would have contained the hostility to be expected in these circumstances. His melancholia at the death of Absalom must have been in proportion to the underlying anger. His failure to punish Joab may also have been the expression of an intense need to defend himself from awareness of such hostility.

Joab's murder of Absalom was probably based on the captain's feeling that this punishment was deserved by such a son and that therefore David must have wanted it. If this was the case, then somewhere within David himself, such knowledge must also have lurked. Joab therefore acted once more in accordance with David's unconscious wishes.

Why therefore did David never forgive this deed? If an unconscious wish was fulfilled, should he not have forgiven Joab and secretly appreciated that his military leader had again acted in his behalf? This area of relationship with a son, however, was a most conflictful one for David, as we have seen. No solution would have been the right one. If Joab represented David's unacceptable aggressive wishes in this respect, then the king's superego would demand his punishment. But because of his ambivalence, which may have been based on a secret awareness of his own involvement in the situation, David could not carry out any punitive measures against Joab. It was only later, on his deathbed, that the king directed his son Solomon to mete out the punishment which he himself was unable to inflict.

Strangely enough, it is in the very last days of David's illness, at the time that his son Adonijah makes an attempt to seize the succession to the throne, that Joab deserts David and takes sides with the rebellious son. This desertion is hard to explain. It may be a final expression of Joab's own ambivalence to the king, in whose cause he had put aside so much of his own personality.

Abishai, the brother of Joab, and one of the mighty champions that surrounded David, also served the same purpose, though to a lesser degree. Like Joab, Abishai wished to dispose of David's enemies for him. Early in David's career, it was Abishai who responded to a call for a volunteer to accompany David into the sleeping camp of Saul, when the latter was pursuing them in the wilderness of Judea. Abishai's first impulse was to slay this enemy of his leader, but David forbids him. Many years later, when the king is fleeing from Jerusalem during the revolt of Absalom and the hostile Shimei insults him and casts stones at him, it is Abishai who wishes to kill the offender, but is again restrained.

There are other occasions when Abishai continues his pattern of wishing to exterminate David's enemies, in a role that resembles Joab's. After the revolt, when David is preparing to return to Jerusalem, among those who come to greet him and pay their respects is this very same obnoxious Shimei. He now comes forward and expresses contrition for his former behavior, asking the king's forgiveness. Abishai then demands as before, "Shall not Shimei be put to death for this, because he cursed the Lord's anointed?" And David replies, as before, "What have I to do with you, ye sons of Zeruiah, that ye should this day be adversaries unto me? shall there any man be put to death this day in Israel? for do not I know that I am this day king over Israel?" And the king said unto Shimei, "Thou shalt not die (II, 19:22–24)."

Abishai is described as one of David's mighty men who "lifted up his spear against three hundred and slew them." It was this champion who defended the aging David in a battle when the king was attacked by one of the Philistine giants. "And Isbi-benob, the weight of whose spear was three hundred shekels of brass in weight, he being girded with new armour, thought to have slain David. But Abishai, the son of Zeruiah, succored him, and smote the Philistine and killed him (II, 21:16–17)."

It is interesting that whenever David rejects or condemns any act of one of these brothers, he always refers to both of them in the expression, "Ye sons of Zeruiah." He thinks of them as a unit, perhaps, because they serve the same purpose for him. These men are evidently the only close relatives who consistently and loyally remain at his side for many years. Sons of his sister, they must have been like good brothers to David and may have filled an important need, since his own brothers seem to have abandoned him. David's frequent gruffness toward them must have expressed his closeness too, particularly if they unconsciously symbolized projections of himself. At the same time, these attitudes may have indicated his ambivalence also, toward sibling figures, whose protection he desired but whose power he may have feared, attitudes characteristic of a younger brother toward older ones.

David and His Champions

A curious and unusual aspect about David's life as a leader is his evident wish to have heroes and champions around him, particularly in the later days of his reign. The Bible and the rabbinic literature go to great lengths and engage in considerable embellishment when describing the stature, size and strength of the mighty men who surround David and serve him with loyalty and devotion. Some of their achievements are related with an abandonment to fantasy and exaggeration that stands in marked contrast to the style of understatement and restraint that characterize other areas of biblical writing.

Similar to the feat of Abishai as mentioned earlier, Benaiah, another of these valiant men, "slew a lion in the midst of a pit in time of snow. And he slew an Egyptian, a man of mighty stature, five cubits high; and in the Egyptian's hand was a spear like a weaver's beam; and he went down to him with a staff, and plucked the spear out of the Egyptian's hand, and slew him with his own spear (II, 23:20–21)."

Four Philistine giants of Gath fought with Israel and were slain by David's mighty men. One of them is called Goliath. He is killed by Elhanan of Bethlehem. Some commentators claim this passage proves that David never did slay a *Goliath* himself and that this later event was displaced to a point early in the story and attributed to him. There seems to be no basis, however, for such a conclusion. It might be more helpful to find a common factor in all these stories of giants and the mighty men who slew them. It is evident that an element of fantasy is at work here.

David's rise to fame and fortune began with his killing of Goliath. Whether fact or legend, such an episode must have had a particular significance for David and therefore one could expect

recurrences of this theme later in his life. The unconscious significance of David's conquest of Goliath has been discussed earlier
in this study. One further aspect might be helpful here. The
fantasy of performing the heroic deed of slaying the evil monster,
which is common in fairy tales, may have been stimulated in
young David by special circumstances. With eight men older
than he in the family, the youth's need for achieving some kind
of recognition would have been especially great. Equally strong
must have been the superego forces of repression which had to
deal with wishes to overcome his siblings and his father. His need
for the love and approval of the good father would therefore be
all the greater as a reaction formation to such competitive feelings. The strength of these wishes may have come out in displacement against the villain who threatened the good father himself.
Such a fantasy would gain power from the background of his
times. To the shepherd youth, King Saul, a man of mighty stature,
must have represented the ideal father figure. Saul may have been
the first giant of young David's fantasies. But this giant, the king,
represented the ideal father, whose love and protection would
be very desirable. What better way to get this love than to save
such a figure from the threat of an even greater giant, an evil
and destructive being? Thus David's need to overcome the father
and to save him at the same time could be fulfilled.

One may question the assumption made here that such unconscious motivations were actually at work within David. What
basis is there for drawing these conclusions? One can only say
that they are hypotheses rather than conclusions and that the
basis for such a formulation lies in the material of the story itself,
as in the latent content of a dream. Competitiveness toward the
father and older siblings is too universal to need substantiation.
It is only the specific forms that this psychological struggle takes
that may require clarification. David's attitudes in the father and
son roles all during his life seem to follow certain patterns, as we
shall continue to point out, that indicate ambivalent feelings with
reaction formations toward father and son figures.

It is in the later years of his life that the fantasy of the giants of Gath return. But now there is a reversal of roles. It is not David who is the hero, protecting a father figure. This task is projected to others and the king himself is the one who is defended by the bravery and devotion of his chiefs. David's need to have heroes and champions about him, men of great size and strength, now becomes more understandable. He identifies with these heroic sons who save the father and thus repeats in fantasy what was probably the most wonderful and gratifying experience of his life, the conquest of Goliath and the rewarding interest and attention from the king that followed. Now he was the father and his champions defend him lovingly. The devotion of these son figures served as a reassurance against any retaliatory aggression toward him. Guilt feelings regarding hostility toward the father that must have been a repressed element in the killing of Goliath could thus more easily be warded off. The fact mentioned earlier that one of the giants is named *Goliath* and is killed by a Bethlemite again points to David's longing to repeat vicariously his own youthful experience.

Another of these four giants of Gath is described as having six fingers on each hand and six toes on each foot. Like a composite figure in a dream, he may symbolize aspects of David's own unconscious at this time. The extra appendages, in their representation by the opposite, a mechanism commonly found in dreams, may express castration anxiety on the part of David, experienced here through projection.[14] The monstrous creature may also be the powerful phallic father, more than usually equipped to avenge himself upon the man who once decapitated another giant of Gath, an act which also symbolized castration. Significantly, he is slain by one of David's champions named Jonathan, the son of Shimea, David's brother. Was David now allowing an *earlier* Jonathan some of the victory once thought to be his due when David replaced the son of Saul as the challenger of Goliath? It is of interest also that when the long list of the champions who surrounded David is mentioned, the name of each is given in terms of his lineage except for that of Jonathan, which here stands alone (II, 23:32). Was the one who held that name in the past merged with the later Jonathan in the mind of David at this point and therefore his true identity confused?

Legend says that the four giants of Gath were brothers, the sons of Orpah, a sister-in-law of Ruth. The two women were also purported to be sisters, both being daughters of the Moabite king.[15] The giants would therefore represent a relationship with David on a collateral level, as with siblings. Again Moab and Gath are brought together in a familial association. The former is the land of David's maternal ancestress, Ruth, while the latter is the *mother-city* of the giants, whose more remote origins are also Moabite. Thus the view is strengthened that the giants symbolize hostile brothers who also represent oedipal fathers.

With the weakening of his defenses brought about by age, David was more vulnerable to unconscious feelings of guilt, that of overcoming his father, his brothers, his friend Jonathan, and most of all, his king, and emerging as the mightiest of them all. David's retreat however is in the form of identification with sons who love and protect him.

The unconscious need to renounce his role of leadership in war gains further credence from the episode that occurs during one of these battles against the Philistines. The king grew faint and would have been killed by one of the giants had not Abishai saved him, as mentioned earlier. Then the men of Israel remonstrated with David and said, "Thou shalt go no more out with us to battle, that thou quench not the lamp of Israel (II, 21:17)."

An incident that brings out vividly the devotion of David's chiefs to their king occurs when the latter expresses a desire for some water from the nearby well of Bethlehem. His boyhood home was then a Philistine garrison. Three of David's chiefs hear the remark of their king. They steal through the enemy lines and bring David the water he wished for. The king is so moved that he cannot drink it. He pours it out as a libation before God, saying, "Be it far from me, O Lord, that I should do this; shall I drink the blood of the men that went in jeopardy of their lives (II, 23:17)?"

This act of sacrifice must also have expressed David's guilt in subjecting the men to this danger. But by pouring out the water he put their deed to naught, in a sense, for he denied himself the pleasure they wished to bring him. Like all sacrifice, the gesture contained ambivalent features.

In the Later Years of David's Rule

It may not be without significance that David's first indication of withdrawing from active leadership in battle, "lest the lamp of Israel be quenched," comes immediately after one of the most gruesome acts of his life.

We are told that there was a famine in the land which lasted for three years. David inquired of the Lord what the cause for this expression of Divine displeasure could be and the Lord said, "It is for Saul, and for his bloody house, because he put to death the Gibeonites (II, 21:1)."

This is the first reference to such an act on the part of Saul. The gravity of this offense would lie in the fact that early in the Hebrew conquest of Canaan, the Gibeonites had made a treaty with Joshua according to which they were to be permitted to live peacefully in the land. If Saul had put any of them to death, he had violated this treaty.

David then summoned the Gibeonites and asked how he could atone for the wrong they had suffered. They demanded blood retaliation, that seven sons of Saul be surrendered to them to be hanged from the walls of Gibeah, former citadel of the first king. David acquiesced to this demand. We are told that he spared the son of Jonathan because of the oath that had passed between the two former friends, but he took the two sons of Rizpah, Saul's concubine, and five sons of Michal, whom she bore to Adriel. This latter statement is quite puzzling, for it was Michal's sister, Merab, who was married to Adriel, while Michal, as we know, was David's wife. Biblical commentary and legend try to explain this strange error by saying that Merab had died and Michal brought up her children and therefore was considered their mother. However, there is no basis for such an assumption. We can only regard this error as a displacement on an unconscious level and try to understand what it means.

One must wonder first of all why this entire incident was introduced at this time. Suddenly, God is displeased because of an act ostensibly committed by Saul many years ago. This remembrance is followed by the punishment of famine upon a whole people and a demand for a *lex talionis* penalty involving the innocent sons of Saul.

It is possible that the alleged earlier betrayal of the Gibeonites might have served as a screen for a much more recent betrayal which David himself suffered at the hands of his own son Absalom, a hurt which had never found expression in real anger on the part of the king. There may have been an unconscious need on David's part to punish someone for the wrong and humiliation he had suffered from his son. His anger at Absalom must have been deeply stifled by his strong identification with the youth, and by the sorrow and guilt stimulated by his untimely death. But a son or sons ought to suffer for the revolt against the father, for the shedding of blood where an eternal covenant of peace should have existed. Who could be more fitting victims than the sons of Saul, the man from whom he had wanted and expected love but received hostility!

The question arises as to why the Gibeonites were selected as the symbol for this acting out, if so we consider it. Shortly before the event referred to above, the expression "at the great stone which is in Gibeon," is mentioned in another context. It is there that Joab perpetrates one of his several acts of treachery. He chanced to come upon Amasa, the recently appointed rival captain of the host, at the stone of Gibeon. Pretending to be friendly, Joab seized the beard of Amasa in the customary gesture preliminary to kissing a friend. While doing so, he stabbed Amasa with his sword. This incident occurred while David's troops were in Gibeon, on their way to the capture of another traitor, Sheba, of the house of Saul, who had tried to stir up the Benjamites to revolt. These incidents must further have influenced the mood of the king at this time. He had been betrayed by all three men, Amasa, Joab, and Sheba, as well as by Absalom. The need for reprisal must have been strong in the weary and bitter heart of David.

The Gibeonites were very likely a symbol of betrayal in the minds of the people of Israel. As will be recalled, this people perpetrated a ruse upon Joshua and the elders of Israel in the early conquest of the land. They sent messengers to bid for peace and portrayed themselves as coming from a distant part of the country, remote from the land in which the Israelites had an immediate interest. On this basis, a treaty of peace was established with them. The trick was soon discovered but the bond, once established, could not be annuled. As a punishment, however, the Gibeonites were made the servants of the children of Israel, the *hewers of wood and the drawers of water*. The great stone in Gibeon may well be a symbolic locality representing the betraying phallic father, where the treacherous murder of Amasa took place.

On the other hand, the Gibeonites were the Cinderellas of the people of Israel, and it may have been this aspect of himself, stemming from early childhood, that moved David unconsciously to identify with them and displace his own cause to theirs.

Let us return now to the question of why the sons of Michal are mentioned instead of the sons of Merab, which was no doubt intended. This error could provide another thread of association to the whole episode, with its repetition of the theme of betrayal. Saul had betrayed David when he promised him the hand of Merab and then gave her to Adriel instead. Michal herself betrayed him by not bearing him any sons and by her rejection of him. The two women may have become identified in his mind. Punishing the sons of Merab, then, would be a way of punishing the imaginary sons of Michal, and thereby his own sons. It may also be that he regarded Michal unconsciously as an incestuous object, a mother who belonged to the father figure, Saul. If this was so, then the grandsons of Saul would indeed be Michal's sons also. David's repressed hostility toward his own disappointing sons could then find appropriate expression by being displaced toward the children of Merab.

The confused identifications between sisters and mothers, as perhaps with his own half-sister, Zeruiah, and his mother, may also find expression here. Since he was the youngest in the family, David may have had sisters who were old enough to be his mother. This whole unhappy episode is blamed on a cause arising in the distant past, as indeed psychologically it was, for David's first disappointments in his family relationships started at an early age. The murder of the seven sons of Saul must also have been associated with David's repressed hostility toward his seven brothers, which would account for the specificity of this number.

It seems that God's displeasure toward the people of Israel was aroused on another occasion during the reign of David, also in the latter years of the king's life. Of the second occurrence we are told, "And again the anger of the Lord was kindled against Israel, and He moved David against them, saying, 'Go, number Israel and Judah (II, 24:1).' "

The word *again* in the above text must refer to the first time that God's anger was expressed, namely on the occasion just discussed, when he caused the people to suffer famine for three years. Evidently God had further need to punish Israel, and in order to find justification for this, he *moves* David to commit the wrongdoing of census-taking. In the account as recorded in *First Chronicles,* this contrary behavior on the part of God cannot be so well tolerated as in the earlier text of *Samuel Two,* and the narrative states that *Satan* was the one who inspired this wicked behavior in the king.

Two questions occur at once. Why did God feel the need to punish Israel again and why was census-taking such a serious offense? Let us start with the latter query. As Frazer points out, there was a common superstition among primitive peoples against counting or enumerating the good things one possessed. Some of the unconscious factors behind such a superstition, may be that the possessor fears to tempt Fate by arousing envy in others, thus risking the loss of these good things. David's lack of such fear in his act of census-taking may have been an expression of arrogance, as if there was no outside power of whom he needed to be afraid. If the king had proceeded on this task of numbering the people for some immediate realistic reason, as he did before the battle with the forces of Absalom, that would have been another matter. It was evidently the spirit in which David embarked on this project that made it so offensive to God. It indicated a vain-glorious attitude on the part of David, a need for a feeling of omnipotence and pride in the numerical strength of the military men who were subject to his command. Its narcissistic nature was immediately sensed by Joab, who tried to dissuade David from the undertaking, but in vain. David had the need to be God-like and to rely on his own strength for future military victory rather than trusting in God.

This, then, was the offense to which God himself tempted David. The text frankly conveys the idea that God stimulated David to an act that merited punishment because he was again angry with Israel. Perhaps the *again* really means *still*. God was still angry even after the expiation David offered by hanging the seven sons of Saul.

Psychoanalytically, this irrational behavior of God can only be seen as a projection of David's own feelings. It must have been David's anger that needed a further outlet. The hostility that prompted David to avenge himself on the seven sons of Saul had not yet been assuaged. This time aggression was directed toward the larger group, his entire people.

What had aroused David's anger to this degree? In order to comprehend this, let us glance briefly at his life situation during this period. Both episodes under consideration took place in that aftermath of David's most successful years of reign, when he returned from exile. The revolt of Absalom and the events that followed must have had a severely traumatic effect upon the aging king. It should not be too surprising if some regressive behavior patterns manifested themselves at this time, as was suggested before.

The need to leave his beloved Jerusalem, although a decision of his own making, must have been experienced by David as a form of abandonment. It was the mother and the people who deserted him. David's return to Jerusalem too was marked by disharmony. The question of who was to have the honor of accompanying the king back to Jerusalem became the occasion of an ugly brawl between the people of the northern tribes and those of the south, to the point where "the words of the men of Judah were fiercer than the words of the men of Israel." During this outbreak, Sheba tried to start a new revolt with his cry,

> "We have no portion in David, neither have we inheritance in the son of Jesse; every man to his tents, O Israel." So all the men of Israel went up from following David, and followed Sheba, the son of Bichri; but the men of Judah did cleave unto their king, from the Jordan even to Jerusalem (II, 20:1–2).

David thus became a kind of object for whose possession the two segments of population were struggling. It must have been a bitter moment for the sad-hearted king. Even before this hour, David had to humble himself by sending messengers to his own people of Judah, suggesting to them that he should be brought back from exile. It seems that they were the last to do so. He humbled himself also by appointing Amasa, who headed the forces of the Absalom revolt, to the post of one of his own chief officers. He endured the apologies of the officious Shimei, who had so vilely cursed him on an earlier occasion.

One wonders if it was really necessary for David to have been so humble and so forgiving at this time. He no longer had a rival for the throne. There was no real obstacle in the way of his return. We must conclude that David's own emotional attitudes were largely responsible for his behavior. He abandoned his throne readily and returned to it humbly.

But such feelings are invariably accompanied by hostility. He who suffers often feels that he has earned the right to make others suffer. The ruler who returns from exile, then, is different from the king of earlier years. His first act after this return is to send his army after the traitor Sheba, for the king feared that the people might again follow him in another rebellion. David seems to have lost his trust in the people.

It is at this time that the punishment of famine falls upon the land and David seeks absolution from God by hanging the seven sons of Saul. Then the text deals with a brief account of further war with the Philistines, highlighted by the great champions who fought for David. It may be that he found it necessary at this point to convince himself of the love and loyalty of the great fighting men, the killers of giants, who surrounded him. David may have been striving here for a strengthening of his old defenses. He was the beloved father, surrounded by mighty sons. They killed the great giants of Gath to protect him. He was not unwanted, he was not abandoned, he was still *the lamp of Israel.*

But the hurts that David suffered must have proved stronger than his defenses. He was still angry with the people and had a need to punish them. In ordering the taking of the census, David unconsciously indicates the true source of his anger. On a manifest level, he is taking undue pride in the number of fighting men that are his to command. On a deeper level, he may have been counting them for the purpose of destroying them. Indeed, this purpose can be seen in the opening statement of the story, that God was angry and moved David to number Israel and Judah. The projection upon God of his own anger may have the further significance of indicating David's identification with God at this point. It is David who numbers the people, thus expressing an unconscious fantasy of omnipotence over them. Such a fantasy would compensate him for feelings of helplessness that he must have suffered at their hands. It is indeed David himself, here playing a God-like role, who is angry at Israel.

In response to the king's command, the reluctant Joab and his men travel throughout the land numbering the military men available to David. It takes them nine months and twenty days to complete the task. The king then acknowledges responsibility for his act and repents.

And David's heart smote him after that he had numbered the people. And David said unto the Lord: 'I have sinned greatly in what I have done; but now, O Lord, put away, I beseech Thee, the iniquity of Thy servant; for I have done very foolishly (II, 24:10).'

But God does not respond to the king directly as in earlier, happier days. He sends the prophet Gad with a message that David may choose one of three punishments for the wrong he had done. Curiously, it is the people who are to be the objects of the punishment, not David personally. Thus, the original impulse of the wish for retribution against them comes through, while David's suffering would be that of the good father who sees his children chastised. The three possible penalties are seven years of famine, three months of being pursued by foes in war, or three days of pestilence throughout the land. David chooses the last of these, declaring that he would rather put his fate into the hands of God than of man. Here again his bitterness toward the people finds expression.

During the plague seventy thousand men throughout the land perish. It is interesting that women and children are not included here. The text definitely says *men*. One might argue that the death of women and children would not be of sufficient significance to mention since they would not decrease David's fighting force. But the Bible is not a book of military strategy. Its emphasis is on the human and the moral. We must assume therefore that this incident deals with David's specific hostility toward men.

The number, *seventy*, occurs here again. We discussed its possible significance in connection with the seventy and fifty thousand men who perished in Beth-shemesh for gazing upon the Ark. Our conclusion then was that the *seventy* may have stood for the elders, or fathers, of the community. Here, combined with *thousands*, we have the impression that David was primarily punishing father figures, multiplied by the thousands. However, it may contain the additional meaning that not only the fathers were punished, but the people as a whole.

Since human behavior is often overdetermined, that is, has

more than one underlying cause, it might be well to consider further why census-taking was given as the act of wrongdoing.

As has been noted before in the present studies, related ideas are often expressed in the Bible by placing such material in juxtaposition to each other. Now immediately preceding the statement that the anger of God was kindled against Israel is *another kind of census-taking* in which David lists in highly specific fashion thirty-seven chiefs who surrounded him. It is clear in the glorified accounts related of their exploits that David relied on them for protection in his old age.

But, one might ask, where was David's faith in God at this point? Why was it necessary to describe in so expansive and even vain-glorious a fashion the beloved *sons* around the king? We have tried to explain the underlying psychodynamics within David that might have motivated this presentation. But a further element should be considered. It may be that a conflict of loyalties was going on within David involving his most precious relationship, his feelings toward God himself.

In contrast to the youthful David who faces Goliath with a confident assertion of his trust in God, the aging king glories in his human defenders. There is a further puzzling aspect. In the very midst of an account describing the exploits of David's military men, content of a totally different nature is suddenly introduced. A lengthy prayer of exceptional intensity of feeling and beauty of imagery (also found in the Bible as *Psalm 18*) is presented. In it David extols God as his Protector, using such expressions as "The Lord is my rock, and my fortress, and my deliverer;/ The God who is my rock, in Him I take refuge." He declares that God is the one who will save him from the violence of his enemies and from the dangers of death: "For the waves of Death encompassed me./ The floods of Belial assailed me." David furthermore attributes to God the victory over his enemies: "For Thou has girded me with strength unto the battle." Even in relation to his own people, God has helped the king: "Thou also hast delivered me from the contentions of my people;/ Thou hast kept me to be the head of the nations."

Thus all the problems with which David was then troubled

are expressed in the psalm, which is too lengthy to be quoted here in its entirety. Yet the abruptness of its appearance in the text creates an element of surprise. Scholars from the school of *Higher Criticism* believe that it was added at a later date, together with the chapters immediately preceding and following (Sam. II, 21–24). One writer describes this content as a kind of *literary miscellany,* stemming from several different sources.[16, 17] There is no convincing reason given however of why the biblical compilers inserted this material in what is evidently regarded as a haphazard fashion.

Psychologically, the sudden appearance of this poignant expression by David of his loyalty and devotion to God makes sense. It may correctly express his conflictful feelings at this point in his life, perhaps serving as an unconscious denial of his lack of trust in God, a state of mind so unusual for him as to cause deep emotional distress.

But the feelings seem to expend themselves in the very length and intensity of verbal expression. The rush of conscience is subdued and dies away. The latter part of the prayer (Chap. 23) is preceded by the phrase, "Now these are the last words of David:" Their meaning is unclear. Perhaps the king would have wished that the matter had ended thus, with these *last words* which consist of a further assertion of his own sense of righteousness. "For I have kept the ways of the Lord,/And have not departed wickedly from my God." This sounds like a further desperate effort at denial of his real feelings at this moment in time. But the conflict within him continues. He returns again to extolling his human defenders, this time enumerating them one by one, a kind of *census-taking* which must have given him gratification.

Thus the two calamities that befell Israel, famine and pestilence, natural ills that the land and the people were frequently heir to, may be utilized here to describe a temporary breaking down of David's life-long defense of being the loving father and the dutiful son. Instead, his repressed hostilities, more successfully defended against in earlier years, find expression in his need to punish and to take revenge. But this need also must be carefully defended from awareness through projection and displacement.

We come now to the dramatic incident of how the plague stopped and the city of Jerusalem was spared. The text says,

> And when the angel stretched out his hand toward Jerusalem to destroy it, the Lord repented Him of the evil, and said to the angel that destroyed the people: "It is enough; now stay thy hand." And the angel of the Lord was by the threshing-floor of Araunah the Jebusite. And David spoke unto the Lord when he saw the angel that smote the people, and said: "Lo, I have sinned, and I have done iniquitously; but these sheep, what have they done? Let Thy hand, I pray Thee, be against me, and against my father's house (II, 24:16–17)."

Interestingly, it is God himself who intercedes with the angel of death for the safety of Jerusalem. It is not hard to imagine David in this fantasied role, sparing the city he loved so much. Nor is it difficult to see the symbolism of the angel by the threshing-floor of the Jebusite, with his hand stretched out toward Jerusalem. It is the memory of the fruitful, sexual mother, the loving woman, that restrains and puts an end to David's hostile wishes. The father forgives the sons out of love for the mother. Here is indeed the picture of Eros conquering Thanatos. Also in his compassionate plea asking God to spare the people, "These sheep, what have they done?", we see a return of the former David, the good shepherd, who now rightly takes the responsibility for his hostile wishes upon himself.

Although anthropomorphic presentations of God are certainly not unusual, such irrational behavior on God's part, first being angry against Israel, then prompting David to behave in a way that would justify punishment of the entire nation, then repenting of the evil, is somewhat anachronistic in this period of Jewish history. But viewed as a consequence of David's inner struggle at this time, it seems to portray an understandable projection of this conflict.

David is instructed by Gad the prophet to build an altar to the Lord on the threshing-floor of Araunah, the Jebusite. The king visits this man to buy the area. Araunah greets his august visitor with ceremony and offers to give him the desired land but David insists upon paying for it. He does so and builds his altar and then makes a burnt-offering upon it.

This transformation of the threshing-floor into an altar is a vivid expression of the process of sublimation. David gives up the sexual mother and transforms his incestuous desires, those wishes which lie at the basis of sibling rivalry and ambivalence to the father, into a worshipful submission to an Idealized Father, with whose moral laws he identifies. It is meaningful that again a stranger is involved in this process. The Jebusite, representative of the original owners of Jerusalem, may represent a defense against the image of the oedipal father.

David refuses to accept the land as a gift. Sublimation must be accomplished through one's own effort and sacrifice. Moreover, that which one pays for is more securely one's own and cannot be reclaimed by the other. So too, did Abraham, in earlier days, insist on paying for the Cave of Machpelah, also purchased from a stranger.[18] Thus David makes his peace with God and, hopefully, with himself. It seems fitting that the book of *Samuel Two* ends with this episode.

David's Last Days

The manner in which a man relaxes his hold upon life during his last days on earth may be revealing of his character. At such a time we may expect defenses to weaken and long-repressed impulses to appear.

The last days of David are recorded at the beginning of *First Kings*. We are told that

> David was old and stricken with years; and they covered him with clothes, but he could get no heat. Wherefore his servants said unto him: "Let there be sought for my lord the king a young virgin; and let her stand before the king, and be a companion unto him; and let her lie in thy bosom, that my lord the king may get heat." So they sought for a fair damsel throughout all the borders of Israel, and found Abishag the Shunammite and brought her to the king. And the damsel was

very fair; and she became a companion unto the king, and ministered to him; but the king knew her not (Kgs. I, 1:1–4).

This intriguing situation brings to mind a number of questions. David was about seventy years old at this time. Among his many wives and concubines there must have been a number considerably younger than he. Why couldn't one of them have performed this function for David? The text states clearly that the king did not use her as a sexual object—"he knew her not." Why then did she have to be a fair virgin for whom a search must be conducted throughout the land? Her two functions are to "stand before him and to minister to him," and also to "lie in his bosom and warm him." This is clearly the task of *mothering*. But wouldn't it have been more understandable and suitable for a middle-aged woman to perform such duties?

Psychoanalytically, we can view this incident as a fulfillment of David's infantile wish to return to the arms of the mother. Abishag lay in his bosom as he had once lain in the maternal bosom. She must be a young and lovely mother, as the child visualizes her; and indeed, the mother of one's youth is generally young. She must be beautiful, too, because this is the mother of one's oedipal dreams and fantasies, the most desirable person in the world. But this object of incestuous wishes must of course be held inviolate; she may not be used sexually. It is also in accordance with childhood fantasy that the young mother should be a virgin. For the child wishes to deny the role of the father in conception.

The good mother stands before the child and ministers to him and is a companion to him. And when he is cold, she takes him to her bosom and warms him. This is what Abishag did for David.

The suggestion for this kind of comforting comes from David's servants, the loyal, loving sons, who here turn over the desired and desirable mother to David for his complete possession. He does not have to compete with them for her attention. They voluntarily yield her to him. No guilt is thus involved.

On another level, further inferences can be drawn from this rather moving and pathetic picture of the old king, once a great and valiant warrior, now lying in the bosom of a young girl for warmth. One thinks of King Lear and the fair young daughter whose love he so desired. Other associations from literature come to mind. Freud's essay, "The Theme of The Three Caskets," reminds us that in mythology the young and lovely maiden may be symbolic not only of love but of death. In a desperate attempt at denial, death takes on the appearance of its opposite, youth and loveliness.[19] May not Abishag also represent this *motif* in her relationship with David? Her youth and beauty may have served as a denial of David's feelings of approaching death against which he thus fought. The two functions, that of maternal love and of death, are indeed opposites, for it is maternal love which saves the infant from death.

It is against this background that we can best understand David's reactions to the final events of his life. Adonijah attempts to seize the throne but is defeated in this purpose by the influence of Bathsheba and Nathan the prophet. At their urging, David bestirs himself from his blissful lethargy and does what is required of him. He gives specific directions for Solomon's anointment and the public announcement of the latter's succession. And he bestows upon Solomon suitable words of fatherly advice and blessing. Thus we see that David's ego was capable of functioning to the last.

However, before the king is roused by Nathan and Bethsheba, he does show a surprising indifference and lack of knowledge about what is going on about him. He does not even seem to be aware of Adonijah's rebellion, which takes place just outside the walls of Jerusalem. What could be the meaning of this? One recalls with what gratitude and deep emotion David once received the good word from God that a son would continue on the throne after him. And now that the moment was at hand, David seemed almost oblivious to his duties and responsibilities.

It is possible that his regression to the arms of the mother may have served the further purpose for David of defense against the pain of being displaced by a son. He would have liked to avoid the whole situation.

One more element of these last days has aroused speculation

among biblical students, together with some harsh criticism of the king. The final injunction which David imparts to Solomon is to inflict the penalty of death upon two men, Joab, the captain of the host, and Shimei, the Benjamite, who reviled David when he was fleeing from Jerusalem. Let us try to understand the basis for David's behavior here.

One can only conjecture the motives that prompted the dying king to this act. Did he perhaps wish to remove from his son's path personalities who might cause trouble for the young king? Some biblical commentators incline to this view. It is true that in Adonijah's revolt and attempted accession to the throne, he had received the powerful support of Joab, who at the very end of David's life thus strangely deserted and betrayed the man whom he had served so well for many years. Such a betrayal did indeed clearly show that Joab was not on the side of Solomon. He therefore would in truth be dangerous to the inexperienced young ruler. The king must have felt keenly such a personal betrayal by one who had shared his good and bad fortunes so closely throughout a lifetime. It must have revived David's anger toward those other betrayals of Joab, the murder of Abner and Amasa, and most of all, of Absalom. As we indicated before, the need to punish Joab for Absalom's death must have remained strongly present within David.

Thus while it seems that reality factors in the situation are sufficient to explain David's feelings and action in this matter, we know that the unconscious plays its role in every situation, whether for good or ill. We can see David functioning here on two levels, the still integrated ego, thinking probably in terms of what was best for his young son Solomon, and the more infantilized David, reluctantly stirred out of his pleasant regression from the arms of the mother. To this latter David, the thought of Joab may have evoked ancient memories of the betraying father and infantile wishes for his destruction. Moreover, if it is true that on many occasions Joab represented a projection of David himself, a part of his own personality which carried out wishes unacceptable to the king's superego, then with David's own death, this rejected part of him should also logically die. Perhaps, on this unconscious basis, too, David could not brook the survival of Joab.

Why was Shimei coupled with Joab for this dread punishment of bringing ". . . his hoar head down to the grave with blood." Again, on a reality level, Shimei, the Benjamite, was a potential enemy to a Davidic successor to the throne. His hatred for the house of David and his wish to restore the dynasty of Saul were made abundantly clear on the occasion when he so cruelly reviled and cursed the grieving king. Such a man too could create difficulty for Solomon.

However, according to the wording of the text, these were not the reasons why David required their punishment at Solomon's hands. They were to be punished because of that which they did to David himself. The long suppressed anger of the king now finds an outlet. He does not try to justify or rationalize beyond this.

Thus we see that David is deeply human to the end. The repressed wishes of both love and hate emerge through his weakened defenses. His strongest emotions of longing and love for the mother, hatred for the hostile father, devotion and duty to his son, and an abiding faith in God, the Good Father, mark his last words and actions.

Summation

David's life history can best be understood in terms of the inner struggle that is the mark of both human frailty and human strength. His need to be conqueror and king, ruler of men, met with the obstacle of unconscious conscience. The guilt of the conquest and of the triumph, which is the guilt of overcoming *the father,* found expression in David's personal life. His defenses gradually weakened and in the latter part of his existence, he regressed to a reversal of the father-son role, and finally, before death, to the infant in the arms of the mother.

David's life seems to follow a normal curve of gradual rise to power and then a gradual descent to the waning strength of old age. Even the length of his life span is the average one, seventy years. He is the first biblical hero whose years are measured according to the standards held valid by the ordinary man. This may be symbolic of the fact that David was a hero on a very human level and should be evaluated on that basis.

Tradition associates the house of David with the coming of the messiah and pictures David himself as the model or prototype of this mystical character. The Jewish conception of the messiah is one who will usher in an era of happiness, peace, and prosperity for all mankind. In that happy day the dead will be resurrected and the Jewish people will be gathered in from the far corners of the world to the land of Zion.

The word *messiah* means the *anointed one* in Hebrew, similar to the word *Christ,* which comes from the Greek. We will not enter here into a discussion of the role played by the concept of the messiah in Jewish lore but rather ask ourselves why a scion of the house of David was elected for this honor.

The reign of David was one of the proudest and most glorious periods in Jewish history. In later centuries, when the people of Israel were dispersed over many lands and suffered many adversities, they clung to this memory of a Golden Age in Jewish history. The idea of a messiah then became associated with a wish-fulfilling fantasy that someone like David would come once more and restore the glories of the past. The point which seems of particular significance for our purpose here is the choice of David in this connection. There must have been something in the personality of David as well as in the splendor of his reign that caused his name to be associated with the messianic hope. Our thesis throughout has been that David tended unconsciously or otherwise to think of himself as a loving father, not only to his sons, but to all the people of Israel. David was passionately devoted to his land and to his people. It is true, according to our thesis, that this fatherliness had a defensive quality. But the nature of one's defenses helps to determine the character of the man, to use a psychoanalytic cliché.

The people must have responded to this important aspect of his personality. In the messianic ideal, the people long for the return of this loving father in the purified and idealized personality of a messiah. It is clear that David himself is not to fill that role. This may be an acknowledgment of his ambivalence in it. But someone of his dynasty, who will be a wonderful king like David, would do so.

Just as the longing for a Golden Age is comparable to the wishes of adults for a return to a fantasied happy childhood, so the messiah of Jewish legend can be compared to a wish for the return of the ideal father, who will soothe all woes and bring to realization all the unfulfilled wishes of that earlier age. David's fatherliness, growing out of his sublimations and reaction formations, made him a suitable figure to form the prototype for such a role among the people of Israel. Together with this image were the concepts of strength, power, and glory associated with the reign of the king.

The life of David does not represent complete achievement. He is a very human figure with whom one can identify in terms of *becoming* rather than being. This aspect may also be symbolized in the longing for his return. The messianic era which one of his house supposedly will usher in, is also in the realm of that which is to come rather than that which is already achieved.

Solomon, the Man
and the Myth

CHAPTER SEVEN

SOLOMON, THE third king of ancient Israel, was strikingly different in personality from his father David. Popular ideas associated with him would concern his wisdom, the magnificence of his court, and his many wives. But little would be forthcoming about the nature of the man himself. While David is revealed to us in all his human strengths and weaknesses, Solomon has remained a kind of symbol. He is an idealized figure, commonly pictured in garments of royal purple, sitting upon a throne of legendary splendor. We visualize him entertaining the Queen of Sheba at a sumptuous feast or regaling her with clever stories and conundrums. In his more serious role, the king is viewed as rendering judgments in the royal courtroom, a symbolic figure of wisdom and justice.

The popular fantasies about Solomon present a curious enigma. Though we tend to view him as leading the rather indolent life of an Oriental monarch, much given to pleasure and pastime, we know it was under Solomon's regime that Israel was transformed from a provincial people to a cosmopolitan nation, related to other countries by far-flung trade routes over land and sea. His era was one of peace and prosperity, marked by ambitious building projects, the exploitation of mines, a tremendous increase in commerce and trade, and a growing urbanization of the people. Yet the forces that Solomon set in motion led to an economic and political collapse of the kingdom, and certain aspects of his personality left a significant impact of a negative kind on the moral and religious life of the people.

Another rather striking incongruity appears when one views the material of this king's life story. Although Solomon is known for his many wives, it is not popularly remembered that he had but one son, Rehoboam. Even the Bible, which tells us that Solomon had seven hundred wives and three hundred concubines, ignores completely the strangeness of this rather remarkable fact, the unfruitfulness of the king. The text refers several times to the *son* of Solomon, never to his *sons*. The reference always takes for granted that Solomon has a *son,* never indicating the peculiarity or the connection of the two facts—a thousand wives and one son! The Talmud, too, usually so open in its commentary on biblical heroes, barely makes mention of this fact. Later legend, which also weaves a rich fabric around the figure of the king, passes rather silently around this aspect of his life.

Solomon evidently had several daughters, at least two, in addition to a son. They are mentioned indirectly when named as the wives of two of his officers. This tendency in the biblical narrative to gloss over Solomon's paucity of offspring in a culture where children were considered so important must have some significance. It offers an indication of the mood and manner in which the biblical picture of Solomon is presented. This mood and manner seems to have a defensive aspect. Indeed, it has a quality uniquely its own. The story of Solomon is told as a kind of wonder tale, extolling the greatness and glory of this king. It is related as if all Israel were the audience, holding its breath and watching with awe the strange and splendid happenings that were being enacted in the once-crude fortress of the City of David and throughout the land. And indeed this must have been so.

One biblical commentator suggests that the motivations of the unknown compiler may have been to present a picture of Solomon as one who is acceptable to God, especially as the builder of the Temple.[1] But Solomon could have been acceptable in an almost infinite number of different roles and characterizations, provided the king was faithful to God's commandments. Is there then any specific meaning to the *actual* way in which his story has been preserved for us, why the style of the narrative dealing with the biography and reign of King Solomon tends to glorify and idealize? The answer must be sought analytically, considering the *form* of the material as part of the content.

The biblical text dealing with the life of Solomon is found in the first eleven chapters of *First Kings*. It is the product of a compiler who had the advantage of contemporary records, court archives, and eyewitness biographers. Yet, curiously, as we have noted, Solomon remains shrouded in legend, more of a myth than a man. Even Abraham, more remote in time and without the benefit of so much contemporary recording, is more real than the king who ruled Israel at the height of its grandeur. We shall assume that there were psychological reasons for this glorified image of Solomon which the Bible presents and which posterity has rather unquestioningly accepted.

At the same time, but in an oddly isolated fashion, the real faults and shortcomings of this intriguing personality are reported in the biblical text about him. Thus Solomon is remembered as the king who built the Temple. That he later went astray after strange gods, while clearly stated, is less known or recalled. There seems to be a kind of tacit agreement in the biblical account and folklore to highlight his positive qualities and to shroud his weaknesses. This effect is achieved by what might be called the process of isolation. We do not get the picture of a person in conflict, as with some other heroes of the Bible. Solomon's positive attributes are presented glowingly, unimpaired by any mention of faults. His more questionable behavior is set forth at another time, as something apart, and is generally presented as a factual statement, without much elaboration. Thus the two aspects of his personality tend to be isolated from each other, a mechanism of defense which, as we shall see, Solomon himself must have employed to a considerable degree. We have here an example of how the *form* of the material, the way in which it is presented, is closely related to some aspect of meaning in the content with which it deals. One wonders if Solomon's scribes, the record-keepers and biographers, in identification with the king's unconscious wishes, presented him in terms of his own self-image. History and legend managed to convey two separate images of him to the world. This analysis will attempt an understanding of both these aspects of the man and their relationship to each other.

Solomon, the third king of ancient Israel, enters upon the stage of biblical history riding upon his father's mule, in all its regal trappings. As we shall see, this fact is not without symbolic significance. The scene is at Gihon, the lower ground outside the eastern slope of Jerusalem, in the Valley of Kidron. The occasion is his anointment as king to succeed David, then on his deathbed. This ceremony of accession is the result of hasty plans to interrupt an attempted *coup d'etat* by Adonijah, at this time the oldest son of King David, who was also outside the city walls, at En-rogel, an adjoining valley, southeast of the city. Adonijah was about to have himself proclaimed king by his followers. This insurrection against the sick and aged ruler was brought to a precipitate halt when forces close to the throne overthrew the plot with the coronation of Solomon, long-promised heir to the kingdom. The sounds of acclamation from Gihon penetrated and paralyzed the festivities at En-rogel, sending the conspirators into flight.

Solomon plays a passive role in these exciting events. He must have had some inkling that Adonijah was conspiring to seize the throne. If he was totally unaware of the plot, then this factor too is meaningful in terms of his personality, indicating a certain detachment from his surroundings. Yet Solomon does nothing in his own behalf to insure his succession. Nathan the prophet and Bathsheba, the mother, acted for him when they influenced the ailing king to order the immediate coronation of this younger son. Thus, Solomon, the great king who makes himself famous for his energy and initiative, enters upon his heritage as a passive instrument in the hands of others. The biblical narrative conveys this feeling.

> So Zadok the priest, and Nathan the prophet, and Benaiah the son of Jehoida, . . . went down, and caused Solomon to ride upon king David's mule, and brought him to Gihon. And Zadok the priest took the horn of oil out of the Tent, and anointed Solomon. And they blew the ram's horn; and all the people said: "Long live king Solomon." And all the people came up after him, and the people piped with pipes, and rejoiced with great joy, so that the earth rent with the sound of them (1:38–40).*

Even in this account there is a kind of forced quality. "The people *said*, 'Long live the king.' " One would have expected a word like *shouted* instead. An element of incongruity is added by the expression, ". . . and the earth was rent with the sound of them," as if, somehow, the narrator is making an effort to compensate for the earlier lack of enthusiasm.

In his first act as the reigning king, Solomon has to deal with the rebel Adonijah. The latter rushes into the Tabernacle and holds on to the horns of the altar, pleading for his life. When Solomon is appraised of the situation, he makes his first judgment, declaring, "If he shall show himself a worthy man, there shall not a hair of him fall to the earth; but if wickedness be found in him, he shall die (1:52)." Solomon thus acts on his own initiative, promptly and decisively. His decision is one of clemency but firmness. It is an attitude strongly similar to David's own ways of judgment.

The aged king is still alive at this time. It may have been an act of sensitivity for his father's feelings as well as his own promptings that moved Solomon thus to blend justice with mercy, setting a standard based on ethical concepts of right and wrong.

---

* Biblical quotations and references in this chapter, unless otherwise noted, are from First Kings, Chapters 1–11.

It is only after the death of David that Adonijah dares to tempt fate. He requests through Bathsheba that David's own concubine, Abishag, should become his wife. Solomon, who receives his mother ceremoniously, quickly loses his politeness when he hears her request, and in a rage declares that Adonijah must die. The concubine of a king belongs to none other than the reigning monarch and is thus a symbol of his rule. Adonijah had gone too far.

Before his death, David summons the new king and imparts his final words of advice and blessing. He says to his son, "I go the way of all the earth; be thou strong therefore and show thyself a man; . . . (2:1–2)." Solomon is adjured to keep the commandments of God according to the law of Moses, for this was the path along which he would prosper. The parting words which David utters also have to do with the recommendation of punishment by death of two men, unfriendly to the new ruler and personally hated by David.

There is no indication of how Solomon reacted to his father in this deathbed scene. The reader is tacitly led to assume that the son has heard and that he will obey. But the attention is focused on David, not Solomon. The latter, here, as in the anointment which came earlier, gives the impression of being acted upon, the object of other people's purposes and decisions. Similiar situations in the lives of earlier rulers come to mind. When Samuel anointed Saul, the latter experienced himself as having a changed heart. Although this was also a passive role, the recipient's feelings are recorded and he remains the significant figure in the scene. When Samuel anointed David, ". . . the spirit of the Lord came down mightily upon him." But in regard to Solomon, neither the anointment nor the father's final words evoke any response, or at least, none considered sufficiently important to be noted in the text.

Yet Solomon picks up the reins of government with swiftness and surety. He acts upon his father's wishes but does so in his own way and in his own time. The new king thus displays two aspects of his personality in these early events. First, he submits passively to the actions of others in the assumption of his kingly role. Secondly, he accepts promptly the responsibilities of this role, acting with forethought and decision. One gets the impression that at the time of his anointment, the young ruler, in response to the dramatic change in his life situation, undergoes an abrupt transition from a passive to an active role.

The next episode in the biblical narrative has a special interest from a psychonanalytic viewpoint. God appears to Solomon in a dream. The frame of reference is clear. It is not that Solomon dreams about God, but that God chooses the medium of the dream in which to reveal his presence. This dream therefore need not be interpreted by wise men or priests. Indeed, its manifest content is clear enough. There is a striking lack of symbolism or imagery of any kind. God simply appears to him at Gibeon, where Solomon has gone to make sacrifices, and he speaks to the king without preamble or preliminary, saying, "Ask what I shall give thee." And Solomon proceeds to ask. He makes quite a lengthy speech, setting forth his request. God is so pleased with the nature of this request that he promises Solomon a great deal more—all those things which the king might have asked for but didn't. God too makes quite a long speech, most of it consisting of his laudatory reaction to Solomon's request. Only at the end does God make the usual condition and then in a limited kind of fashion. He says that if Solomon will walk in his ways and keep his statues and commandments as David his father did, then God would lengthen his days. The episode concludes with the words, "And Solomon awoke, and behold, it was a dream." Only here is there clearlv an acknowledgment of the nature of this experience.

Interestingly, at a later date, when God again appears to Solomon, this time not in a dream, the narrative states that this is the second time God appeared to him, thus not disinguishing beween the manner of the first appearance and that of the second. It is apparent therefore that Solomon accepted his dream, not as a subjective experience but as a reality. We know that in those days dreams were regarded as one of the ways in which revelations prophetic of future happenings or the will of God were made.

As is well-known, the request that Solomon makes of God is for an understanding heart. His reply to God's generous offer has important psychological implications and will therefore be quoted in its entirety.

> And Solomon said: "Thou hast shown unto Thy servant David my father great kindness, according as he walked before Thee in truth, and in righteousness, and in uprightness of heart with Thee; and Thou hast kept for him this great kindness, that Thou hast given him a son to sit on his throne, as it is this day. And now, O Lord my God, Thou hast made Thy servant king instead of David my father; and I am but a little child; I know not how to go out or come in. And Thy servant is in the midst of Thy people, that cannot be numbered nor counted for multitude. Give Thy servant therefore an understanding heart to judge Thy people, that I may discern between good and evil; for who is able to judge this Thy great people (3:6–9)?"

What feelings and attitudes does this prayer reveal in the youth who has only recently assumed the kingship? First of all, there is a feeling of inadequacy in regard to the great responsibility involved. Such a feeling can be considered normal and understandable under the circumstances. Solomon's definition of wisdom is also wise. He asks, not for intellectual acuity but for an *understanding heart* that can distinguish between good and evil. He seems to show cognizance here of the complexity of human behavior and he again makes morality the basis for judgment.

In what frame of reference does Solomon relate to God? He bases the claim for the acceptance of his plea on the strength of God's love for David. He himself is only David's son, and it is as such that he addresses himself to God.

This image of himself must indeed have loomed large in the mind of Solomon. He was important chiefly as his father's son. It seems safe to conjecture here that, at this point in his life, Solomon was suffering from feelings common to the sons of great fathers—a dwarfing of his own sense of self-importance when measured against the stature of the father. Solomon must have described his feelings truly when he said, "I am but a little child, ..."

And indeed he relates to God in this fashion. The small child wants and expects help from the father. Solomon asks for what he wants in a simple and direct manner. He does not question the omnipotent power of God to grant this request. Moreover, he must have been quite certain that God would approve such a wish. And indeed, the text immediately goes on to say, "And the speech pleased the Lord, that Solomon had asked this thing." Thus, not only the *content* of Solomon's plea met with approbation, but the speech itself, the form that this prayer took was pleasing to God. We see here a manifestation of narcissism in which verbal expression, a form of potency, plays a role. It will be helpful for our purpose to quote God's reply fully.

> And God said unto him: "Because thou hast asked this thing, and hast *not* asked for thyself long life; neither hast asked riches for thyself, nor hast asked the life of thine enemies; but hast asked for thyself understanding to discern justice; behold, I have done according to thy word: lo, I have given thee a wise and understanding heart: so that there hath been none like thee before thee, neither after thee shall any arise like unto thee. And I have also given thee that which thou hast not asked, both riches and honour—so that there hath not been among the kings like unto thee—all thy days. And if thou wilt walk in My ways, to keep My statutes and My commandments, as thy father David did walk, then will I lengthen thy days (3:11–14)." *(italics added)*

God's answer to Solomon's seemingly modest and praise-worthy request for an understanding heart is all that the most narcissistic personality, in its most imaginative mood, could wish for. God's reply is, of course, also a part of Solomon's dream and therefore expressive of the dreamer. We know that the word *not* doesn't occur in a dream, for negation cannot be expressed directly in the unconscious.[2] Solomon therefore *did* expect all those other things that he could have asked for but didn't. There is a certain charming naiveté about this whole episode despite its underlying complexity. It has the tone of a little boy telling his father that he wishes to perform his duties well and does not really expect a reward, although assuredly he does.

What Solomon asks for is omniscience. He also expects those things which will help to make him omnipotent—riches and a long life. The king thus craves to be all-knowing and all-powerful, the very opposite of the *little child* he feels himself to be. Moreover, there is an emphasis on the quality of *uniqueness,* in terms of the superlative. God promises to make him wise, "so that there hath been none like thee before thee, neither after thee shall any arise like unto thee."

The desire for wisdom, even in this exaggerated form, could be openly expressed because it was ego-syntonic. It is significant of the social and cultural standards among the ancient Israelites that wisdom, especially as it is related to human values and ethical standards, should have occupied so high a rank, preceding those of riches and honor in terms of prestige.

The biblical description of Solomon's wisdom is in striking contrast to the style of restraint and understatement so characteristic of other parts of the Bible.

> And God gave Solomon wisdom and understanding exceedingly much, and largeness of heart, even as the sand that is on the sea-shore. And Solomon's wisdom excelled the wisdom of all the children of the east, and all the wisdom of Egypt. For he was wiser than all men: than Ethan the Ezrahite, and Heman, and Calcol, and Darda, the sons of Mahol; and his fame was in all nations round about . . . (5:9–11).

The personalities with whom Solomon is here compared are obscure in terms of their names. Research revealed that Jewish tradition identifies Ethan the Ezrahite with *Abraham.* And interestingly, the same expression, the sand that is on the sea-shore, is also used in connection with Abraham. There it describes the countless number of progeny which God promises to the Patriarch. The limitless nature of the promise has a defensive function in that setting, too, being a reversal of the reality of Abraham's long period of childlessness. The same situation may be true of Solomon. Was this need to be the wisest of all men a compensatory one, to make up for feelings of inadequacy, particularly in the sexual role? Wisdom is a sublimated form of potency.

The second of these rather mysterious personalities with whom Solomon is favorably compared is Heman, *the confidant* (of God). He is identified with *Moses*. Calcol, the *giver of food,* is suggestive of *Joseph*. Darda refers not only to an individual, but to a whole group, the *wise generation,* the sons of *Mahol,* that is, the *sons of pardon*. There is a legend that the generation of Israelites who lived in the desert after the exodus from Egypt, were miraculously healed of any physical defects, such as lameness, blindness, or deafness, because God wanted to give the Torah to a people without blemish.[3]

We have here an interesting condensation of meanings. Solomon competes successfully with three father figures of his people but dares to do so only when they are presented in disguised form. Moreover, in identification with the sons of Mahol, he hopes that he too will be healed of any physical defects, symbolic of castration, and that the form this healing is to take will be an abundance of wisdom.

Solomon's competitiveness with his own father David is not even mentioned in this context. The only reference that might obliquely be associated with David is God's approval that Solomon did not wish for the life of his enemies. On his death-bed David did make such a request of Solomon, as we have seen. An implied criticism of David may therefore be present here. But rabbinic literature does make reference to a competitive attitude, saying that in his great wisdom, Solomon was not only able to supplement the words of his father David, but also sometimes to correct them. A number of tales have been collected that deal with the theme of Solomon's superiority over David in regard to wisdom. Although a production of later times, these stories contain old material.[4] It seems that the earlier Jewish literature was a little averse to seeing this competitive spirit between Solomon and David.

It is the thesis of this study that Solomon's need for grandeur, for power, for riches, for peaceful conquest, all have a defensive aspect, together with a hidden competitive attitude toward David. A large part of this defensive structure serves the function of overcoming feelings of inadequacy. To the extent that the desire to be wise was bound up with the wish to be a *good* king, it was a form of sublimation and found socially accepted outlets.

Let us try to understand the development of this personality by viewing further some of the influences of Solomon's life that are implicit but not always expressed in the biblical material.

According to the account in *Second Samuel,* Solomon was born to Bathsheba and David after the mother lost her first offspring. The latter had been the product of her illicit union with the king. It will be recalled that it was the death of this infant that David lamented so movingly. The second child comes therefore as a kind of restitution after Bathsheba becomes the wife of David. The Bible says, "And David comforted Bathsheba, his wife, and went in unto her, and lay with her; and she bore a son, and called him Solomon. And the Lord loved him; and He sent by the hand of Nathan the prophet, and he called his name *Jedidiah,* 'beloved of the Lord,' for the Lord's sake (II, 12:24–25)."

After the time of his birth Solomon is not mentioned again in the biblical story until the occasion of his accession to the throne. He was one of the younger sons of the king, it is true. But Solomon should have occupied a place of special importance since David had promised Bathsheba that this son would inherit the kingdom. One wonders how seriously David regarded this promise. We know that he had to be reminded on his death-bed by Bathsheba and Nathan the prophet of his given word that Solomon would succeed him. Not without significance, also, is the fact that such a promise is not referred to in the text until the time comes for its fulfillment. This brings us to the larger theme of the relationship between David and Solomon.

Are there any indications in the biblical text of how the father felt toward this son whom he had chosen to succeed him? David had many sons. In the first seven and a half years of his reign, when he ruled from Hebron over the tribe of Judah, he became the father of six sons. In the longer period of his king-ship at Jerusalem, thirty-three years according to the biblical chronology, he produced more offspring. Solomon was among the latter, mentioned as the fourth son born to David in the new capital of the united monarchy. Solomon therefore had at least nine older brothers.

Although the promised heir to the throne, Solomon must have lived rather obscurely in the background of the royal family. The older brothers managed to capture the center of the stage. There was Amnon, who as the eldest had an important claim on the attention of the king. There was Absalom, the son of a princess. He was bold and arrogant, beautiful of face and form, and beloved of the king. There was Adonijah, also ambitious and daring, who emulated Absalom.

One pictures the young prince Solomon as quiet and unob-trusive of temperament, remaining aloof like his mother Bath-sheba, until called to the scene of action. Actually, he was con-siderably younger than the first sons of David and thus realistically unable to compete with them. On the basis of his later develop-ment, we can visualize this young heir to the throne as occupying himself a good deal with dreams and fantasies of what he would do when he became king, as his mother must have told him he some day would. Evidently he was not openly recognized as potential successor to the throne or Absalom might have made short shrift of him in the days when that ruthless prince was plotting treacherously against David. While Absalom and Adoni-jah planned their successive rebellions, the young Solomon may have accepted in good faith the promise of the king, a belief supported by Nathan the prophet and nourished by Bathsheba that he and no other would some day be king of Israel. Solomon's plans must early have taken the path of peaceful conquest, for how else could he cope with such powerful figures as his father and older brothers? His fantasies of omniscience and omnipo-tence as forms of mastery must have had a start early in life.

A father is always someone of tremendous power to a child at a certain age. When this father is a king, when he is beloved by the people and by God, then indeed he is a figure that can

be almost overwhelming to a small boy. All this may be counter-
acted to a large degree if there is a warm, accepting relationship
between the two. But we know that the role of fatherhood was
one of David's greatest weaknesses. We can assume therefore
that he must have failed Solomon in some aspects of this relationship, an assumption that will be further explored in the present
study. Would David, for example, have preferred that Adonijah's
attempted *coup d'etat* be successful? Did he perhaps feel that
Solomon was not the best choice for the kingship? These are
conjectures that will require more substantiation.

We have only one record of a direct communication between
David and Solomon, the deathbed scene. It might be helpful to
return to this episode. The tone in which David utters these
last words is not one of direct command. The dying king takes
the youth into his confidence, speaking as one who is revealing
secret thoughts to an equal. He infers that Solomon, *being a wise
person,* will act in accordance with the father's suggestions. Twice
during this speech David refers to Solomon's wisdom, saying
openly, "Do therefore according to thy wisdom . . ." yet he makes
very specific what he thinks the new king's action should be in
regard to the final fate of a certain personality at the court. Concerning another of his enemies David says, "Now therefore hold
him not guiltless, *for thou art a wise man;* and thou wilt know
what thou oughtest to do unto him, and thou shalt bring his
hoar head down to the grave with blood (2:9)." *(italics added)*

This manner of speaking is clearly a way of enforcing suggestion by means of flattery. David must have known that Solomon wanted to be considered wise and therefore used this
avenue of appeal. The tone of this relationship is not one of
straightforwardness, honesty, and genuine acceptance on the part
of the father. It implies rather an attitude of condescension which
may have covered a distrust of Solomon's real capacity for wisdom.

In view of this evidence, Solomon's wish to be granted wisdom
is even more understandable. So is his later rebellious desertion
of the ambivalently-held father-ideal.

In the parallel account of this period given in *Chronicles,* these attitudes of David are expressed more directly. One of Solomon's major tasks was to be the building of the Temple. But it is David who spends a goodly portion of time and energy in the preparation for this task. This text goes into great detail describing all the preliminary work done by the father. He provided the plans and arranged for all the materials. David evidently wished to leave nothing to Solomon or to chance. It was indeed David's Temple that Solomon built. He merely carried out the commands of his father (Chron. I, 22).

While it may be true that this later and more priestly-oriented account in the Bible may have wished to credit David with this accomplishment and thus emphasized his share in it, some basic truth may here be revealed about the attitude of David toward Solomon. The king pleads with the people to support his son after his own death, asking that they help him in the building of the Temple. David says, "Solomon, my son, whom alone God hath chosen, is yet young and tender, and the work is great." Some concern is here expressed about Solomon's ability to carry out the task before him.

Did David have some unconscious hostility toward this very son that was destined to displace him? As noted earlier, Solomon came after Bathsheba's bereavement of her first child. Her affective ties to this second son may therefore have been quite strong. He was the symbol of God's forgiveness and a testimony of her reinstatement as a wife and mother in Israel. The father's grief at the death of the first child must also have given way to joy at the arrival of this son. But Solomon was also the first person to intrude between him and Bathsheba. David was no longer the sole recipient of his wife's love and interest. As we know from an earlier study of David's own life, this eighth son of the family of Jesse was sensitive to displacement in the mother's love. If so, his identification with the small boy, an unstable relationship at best, could easily give way to feelings of hostility arising from unconscious jealousy of this rival. The defense against such unwelcome feelings may have come as the wish that Solomon might represent an idealized image of David himself, a mechanism which we found operative in his personality in other situations. Through this child, "beloved of the Lord," David might have a renewed claim on God's approval and love.

The question might well be raised: What real evidence is there in the biblical material for such a reconstruction? First, we have seen indications pointing toward some unconscious hostility on the part of the father toward the son, and a tendency to belittle him. If Solomon is a symbol of what David expected of himself and yet could not fully attain, then Solomon's real qualities and achievements would always fall short of what the father really wanted and expected of him. Secondly, we have seen that Solomon's own sense of self-identity was largely in terms of being his father's son and of fulfilling his father's wishes. We know that children tend to carry out the unconscious fantasies of the parent in regard to them.

Are there any positive aspects of David's attitudes toward Solomon? The father did indeed rouse himself on his deathbed and give orders that this younger son be announced as his successor. But even more significant in this respect was David's influence upon the personality of Solomon. This son must have identified in a special way with certain of his father's character qualities. We have noted earlier a strong sense of justice and a tendency to the mellowing ingredient of mercy. The wish expressed at Gibeon to be a good king and to follow in the footsteps of David must have been based on many years of emulation in fantasy of the admired father. Such aspirations, while colored by ambitious and competitive needs, would nevertheless have a spiritualizing effect upon the youth and aid in the process of sublimation.

What indications are there of the role Bathsheba played in the character development of Solomon? The only direct verbal exchange between the two in the biblical narrative occurs in the little scene when, as the Queen Mother, Bathsheba appears before the recently appointed monarch and presents Adonijah's fateful request for the hand of the concubine, Abishag. Solomon receives here ceremoniously. The text says,

And the king rose up to meet her, and bowed down unto her, and sat down on his throne, and caused a throne to be set for the king's mother; and she sat on his right hand. Then she said, "I ask one small petition of thee; deny me not." And the king said unto her: "Ask on, my mother; for I will not deny thee." And she said: "Let Abishag the Shunammite be given to Adonijah thy brother to wife." And king Solomon answered and said unto his mother: "And why dost thou ask Abishag the Shunammite for Adonijah? ask for him the kingdom also; for he is mine elder brother; even for him, and for Abiathar the priest, and for Joab the son of Zeruiah." Then king Solomon swore by the Lord, saying: "God, do so to me, and more also, if Adonijah have not spoken this day against his own life . . . (2:19–23)."

The perception is inescapable that Bathsheba not only agrees to perform the mission Adonijah requests of her but makes that mission her own. She clearly wanted the king to grant this petition, for she asks it on her own behalf as well as on his who requested it. The words, *deny me not,* make this attitude clear.

As indicated in my study of David, Bathsheba's motive may have been to remove Abishag from the royal harem. Understandably it must have been distasteful to her that Solomon should inherit David's concubine. An unconscious identification with Abishag on the part of Bathsheba would have made such a relationship tantamount to incest. On the other hand, jealousy of the concubine may also have played a role. Perhaps Bathsheba feared that Abishag would detract from her own influence over the king, thus possibly repeating a similar situation with David.

But the young ruler does not identify with his mother's feelings on this occasion, thus indicating a will and strength of his own. He must have experienced his mother's request as a surprising and bewildering lack of regard for himself. His reply is a sharp one—"ask for him the kingdom also."

The sudden change of mood in the king when he learns the nature of her petition, indicates that he is indeed capable of a quick reversal in his attitude, under strong provocation. While the king's anger is directed mainly toward Adonijah, his reproach toward Bathsheba is also clear. Although Solomon owed his mother much and evidently wished to show his gratitude, it is also apparent that he was not intimidated by her.

This incident tells us little enough about the relationship between Solomon and Bathsheba. Perhaps as the story develops further and we understand some of Solomon's own attitudes toward other women, we may be able retrospectively to get a wider view of this first woman in his life.

It is interesting that right after Solomon's famous prayer for an understanding heart, the opportunity to prove his wisdom occurs in regard to a mother and child relationship. The Bible relates the well-known story of the two harlots and their simultaneous claim to be the mother of an infant child. The dispute is brought to Solomon's court for settlement. He orders a sword to be brought and declares that he will divide the child and give half to each of the two claimants. The woman who is making a false claim agrees to this proposed settlement but the real mother pleads with the king to spare the child and give him to the other woman. The infant is then restored to its rightful mother.

Biblical critics point out that similar stories are found in other ancient Oriental literature and that therefore Solomon's biographers must have derived the biblical episode from such sources. Actually, there is no way of knowing whether legends of this kind could have been created independently or, if not, who borrowed from whom. Psychoanalytically, this factor is not important. Solomon used this material, whether originally or not, because it met his needs. He therefore made it his own. The main theme of the incident seems clear enough. The love of a mother will triumph over more self-centered needs.

One wonders, however, why Solomon had to choose harlots for the characters in his story. Socially accepted married women would have served the same purpose. It may be that the concept *mother* and *harlot* were associated in Solomon's unconscious in a particularly close fashion. Although he was the legitimate child of David and Bathsheba, Solomon must have known about his mother's earlier history with the king. It is safe to assume that as a boy he must have utilized this episode to mobilize oedipal jealousy and anger against his father and to nurture distrust against the mother. In the unconscious of many children, the mother, who is a partner in the secret sexual life with the father, has an aspect of the harlot. This aspect would be considerably increased where so much reality basis existed.

On a conscious level, however, Solomon's positive feelings of love and honor for his own mother seemed to prevail. Perhaps they had to be overly-strong as a defense against the repressed doubt. The legend of the two harlots seems to say, "The *mother* is good; the *woman* is evil." Even more significantly, Solomon shows that a mother, *even if she is a harlot,* can have a genuine love for her child. Perhaps the king had a need for this kind of reassurance. That he chose this situation as the first in which to demonstrate his newly-acquired wisdom is certainly meaningful. The warm response of the people to this manifestation of his wisdom indicates how universal is this need to believe in the sincerity of a mother's love.

One of the outstanding achievements associated with the reign of Solomon is the building of the Temple. The Bible devotes considerable space to the description of this task. Yet this portion of the text, in spite of its highly specific detail, manages to be quite confusing. A noted biblical commentator refers to it as "one of the most difficult sections in the Old Testament." He thinks that Hebrew scribes did not understand architectural terms and that the particular author involved lacked the capacity to write clearly. He also believes that the account has gone through a number of revisions and additions.[5]

On the other hand, another commentator of high repute declares in reference to the same content, "The present document is particularly original. . . . We actually possess in these chapters concerning the construction and furnishings of the temple the fullest and most detailed specifications from the ancient Oriental world."[6]

The fact of such diametrically opposing opinions from two scholars is in itself interesting. The present writer tended to agree in certain respects with both views. While many of the architectural details are presented with admirable exactness, a repetitive account of the same procedures but with variations in details, and a certain repetition of descriptive phrases, often without clearness of pronoun antecedents, are some of the factors that help to obscure rather than to clarify. Another disturbing element is the sudden disruption of logical sequence at several points in the presentation of material. Thus, after a lengthy description of how the Temple was built, the statement is made, "So he built the house and finished it." The narrative continues in the very same sentence with a further description of how the Temple was being constructed, quite oblivious of the fact that it was already completed. The interpolation of this particular phrase occurs several times in the same fashion. At another point, after an elaborate description of the buildings comprising the royal palace, also built by Solomon, the text suddenly reverts to the Temple again and continues with an account of its furnishings, ignoring this break in continuity.

Such blatant elements leading to confusion are hard to understand. Solomon had official scribes and keepers of the royal archives. The complex organization of his many and far-flung activities required and, in other situations, apparently received, careful recording. The building of the Temple was of special importance. Why then would eye-witnesses not be able to write down in clear and legible terms what they saw before them?

If we assume that the *manner* of presentation has some meaning, then this confusion may have psychological significance in regard to the person most involved, Solomon himself. Such an interpretation may sound far-fetched but other instances of corrupt text have yielded rather convincingly to this kind of exploration, as we have seen.

What, for example, might the repetitive interpolation of the phrase, "So he built the house and finished it," signify? Shortly after its first occurrence Solomon receives a communication from God. It is brief and to the point.

And the word of the Lord came to Solomon, saying, "As for this house which *thou art building,* if thou wilt walk in My statutes and execute Mine ordinances, and keep all my commandments to walk in them; then will I establish My word with thee, which I spoke unto David thy father; in that I will dwell therein among the children of Israel, and will not forsake My people Israel (6:11–13)." *(italics added)*

We had been told just before that the house was completed but God refers to it as in the process of being built. Immediately following this Divine revelation, the text reiterates, "So Solomon built the house and finished it." This is again followed by a continuation of how the Temple was being built.

Perhaps the most helpful question to ask at this point is why God chooses this occasion to communicate with Solomon. In the midst of the doubt about whether the Temple is completed or still in the process of being built, God expresses a *conditional promise;* He will bless this project only if Solomon proves himself worthy of it.

The communication with God at this time may indicate that Solomon was going through a period of conflict, of inner stress. *He may have felt both a wish to complete his great undertaking and a fear of doing so.* The king must have needed some reassurance at this point that his work would not be in vain, that it would indeed be acceptable to the Heavenly Father.

The repetitive and confused details in regard to some aspects of the Temple architecture may indicate a *resistance* on the part of Solomon to seeing clearly. *Confusion* serves a defensive function of the ego, protecting one from full awareness of a situation which is unconsciously disturbing.

The completion, or near-completion, of the Temple may have called forth varying strong emotions in the son of David. This achievement, which was an impressive one on a reality basis and even more significant psychologically, must have fed his narcissism, his sense of power and importance. He had carried out what David had not been able to accomplish. This structure represented not only Solomon's obedience to the father but also a victory over him. While the son must have felt superego approval at fulfilling the obligation placed upon him, he may also have experienced guilt at thus overcoming the father.

Oedipal and superego feelings must indeed have been deeply involved, both in the task and also in the symbolism of the Temple itself. The house of the Father is, symbolically, the mother. The building of this place of worship may therefore have represented to David not only a victory over the father in a real sense, but also a fantasied conquest of the mother. As will be seen in his dedication prayer, Solomon was much concerned with the question of whether God would indeed dwell in the Temple he had built. This doubt, and the conflict of which it was a part, may be expressed not only in the communication from God at this point but also in both the wish and the fear to get the task completed. As long as he was in the process of building, the final outcome regarding its acceptance might more easily be postponed.

In spite of some of the confusion concerning the architecture of the Temple, its main outlines stand out clearly. One of its unusual features consisted of two large pillars of burnished copper which stood on either side of the porch leading to the Temple. Solomon called them Jachin (*He establishes*) and Boaz (*in Him is strength*). Another impressive object was the great laver, the *molten sea,* of cast copper alloy which stood in the courtyard near the altar of sacrifice. The gracefully-shaped bowl of huge dimensions stood on the backs of twelve oxen, with three facing in each direction of the compass.

In both of these two rather dramatic elements of *decor,* the symbolic sexual images of man and woman are vividly delineated. The symbolism of the Temple structure itself, with the Ark deposited in the comparatively small chamber known as the Holy of Holies, is also easily apparent.

Legend says that when the Ark was about to be brought into the Holy of Holies, the door of the sacred room locked itself and could not be opened. Solomon prayed to God with all his heart but not until he uttered the words, "Remember the good deeds of David thy servant," did the door open of itself.[7] The story indicates that the Temple *belonged* to David and became Solomon's only as the son of his father.

Another puzzling aspect in regard to the Temple is the obscurity regarding the time of dedication. This situation is highlighted by the fact that the Bible states very clearly when the building of the Temple was begun. "And it came to pass in the four hundred and eightieth year after the children of Israel were come out of Egypt, *in the fourth year of Solomon's reign over Israel, in the month Ziv, which is the second month,* that he began to build the house of the Lord (6:1)." We are also told that it took seven years to complete the project (6:38). According to the sequence of events as recorded, the royal palace, which took thirteen years to finish, was also completed before the Temple dedication took place. The biblical text explains that it took Solomon twenty years to complete both these undertakings (9:10).

It has been a matter of note that Solomon spent about twice as much time in building the palace as in the construction of the Temple. And indeed the former, consisting of a number of buildings, was a far more elaborate and ambitious undertaking than the comparatively small house of worship. Actually, the Temple was not intended to house the worshippers, for the services took place in the spacious Temple courts where the great altar of sacrifice was located.

One wonders if Solomon wished to postpone the dedication ceremonies until his own palace, close by on the Temple Mount, was completed. Was this an expression of his competitive spirit with a father image as well as doubt about the acceptability of what was, on one level, *his* Temple, and on another, the Temple of David?

One cannot dismiss as purely accidental that the date when the Temple was begun is so carefully recorded while the more important occasion, the year of its dedication, is thus left to conjecture except to note that it took place during the festival of the seventh month (8:2). Psychologically, one can conclude that this is a purposeful forgetting. It may be significant of the inner conflict within the king.

Did the Temple stand idle and unused all these years? We do not know; probably it was used unofficially, but not as a central place of worship by the nation.

Solomon's prayers are presented with a degree of fulness not found in any of his other communications. This fact is understandable on the basis of the function and purpose of the biblical narrative. But there may be a further reason for this situation. The young man from whom not a word is recorded during all the tumultuous events of Adonijah's attempted *coup d'etat,* his own anointment and succession, and the farewell scene with his dying father, speaks fully and freely with God. It is possible that the inhibitions and repressions which may have hampered him with earthly father figures were loosened, and found increased expression in this sublimated form.

We have noted that in Solomon's first communication with God, which occurred at Gibeon, the young king's attitude was that of a suppliant child, humble, yet unconsciously expecting much from the Omnipotent Parent. It is in the prayer of dedication, however, on the occasion when the Temple is ready to be utilized as a national shrine, that Solomon's attitudes toward God are expressed most expansively. An entire chapter (Kings I, 8), is devoted to this momentous occasion.

People from all over the land gather in Jerusalem. Heads of tribes, the princes and elders of Israel, assemble in the city of Zion. The priests take up the Ark from its abode in the Tent where it had been placed by David. With much ceremony and with sacrifices, the sacred object is carried to the Holy of Holies in the resplendent new Temple and placed under the spreading wings of the two cherubim that cover the farthest wall. This moment is one of unparalleled importance in the religious life of the people. The text says,

> And it came to pass, when the priests were come out of the holy place, that the cloud filled the house of the Lord, so that the priests could not stand to minister by reason of the cloud, for the glory of the Lord filled the house of the Lord . . . (8:10)

Then Solomon begins his prayer. According to the account in *Chronicles,* Solomon had built a metal scaffold for the occasion and upon this platform he stood before all the congregation of Israel (Chron. II, 6:13).

> Then spoke Solomon: "The Lord hath said that He would dwell in the thick darkness. I have surely built Thee a house of habitation, A place for Thee to dwell in forever (8:12–13)."

Solomon thus begins with a pronouncement of his great accomplishment. But what follows? As if overawed by his own words, the king now retreats. Not to him does the honor belong, but to David, his father. Again, as at Gibeon, Solomon seeks acceptance and protection in the shadow of David's greatness. The son declares that he has served only as the instrument of the plan agreed upon by David and by God.

> And he said: "Blessed be the Lord, the God of Israel, who spoke with His mouth unto David my father, and hath with His hand fulfilled it, saying: 'I chose David to be over My people Israel.' Now it was in the heart of David my father to build a house for the name of the Lord, the God of Israel. But the Lord said unto David my father: 'Whereas it was in thy heart to build a house for My name, thou didst well that it was in thy heart; nevertheless thou shalt not build the house; but thy son that shall come forth out of thy loins, he shall build the house for My name.' And the Lord hath established His word that He spoke; for I am risen up in the room of David my father, and sit on the throne of Israel, as the Lord promised, and have built the house for the name of the Lord, the God of Israel (8:15–20)."

In this portion of the prayer alone, consisting of six verses, the name *David* is mentioned five times. Some may point out that Solomon was merely utilizing the prestige and popularity of his father's name in order to establish more firmly the importance of the Temple as a central place of worship for the nation. This must certainly have been so. But there is nothing in the way the material is presented to suggest that Solomon did not himself accept and sincerely believe the words he uttered.

If the dedication of the Temple took place some twenty-four

years after Solomon became king, as the text implies, he certainly had already established a name and a reputation of his own. He had achieved much for the nation on a reality basis. In spite of this fact, Solomon still felt a psychological need to appear before the people and before God under the aegis of David's greatness. This is not surprising, for unconscious attitudes can be timeless, as we know.

It becomes increasingly evident that Solomon's sense of importance in the eyes of God seems to rest largely on a fact extraneous to his real self. Such a feeling must have been basic in the development of his personality from earliest times, as suggested before. Solomon, the child, Solomon the youth, even Solomon the king and the builder of the Temple, had significance in the scheme of things, not for any virtues of his own, not from an inherent sense of personal destiny, but only because he happened to be the son of David.

The terms of the relationship having been repeated and clarified in this portion of the prayer, what concept emerges next? Solomon extols the greatness of God, declaring,

> "O Lord, the God of Israel, there is no God like Thee, in heaven above, or on earth beneath; who keepest covenant and mercy with Thy servants, that walk before Thee with all their heart; who hast kept with Thy servant David my father that which Thou didst promise him; . . . (8:23–24)."

At this point an element of doubt enters into the mood of exaltation and supplication. Solomon asks,

> "But will God in very truth dwell on the earth? behold, heaven and the heaven of heavens cannot contain Thee; how much less this house that I have builded! Yet have Thou respect unto the prayer of Thy servant, and to his supplication, O Lord my God, to hearken unto the cry and to the prayer which Thy servant prayeth before Thee this day; that Thine eyes may be open toward this house day and night, even toward the place whereof Thou hast said: My name shall be there; . . . (8:27–29)."

What does this aspect of the prayer connote? Does Solomon really have a concept of the universality and transcendental nature of God? Some biblical commentators theorize that this prayer is an expression of priestly theology, inserted at a later date. We will however continue to deal with the material as it stands. From a psychological viewpoint, what attitudes might these lofty words convey? The king may here be voicing feelings of awe, helplessness, and doubt. Would God indeed dwell in the house which Solomon had built? Now that the task was finished, now that the superego demands were fulfilled, Solomon may have felt more free to allow repressed feelings of doubt and uncertainty to come to the surface. Heretofore, he had been occupied with a clearly defined task—the building of the Temple. The completion must, in a certain sense, have created a void. The need for inner meanings of the accomplishment must have confronted the king.

Together with the awe and doubt, this portion of the prayer may be trying to express a wish also. *If only* God would indeed dwell in this habitation, if he could be thus encompassed and contained, Solomon might feel more secure. His need for active mastery and control may be manifested here rather than a profound philosophical conception of God. Solomon's prayers have a quality of *demand* underlying the supplications. But this wish and hope which find such spontaneous expression at the opening of the prayer in the words, "I have surely built Thee a house of habitation, A place for Thee to dwell in forever," fades rapidly. Solomon quickly settles for the lesser good, the request that God might incline his ear toward this holy place and that his Name might be there. The symbolic Presence of God rather than the actual Presence is as much as Solomon dares to hope for. It is a compromise that indicates a decrease in the feelings of omnipotence on the part of the king, an acceptance of reality that even he, with all his power, could not confine and thus control the Presence of God.

In this prayer of dedication, Solomon considers at some length the problem of sin and repentance. There are moments when one senses within the king a growing apprehension about his own state of grace. Although he speaks in the name of all Israel, there must have been a strong feeling of personal involvement in the words,

> ". . . what prayer and supplication soever be made by any man of all Thy people Israel, *who shall know every man the plague of his own heart,* and spread forth his hands toward this house; then hear Thou in heaven Thy dwelling-place, and forgive . . . for there is no man that sinneth not . . . (8:38–39; 46). (*italics added*)

There seems to be some inconsistency in the way Solomon deals with the two concepts, justice and compassion. At some points he demands stern justice from God, declaring,

> ". . . do and judge thy servants, condemning the wicked, to bring his way upon his own head; and justifying the righteous, to give him according to his righteousness (8:32); . . . forgive, and do, and render unto every man according to all his ways, whose heart Thou knowest . . . (8:39)."

Here forgiveness does not seem to be distinguished from the sterner concept of justice. Was it difficult perhaps for Solomon to believe in forgiveness apart from justice? When we remember the strict superego of the man who helped to educate him, Nathan the priest, such a consequence should not be surprising.

One clear distinction Solomon does make repeatedly. Forgiveness and compassion should be granted to those who pray and confess their sins in association with the locale of the Temple. If God should show his displeasure by causing the various disasters to which the people were heir: defeat in war, lack of rain, famine, pestilence, siege, exile to a strange land—and if the people pray *in or toward the Temple* and confess their sins, then God should forgive them and end their suffering. This is the tenor of a large part of Solomon's supplications. He begs God to pay special heed, not only to prayers uttered in the Temple itself, but also to those that are recited when the worshipper faces in the direction of the Temple or stretches out his hand toward it, even from a distant city or a foreign land.

Such repetition of a single theme certainly indicates its importance for the king. An actual counting shows that at *ten separate times,* in the course of twenty verses, Solomon repeats this request.

One could readily infer that the king's purpose in this matter was to impress upon the people the importance of the Temple as a national shrine and thus help bring about a closer religious unity throughout the tribes of Israel. This may well be so but it would not obviate additional meanings on a more personal basis for Solomon himself. It is this aspect which will be of special interest here.

Solomon clearly wants the Temple to be a place endowed with special powers, particularly in regard to confession of sin and forgiveness. Underlying such an approach to Deity must be a strong need for magic and omnipotence on the part of Solomon himself. In this situation he is identified with the Temple. It is he therefore who wishes to be the intermediary between God and men and to have the power of punishment and forgiveness. Solomon thus felt related to the Temple in a special sense. If God too had a particular relationship to the house of worship, then the king and God would share this bond between them.

What might be the specific nature of this bond? If we translate the symbolism of the Temple and God (Mother and Father), the answer is clear. *Solomon must have felt unconsciously that the surest way to reach the father is through the mother.*

This situation must indeed have been a familiar one in his own life experience. Solomon was of special importance to David because of Bathsheba. His wishes were fulfilled by the father via the mother. He became the successor to the throne, first because of the promise made to Bathsheba and, at the critical moment, through her intercession. This pattern of how Solomon related to David must have been repeated on many other occasions during his life. When the youth had a request to make of the king, it is likely that Bathsheba was the bearer of the message. Did she not perform this service even for Adonijah, when Solomon himself was king? Perhaps it was a role to which she was accustomed.

The mother may also have been the intermediary on occasions of family discipline. If Solomon had done some wrong and feared the displeasure of his father, Bathsheba may have helped to secure the king's forgiveness. This is not an unusual role for a mother. It will be recalled that another woman in Israel performed such a function when Joab sought a way of obtaining David's forgiveness for Absalom. We know that David was humanly susceptible to the charms of women. He even stayed the punishment of the miserly Nabal because of Abigail's plea. This family background helps to explain the repetitive element in Solomon's prayer of dedication, the urgency of his need and wish to control the actions of the Heavenly Father through the powers centered in the Temple.

There are other indications of Solomon's tendency to relate to the father through the mother. His many alliances with foreign monarchs were generally implemented by marriages with the daughters. While this procedure is common enough among royalty, it was practiced by Solomon to an unusual degree.

An interesting, perhaps significant, detail concerning the description of the buildings on the Temple Mount, mentions that the separate palace he built for his first and probably favorite wife, the daughter of Pharaoh, was situated *between his own palace and the Temple*. The biblical story, for some reason, goes to the trouble of mentioning this fact.

One might conjecture to what degree Solomon actually identified with the woman and related to the man accordingly. More important than any latent homosexuality as such must have been the need to identify with the Omnipotent Parent. The mother serves first as the model for this image. But if he saw Bathsheba as a way of reaching the father, his first tendency may have been to develop a passive-feminine role toward David. After his anointment as king, the youth may have undergone a dramatic change, moving from a narcissistic identification with the mother to an identification with the father, whose position he now occupied. He was therefore a man of action and could achieve greatly in reality. But the basic pattern of relating to the woman as a bridge to the man may have remained. Solomon's attitude toward the Temple, the symbolic mother, the intensity of his need to endow the house of worship with some kind of personal, magical power through which he could reach God, may thus be better understood.

An aspect of particular interest in this lengthy prayer of dedication is Solomon's plea in behalf of the stranger. Specifically,
Solomon asks God to hear the prayers of the stranger also,

> ". . . when he shall come out of a far country for Thy name's
> sake—for they shall hear of Thy great name . . . and do
> according to all that the stranger called to Thee for; that all
> the peoples of the earth may know Thy name, to fear Thee,
> as doth Thy people Israel, *and that they may know Thy name
> is called upon this house which I have built* (8:41–43). (*italics
> added*)

The first mention of the stranger in the quotation given above
seems to refer to the proselyte. The second time, Solomon wants
all the peoples of the earth to acknowledge God's greatness. The
motive here is a narcissistic, or self-centered one, as the italicized
words in the verse quoted make clear. Solomon wants to share in
God's omnipotence. He wants to prove to the whole world that
the God whose name is associated with the Temple which the
king has built, is the most powerful God of all.

Solomon's attitude to the stranger, then, may be a wish to ex-
tend the sphere of his own influence, as well as that of God's. This
motivation may have been a significant aspect of Solomon's cosmopolitanism. It seems that the son of David needed a larger stage
upon which to portray his greatness and his glory.

While David too was friendly with strangers and could maintain a good neighbor policy if he so desired, his deepest feelings
were centered in his own land and his own people. Solomon's
cosmopolitanism could be understood psychoanalytically as an
extension of his own ego boundaries, enlarged for the purpose of
personal gratification. It may have had a further purpose of a defensive nature. Solomon took the women of many strange lands
to wife; he made alliances with rulers of foreign lands. This
reaching out for the stranger may have been a way of countering
the close relationship with the mother and, perhaps, with the
father as well.

As a background for these interpretations it should be remembered that Israel was strongly ethnocentric. True, it shared many

cultural aspects of life with its neighbors. But the thing that set Israel apart was a sense of its uniqueness, based on its religious and moral concepts. Solomon, who wanted to include the whole world within the boundaries of his group, as worshippers of his God, in the latter part of his own life broke down those boundaries and lost his own sense of spiritual identity.

It might be noted here that Solomon's prayers have none of the ecstasy and joyousness expressed so often by David and repeated so variously in the psalms attributed to the latter's authorship. David had a sense of closeness and intimacy with the Deity; Solomon bowed before him and pleaded for grace on the basis of another's virtues.

This long biblical chapter closes with a description of the sacrifices that were offered on the great occasion and the celebration that was held throughout the whole land of Israel for fourteen days. It seems appropriate that the last verse should state,

> On the eighth day he sent the people away, and they blessed the king, and went unto their tents joyful and glad of heart for all the goodness that the Lord had shown *unto David His servant,* and to Israel His people (8:66). (*italics added*)

The space devoted to the description of the Temple and the prayer of dedication by the king indicates the importance attributed to this subject by the compilers of the biblical text. These matters must have been important also in the life of Solomon.

After the dedication ceremonies, God appears to Solomon for the second time, "as He had appeared unto him at Gibeon." Thus, the fact that God *spoke* to Solomon in the interval is here ignored (6:11–13).

The second visitation is clearly likened to the earlier one at Gibeon, after an interval of over twenty years. It will be interesting to compare the content and mood of this communication with the first one. This time God appears without the framework of the dream. This aspect, in itself, may have some meaning. It may indicate an increase in narcissism, a greater degree of a sense of omnipotence on the part of the king. True, communications from

God were not unusual among the heroes of ancient Israel. But the psychological significance of these events should be related both to the period of history and the type of personality involved. Solomon's relationship to God was quite different from that of his father, as suggested before. God appeared to Solomon rarely. Such occasions must therefore have indicated unusual intrapsychic activity or tension. The very fact that Solomon experiences God in a dream the first time indicates psychological distance between the king and the Heavenly Father. The bridging of this distance during the second appearance cannot be viewed as a closer relationship in a positive sense. The context of the material points more readily to a greater feeling of grandiosity on the part of Solomon, accompanied, however, by an increasing sense of foreboding and insecurity.

In this latter visitation God speaks to Solomon at some length, but it is a one-way communication. In this respect too it differs from the earlier one at Gibeon, where a *verbal exchange* took place. The psychological bridging of the distance therefore does not bring about a closer feeling of intimacy.

God begins by acknowledging Solomon's prayer of dedication.

> "I have heard thy prayer and thy supplication, that thou hast made before Me: I have hallowed this house, which thou hast built, to put My name there for ever; and Mine eyes and My heart shall be there perpetually . . . (9:3)."

Then this promise is made conditional upon Solomon's good behavior which, as usual, is expressed in the formula that he should follow the example set by David, his father. The consequences of his failure to do this are then expressed in strong terms.

> "But if ye shall turn from following Me, ye or your children, and not keep My commandments and My statutes which I have set before you, but shall go and serve other gods, and worship them; then will I cut Israel out of the land which I have given them; and this house, which I have hallowed for My name, will I cast out of My sight; and Israel shall be a proverb and a by word among all peoples; and this house which is so high (shall become desolate), and every one that passeth

by it shall be astonished, and shall hiss; and when they shall say: Why hath the Lord done thus unto this land, and to this house? they shall be answered: Because they forsook the Lord, their God, who brought forth their fathers out of the land of Egypt, and laid hold on other gods, and worshipped them, and served them; therefore hath the Lord brought all this evil upon them (9:6–9)."

How different is the tone of this visitation from the earlier one at Gibeon! There, the young king was filled with the desire to be a good ruler and with the expectation of being loved and favored by God. His wishes for omniscience and omnipotence, although narcissistic and defensive, were nevertheless strongly colored by social purposes. Now, on the auspicious occasion when the king's long years of effort are over and success in this important project of building the Temple has been accomplished, there is a strange tone of warning and foreboding in the reply God makes to Solomon.

The conditional promise is a familiar element in the relationship between the children of Israel and their God. It finds expression however in different ways and with varying degrees of emphasis. In the three communications God makes to Solomon, before the latter's digression from religious loyalty, the form and spirit of the conditional promise changes considerably. We have noted that at Gibeon, *the promise itself,* that of God's acceptance and reward, occupies a large part of the content, while *the conditions* are stated in brief form and muted tones. On the occasion when God speaks to Solomon but does not appear to him, the conditional aspect of the promise is made more emphatic but the chief function of the message seems to be one of reassurance. In the final and more lengthy communication with which we are here concerned, the conditional part of the promise takes precedence over God's words of acceptance, imparting a mood of gloomy prediction.

In further comparison, it could be said that God's appearance at Gibeon marked Solomon's psychological ascendancy to his role as spiritual leader, accompanied by a sense of comparative security in God's acceptance of him. On the other hand, this second visitation, coming at the climax of the king's glory, was also the beginning of his decline. Both his rise and fall have their roots in Solomon's relationship to God. These Divine revelations can be understood as projections of Solomon's intrapsychic state. They are indicative of his changing attitudes toward God, significant of the changes in his psychological defenses.

Solomon must have sensed within himself a growing weakness of his powers of sublimation and a consequent increase in the temptation to rebel against the father figure. The stern words of warning uttered by God may be an effort on the part of the king to maintain his defenses. God distinctly warns him against the very evils of which Solomon is later guilty—the worship of other gods.

Some biblical critics point out that this material also may be *ex post facto,* inserted after the fact. But other scholars feel that there is no real authority in many situations for this kind of re-shifting of the text. Certainly on a psychological basis, the material as it stands makes good sense, for it portrays consistently a developmental picture of the king's psychic life.

What indications do we have of personal relationships in the life of Solomon beyond the parental figures already considered? The Bible gives very little information on this important aspect of life in regard to the king. Indeed, the total picture of his life leaves one with the impression that he had few such relationships, if any. There is no other outstanding personality in the story of Solomon during the period of his adulthood. He and he alone occupies the center of the stage.

This situation differentiates Solomon from the early patriarchs of Israel and from the two monarchs who preceded him. In a culture where family life was of special importance, Solomon gives the picture of a man without significant personal involvements, despite all his royal splendor, his crowded court, and a thousand wives. However, we shall explore here, in the light of available material, some of the people in his life.

Solomon's most notable friendship was with Hiram, king of Tyre. It is to him that the young Solomon, early in his reign, appeals for help in the building of the Temple. This royal neighbor responds with a degree of warmth that has an unusual quality. The text says,

> And it came to pass, when Hiram heard the words of Solomon, that he rejoiced greatly, and said, "Blessed be the Lord this day, who hath given unto David a wise son over this great people (5:21)."

Like Solomon's own father, Hiram refers to the young king's wisdom. One wonders if this ardor, expressed by one who was a peer and close friend of David himself, may not have been a displacement, a wish-fulfillment on the part of Solomon. More than anything else, the young ruler must have wanted the approval and esteem of his own father. This ungratified need and wish may thus find expression by utilizing the genuine friendliness and good-will of the man who must have been a father figure for many years.

Solomon's ambivalent feelings in such a relationship come out in one of the commercial transactions with Hiram. It is not without interest that this episode follows immediately the account of God's second visitation, with its warning of possible disloyalty to the Heavenly Father himself. Solomon gives the king of Tyre twenty cities as part of the payment for the cedar and cypress trees and the gold furnished by the latter. The biblical narrative states, "And Hiram came out from Tyre to see the cities which Solomon had given him and they pleased him not (9:12)." Hiram's attitude is one of disappointment rather than anger or unfriendliness. He says, "What cities are these that thou hast given me, my brother?" The inference to be drawn therefore is that it was Solomon who was at fault and that he repaid Hiram's generous help in a manner that indicated a lack of appreciation.

Oddly, one of the most skilled workers in metal, who made important objects for the Temple, was a young man whom Solomon imported from the city of Tyre and who was named *Hiram*. The text goes to the trouble of telling us something about his ancestry and describes him in rather glowing terms. "He was the son of a widow of the tribe of Naphtali, and his father was a man of Tyre, a worker in brass, and he was filled with wisdom and understanding and skill, to work all work in brass. And he came to king Solomon and wrought all his work (7:13–14)."

This young man resembles Solomon himself in certain respects. Both are "filled with wisdom and understanding." Both are commissioned to build the Temple. Hiram is identified with the king of Tyre through the similarity of names and in being inhabitants of the same city. He is a *son of Tyre,* subject of the king, and therefore a son figure with whom Solomon can identify. Like the Hebrew ruler, Hiram was fatherless.

Isn't this analogy based on a factual statement in the text that might be purely coincidental, the reader may ask? Perhaps so. But there is little in the Bible that is *purely coincidental.* Moreover, why should a mere worker in the Temple be described in such glowing terms and his ancestry carefully noted? Less has been said about many more important personalities than the young metal worker from Tyre. King Solomon must have experienced a strong sense of identification with this person and wished to be like him. Hiram's skill in working with his hands must have been one that Solomon both admired and envied. And indeed the young Hiram executes some of the most important and unusual tasks associated with the furnishings of the Temple, among them the two bronze pillars, Jachin and Boaz, and the *molten sea,* resting on the twelve oxen.

Clinically, we often find that men who suffer from feelings of sexual inadequacy also have difficulty in activities that require manual dexterity. Solomon must have interpreted Hiram's skill as the equivalent of wisdom and understanding, the latter being the king's own ways of compensating. Through a narcissistic identification with the metal worker from Tyre, Solomon may have satisfied in fantasy his wish to fulfill his father's directives in regard to the building of the Temple and, at the same time, to derive gratification from the unconscious, symbolic connotations which these objects may have represented. The young metal worker from Tyre may have been a projected idealized image of Solomon himself at a more youthful age.

Among the father figures in Solomon's life, the head priests, who had official positions at the royal court, must have played important roles. It is significant to note the young king's attitude toward Abiathar, the priest who supported Adonijah in the latter's attempt to seize the throne. The Bible says,

> And unto Abiathar the priest said the king: "Get thee to Anathoth, unto thine own fields; for thou art deserving of death; but I will not at this time put thee to death, because thou didst bear the ark of the Lord God before David my father, and because thou wast afflicted in all wherein my father was afflicted (2:26)."

Thus Solomon shows respect and compassion for one associated with his father, even though Abiathar could have been considered as an enemy and a traitor. We see here again that the son resembles the father in tempering justice with mercy.

The priest who was most closely and positively related to the life of Solomon was Nathan, chief counselor of David, a man of great moral strength and courage. It was he who rebuked the latter for his illicit romance with Bathsheba. It was Nathan who named the infant Solomon *Jedidiah,* "beloved of the Lord." It was also Nathan who encouraged and prompted Bathsheba to appear before the dying king David and remind him of his promise that Solomon would succeed him. In fact, it is Nathan's own appearance before David's bedside for the same purpose that causes the king to take action. We can view Nathan therefore as a strong and loyal father figure for Solomon, from the time of the latter's birth. The fact that Nathan also had a superego function for David must have strengthened this kind of influence over Solomon too.

There is no real love story in the life of Solomon, the man with a thousand wives. The only time the word *love* is mentioned in this connection is in the statement, "Now king Solomon loved many foreign women, besides the daughter of Pharaoh . . ." To love many is indeed to love none. His chief wife seems to have been this daughter of Pharaoh whom he married in the early years of his reign. But this romance is rather unromantically presented in the factual pronouncement,

> And Solomon became allied to Pharaoh king of Egypt by marriage, and took Pharaoh's daughter, and brought her into the city of David, until he had made an end of building his own house, and the house of the Lord, and the wall of Jerusalem round about (3:1).

Legend says that he married the Egyptian princess right after the Temple was completed and that his whole mode of life then changed. This astute observation implies the relationship between id and superego in the personality of the king. Only after he had fulfilled his obligations to God and to David could Solomon allow himself a life of his own. But even this kind of adjustment did not go altogether smoothly. The conflict is expressed in a legend dealing with psychologically significant detail.

The story says that the day after his marriage, when the wedding feast was to be held, was the same day that the Temple was to be dedicated. During the nuptial night, the princess artfully beguiles the bridegroom with the music of a thousand different instruments played by her attendants. Moreover, this wily woman had spread a tapestry over the king's bed, studded with jewels so that they gleamed and glittered like stars. Whenever Solomon tried to get up, thinking it was morning, he saw these starry lights above him and thought it was still night. In this fashion he slept on, long after the hour set for the dedication of the Temple. Even the daily sacrifice could not be performed because the keys to the Temple lay under Solomon's pillow and none dared disturb him. Finally Bathsheba's help was sought. She awoke her son and rebuked him, saying, "Thy father was known to all as a God-fearing man, and now people will say, 'Solomon is the son of Bathsheba, and it is his mother's fault if he goes wrong. . . . Take care, give not thy strength unto

women nor thy ways to them that destroy kings, for licentious-
ness confounds the reason of man. . .' ''[8]

As one so often observes clinically, conscientious effort toward
a goal can be suddenly undone at the very moment when success
is at hand. So in this legend, Solomon, after all his work and devotion in building the Temple, fails the people on this very day
which was to see the crowning of his achievement.

What can be the meaning of such a legend? How did it arise?
It expresses an intuitive insight that Solomon was ambivalent in
his task of building the Temple. For this reason perhaps he did
not dare to be entirely successful, to accept the homage and
acclaim of the people on the day of its dedication. Solomon's religious fervor is clearly portrayed here as being a sublimation of
sexuality. Submission to the will of the father involves a renunciation of the woman. In the instance described here, sexuality re-
asserted its claim, even though the responsibility for this regression was placed squarely upon the seductive woman.

It is interesting that the king's recall to conscience is made
through the mother. She acts here as the superego, a role that is
usually predominantly played by the father. Her appeal, however, is on a personal basis. Solomon's dereliction from duty will
be a reflection upon her. It should be noted though that Bathsheba upholds David as the model of a God-fearing man. There
is no conflict between the superego ideals of the parents. However, we see again that Solomon is put in a position where he has
to relate to the father through the mother. The king is not even
allowed a nuptial night unharassed by conscience. The keys to the
Temple under his pillow are a reminder of the sublimation
which David seemed to have demanded of him, a duty reinforced
by his mother's voice intruding upon his wedding night.

While these legends seem to portray Solomon as a passive object in the hands of seductive and controlling women, the reverse
may also be true. It may have been the king who wished to
possess and control the woman but desired unconsciously to
place the responsibility for his conduct upon their aggressive behavior. Certainly a king with such a large harem could not have

been overtly timid with women. Both needs, to possess and to be possessed, are not contradictory for the unconscious.

One of the colorful episodes in Solomon's life is his meeting with the beauteous Queen of Sheba, who comes to visit him in Jerusalem. The manner in which he entertains and honors her shows his ceremonious and gallant attitude toward women. It seems strange therefore that folklore should treat him so differently in this respect. There are a number of legends attributed to his authorship where hostility and distrust of the woman provide the main theme.[9]

The visit made by the Queen of Sheba is the closest to a romantic interlude that we have in the life of this man of many wives. And even here the romantic aspect can be questioned. The relationship between the two monarchs resembled more a strong but friendly competition. Solomon exhibits his magnificence and wisdom before the awestruck Queen to such a degree that she gasps, ". . . the half was not told me; thou hast wisdom and prosperity exceeding the fame which I heard. Happy are thy men, happy are these thy servants, that stand continually before thee, and that hear thy wisdom . . . (10:7–9)." These are words that a clever woman would utter to a man whom she intuitively sensed as having a great need for self-importance. Thus the Queen greatly admires Solomon but there is not a word in the biblical story to give credence to the romance which the world likes to attribute to them. Legend, in feeble attempt to make amends for this rather striking omission on the part of a king who supposedly had a voluptuous nature, says that a marriage did occur between them.[10]

The image of this Queen is itself shrouded in legends of mystery and magic. The Talmud expresses the opinion that she may herself be a legendary character. She is presented in both Arabic and Jewish sources as a sorceress or demon, a daughter of the jinn, or genii.

In the legendary marriage with this mysterious Queen further obscure aspects enter. There is an Arabic story that the genii wanted to prevent the union so they called Solomon's attention to a defect in the Queen's feminine charm. She had hair on her legs. It seems that this characteristic also marked her as belonging to the family of jinn. Jewish sources too comment on this blemish to the lady's beauty. Legend says that Solomon discovered this unromantic detail when he sat in a house of glass to receive her. The Queen, thinking that he sat in water, lifted her dress to keep it dry, as she approached him. He then noticed her bare legs and remarked rather bluntly, "Thy beauty is the beauty of a woman, but thy hair is masculine; hair is an ornament to a man but it disfigures a woman." The king orders a depilatory made of arsenic and unslaked lime, which successfully removes the defect.[11]

During her visit, the Queen tests Solomon by presenting him with riddles and conundrums and he delights in the exhibition of his wisdom, grandeur, and power. What psychological significance, if any, can be attributed to this rather bizarre relationship? The Queen of Sheba can be recognized as the phallic mother, who admires the *mind* of man, the displaced phallus. She can be understood here as a projected image of Solomon himself, representing an important aspect of his personality.

Solomon may have been able to relate to a woman most fully on the basis of a narcissistic identification, someone who resembled important aspects of himself. Perhaps the Queen was his ideal image of a woman, a ruler like himself, but a feminine counterpart, who would acknowledge his superiority. Yet it had to be a woman with an illusory phallus, even though he defensively tried to remove it. Solomon's need for wisdom, grandeur, and power, as suggested earlier, was evidently a compensatory reaction to feelings of sexual inadequacy, deepened no doubt by the limited number of his offspring.

Solomon's treatment of women throughout his life shows a tendency to honor them, as he honored his mother Bathsheba when she appeared before him, even though he could not grant her request. He showed his esteem for the daughter of Pharaoh by building a separate palace for her. Later in his life he honored many of his foreign wives by building temples for their gods. It could be said of Solomon that he did not underestimate the power of a woman. Perhaps it was because he overestimated her influence that she remained an object to be honored and feared, someone with whom to compete at times, but not one with whom a true love relationship was achieved.

Solomon was both a man of action and a man of dreams. His wishes reached grandiose proportions, as we have seen. His longing for power in both the mental and material spheres of life seemed to border on what could be regarded as pathological. Perhaps the saving feature was his ability to carry out in reality a considerable part of his wishes and dreams. This opportunity, however, was not just a consequence of his kingly role and of the favorable position of Israel at this period. It was also a genuine capacity to act, to carry out the envisionings of a mind that was creative, imaginative, and daring. Solomon showed great aptitude for opening new paths in different areas of life. He was not dependent on precedent. Based on a united monarchy whose boundaries had been considerably enlarged by David, Solomon's reign of peace and prosperity provided a background for the development of material and cultural projects. Archaeology has amply confirmed biblical accounts of Solomon's accomplishments.

The geographic, cultural, and social world in which he moved was also one of enlarged boundaries. Solomon carried on trade by caravan and ship to the far corners of the known world. His copper mines at Ezion-geber, on the Gulf of Aqabah, the southernmost portion of his realm, has been the scene of recent archaeological findings. Solomon's copper refineries in this area, as Nelson Glueck's work shows, were of a size and degree of elaborateness unknown in any other area of the ancient Near East. And yet, ". . . it was so relatively insignificant an enterprise that it is not even mentioned in our sources."[12]

Another accomplishment which shows initiative on the part of Solomon was his building of a chain of chariot cities as part of his standing army, and of store cities to house supplies. The well-known archaeological findings at Megiddo, located in the

north-central part of the country at the juncture of two important trade routes, revealed excellently constructed stables
for over four hundred horses, perhaps many more. Similar cities
were found on other sites.

Solomon's building program was one of his outstanding
achievements. It is understandable that Jerusalem, the capital
city, should have benefited particularly by this interest on the
part of the king. He transformed the fairly modest *City of
David* into one of international character and atmosphere. The
group of royal buildings on the Temple Mount, an elevation
rising almost twenty-five hundred feet above sea level, faced eastward toward the point where the sun rose over the still higher
Mount of Olives.

The Bible gives a lively picture of these structures constituting
the palace of the king. They stood on an artificially broadened
hilltop that provided a level area of sufficient scope. There was
the House of the Forest of Lebanon, so called because of the four
rows of cedar pillars which characterized it. Then there were the
Porch of Pillars and the Hall of Judgment, the latter of which was
the throne room. His own dwelling and the palace for his Egyptian queen were significant edifices. These buildings ran in a
south to north direction, the most northern being the Temple
itself.

Solomon's throne was a thing of glory, of almost fantastic
design. The Bible describes it as follows:

> Moreover the king made a great throne of ivory, and overlaid
> it with the finest gold. There were six steps to the throne, and
> the top of the throne was round behind; and there were arms
> on either side by the place of the seat, and two lions standing
> beside the arms. And twelve lions stood there on the one side
> and on the other upon the six steps; and there was not the
> like made in any kingdom (10:18–20).

One wonders what kind of man would want such a throne
and what his feelings were as he sat upon it and judged the
people who came before him.

Solomon showed great ability as an organizer. The Bible gives
a detailed description of his orderly division of the kingdom into

twelve geographic districts, each with a chief officer in control. It was the responsibility of each of these provinces to provide food supplies for the royal household one month each year.

Solomon also introduced a limited form of the corvée, or forced labor. Each man was required to serve a certain amount of time on the national building projects. We see this king therefore as a man who was strongly reality-oriented in the management of material things.

Solomon also achieved in another kind of reality, the world of the intellect. He was known not only for wisdom but also for knowledge, especially regarding the world of nature. The text says in this respect,

> And he spoke of trees, from the cedar that is in Lebanon even unto the hyssop that springeth out of the wall; he spoke also of beasts, and of fowl, and of creeping things, and of fishes. And there came of all peoples to hear the wisdom of Solomon, from all kings of the earth, who had heard of his wisdom (5:13–14).

In regard to his accomplishments in the field of wisdom literature and lyrics, the Bible says, "And he spoke three thousand proverbs; and his songs were a thousand and five (5:12)." Apart from the question of numerical accuracy involved, there must have been some factual basis for this kind of reputation. Solomon is credited by tradition with the authorship of the biblical *Book of Proverbs* and the *Song of Songs, Which is Solomon's.*

Here then was a person who was an excellent organizer and executive, endowed with a keen intellect, having a complex, philosophic outlook on life, and capable of creative ability in the fields of art and science. Despite the increased burdens that he put upon his people in the form of taxes and forced labor, it is of his era that the Bible says, ". . . and he had peace on all sides round about him. And Judah and Israel dwelt safely, every man under his vine and under his fig-tree, from Dan even to Beer-sheba, all the days of Solomon (5:4–5)."

From the style of his personal throne to the scope of his international relationships, Solomon functioned on a grand scale. In the words of a noted archaeologist and student of the Bible,

"The age of Solomon was certainly one of the most flourishing periods of material civilization in the history of Palestine."[13]

Yet Solomon, as we have seen, had his failings. It is these very weaknesses that make him a meaningful human figure, a man who struggled with inner conflict and was able to achieve in spite of them.

Solomon ruled over his kingdom for forty years, according to biblical chronology. Yet the full second half of his reign is dealt with in about two-and-a-half of the eleven chapters devoted to the story of his life. It is not until the very last chapter that Solomon's fall from grace is recorded, in a manner and with a brevity that is out of proportion to its real significance and the enormity of its possible consequences upon the spiritual life of his people. The text says, "For it came to pass, when Solomon was old, that his wives turned away his heart after other gods; and his heart was not whole with the Lord his God, as was the heart of David his father (11:4)." The responsibility for his behavior is placed upon his wives and the extent of his wrongdoing is phrased, not in terms that would describe his real apostasy, but merely as a deviation from a wholehearted worship of God.

Yet the gods Solomon worshipped were among the most degrading and cruel of the Canaanite deities. There were the Ashtoreth, various goddesses of fertility, whose temples were centers of sacred prostitution, the practice of which was generally accompanied by widespread sexual orgies. He built altars to Chemosh and Molech, to whom living children were sacrificed by being thrown into a burning furnace. The same man who worshipped the God of the universe in transcendental terms, who spoke so eloquently of the God of justice and compassion, now participated in the demoralizing cults of his pagan wives.

The reproof and punishment meted out by God is in the same tone of comparative mildness.

> And the Lord was angry with Solomon, because his heart was turned away from the Lord, the God of Israel, who had appeared unto him twice, and had commanded him concerning this thing, that he should not go after other gods; but he kept

not that which the Lord commanded. Wherefore the Lord said unto Solomon: "Forasmuch as this hath been in thy mind, and thou hast not kept My covenant and My statutes, which I have commanded thee, I will surely rend the kingdom from thee, and will give it to thy servant. Notwithstanding in thy days I will not do it, for David thy father's sake; but I will rend it out of the hand of thy son. Howbeit I will not rend away all the kingdom; but I will give one tribe to thy son, for David my servant's sake, and for Jerusalem's sake which I have chosen (11:9–13).

This is the tone of a kindly father reproving a disobedient son and saying, "Didn't I warn you not to do that!" Should Solomon really have required such warnings in the first place? At this period in the religious life of Israel, the principal of monotheism had already been long established. We hear of no such temptation in the life of David, or even in the history of the unstable Saul. Moreover, the real consequences of his behavior are postponed until Solomon's death. It will be recalled that when Samuel predicted the same kind of punishment for Saul, involving deeds far less reprehensible, the mood of condemnation and righteous wrath was much more intense. Solomon's self-protectiveness is carried over into the tone of his biographers. On the other hand, it might be pointed out that even this tendency did not save him from disapproval and punishment.

What was the nature of the temptation that led Solomon to worship idols, thus incurring the anger of God and undoing a large part of his influence as religious leader over his people? This development must have been a gradual one. There are signs of increasing inner awareness on his part of weakness in this area and a wish to defend himself against it. As we have noted, the conditional promise of God's continued acceptance and love assumed a more warning note as time went on. But there seemed to be an irresistable quality to the process. And it is clear in viewing the totality of Solomon's life that a basic inner rift must have existed from the beginning. The devotion to the God of Israel was one side of the coin; the desertion of this God was the other, potentially present from the beginning.

It is in the light of this later development that we can better understand the true significance of Solomon's earlier ways of behaving. Let us review some of the factors that may have entered into the development of his character structure.

The basic element in the personality of the king was his narcissism, or self-love, especially in the need for self-aggrandizement. This was obvious in his quest for the superlative in all areas of life, so well reflected in the biblical narrative, where he is described as the wisest and greatest of all kings. It is obvious in his need to be all-knowing and all-powerful.

This over-evaluation of self was probably fed from several sources and served strong needs, judging from its proportions. A major function of this character trait must have been to provide a defense against feelings of a directly opposite kind, a sense of inadequacy and inferiority. Such feelings are often dealt with through the mechanisms of denial and reaction formation, the whole process, of course, being on an unconscious level. Another source of his grandiosity may have been the sense of shared omnipotence with a powerful father, a phase of development which Solomon may have been particularly loth to relinquish, especially in his role as a crown prince.

But most significant of all, it seems to this writer, was the specific nature of Solomon's *ego ideal,* that which he aspired to be. There is a close relationship between this psychic structure and the *father ideal* held by the child. The idealized image of the father is based on identification with him.[14] Normally, the father ideal merges into and becomes part of the ego ideal. In Solomon's case, this seems not to have happened. The idealized image of the father would therefore lack stability and remain as a kind of foreign body within the larger structure of what is more generally known as the superego, or conscience, a term which Freud used synonymously with *ego ideal.*

The *father ideal,* common in early childhood, must have assumed exaggerated proportions in Solomon's situation, not only because of the real power of the father-king and the magnetic influence of David's personality, but also because this idealization of the king was needed by Solomon as a mechanism of defense against his ambivalent feelings, which might otherwise have led to a devaluation of the father. An idealized image of David helped to maintain him as an omnipotent figure with whom Solomon could identify and thus protect himself from feelings of inner weakness as well as from guilt.[15]

A further source for the idealization of David may have been the influence of Bathsheba. According to legend, she upheld David as the model for the son to follow. There would hardly be any reason for her to do otherwise. In addition to her own probably warm feelings for David, there must have been a competitive element for the attention of the king among the various wives and their sons. Bathsheba's continued prestige and her hope of becoming Queen Mother depended on Solomon's success. If he was to be a good son and please his father, Solomon must become like him.

In order to evaluate correctly the weight of the mother's influence, it is well to remember that in a non-monogamous family, the mother belongs to the child in a more personal and closer bond than does the father, who must be shared with the children of all his wives. The danger of loss of love from the mother thus becomes particularly threatening. As we have seen, the relationship between Solomon and his mother must have been especially close.

Since Solomon tended to relate to the father through the mother, his identification with the father would be strengthened by the mother's support. The vigor and resolution with which Solomon fulfilled the demands of his ego ideal indicate the degree of emotional investment in it. However, there was no serious problem as long as the real ego worked in harmony with the ego ideal, deriving gratification from the attainment of this ideal.[16]

And indeed, Solomon's narcissism was not of the pathological type. There was no loss of contact with reality, no signs of megalomania. Solomon did not consider himself omnipotent; he merely *wished* to be so. The distinction is all important. His wish found partial expression in reality achievement. Those wishes incapable of realization found release in creative imagination. Folklore and legend abound with stories of Solomon's powers over the world of nature. He has contact with the *demi-monde* of mythological creatures, some of whom have to perform his bidding. Both Jewish and Arabic folklore are rich in tales of Solomon's adventures in the realm peopled by these inhabitants of the world of fantasy.

There must be some reason why Solomon was chosen as the figure around which stories of this kind were woven. Rabbinic scholars of early times, many of whom devoted their lives to the study of this text, sensed acutely the quality of character and personality that emanated, as it were, from the style and wording of the biblical story. They intuitively read between the lines.

How did the kind of ego ideal described above affect the character structure of Solomon? The hypothesis presented here is that in the first part of his life, Solomon acted on the basis of an ego ideal taken over almost wholly from the wishes and commands of his father. This internalized father image may have functioned as a kind of hypnotic influence which expressed itself in what could be called auto-suggestion.[17] David's incorporated wishes and commands would then continue their potency.

However, this kind of development, not being fully integrated with the rest of Solomon's ego or with the more mature aspects of his superego, would lack a certain genuineness and stability. It would act as a foreign body which the rest of the personality would seek to expel. Such a process is more likely to occur when the father ideal *takes the place* of the ego ideal rather than forming one of the ingredients of the latter.

Such a hypnotic influence would maintain its positive aspect only as long as the ego-syntonic features of the ego ideal were in the ascendancy. In Solomon's case we know that ambivalent factors were present but repressed in the structure of the father ideal. When the appropriate situation arose therefore, the positive elements of the auto-suggestive influence gave way to the counter-suggestions of a negative character that had always been potentially present. The rebellious feelings against the father came to the surface. One gets the impression that Solomon's behavior when he "went astray after other gods" had a compulsive quality, as noted before.

This latter phase of Solomon's life can be understood as the period when his ego ideal, which represented the demands of his father, his God, and society in general, was abandoned. For a long time, Solomon had lived in accordance with the introjected demands of his unconscious conscience. Later came the need to overthrow this ego ideal, an expression of hostility toward the father which had never found an outlet during the latter's lifetime. Having fulfilled his duty, having carried out the wishes of his father, Solomon then allowed the underlying hostility to come to the surface. The forces of repression gave way, the pseudo-sublimations crumbled, and Solomon's weaknesses revealed themselves in a way that was essentially human and psychologically understandable.

When aggressive factors began to operate in the personality of Solomon, the development described earlier may have reversed itself. The ego ideal was undermined by the inherent ambivalence. The narcissistic libido that is invested in the ego ideal, a form of libido that is largely derived from homosexual sources, now sought to find its way back into those original sources. The pattern of reaching the father through the woman remained. But instead of the *Idealized Father*, the *Evil Father* of repressed instinctual forces is chosen. Sexuality must have been closely associated with a sense of sin and disobedience in the mind of Solomon. The gods after whom he went astray were symbols of his own projected feelings of wickedness. As a woman was once responsible for his rise to grace, so women are now made responsible for his fall. It seems to be characteristic of some personalities, known for their narcissism, that together with a wish for omnipotence there is also a need to avoid responsibility for their acts. In this sense the underlying wish for childlike dependency remains.

The striving toward monotheism represents a movement toward a unified superego, the consequence of a successful resolution of the oedipal conflict. Regression from this position would indicate that the original monotheistic attainment was not a genuine one and therefore subject to dissolution. The elements that combined to form the superego now regress to their former state of component instinctual activities. Their expression in overt behavior can therefore be regarded in the area of perversions. The worship of idols who demanded child sacrifice and licentious sexual practices in the temples was a return to primitive concepts of religion and morality. It typified the regressive forces within Solomon himself.

Solomon's personality development can be considered as the opposite to that taken by Abraham, the traditional founder of monotheism. The Patriarch struggled with his conflicts, gradually attaining more inner strength and greater confidence in God. Solomon began with a full, childlike faith in God and with expectations of omnipotence and omniscience. He ended with a weakening of the moral fibre and an abandonment of the moral God. In Abraham's first communication with God, the Patriarch is given a task and a mission. In the case of Solomon, the youthful king is at once rewarded with wisdom, power, and riches. We see here the contrasting views of Deity with which these two men began their leadership. Abraham's life resulted in a closer union of his people, a union fostered by the emergence of a genuine group ego ideal. Solomon's period of rule, although profitable and positive in many ways, led to a dissolution of the united monarchy and a lowered level of religious and moral life.

A Psychoanalytic Note on the
Function of the Bible

 CONCLUSION

O NE OF the concepts that emerged from the present study has to do with the nature and function of the Bible as a whole. I see this body of literature (*Old Testament*) as an expression of the Hebraic approach to what is regarded from a Freudian viewpoint as the nuclear psychological conflict of each human being—the oedipal struggle.

These writings might be considered as performing the same function for the Hebrews as the *Oedipus Rex* dramas did for the ancient Greeks. However, instead of their heroes acting out the primordial crime as Oedipus did, the Hebrews, over a long period of time, evolved a form of sublimation, a *working through* of the conflict, which led to new paths in the fields of morality and religion.

The text of the Bible contains the story of this evolution. It is a remarkable expression of the development of the superego, outgrowth of the oedipal conflict, portrayed as a group drama, with its leaders as the representative actors.

The particular aspects of the conflict, its massive repression both of incestuous wishes toward the mother and the ambivalence between father and son, the efforts to overcome this hostility along constructive lines, the instinctual renunciations that led to identification with a monotheistic Father-God and increased feelings of kinship in the group, all these forces can be observed in the lives of many of the biblical heroes.

The theme that runs like a unifying thread through the various books of the Bible is the story of man's struggle between his instinctual impulses and his wish and need for socialization. This is indeed the kernel of the oedipal conflict. In the studies of the personalities that comprise this volume, it was disclosed that the oedipal theme was indeed the dominant one in their lives, with the exception of Joseph, where sibling rivalry seemed to take precedence. There were many instances in the text of the *return of the repressed,* the longing for the mother, which came out in disguised and symbolic ways, indicating a resistance to the process of identification with the commandments of the Father.

The Bible repeats the oedipal theme through various media, in the realistic personal conflicts of its leaders and heroes, through legend and symbolism, in poetic and prophetic expression, and through song and proverb. It is because the struggle in itself and the significance of its outcome was so important, that the Bible did not hesitate, in many instances, to reveal with a frankness often embarrassing to readers, the faults and shortcomings of its heroes. At the same time, since aspects of this struggle were on the level of unconscious conflict, the mechanisms of defense employed by the ego sought to deny and to disguise the forbidden impulses.

Thus the Bible is a story of human conflict and endeavor rather than the portrayal of heroes as perfect examples to be emulated. As the civilization of Israel progressed from early times through the centuries, this struggle took on a more purified form until it reached a high degree of sublimated expression in the writings of the prophets. But its basic nature was the same—

man's efforts to find a *modus vivendi* between his instinctual wishes and his conscience.

Different stages of civilization create areas of special psychic significance common to a people as a whole. "Men who share an ethnic area, an historical era, or an economic pursuit, are guided by common images of good and evil," said Erik Erikson.[1] The Bible can be seen as a unique product of the Hebraic group at a certain period of its development. It can be understood as an expression of the group culture, a folk literature brought into being through its gifted storytellers and mythmakers, who made vocal the thoughts and feelings of the people. The leaders through whose experiences the stories are told reflect, not only their individual struggles and aspirations, but also those of the group. It is because their conflicts are typical and yet new solutions are attempted that these people are leaders.

In the mass oedipal involvement which the Bible expresses, the feelings for the mother were sublimated in a love for the *land*, which became the good mother, *flowing with milk and honey*, and in an acceptance of the Torah, or religious law, *the words of the Father*.[2, 3]

It is significant that after the first loss of the land suffered by the Hebrews through the Babylonian conquest, followed by the burning of the Temple in 586 B.C.E., the subsequent happy return to Canaan fifty years later was marked by two events, the rebuilding of the Temple and a renewed emphasis upon the study and observance of the Torah. The relationship is clear. Only by worshipping God and obeying his commandments would they feel any security in possessing the land.

In the later destruction of the Kingdom of Judah by the Romans (70 C.E.) and the more widespread exile of Jews to other lands, a further substitution of the *Law* for the *Land* was achieved, and the Jews became the *People of the Book*. Thus, even the symbolic mother had to be renounced and in its place came a more spiritualized, internalized identification with the commandments of the Father. He thus granted his followers a *way of life* in which adult sexuality was sanctioned and a benign

Superego exerted a controlling but permissive influence over the whole of existence.

This concept of the purpose and function of the Bible offers some explanation of the unique role which it has played in the Judeo-Christian culture of the Western world. The powerful affects associated with the oedipal conflict and the formation of the superego are related to this body of literature. Perhaps that is the reason, also, why even psychoanalytic investigation of the text has been so surprisingly limited in this field. To look at *the father* critically can become a forbidden form of voyeurism. But only by daring to do so can we fully appreciate how the very human struggles of these group fathers led to the growth and development of the social and moral concepts which are the foundation of our own present day Judeo-Christian culture.

Some Brief Remarks
on Biblical Exegesis

As one reviews the history of man's efforts to probe into the origins of the Bible, one fact stands out impressively—how little we know with certainty about the true birth-pangs of this priceless literature. Yet it seems safe to say that the Bible has evoked more scholarly interest and research than any other comparable number of written words.

The following brief discussion of the complex area of biblical criticism is intended to provide some background for the lay reader. For him, also, several *Introductions* to this field and some other volumes of related interest are suggested.[1]

The Bible is a body of literature made up of a number of books which deal with a variety of material in a diversity of literary forms. Yet all are tied together by a common theme—the religious life and history of a people.

Just the process of gathering this content together and the tasks of compiling, editing, and putting it into the form familiar to us today, went on for about a thousand years, approximately from the tenth century B.C.E. to the first century of the present era. Some of the material it contains goes back even farther, perhaps to the middle of the second millenium B.C.E. In the words of one scholar, "written sources for this period may have existed at a much earlier date than has been commonly supposed."[2]

Not only does obscurity veil the beginnings of the Bible, but

315

even the time of its final canonization is indefinite. This latter procedure is one which declares the writings to be holy, thereby no longer subject to change.[3]

Most scholars agree that the *Pentateuch* attained the status of canon sometime in the days of Ezra and Nehemiah, around 400 B.C.E. These *Five Books of Moses* (the *Torah*) came down to us as a unit. If they were ever known as separate scrolls, we have no record of such a time.[4] It is possible however, that the book of *Deuteronomy* does have such a distinction and is synonymous with the book of laws discovered by King Josiah in the Temple in 621 B.C.E.[5]

What we know with certainty about that part of the Bible called the *Prophets* is that it was obviously made up of independent scrolls and that it existed pretty much in its present order by the middle of the second century B.C.E. The third division of the *Scriptures,* the *Writings,* was probably a long time in the process of formation. Its canonization date is indefinite, opinion regarding it ranging from the second century B.C.E. to a period two hundred years later.

Regarding the *Pentateuch,* it is thought that a standard copy of it was deposited in the Temple long before the Common Era and was used as a guide by scribes to correct their own scrolls.[6] Thus, in spite of the human tendency to error, much effort went into the preservation of the text from earliest times.

Tradition ascribes the final compilation of the Bible to a synod of Jewish scholars at some time around the end of the first century of the present era. Their motivation evidently was to preserve this literature during the period of turmoil following the destruction of Jerusalem at the hands of the Romans in the year 70 C.E. Modern scholars however vary in their opinion about the date of final canonization, some placing it as far back from that time as two hundred years and others moving it forward from this catastrophic event for the same length of two hundred years. Suffice it to say, we have known the Bible in its present form, with variations in the versions of that form, for about two thousand years.

For many centuries the Bible was regarded as a divine revelation and therefore not subject to imperfections. Problems involving the obscurities of the text were attributed to man's limited capacity to understand. Nevertheless, critical approaches to the study of the biblical text were not wanting even among the rabbis of Talmudic days. They were cognizant of the many inconsistencies and puzzling features of the text that centuries later became the subject of so much intensive study among the scholars of modern biblical criticism. Nor was this kind of awareness lacking during the Middle Ages when the atmosphere of the church was even more forbidding. Scholarly and inquiring minds covertly expressed and sought answers to the mysteries of the holy text.

The critical study of the Bible in modern times is generally regarded as having its beginnings in the middle of the eighteenth century, reaching its peak among the German theologians of the mid-nineteenth, and continuing into the twentieth. There was a new aura of excitement in the freedom with which scholars now felt able to penetrate boldly into this hitherto sanctified field and face the challenging problems of the Bible's origins and structure.

Under the impetus of the scientific method and the Darwinian theory of evolution, an increased number of scholarly investigators became involved in biblical research, producing a large body of material dealing with theories about the authorship of the Bible and the history of its development.

Certain criteria were formulated on the basis of which the biblical content, particularly of the *Pentateuch* and *Joshua* was separated into what was thought to be the original sources, or documents, from which the Bible as we know it now was compiled and edited. These criteria, growing out of the internal evidence of the Bible itself, were based upon intensive study of its literary characteristics and an analysis of the historical data it contained. Thus evolved the *Documentary Theory*. Its proponents came from the school of *Higher Biblical Criticism,* so called because its areas of interest transcended *Lower Biblical Criticism,* the study of textual problems as such. The theory that the *Pentateuch* was a composite work was then used to explain most of the puzzling features of the text.

One of the major conclusions of the *Documentary Theory* was that these first six books of the Bible, now called the *Hexateuch,* were mainly the work of four writers, each of whom had produced his material at different times. These accounts were later combined into one narrative by various redactors or editors. This theory of composite authorship reached further proportions in which the four chief sources were either subdivided or added to again and again, indicating a much larger number of original authors and redactors. Many times, even a single verse of the Bible was divided into parts and attributed to different sources. This process became known as the *Fragmentation Theory* and led others to challenge this whole area of scholarship and to wonder how such a patchwork could have resulted in so effective a body of literature.[7]

Some of the more basic assumptions of the *Documentary Theory,* such as its division into four major sources, were widely accepted during the better part of the past two hundred years and still provide a basic foundation for *Higher Criticism,* although much more subject to prevailing winds of change. It might be stated, however, that at no time was there unanimous agreement on any of the theories even in regard to its major premises, while concerning details, there was always wide room for differences of opinion.

The zeal for this so-called scientific approach to the understanding of the biblical text led to other departures. There was a reformulation of early Hebrew history, one of the chief proponents of which was Wellhausen, a German scholar of the late nineteenth century. He saw the ancient Hebrews as a group that had a long evolutionary history, beginning as an illiterate, nomadic tribe with a polytheistic religion. He questioned the historical value of the *Pentateuch,* declaring that the early history of the Hebrews it described was legendary, made up at a later date and projected backward in time to provide a suitable background for the later, more authenticated historical epochs. This viewpoint, usually modified in terms of the length of time thus treated, found widespread acceptance until disproved by later scholarship. The Patriarchal Period, especially, was regarded as legendary, a concept that is no longer held valid.

While the work of literary and historical analysis of the

biblical sources still continues, it has diminished in importance. Its task seems to have been largely accomplished. The one outstanding conclusion to which most modern scholars would subscribe is that the *Pentateuch* is a composite work. The *Documentary Theory*, with its four basic sources, together with some variations, is still more widely accepted than any other single theory in spite of the setbacks to which it has been subjected in the last half century. In regard to this whole field, the esteemed scholar, H. H. Rowley, comments, "To treat modern theories as the older traditions were so long treated, as dogmas to be defended at all costs, whose difficulties are to be resolved by special pleading in so far as they are openly recognized at all, is to deny the modern method whereby they were reached. It is wise to recognize that, like all scientific theories, they only hold the field until more satisfactory theories are forthcoming, and that from the ferment of recent challenge something more satisfactory may yet emerge, though in few cases does it seem yet to have done so."[8]

Another important school of thought was that which emphasized the role of oral traditions, a process believed to have preceded the written form. These traditions, it was believed, arose in different localities, perhaps at similar times, a mode of group communication reaching back to the very beginnings of Hebraic life. The scholar's task, as this school saw it, was to penetrate the facade of the written material and find the original nucleus of the oral tradition that had gone into its making. It was felt that the tendency of the redactors had been to preserve as much of the original form and content as possible and thus had kept intact the literary characteristics of its popular origin. The documentary sources were now seen by these scholars, not so much as the work of individual authors, but rather reflecting *schools of writers* in various areas, who gathered the folk traditions and compiled them. In these terms, the biblical material would represent more genuinely the collective expression of a people.[9,10] Regarding both the antiquity of the *Torah* and the authenticity of its language, Solomon Goldman refers to the opinion of the noted Israeli scholar, Y. Kaufmann, as follows ". . . although he readily admits that the Pentateuchal Canon might not date back earlier than the age of Ezra (about 400 B.C.E.), he is convinced that the documents it comprises stem not alone in part or general content but in actuality of composition, in style, and in their very letters from remotest antiquity."[11] The most far-reaching and dramatic influence on biblical scholarship in recent times has come through the revelations stemming from archaeological research. Hundreds of sites throughout the entire Near East have been excavated. A whole new world which had been buried for centuries beneath the sand was brought into the light of day. Thousands of clay tablets and other forms of written records, the most exciting example of the latter being the Dead Sea Scrolls, made available an increasing body of knowledge about the previously shadowy backgrounds of early biblical life. Discoveries in this field not only brought to vivid reality the world of those days but also made possible comparative studies of the literature and history of Israel and her neighbors at a period contemporaneous with the very beginnings of Hebrew existence.

It became evident that the whole ancient Near East, though made up of various peoples and political entities, was united by many bonds of cultural and economic ties and characterized by an advanced state of civilization. Clearly, the Hebrews had emerged as a distinctive people, not from a primitive state as Wellhausen had thought, but against the background of a complex culture in which they had shared. Thus the earlier reconstruction of Hebrew history based on an evolutionary concept was seen as invalid.

One of the consequences of archaeological research was to restore the Patriarchal Period as described in the Bible to its traditional place as the true beginnings of Hebrew life. Although no evidence was unearthed to prove the existence of the specific personalities immortalized in its narratives, the whole social and economic background so colorfully described in the Bible was indeed an authentic picture of those days.

Albright, an outstanding authority on biblical archaeology, says in this connection, "Abraham, Isaac, and Jacob no longer seem isolated figures, much less reflections of later Israelite history; they now appear as true children of their age, bearing the same names, moving about the same territory, visiting the same towns (especially Haran and Nahor), practicing the same customs as their contemporaries. In other words, the patriarchal narratives have a historical nucleus throughout. . . ."[12]

Salo Baron, noted historian of the Jews, also comments on this theme, referring to ". . . the now prevalent assumption of a solid kernel of authentic historic tradition in the biblical narrative." He goes on to say, "The lifelike description of the human strengths and weaknesses of Abraham, Isaac, Jacob, and Joseph, in the book of *Genesis* is also more likely to reflect actual historical personalities than mere personifications of later Hebrew tribes. Few biblical historians would still profess to be shocked by even the extreme statement that 'it is no longer a matter of argument that behind the biblical Abraham an eminent historical personality is manifest. . . .' "[13]

A. E. Speiser, an esteemed authority on the biblical Near East, commented on the reality of the functions which these leaders carried out in the early formation of a people. He writes, "Although there is no proof so far of Abraham's historicity, many biblical historians would probably agree that if some such figure had not been recorded by the ancients, it would have to be conjectured by the moderns."[14] He continues, "While it is true that Israel as a nation would be inconceivable without Moses, the work of Moses would be equally inconceivable without the prior labors of the Patriarchs. The covenant of Mount Sinai is a natural sequel to God's covenant with Abraham . . . the internal evidence of the Bible itself goes hand in hand with the results of modern biblical study based in large measure on the testimony of outside sources. Both sets of data point to the Age of Abraham; each in its own way enhances the probability of Abraham as a historical figure."[15]

In the first comparative studies made possible by archaeological discoveries, the tendency of certain scholars was to point out the similarities between the culture and literature of ancient Israel and that of her polytheistic neighbors, with the implication that the contribution of Israel was therefore not as great as originally thought. But the work of other able scholars, through their translation of the ancient texts, demonstrated that it was the *differences* that were important and which gave to the Hebrew religion and to the biblical writings their unique and distinctive aspects.[16]

The field of biblical exegesis is so comprehensive in scope and content that the numerous other approaches cannot even be touched upon in these few pages. The purpose here is to indicate to the layman the existence of this vast school of thought that the Bible has stimulated, as it continues to exert its profound influence, not only upon the hearts, but also upon the minds of men.

A predominant characteristic of the present era in this field is the tendency to find greater unity in the biblical literature in contrast to earlier tendencies to fragment it. The quest is to deepen the understanding of what held this diverse body of writings together and gave it so important a place in the world of religion. It was recognized that the underlying motive animating those who wrote down and preserved this literature was primarily religious. As one scholar put it, "This recognition of the unifying religious motivation of Hebrew historiography was the most important development in *Old Testament* criticism of the last two decades."[17] It can be said that the same holds true for the several decades that have followed since that statement. And as religious feeling is part of the psychological nature of man, it seems fitting that psychoanalysis should also have a voice in this quest for understanding.

References and Notes

Introduction

1. Ricoeur, Paul. *Freud and Philosophy: An Essay on Interpretation,* Trans. by Denis Savage (New Haven, 1970), pp. 544–545.
2. Freud, Sigmund. (1939) *Moses and Monotheism* (New York, 1949).
3. Goldman, Solomon. *The Book of Books: An Introduction* (Phila., 1948), pp. 60 f.
4. Morgenstern, Julian. *The Book of Genesis* (Cincinnati, 1920).
5. Speiser, A. E. *The Anchor Bible: Genesis,* Trans. with Introduction and Notes (New York, 1964), pp. XVII f.
6. Goldman, *Op. cit.,* p. 48.
7. Roheim, Geza. "Some Aspects of Jewish Monotheism." *Psychoanalysis and the Social Sciences* (New York, 1955), Vol. IV, p. 169 n.
8. Speiser, *Op. cit..* pp. XLV; XLXI f.
9. Goldman, *Op. cit.,* pp. 63 f.
10. Kaufmann, Yehezkel. *The Religion of Israel, From Its Beginnings to the Babylonian Exile,* Trans. & Abridged by Moshe Greenberg (Chicago, 1960) p. 223.
11. Arlow, Jacob. "Ego Psychology and the Study of Mythology." *Jour. Amer. Psychoan. Assn. 9:*375, 1961.
12. Slochower, Harry. "Psychoanalytic Distinction between Myth and Mythopoesis." *Jour. Amer. Psychoan. Assn. 18:*150–164, 1970.
13. Freud, Sigmund. (1922) *Group Psychology and the Analysis of the Ego* (New York, 1949), p. 80.

14. Slochower, Harry. *Mythopoesis: Mythic Patterns in the Literary Classics* (Detroit, 1970).
15. Jones, Ernest. *The Life and Work of Sigmund Freud* (New York, 1955), Vol. II, Chap. 14.
16. Ginzberg, Louis. *The Legends of the Jews* (Phila., 1909–1938), Vols. I–VII.
17. Rank, Otto. (1907) *The Myth of the Birth of the Hero* (New York, 1952), p. 81.
18. Freud, Sigmund. (1908) "The Relation of the Poet to Day-Dreaming." *Collected Papers* (London, 1950), Vol. IV, pp. 173–183.
19. Erikson, Erik. H. "Identity and the Life Cycle." *Psychological Issues* (New York, 1959), Vol. I, No. 1, p. 18.
20. Reik, Theodor. *Listening With the Third Ear* (New York, 1948).
21. Freud, Sigmund. (1928) *The Future of an Illusion* (New York, 1953).
22. Ricoeur, *Op. cit.,* p. 546.
23. Freud, Sigmund. *The Future of an Illusion, Op. cit.,* p. 57.
24. —— (1913) *Totem and Taboo* (New York, 1952), p. 147.

Chapter One
Abraham, A Study in Fatherhood

1. Morgenstern, *Op. cit.,* p. 19.
2. Freud, Sigmund. *Moses and Monotheism* (New York, 1939), p. 211.
3. Ginzberg, *Op. cit.,* Vol. I.
4. Sarna, Nahum M. *Understanding Genesis, The Heritage of Israel* (New York, 1970), p. 108.
5. Kasher, Menachem M. *Encyclopedia of Biblical Interpretation: Genesis* (New York, 1955), Vol. II, p. 105.
6. Ginzberg, *Op. cit.,* Vol. V, p. 208.
7. *Ibid.,* Vol. I, pp. 186 f.
8. *Ibid.,* Vol. V, p. 210.
9. *Ibid.,* Vol. V, p. 214.
10. *The Torah, The Five Books of Moses, A New Translation of the Holy Scriptures* (Jewish Publication Society, Phila., 1962), p. 19.
11. Kasher, *Op. cit.,* pp. 102–103: see also, Hertz (#14 below) Vol. V, p. 214.
12. Speiser, *Op. cit.,* pp. 91 f.

13. Patai, Raphael. *Sex and the Family in the Bible and the Middle East* (New York, 1959), pp. 23 f. *(Paperback)*

14. Hertz, Joseph H. *The Pentateuch and Haftorahs: Genesis, With Commentary* (New York, 1929), p. 115; See also, Speiser, *Op. cit.*, p. 87.

15. Zeligs, Dorothy F. "The Role of the Mother in the Development of Hebraic Monotheism: As Exemplified in the Life of Abraham." In: *The Psychoanalytic Study of Society* (New York, 1960), Vol. I, pp. 287–310.

16. Cohen, A. (Ed.) *The Soncino Chumash* (England, 1947), p. 62.

17. Garma, Angel. *Unpublished paper.* "Ancestral Traumata and Destructive Identifications in Religion and Anti-Judaism.

18. Ginzberg, *Op. cit.,* Vol. I, pp. 234–235.

19. Zeligs, Dorothy F. "Abraham and the Covenant of the Pieces, A Study in Ambivalence." *Amer. Imago, 18:2,* 173–186, 1961.

20. Smith, W. Robertson. (1889) *The Religion of the Semites* (New York, 1959), pp. 314 f.

21. Otto, Rudolf. *The Idea of the Holy* (London, 1923), p. 31.

22. Zeligs, "Role of the Mother . . . *Op. cit.* Contains a fuller description of the seeming inconsistencies in these biblical verses.

23. Jones, Ernest. (1923) "The Symbolic Significance of Salt." In: *Essays in Applied Psychoanalysis* (London, 1951), Vol. II, pp. 22 f.

24. Goldmon, Solomon. *In the Beginning* (Phila., 1959), p. 734.

25. —— *The Book of Books, Op. cit.,* p. 48.

26. Roheim, Geza. "Some Aspects of Jewish Monotheism." In: *Psychoanalysis and the Social Sciences* (New York, 1955), Vol. IV, pp. 169–222.

27. Brenner, Arthur B. "The Covenant with Abraham." *Psychoan. Review, 39:38,* 1952.

28. Reik, Theodor. (1931) *Ritual: Psychoanalytic Studies* (New York, 1958), pp. 72 f; 282 f.

29. Freud, Sigmund. (1930) *Civilization and Its Discontents* (New York), 1951, p. 63.

30. *Ibid.,* pp. 136–137.

Chapter Two
Two Episodes in the Life of Jacob

1. Reik, Theodor. "The Wrestling of Jacob." In: *Dogma and Compulsion* (New York, 1951).

Reik connects these two experiences. He maintains that the latter episode was displaced by editors of the Bible and is really an integral part of the earlier experience. According to Reik, both belonged to the puberty rites through which Jacob passed. The wrestling with the stranger signified the initiatory hostile attack by the father during which Jacob undergoes a partial mutilation, or circumcision, and the second part is the bestowal of the blessing and the consequent rights and privileges of the youth as an adult member of the group. Reik thus sees Jacob as a mythical, or allegorical, figure, representing the entire tribe.

2. Ginzberg, *Op. cit.,* Vol. I, p. 316.

3. *Ibid.,* Vol. VI, p. 234; Vol. V, p. 194; see also, Patai, *Op. cit.,* pp. 194 f.

4. These concepts grew out of a personal communication by Dr. Jacob Arlow suggesting that the possible effects of twinship be more fully explored.

5. Speiser, *Op. cit.,* pp. 212–213.

6. *Ibid.,* p. 196; Speiser comments, "Business transactions in the Near East, while subject to strict legal norms, have also been looked upon to some extent as a game, one in which the contestants match wits with one another."

7. Hertz, *Op. cit.,* p. 220, for the rabbinic viewpoint of Jacob's transaction.

8. Patai, *Op. cit.,* pp. 221 f.

9. Bailey, Albert E. *Daily Life in Bible Times* (New York, 1943), pp. 211 f.

10. Friedman, Paul. "The Bridge: A Study in Symbolism." *Psychoan. Quart.* 21:49, 1952.

11. Reik, "The Wrestling of Jacob," *Op. cit.*

12. *Ibid.,* p. 249.

Chapter Three
The Personality of Joseph

1. Hahn, Herbert F. *Old Testament in Modern Research* (Phila., 1954), p. 193.

2. Patai, *Op. cit.,* p. 43.

3. Jones, Ernest. *The Life and Work of Sigmund Freud* (New York, 1953), Vol. I, p. 5.

4. Feldman, S. S. "The Sin of Reuben, First-Born Son of Jacob." In: *Psychoanalysis and the Social Sciences* (New York, 1955), Vol. IV, p. 282 f.
5. Suggested by Dr. Jacob Arlow in a personal communication.
6. Goldman, *In the Beginning, Op. cit.,* p. 828.

Chapter Four
A Character Study of Samuel

1. *Cambridge Bible for Schools and Colleges: Samuel* (Ed.) Kirpatrick, A. E. (London, 1918).
2. Freud, Sigmund. (1914) "On Narcissism: An Introduction." *Collected Papers* (London, 1950), Vol. IV, pp. 46 f.
3. —— (1927) *The Ego and the Id* (London, 1950), p. 49.
4. Arlow, Jacob. "The Consecration of the Prophet." *Psychoan. Quart.*20:274, 1951.
5. Freud, Sigmund. (1922) "Dreams and Telepathy." *Collected Papers* (London, 1950), Vol. IV, pp. 408 f.
6. —— *The Ego and the Id, Op. cit.,* p. 49.
7. —— (1922) "Certain Neurotic Mechanisms in Jealousy, Paranoia, and Homosexuality." *Collected Papers* (London, 1950), Vol. II, p. 243.
8. —— (1922) *Group Psychology and the Analysis of the Ego* (London, 1950), p. 80.
9. *Cambridge Bible for Schools and Colleges: Samuel, Op. cit.,* p. 69.
10. Kaufmann, *Op. cit.,* pp. 263–265.
11. Freud, "On Narcissism: An Introduction." *Op. cit.,* pp. 45–47.
12. —— "On Narcissism: An Introduction." *Op. cit.,* p. 59. Samuel's manifestation of a sense of guilt here corresponds interestingly to Freud's description of what happens when the social esteem on which, in part, the harmony between the ego and the ego ideal is maintained, is felt to be withdrawn. He says, "The dissatisfaction due to the non-fulfillment of this ideal liberates homosexual libido, which is transformed into a sense of guilt (dread of the community).
13. Greenacre, Phyllis. *Affective Disorders* (New York, 1953), p. 26.
14. Oldine, Christine. "About the Fascinating Effect of the Narcissistic Personality." *Amer. Imago,* 2:347, 1941.
15. Freud, Sigmund, *Group Psychology and the Analysis of the Ego, Op. cit.,* p. 122.

16. Reik, *Dogma and Compulsion, Op. cit.,* pp. 265 f.
17. Freud, *Totem and Taboo, Op. cit.,* pp. 140 f.

Chapter Five
Saul, the Tragic King

1. *Cambridge Bible for Schools and Colleges, Samuel, Op. cit.*
2. Albright, *From the Stone Age to Christianity, Op. cit.,* pp. 279–280.
3. *Loc. cit.*
4. Kaufmann, *Op. cit.,* pp. 247–254.
5. Freud, Sigmund. (1917) "Mourning and Melancholia." *Collected Papers* (London, 1950), Vol. IV, p. 159.
6. Suggested by Theodor Reik in a personal communication.
7. Freud, "Certain Neurotic Mechanisms in Jealousy, Paranoia, and Homosexuality," *Op. cit.,* p. 242.
8. *Loc. cit.*
9. Freud, Anna. *The Ego and Mechanisms of Defense* (New York, 1946), Chap. X.
10. Rank, *Op. cit.,* p. 77.
11. Reik, Theodor. *Ritual: Psychoanalytic Studies, Op. cit.,* p. 105.
12. Abraham, Karl. (1927) "Melancholia and Obsessional Neurosis." In: *Selected Papers on Psychoanalysis* (London, 1949), Vol. I, p. 422.

Chapter Six
David, the Charismatic Leader

1. Ginzberg, *Op. cit.,* Vol. VI, p. 272, n.128.
2. *Ibid.* p. 249, n.22.
3. *Ibid.,* p. 249, n. 23; p. 287; Vol. IV, p. 82.
4. Rubenstein, Richard L. *The Religious Imagination, A Study in Psychoanalysis and Jewish Theology* (New York, 1968), Chap. 2.
5. Freud, Sigmund. (1909) "Family Romances." *Collected Papers* (London, 1950), Vol. V, pp. 74 f.
6. Rank, Otto. (1907) *The Myth of the Birth of the Hero* (New York, 1952), p. 81.
7. Frazer, Sir James. *Folklore in the Old Testament* (New York, 1923), p. 175; see also, Speiser, *Op. cit.,* pp. 212–213.

8. Heaten, W. E. *Everyday Life in Old Testament Times* (New York, 1956), pp. 78–79.
9. Freud, *Group Psychology and the Analysis of the Ego, Op. cit.,* p. 113.
10. *Cambridge Bible for Schools and Colleges, Samuel, Op. cit.,* p. 81.
11. Samuel, Maurice. *Certain People of the Book* (New York, 1955), pp. 186 f.
12. Ginzberg, *Op. cit.,* Vol. IV, p. 91; Vol. VI, p. 254, n. 51.
13. *Ibid,* Vol IV, p 81.
14. Freud, Sigmund. (1900) *The Interpretation of Dreams* (New York, 1955), p. 343.
15. Ginzberg, *Op. cit.,* Vol. VI, p. 85.
16. Pfeiffer, Robert. *Introduction to the Old Testament* (New York, 1948), p. 373 n.
17. Oesterly & Robinson. (1934) *An Introduction to the Books of the Old Testament* (New York, 1958), p. 87.
18. Rabbi Arthur Lelyveld called this analogy to my attention.
19. Freud, Sigmund (1913) "The Theme of the Three Caskets." *Collected Papers* (London, 1950), pp. 253–254.

Chapter Seven
Solomon, the Man and the Myth

1. *The Cambridge Bible for Schools and Colleges: Kings I.* (Ed.) Lumby, J. H. (Cambridge, 1894).
2. Freud, Sigmund. (1900) *The Interpretation of Dreams, Op. cit.,* p. 318.
3. Ginzberg, *Op. cit.,* Vol. VI, p. 283; Vol. III, p. 78.
4. *Ibid.,* pp. 283, 285.
5. Pfeiffer, Robert. *Introduction to the Old Testament* (New York, 1948), p. 385.
6. Montgomery, J. A. *International Critical Commentary, Book of Kings* (New York, 1951), p. 142.
7. Ginzberg, *Op. cit.,* Vol. IV, p. 156.
8. *Ibid.,* Vol. IV, p. 129.
9. *Ibid.,* Vol. IV, p. 135; Vol. VI, pp. 286–87, n. 32.
10. *Ibid.,* Vol. VI, p. 389, n. 21.
11. *Ibid.,* Vol. IV, p. 145; Vol. VI, p. 289, n. 41
12. Albright, *From the Stone Age to Christianity, Op. cit.,* p. 291.
13. ——— *The Archaeology of Palestine* (London, 1954), p. 123.

14. Freud, Sigmund. (1927) *The Ego and the Id* (London, 1950), p. 39.
15. Jacobson, Edith. *The Self and the Object World* (New York, 1964), pp. 109 f.
16. Freúd, "On Narcissism: An Introduction," *Op. cit.*, p. 57.
17. Jones, Ernest. (1923) "The Nature of Auto-Suggestion." In: *Papers on Psychoanalysis* (Boston, 1960), pp. 273–293.

Conclusion

1. Erikson, Erik H. "Ego Development and Historical Change." *Psychological Issues* (New York, 1959), Vol. I, Monograph I, No. 1, p. 18.
2. Brenner, A. B. *Op. cit.*
3. Rosenzweig, E. M. "Some Notes, Historical and Psychoanalytical, on the People of Israel, with Special Reference to Deuteronomy." *Amer. Imago* (1940), 1: 4.

Some Brief Remarks on Biblical Exegesis

1. (a) Oesterly, W. & Robinson, T. (1934), *An Introduction to the Books of the Old Testament* (New York, 1958). (*Paperbook*)
(b) Driver, S. R. *An Introduction to the Literature of the Old Testament* (New York, 1913).
(c) Rowley, H. H. *The Old Testament and Modern Study* (Oxford, 1951).
(d) ——— *The Changing Pattern of Old Testament Studies* (London, 1959).
(e) Robinson, H. W. *The Old Testament: Its Making and Meaning* (London, 1937).
(f) Hahn, Herbert. *Old Testament in Modern Research* (Phila., 1954).
(g) Burrows, Millar. *What Mean These Stones?* (New Haven, 1941).
(h) Orlinsky, Harry. *Ancient Israel* (Ithaca, 1956).
(i) Sandmel, Samuel. *The Hebrew Scriptures* (New York, 1963).
(j) Gordon, C. H. *The World of the Old Testament* (New York, 1958).
2. Kenyon, Sir Frederic. *The Bible and Archaeology* (New York, 1940), p. 278.

3. Rowley, H. H. *The Growth of the Old Testament* (New York, 1961), p. 169. (*Paperback*)
4. Goldman, Solomon. *The Book of Books* (Phila., 1948), p. 30.
5. Rowley, *The Growth of the Old Testament, Op. cit.,* p. 29.
6. Goldman, *The Book of Books, Op. cit.,* p. 37.
7. *Ibid.,* p. 48.
8. Rowley, *The Growth of the Old Testament, Op. cit.,* p. 10.
9. Hahn, *Op. cit.,* pp. 135 f.
10. Nielson, Eduard. *Oral Traditions: A Modern Problem in Old Testament Introduction* (London, 1954).
11. Goldman, *The Book of Books, Op. cit.,* p. 62.
12. Albright, *The Archaeology of Palestine, Op. cit.,* pp. 236–237.
13. Baron, Salo. *A Social and Religious History of the Jews* (Phila., 1952), Vol. I, p. 34.
14. Speiser, E. A. *The Anchor Bible: Genesis* (New York, 1964), p. XLV.
15. *Ibid.,* p. L.
16. Sarna, Nahum M. (1966), *Understanding Genesis: The Heritage of Biblical Israel* (New York, 1970). (*Paperback*)
17. Hahn, *Op. cit.,* p. 260.

Glossary of
Psychoanalytic Terms

Affect: A feeling-tone, pleasurable or unpleasurable.

Alter ego: Someone who represents an externalization of one's own ego or self; another "I."

Altruistic surrender: Withdrawal from a more advantageous position in favor of someone else, usually accompanied by an identification with the other and a vicarious enjoyment of the latter's gratification.

Ambivalence: The coexistence of opposite feelings, especially love and hate, without either feeling modifying the other; in neurotic conflict, one aspect of the feelings is unconscious.

Analysand: One who is being analyzed.

Castration anxiety: An unrealistic fear, usually unconscious, of genital injury or loss, related to the oedipal stage of psychosexual development; may be displaced in later life to other parts of the body; includes the childhood fantasy that female genitals result from loss of a penis.

Cathexis: The investment of psychic energy in a mental representation.

Compensatory (also over-compensatory): Descriptive of a process, generally unconscious, by which an individual tries to make up for real or fancied deficiences.

Compulsion: An urge to perform an action which may seem incomprehensible to the subject or against his conscious wishes and standards, but the omission of which would cause anxiety; may represent the acting out of an unconscious fantasy or a defense against unacceptable wishes.

Condensation: A psychic process, often present in dreams, in which two or more concepts are fused so that a single symbol represents the multiple components.

Conflict, intrapsychic: The clash between opposing emotional forces within the self; a common characteristic of psychic life and a significant cause of psychologic disorders.

Defense mechanisms: Specific intrapsychic processes, working unconsciously, which are used by the ego to protect itself from anxiety or guilt in relation to forbidden wishes or drives.

Déjà vu: (Already seen); The feeling, somewhat uncanny, of having perceived or experienced something before of a similar nature; the feeling may stem from an association with something in the unconscious.

Defusion: The separation of emotions, especially love and agression, so that the former fails to modify and restrain the full force of the latter.

Denial: An unconscious mechanism of defense by which the ego seeks to protect itself from an intolerable idea or feeling by denying some aspect of reality.

Displacement: The transference of emotions from the original idea or person to which they were attached, to less significant substitutes; the motive is to spare the ego the pain of knowing the real source of the feelings while, at the same time, allowing discharge of these emotions.

Ego: That part of the psyche which develops through the influence of the external world upon the more primal structure of the id; serves as the regulatory part of the personality, guiding perception and muscular activity; acts as the mediator between the demands of the id and the world of reality.

Ego Ideal: That part of the personality, related to the superego, which has to do with the self-image of how the person feels he should be; based on identifications with admired and significant figures in early life, especially the parents; partly unconscious; narcissistic ego ideal—a childish image of the perfect self as the individual would like to believe he is or ought to be.

Ego-syntonic: That which is in harmony with the standards of the ego (and ego ideal), therefore causes no anxiety.

Empathy: The capacity to think and feel oneself into the psyche of another person for the purpose of understandng him.

Free association: The psychic process in which one thought leads spontaneously to another, together with the accompanying emotions, because these ideas are unconsciously related or *associated* with each other in some manner; because of reality factors, this kind of thinking is customarily controlled and censored so that unacceptable ideas can be withheld; Freud discovered the technique of *free association* as a path to the unconscious and established it as a fundamental tool in psychoanalytic therapy.

Id: That part of the personality structure which comprises the instinctual strivings and repressed, unconscious content; aspects of the id can reach consciousness only through some form of representation in the ego or find discharge through derivatives expressed in dreams or symptoms.

Identification: A psychic, unconscious process by which an individual patterns himself after another; an important mechanism for the development of one's personality, in which the parents and other significant figures of early life play a major role.

Imago: An unconscious mental image, usually idealized, of an important person in the early life of an individual.

Incorporation: A primitive defense mechanism, functioning unconsciously, in which a person, or parts of him, are figuratively ingested, and thus felt to be within, or part of one's self.

Internalized object: The mental representation of someone, with accompanying emotions, with whom one formerly had a relationship in the external world.

Inhibition: Interference with, or restriction of, specific activities or functions; may result from an unconscious defense against forbidden instinctual drives.

Intrapsychic: Taking place within the psyche.

Introjection: The psychic act of taking into one's ego system the

image of a person, as one perceives that person to be, together
with the accompanying emotions that one had toward him in
the external world; related to the more primitive method of
incorporation.

Isolation: An unconscious mechanism of defense in which an
unacceptable impulse, idea, or act, is separated from its original memory source, thereby removing the emotional charge.

Latent content: The hidden, unconscious meaning as opposed to
the *manifest content,* or the surface meaning; especially related to dreams, fantasies, and works of art and literature.

Masochism: Sexualized pleasure in association with physical or
psychological pain; often related to an unconscious sense of
guilt and a consequent need for punishment to obtain relief.

Melancholia: A severe depression characterized by an intrapsychic
conflict in which a severe superego berates the ego, leading to
a loss of self-esteem.

Narcissism: Self-love as opposed to object love; an over-estimation of
self; *narcissistic identification*—identifying with another person who unconsciously represents aspects of oneself; a love
relationship on this basis is thus largely a form of externalized
self-love; *narcissistic injury*—an injury to one's sense of self-
esteem; a certain amount of narcissism, or self-love, is necessary
for a healthy psyche.

Libido: Psychic drive, or energy, usually associated with or derived from the sexual instinct; in its broad sense used to include all warm relationships and pleasurable feelings.

Object love: Love for another person outside the self.

Oral stage: The earliest period of psychic development in the
infant, when the mouth is the main erotegonic zone; it is the
chief organ with which he experiences the world, taking in
good objects, like mother's milk, and spitting out what he
doesn't like.

Overdetermination: The multiple causality of a single symptom
or emotional reaction.

Paranoid: Characterized by oversuspiciousness; paranoid trends
can vary from mild tendencies within the range of normalcy,

to severe pathology involving grandiose or persecutory delusions.

Passive-aggressive personality: Descriptive of aggressive behavior expressed in passive or covert ways in order to conceal the underlying hostility.

Phallic mother: Refers to the fantasy of the child that the mother, being a powerful person, must also have a penis, perhaps a hidden one; the fantasy is repressed but may remain active in the unconscious.

Pleasure principle: The concept that man instinctively seeks gratification and pleasure and strives to avoid pain and discomfort; related to early stages in personality development; soon comes in conflict with the frustrations imposed by reality and, normally, is modified as one matures, by an acceptance of the *reality* principle.

Primal scene: The real or fantasied observation by the child of parental or other heterosexual intercourse.

Preoedipal: Preceding the oedipal period; refers to the oral and anal stages of psychic development; *preoedipal mother*—the infant's image of the mother during this period.

Projection: A defense mechanism which unconsciously attributes to others that which is unacceptable to the self; these qualities, however, are real to the self and influence the person's behavior accordingly.

Rationalization: The process, frequently unconscious, of finding reasons for that which one wishes to belief or do, without regard for the real, underlying motives.

Reaction-formation: Development of a character trait that conceals and tries to keep under control another trait, which is usually of the exactly opposite type.

Regression: Reverting to an earlier pattern of mental functioning, usually in periods of stress.

Repression: The process of keeping unacceptable ideas from consciousness; these ideas may remain active in the unconscious and seek an outlet in disguised ways, such as dreams or symptoms.

Sadism: Sexualized pleasure derived from inflicting physical or psychological pain on others.

Sublimation: A diversion of psychic energy from instinctual drives which are unacceptable to the self to channels which are personally and socially approved, as in the fields of art, religion, or social service.

Superego: That part of the psyche out of which conscience develops; formed in early childhood by identification with the standards and wishes of the parents and other significant adults, as the child perceives these to be; the self-criticising aspect of the personality which, under certain conditions, can become overly severe and even sadistic, causing guilt and anxiety.

Index to Biblical References

GENESIS

11:26...5
11:28...8
11:29...8
12:1-3...3
12:4...5
12:6-7...9-10
12:10...11
12:11-13...11
13:8-10...13
13:14-15...14
15:1-2...15
15:4-8...18
15:11...19
15:12-18...19-20
17:1...3
18:1-8...22-23
20:12...9
21:10...29

22:1-19...32
24:17-19...37
24:67...37
25:23...36
25:27-28...38
25:29-32...40
27:11-13...41
27:34-38...42
29:19...48
29:26-28...48
32:25...50
32:25-27...52
32:27-31...50-51
35:7...57
37:6-11...67
37:8...68
37:10...69
37:19-20...70
41:17-24...77
41:51-52...79

42:18-20...81
42:36...73
42:37-38...73
43:9...74
44:15...83
44:17...84
44:33-34...84
45:4-8...84-85
45:13...85
48:5-6...89

EXODUS

28...176

JUDGES

17:5...177

FIRST SAMUEL

1:8...94
1:22...96
1:26–27...97
2:1–10...97
3:3–9...100–101
3:9–14...101
3:11...104
3:19–20...106
6:19...223
9:19–10:1...113
10:27...125
11:6–7...126
12:3–4...116
13:2...122
14:39...130
14:45...131
14:47–48...134
15:22–23...135
16:7...163
16:11...163
17:28...167
17:37...171
17:45...171
17:55–58...139
18:1–4...139
18:15...147
18:17...147
18:27...148
21:10...176
22:18...176
23:2...217
23:11–13...217
24:15...175
26:19–21...153
27:5...180
27:8...168
28:2...181
30:23–25...228

SECOND SAMUEL

1:17–27...183
1:20–27...211
4:9–11...229

5:6–9...212
5:19...218
5:20...219
5:23–24...218
6:7...221
6:14...176
6:20...204
7:2...216
8:1...181
10:4...231
11:4...186
12:24–25...270
12:27–28...231
12:29–31...231
13:1–22...183
13:15–19...184
13:20–22...185
13:25–26...186
13:32...187
14:25...189
15:13...192
15:14...191
15:15...192
15:30...194
15:31...195
16:3...195
16:7–12...196
19:1–9...197–198
19:22–24...236
20:1–2...246
21:1...241
21:16–17...236
21:17...240
21:19...211
21–24...250
23:17...240
23:20–21...237
23:32...239
24:1...244
24:10...248
24:16–17...251

FIRST KINGS

1:38–40...263
1:52...263

2:1–2...264
2:9...272
2:19–23...275
2:26...296
3:1...297
3:6–9...266
3:11–14...267
5:4–5...303
5:9–11...268
5:13–14...303
5:21...294
6:1...281
6:9...291–292
6:11–13...279, 290
6:38...281
7:13–14...295
8:2...281
8:10...282
8:12–13...283
8:15–20...283
8:23–24...284
8:27–29...284
8:38–39; 46...286
8:41–43...289
8:66...290
9:3...291
9:6–9...291–292
9:10...281
9:12...294
10:7–9...299
10:18–20...302
11:4...304
11:9–13...304–305

FIRST CHRONICLES

1:22...273
18:1...181

SECOND CHRONICLES

6:13...283

Index

Abiathar, 218, 296
Abinadab, 204–207, 221, 225, 227
Abishag, XII, 207, 274–275
Abishai, 196, 237
Abner, 153, 173, 179, 183
   see also; Saul and David
Abraham, 1–34
   ambivalence of, 5, 6, 13–16
   anxiety of, 10–12, 15, 17, 23
   attitude toward son figures, 16–17
   bargains with God, 24–26
   circumcision of, 23, 30–31
   compared with Solomon, 301
   Covenant of the Pieces, 18–21
   entertains angels unawares, 26
   feelings of guilt, 10–11, 24
   hospitality of, 22–24
   incestuous feelings of, 9

   defense against, XXII, 213
      related to oedipal complex, 213
   need for self-righteousness, 25
   Post-biblical legends regarding, 4–6, 16, 30
   psychodynamics of, 16–21, 25
   relationship to mother, 5–8
   sibling rivalry of, 7, 15–16
   significance of in Judaism, XVIII–XIX, 1–3, 33–34
   theophanies of, 3, 5, 9–11, 13–18, 22, 31
   unconscious fantasies of, 10
   and Hagar, 28–31
   and Ishmael, 28–31
   and Lot, 7, 13–18, 24, 28
   and near-sacrifice of Isaac, 31–33
   and Sarah, 3, 8–15, 28–31

341

Abraham (cont.)
  and Terah, 2, 4–5
  as father figure, 2, 34
  as leader, 3
  at Shechem, 10
  in Canaan, 8–11
  in Egypt, 10
Abram, see Abraham, 2, 7
Absalom, 184–196, 271
  see also; David and Absalom
Absalom's Pillar, 200
Achish, King, 153, 178–181
  see also; David
Adonijah, 200, 207, 262, 264, 271, 274
Aegean seacoast, 92
Agag, 135
Aggression, feelings of, 17, 30;
  see also entries under major per-
    sonalities
Ahimelech, 176, 178
Ahinoam, 227
Ahitophel, 195, 196
Ambivalence, XXIII, 2–3, 31;
  see also entries under major per-
    sonalities
Ammonites, 126, 231
Amnon, 183–185, 271
Anxiety, 8, 11;
  see also entries under major per-
    sonalities
Applied psychoanalysis, XIX–XXI
Archaeology 320–321
Ark, 216, 220, 222
  returned by Philistines, 108
Arlow, Dr. Jacob, 101, 103, 326–327
Asahel, 170
Asenath, 78
Asher, 62

Babylonia, 4
Baron, Salo, 321
Bathsheba, 262, 270, 275, 288
  see also; David; Solomon and Abi-
    shag
Benaiah, 237
Benjamin, 57, 58, 63, 73–74
Bethel, 56, 57

Bethlehem, 117, 173
Beth-Shemesh, 223–224
Bible,
  development of, 315–316
  Higher Criticism, XVII
  importance of, XV
  understanding the, XV–XIX
  and development of superego, 311
  and oedipal conflict, 314
  as folk literature, 313
Biblical commentators, 26, 95, 177,
    261, 277–278
Biblical exegesis, XVII
  Documentary Theory of, 317–319
  Fragmentation Theory of, 318
  present status of, 319, 321–322
  scope of, 322
  Theory of composite authorship,
    318
  in antiquity and Middle Ages, 317
  in modern times, 317
Bilhah, 62
Birthright, 40
Blessing, 44
Boaz, 295
Book of Proverbs, 303
Bride price, 48, 63, 204

Calcol, 268
Canaan, 5, 9, 12, 20
  see also; Promised Land
Canaanites, 10, 14, 105, 172, 177
Castration anxiety, 19, 148, 151
  see also entries under major per-
    sonalities
Cave of Machpelah, 213–214
Children, importance of, 260
Children of Israel, XVII
Chronicles, 283
Circumcision, 23, 30–31
  see also; Abraham
  see also; castration anxiety
Cities of the Plain, 27
City,
  as mother symbol, 27, 173, 193, 211
  of David, 200, 302
  see also; Jerusalem

Collective superego, XXIII

Concubines, 28–29, 62, 75, 193, 241, 264

Covenant,
  concept of, 21
  conditional promise of, 265, 279, 291–292, 306
  of the Pieces, 18–22

Damascus, 16
Dan, 62
Darda, 268
Darwin, 317
David, XII, 161–258
  accomplishments of, 161–162
  ambivalence of, 179, 201, 216, 222–223, 225
  anointment of, 162–164, 218
  anxiety of, 179–180
  guilt feelings of, 188, 192–193, 196, 199, 216
  laments death of Absalom, 189–191; of Saul and Jonathan, 210–211
  later years of reign, 241–252
  meaning of name, 169
  myth of birth of hero, 165–166
  oedipal conflict of, 171, 173–174, 182, 193, 212, 222–223
  period of exile, 169, 174–175
  personality of, 162, 182, 191, 209
  psychodynamics of, 175, 177–178, 180, 187–188, 241–252
  relationship to God, 171–172, 188, 196, 209, 217–220
  and Abigail, 204–206, 209–210
  and Abishag, 208
  and the Ark, 194, 203–204, 216, 220–226
  and Bathsheba, 186, 202–209
  and Goliath, 167–177
  and his champions, 237, 241
  and his sons, 183–185, 189–207, 272–277
  and Jerusalem, 172–173
  and Michal, 203–204, 206–207, 209–210
  and Samuel, 175, 182

  and Saul, 162, 174–176, 178–180, 183, 201
  and sword of Goliath, 171, 176–178
  as father, 183, 185–187, 189, 191, 201–202
  as leader, 227, 230–231
  associated with Messiah, 161, 257
  compared with Joseph, 166–167
  relationship to:
    concubines, 193
    mother, 169–170
    women, 202, 209–210
  relationship with Joab, 232–237
  ruthlessness in war, 230, 232
  wishes to build the Temple, 215–216
  see also; Post-Biblical legends

Dead Sea Scrolls, significance of, 320

Death, 201
  as punishment, 52
  as sacrifice, 58

Deborah, nurse of Rebekah, 57–58
Deuteronomy, 316
Dinah, daughter of Jacob, 27, 79
Documentary theory, 317
Doeg, 151, 176
Dothan, 74
Dreams,
  symbolism in, 21, 177, 225
  see also entries under major personalities

Edom, 151
Edomite, 151, 176
Egypt, 9–11, 61
Eli,
  ambivalence of, 105
  attitude toward Hannah, 95
  death of, 107
  death of sons, 106–107
  guilt feelings of, 103–104
  personality of, 95

Eliab, 163, 167–168
Eliezer, 37
Elihu, 168
Elkanah,
  personality of, 98–99
  role as father, 98

Emtelai, 6
Endor, woman of, 118
En-Rogel, 262
Ephod, 176–178
Ephraim, 66
Erikson, Erik, 313
Esau, 151
    Birth of, 38, 55, 42
    compared with Jacob, 38
    effect of twinship on, 38–39
    grief over loss of blessing, 41–43
Ethan the Ezrahite, 268
Exegesis,
    see Biblical exegesis
Ezion-geber, 301
Ezra, 316, 320

Father, role of, XXIII, 2, 266
    see also entries under major per-
        sonalities
First Kings, 261
First Samuel, 107
Five Books of Moses, 316
Flescher, Dr. Joachim, X
Folk literature, XIX
Freud, Sigmund, XX, XXIV, 2, 3, 34,
    64, 65, 140, 169, 182, 254, 306,
    311

Gad, 62
Gath, 178–182, 211
Gerar, 9
Gibeah, 129, 132
Gibeon, 282, 290, 292
Gibeonites,
    betrayal of, 243
Gihon, 262
Gilgal, 128
Gittite, 225
God, XXIII–XXIV; see also entries
    under major personalities
Golden Age,
    longing for, 258
Goldman, Solomon, 319
Group
    feelings of kinship in, 312
    relationship of heroes to, XVI–
        XVII

Guilt feelings and religion, XXIII;
    see also entries under major per-
        sonalities
Gulf of Aqabah, 301

Hagar, 28–31, 37
    see also; Abraham and Sarah
Hammurabi, Code of, 29
Hannah
    attitude toward Samuel, 97–99
    character of, 94–100
    misjudged by Eli, 95–96
Hanun, 231
Haran (city), 5, 7, 18, 321
Haran
    Abraham's relationship to, 7–8
    death of, 7
Hebron, 183, 191
Herma, Dr. John, X
Heman, 268
Hero, XVIII–XIX, XXI
    see also entries under major per-
        sonalities
Heth, 213
Hexateuch, 317
Higher Criticism, XVII–XVIII, 134,
    250
    see also; Biblical exegesis
Hiram, King of Tyre, 293, 294
Hiram, son of Tyre, 294
Hittites, 213–214
Hospitality, law of, 22
    see also; Sodom and Gemorrah
Hushai, 195–196, 198
Hurrian law, 61

Idol–worship, 4
Incest, 27
    taboo, 213
Incestuous
    objects, XXII
    wishes, 312
Instinctual
    impulses, 312
Isaac
    birth of, 29–30
    deceived by Jacob, 41–42

favors Esau, 38
near-sacrifice of, 31–33
position in family, 36
psychodynamics of, 36–38
and Ishmael, 29–31
Iscah, 8–9
Ish-boseth, 183, 229
Ishmael,
birth of, 30
descendants of, 29
see also; Hagar and Isaac
Israel, Children of, 16–17
Ittai, 194, 196

Jabbok River, 49–50
Jabesh-Gilead, 115, 126
Jachin, 295
Jacob,
ambivalence of, 72, 90
anxiety of, 71
attitude toward God, 46
change of name, 50–51, 54
comparison of two dreams, 55–56
death of, 88
dream of, XX, 35, 44–46, 51–54
symbolism in, 44–46
effect of twinship on, 38–39
flight from home of, 35, 44
incestuous feelings of, 47, 61, 63
maturity of, 60
meaning of name, 36, 50–51
oedipal conflict of, 56–58, 63
predilection for younger son, 66, 90
relationship to mother, 38, 40–44
relationship to Rachel, 47, 48, 61, 63
separation anxiety of, 40
sibling rivalry of, 35–36
wrestles with the stranger, 50–54
and the birthright, 40–41
and the blessing, 41–44
at Beth-el, 56–57
Jebusites, 172–173, 213
Jedidiah
meaning of, 27, 296
Jerusalem, 172, 192, 196, 200, 282, 302
see also; City of David
Jesse, 164, 167, 187

Joab, 170, 189–190, 196–197, 200, 209, 211, 231
see also; David
Jonadab, 183, 187
Jonathan,
attitude toward God, 142
psychodynamics of, 140–143
and David, 139–140
as hero figure, 132–133, 138–141
see also; Saul
Jones, Ernest, 27
Jordan River, 115, 126, 196
Jordan Valley, 195
Joseph, 59–90
capacity to forgive and love, 88
death of, 88
defensive attitudes of, 68, 76
dreams of, 67–69
ego strength of, 74–75
faith in father figures, 75, 77
faith in God, 87–88
favored by parents, 63–64, 66
guilt feelings of brothers, 80
integrity of, 75
interprets dreams, 77–78
loss of mother, 65
narcissism of, 83
oedipal situation of, 65
popular appeal of, 59
relationship to: Benjamin, 81–82;
to father figures, 77, 89;
to Reuben, 70, 75
signs of maturity, 87–88
sons of, 79
superiority of, 65
symbolism of the cup, 82–83
vulnerability of, 64–65
and his brothers in Egypt, 74, 79–89
as a son figure, 88–89
in Egypt, 74–89
in prison, 76
Joshua, 92, 317
Josiah, King, 316
Judah, 73, 81
Judaism, XXIII, 2
development of, 33
Judeo-Christian culture
and the Bible, XVIII

Judeo-Christian culture (*cont.*)
  growth and development of, 310–
    314

Kaufmann, Y, 319–320
Keilah, 211, 217–218
Kenites, 135
Kiriath-jearim, 108, 221–222
Kish, 124

Laban, 42
  competitive toward Jacob, 48–49
Language
  as symbol, XVI, XXIII
Leader, XVI–XIX
  see also; hero; and entries under
    major personalities
Leah, 48, 64
  sons of, 62
  see also; Jacob and Laban
Lelyveld, Rabbi Arthur J., XI–XII
Levi, Tribe of, 55
Levites, 194
Lex talionis, 73, 242
Lot, 7, 15, 25–26, 28
  see also; Abraham
Lower Biblical Criticism, 317

Mahanaim, 196
Mahol, 268
Malcam, 232
Margalith, Mrs. Helen, X
Meerloo, Dr. Joost A. M., XII–XIII
Mephi-boseth, 195
Metheg-ammah, 181–182
Michal, 147, 203
  see also; Saul and David
Michmas, 129
Midrash, 38, 86
Milcah, 8–9
Mizpah, 108
Myth of birth of the hero, 166
Moabites, 230
Monotheism, XVII, 1, 310
  and polytheism, 312
Morality, development of, 34, 310–
    314; *see also;* Freud

Moses, 93, 321
  and daughters of Jethro, 60
Mount Gilboa, 118, 210
Mount Moriah, 33
  Myth of birth of the hero, 166
Mythopoeic hero, significance of,
    XIX, XXI

Nabal, 204–205
Nabash, 126
Nahor, 7, 321
Naphtali, 62, 295
Nathan the Prophet, 200, 207, 209,
    254, 262, 270, 296
Nehemiah, 316
Nile, 79
Nimrod, 4
Nob, 176, 179, 211

Oak of Weeping, 57
Obed-Edom, 225,
  see also; Gath
Oedipal dilemma, XVIII, XXIII
  conflict of, 312–314
  see also entries under major per-
    sonalities
Oedipus Rex, 311
On, Priest of, 79
Oral tradition, role of, 319
Otto, Rudolf, 21

Patai, Dr. Raphael, X
Patriarchal period
  authenticity of, 318, 320–322
Peniel, 56
Peninnah, 94
  see also; Hannah
Pentateuch, 316–317
  composite nature of, 319
  see also; Bible
Phenix, Prof. Philip, IX
Philistines, 92, 108–109, 126, 167, 211
Pidyon Ha-ben, significance of, 55
Polytheism, 4, 321
Post-biblical legends, 4–8, 16–17, 213–
    215, 240

Potiphar, 75
Potiphar's wife, 75
Poti-phera, priest of On, 78
  see also; Potiphar
Prayer, 94, 108, 266
  see also entries under major personalities
Primogeniture and ultimogeniture, 168
Promised Land, 12
  see also; Canaan
Prophets, 92, 114, 124, 312, 316
Proselyte, attitude of Solomon toward, 289
Psychoanalysis, applied, XIX–XXI

Queen of Sheba, 259, 299–300

Rabbah, 231
Rabbinic sources, 14, 269
  see also; Solomon and David, 269
Rachel, 50, 57, 60–63
  see also; Jacob and Laban
Ramah, 96, 108
Rank, Otto, 166
Rebekah, 37–39
Rehoboam, 260
  see also; Solomon
Reik, Dr. Theodor, IX, 47, 325
Religion, development of, 34, 105, 177, 311, 315, 322
Return of the Repressed, 211, 312
Reuben, 62, 65, 73
Ricoeur, Paul, XVI
Rowley, H. H., 319
Ruth, 230

Salt, symbolic meaning of, 27
Samuel, 91–120
  attitude toward God, 99, 104, 112
  attitude toward kingship, 109–111
  called by God, 93, 102–103
  childhood influences of, 93–99
  death of, 118, 152
  development as leader, 118–120
  psychodynamics of, 111–120

  relationship to Eli, 102–106
  role as leader, 92–93, 116
  Samuel and Saul, 112–118
  shocked by defeat of Israel, 106–109
  as father, 111–112, 116
  see also; David, Saul
Samuel, Maurice, 206
Sanhedrin, 223
Sarah
  birth of Isaac, 29
  relationship to Abraham, 8–13
  and Hagar, 28–30
Sarai
  see, Sarah
Samaritan text, 5
Saul, 121–160
  abandonment of by Samuel, 128, 134–135
  accomplishments of, 159
  ambivalence of, 136, 152
  anointment of, 124, 128
  castration anxiety of, 157, 158
    symbolically expressed, 136
  death of, 118, 155
  psychopathology of, 133, 144, 157–158
  relationship to God, 130, 133, 154
  relationship to Jonathan, 130–133, 140–142
  and the woman of Endor, 154
Second Samuel, 270
Sexuality,
  sanction of in Judaism, 313
Shechem, 9–10, 27, 79
Shiloh, 96, 108
Shimeah, 183
Shimei, 195–196, 256
Simeon, 73
Snow, Rev. John Hall, X
Sodom, King of, 15
Sodom and Gemorrah, 14–16, 24–27
Solomon, 259–310
  ambivalence of, 274, 294, 298, 307
  anointment of, 262–263
  anxiety of, 269
  attitude toward David, 264–265, 271–274, 269, 287
  attitude toward the stranger, 289

Solomon (*cont.*)
    attitude toward women, 276, 288,
        297–301
    character traits of, 263
    defensive aspects of character, 261–
        262, 269–270
    competitiveness of, 269–270, 281
    cosmopolitan interests of, 260, 289
    creative imagination of, 307–308
    diversity of interests, 301–302
    dreams of, interpreted, 265–270
    ego-ideal of, 306–310
    era of peace and prosperity, 301–304
    father ideal of, 296
    harem of, 275
    legends regarding, 269, 280
    narcissism of, 267, 279, 295, 306, 309
    popular images of, 259–260
    position in family, 271
    prayers of, 282–286, 290
    regression in religious life of, 304–
        308
    relationship to God, 265, 267, 270,
        284, 290–293
    see also; conditional promise
    theophanies of, 290, 292–293
    and Adonijah, 262–263, 274, 276,
        282
    see also; Adonijah
    and Bathsheba, 262–263
    see also; Bathsheba
    and Hiram, King of Tyre, 293–294
    and Hiram, son of Tyre, 295–296
    and Nathan, 262–263
    and Queen of Sheba, 259, 299–300
    and the Temple, 261, 273, 277, 278–
        298
    as depicted in the Bible, 260–262,
        282, 284
Song of Songs, 303
Speiser, A. E., 321
Sublimation
    in the development of Judaism, 31
Superego,
    as controlling influence of behavior,
        314

Sword of Goliath, 177–178
    see also; David, 177
Symbols, use of in religion, 313
Syria, 10

Talmud, XVI, 260, 299, 317
Tamar, 183, *see also;* David
Tanner, Rev. Eugene S., X
Theophany,
    see entries under major personali-
        ties
Torah, antiquity of, 319
    authenticity of language, 319
Temple, 93, 313
    see also; Solomon and David
Temple Mount, 288, 302
Terah, 2, 4, 5, 7
    see also; Abraham
Teraphim, 61
Terebinth of Moreh, 10
Thanatos and Eros, 251
Theme of the Three Caskets, 254
    see also; Freud
Torah
    as symbol of father, 313

Ur of the Chaldees, 5, 7, 18
Uriah the Hittite, 208–209
Urim and Thummim, 176–177
Uzzah and the Ark, XI, 221–225

Valley of Kidron, 262

Wellhausen, Julius, 318–320

Zeruiah, 170
Ziba, 195
Ziklag, 180–181, 210
Zilpah, sons of, 62